Biomedicine is often thought to provide a universal, scientific account of the human body and illness. In this view, non-Western and folk medical systems are regarded as systems of "belief" and subtly discounted. This is an impoverished perspective for understanding illness and healing across cultures, one that neglects many facets of Western medical practice and obscures its kinship with healing in other traditions. Drawing on his research in several American and Middle Eastern medical settings, Professor Good develops a critical, anthropological account of medical knowledge and practice. He shows how physicians and healers enter and inhabit distinctive worlds of meaning and experience. He explores how stories or illness narratives are joined with bodily experience in shaping and responding to human suffering. And he argues that moral and aesthetic considerations are present in routine medical practice as in other forms of healing.

Medicine, rationality, and experience

THE LEWIS HENRY MORGAN LECTURES 1990

presented at
The University of Rochester
Rochester, New York

Lewis Henry Morgan Lecture Series

Fred Eggan: *The American Indian: Perspectives for the Study of Social Change*
Ward H. Goodenough: *Description and Comparison in Cultural Anthropology*
Robert J. Smith: *Japanese Society: Tradition, Self, and the Social Order*
Sally Falk Moore: *Social Facts and Fabrications: "Customary Law" on Kilimanjaro, 1880–1980*
Nancy Munn: *The Fame of Gawa: A Symbolic Study of Value Transformation in a Mussim (Papua New Guinea) Society*
Lawrence Rosen: *The Anthropology of Justice: Law as Culture in Islamic Society*
Stanley Jeyaraja Tambiah: *Magic, Science, Religion, and the Scope of Rationality*
Maurice Bloch: *Prey into Hunter: The Politics of Religious Experience*
Marilyn Strathern: *After Nature: English Kinship in the Late Twentieth Century*

Medicine, rationality, and experience

An anthropological perspective

BYRON J. GOOD

Harvard Medical School

CAMBRIDGE
UNIVERSITY PRESS

CAMBRIDGE UNIVERSITY PRESS
Cambridge, New York, Melbourne, Madrid, Cape Town, Singapore,
São Paulo, Delhi, Dubai, Tokyo, Mexico City

Cambridge University Press
The Edinburgh Building, Cambridge CB2 8RU, UK

Published in the United States of America by Cambridge University Press, New York

www.cambridge.org
Information on this title: www.cambridge.org/9780521425766

First published 1994

A catalogue record for this publication is available from the British Library

Library of Congress Cataloguing in Publication Data

Good, Byron.
Medicine, rationality, and experience: An anthropological
perspective / Byron J. Good.
p. cm. - (The Lewis Henry Morgan lectures: 1990)
Includes bibliographical references and index.
ISBN 0 521 41558 6 (hardback). - ISBN 0 521 42576 X (pbk.)
1. Medical anthropology. 2. Social medicine. I. Title.
II. Series.
GN296.G66 1994.
306.4'61 - dc20 92- 45254 CIP

ISBN 978-0-521-41558-3 Hardback
ISBN 978-0-521-42576-6 Paperback

Contents

Figures

Foreword

Byron Good delivered the Lewis Henry Morgan Lectures on which this book is based in March, 1990. This marked the twenty-eighth year in which the Lectures were offered to the public by the Department of Anthropology at the University of Rochester. As I write, the thirty-first Lectures are less than two months away. The Lectures were launched under the leadership of the Department's founding Chair, Professor Bernard S. Cohn, with generous support from the Joseph R. and Joseph C. Wilson families. For twenty-eight years, from 1964 through 1991, the Editor of the Lectures was Professor Alfred Harris. The first five published volumes in the series were Meyer Fortes' *Kinship and the Social Order*, Fred Eggan's *The American Indian*, Robert McC. Adams' *The Evolution of Urban Society*, Victor Turner's *The Ritual Process*, and Ward Goodenough's *Description and Comparison in Social Anthropology*.

The Lectures serve in part as a memorial to Lewis Henry Morgan, a prominent Rochester attorney as well as a founder of modern anthropology. Morgan was never dependent on the perhaps dubious pleasures and rewards of an academic position in mid-nineteenth century America. Nevertheless, as Professor Harris noted in his Foreword to Meyer Fortes' inaugural Lectures, Morgan was connected with the University of Rochester from its beginning. A major early benefactor, he left the University money for a women's college as well as his manuscripts and library. Until the creation of the Morgan Lectures, however, the only memorial to him at the University was a residence hall wing named in his honor.

The Morgan Lectures, the published volumes as well as the public lectures in Rochester, also are the site of a complex series of intersecting and overlapping conversations. Most importantly, of course, the Lecturer addresses other anthropologists and scholars in a variety of allied fields on his or her own behalf. The Lectures also provide an opportunity for the Department – undergraduates, graduate students and faculty alike – to engage in close interaction with scholars working on a wide range of problems in our discipline, many of which we cannot hope to represent in a single department. Ideally, their work challenges as well as complements our own. Through its selection of Lecturers, the Rochester

Department of Anthropology is able to convey its sense of the growing points of the discipline as a whole. Here our audience is both local and international, anthropological and interdisciplinary. First through the public lectures in Rochester and then through the published volumes, the Lectures serve as a forum in which scholars from a variety of disciplines and members of the public may meet to discuss matters of general as well as academic interest.

I rehearse all of this for two reasons. The first is to honor the work of my predecessors. It is a considerable privilege and responsibility to take up the legacy of Professors Cohn and Harris and their distinguished Lecturers. The second is to make clear that my appreciation of Professor Good's book is necessarily partial and incomplete.

Medicine, Rationality, and Experience is a large work. As Morgan "discovered" or "invented" kinship as a cultural domain and an object of anthropological investigation, so Good here finds a definition of illness, providing medical anthropology with an object of study and a program of research. For Good, illness is an aesthetic rather than a biological object. His approach is interpretive rather than positivist.

Annie Dillard observes in *The Writing Life* that

> When you write, you lay out a line of words. The line of words is a miner's pick, a woodcarver's gouge, a surgeon's probe. You wield it, and it digs a path you follow. Soon you find yourself deep in new territory. Is it a dead end, or have you located the real subject? You will know tomorrow, or this time next year . . .
>
> The writing has changed, in your hands, and in a twinkling, from an expression of your notions to an epistemological tool.

With observations such as this in mind, I say advisedly that Good "finds" a definition of illness. This outcome is prefigured in Good's earlier work and in the first chapters of this one, but one of the charming features of this book is that it provides glimpses of the way in which its final destination emerged after much hard work. On the opening page of chapter 7, Good writes that

> Shortly after I finished writing the last major chapter of this book – on the narrative representation of illness – a former professor of mine asked what I had discussed in the Morgan Lectures. I replied that I was developing a theory of culture and illness from the perspective of aesthetics, examining how illness is formulated as an "aesthetic object." I later thought back on what I had said with considerable anxiety, because with the exception of reviewing some of the literature on narrativity the book hardly addresses the issue of aesthetics at all. Furthermore, this surely represents a small part of what this book has been about and a very partial way of conceiving a program for medical anthropology. Nonetheless, my rather offhand comment suggested an interpretation of where I had emerged after nearly two years of work on this project, and may serve as the starting point for work to come (p. 166).

We have in this volume the record of a difficult voyage of discovery.

By my reckoning, Good's argument may be divided into two parts. The first, chapters 1 through 3, consists of preparatory work. Here Good severs the subordinate relationship of medical anthropology to medicine and biology and cuts its moorings in positivist epistemology. Medical science, he argues, is in part an ideological formation. It does not mirror nature in any direct way and cannot provide the foundations for a medical anthropology concerned with experience and comparison. Instead, a meaning-centered approach is required, one which recognizes that the language of medicine is a *"cultural language"* (p. 5) and a historical formation.

In the latter part of chapter 1, Good argues that, in spite of the many advances in medical diagnosis and therapy, the notion that medical science mirrors nature rests on a culturally specific distinction between knowledge and belief. In medical practice, public discourse and much anthropological writing, the other is regarded as holding culturally determined beliefs, often erroneous, while "we" have attained objective, empirical knowledge. Patients may have beliefs about their illnesses; doctors have knowledge. As Good observes, however, following Wilfred Cantwell Smith, our current concept of belief as something held to be true without certain knowledge is itself historical in character, arising in English usage only in the last three centuries. In earlier usage, belief had to do not with propositions but with activity, being loyal to or loving. Specific to our own culture, our modern concept of belief may be badly misleading when applied to other times or other places. At the same time, our conception of scientific knowledge as an objective mirror of nature has come to be less convincing. In some quarters, at least, it, too, is seen to be shaped by culturally specific practices.

Good pursues the conflict between positivist and interpretive epistemologies in chapters 2 and 3. Chapter 2 provides a broad overview of medical anthropology in the twentieth century. It is focused on contrasting representations of illness, their epistemological presuppositions and their implications for programs of research. A preliminary account of writings about concepts of illness and healing from before the Second World War grounds the discussion in mainstream anthropological concerns. The greater part of the chapter is devoted to an account of debates among representatives of the continuing "empiricist tradition," cognitive and "meaning-centered" approaches, and "critical" medical anthropology in the period since the 1950s when medical anthropology emerged as a distinct subfield of anthropology concerned with work in international public health. The divergent theories of knowledge inherent in these competing positions are not, Good argues, mere philosophical window dressing. They have important consequences for programs of research and for the ways in which anthropologists interact with and write about the people they study and with whom they live. In Good's view an interpretive or meaning-centered approach that remains "conversant with critical theory" is essential if medical anthropology is to comprehend the claims of medical science and biology while still recognizing "the validity of local knowledge in matters of sickness and suffering" (p. 63).

Chapter 3 is the first ethnographic chapter of the book. (Here as elsewhere Good discusses material gathered jointly with his wife, Mary-Jo Good, also a distinguished medical anthropologist.) A fascinating preliminary report on a study of Harvard Medical School's New Pathway to General Medical Education, the chapter uses Ernst Cassirer's theory of symbolic forms to construct a picture of medical practice as embedded in culture, "a symbolically mediated mode of apprehending and acting on the world" (p. 87). Medical students enter the world of medicine, Good contends, by participating in a distinctive set of what Marilyn Strathern might call knowledge practices, "specialized ways of 'seeing,' 'writing,' and 'speaking'" that "formulate reality in a specifically 'medical' way" (p. 71). This ethnographic account serves as a bridge between the two parts of the book. Looking backward, it provides evidence in support of the claim, developed in the first two chapters, that medicine is embedded in culture. Looking forward, it is a first concrete illustration, using relatively familiar materials, of an interpretive approach that takes as its "analytical focus the 'formative processes' through which illness is shaped as personal and social reality . . . " (p. 66).

The second part of the book, chapters 4 through 6, consists of a series of ethnographic analyses, using material gathered in Iran, Turkey, and the United States. Together, these analyses give substance to Good's suggestion that medicine is a symbolic form and to his proposal for an interpretive approach to medical anthropology.

In chapter 4, Good applies the notion of semiotic networks to a Boston woman's account of her difficulties with rectal bleeding and to the account of digestion in Galenic-Islamic humoral medicine. This amounts to a sustained attack on the notion that medical terms in different cultures or in different segments of a single culture have a common reference to biological facts external to culture that can provide a basis for comparison and translation. Their meaning derives instead, Good shows, from their place in dense semiotic networks. Medical terms have meaning "in relation to a field of signs" (p. 112). They have as much to do with experience, gender and society as with biology. Their interpretation requires attention to the complex array of conceptual systems in which they participate as well as to the practices through which these systems are enacted and reproduced.

Good has been concerned with the analysis of semiotic networks since 1977 and the approach has been widely emulated in medical anthropology. Chapters 5 and 6 push the interpretive perspective into fresh territory. Like chapter 3, chapter 5 proposes a phenomenological account of the construction, and destruction, of lifeworlds. But, where chapter 3 focused on medical students, chapter 5 revolves around a Boston man's moving account of his life with chronic pain and is concerned with the experience of illness. Here Good suggests that medical anthropology "can bring method to the cross-cultural investigation of illness experience" (p. 134) by examining the phenomenology of these experiences, the ways in which they are narrated and the rituals employed to reconstruct the world that suffering has unmade.

Chapter 6 extends the analysis of the representation of illness in narrative, now focusing on Turkish informants' accounts of seizure disorders. Two aspects of the analysis in this chapter strike me as particularly interesting. Good draws upon Wolfgang Iser's theory of reading to argue that the "formative practices" that shape illness and illness experience are inherently social. For Good the meaning of illness is constructed through narrative practices in which sufferers, their families and other associates, and healers all participate. Like the meaning of a text, the meaning of an illness narrative, itself often the complex product of multiple authors, lies neither in the text itself nor in the reader/hearer but is a social product. It is socially distributed. Good draws upon Jerome Bruner to argue that illness narratives succeed by "subjunctivizing reality" (p. 153). Narratives are not closed accounts but endorse alternative perspectives and alternative readings, both retrospectively, looking toward the origins of suffering, and prospectively, looking toward the possibility of cure or alleviation of suffering.

In its own way, the narrative strategy that Good uses in *Medicine, Rationality, and Experience* also is socially distributed and subjunctivizes reality. As Good argues in chapter 2 and repeats in the concluding chapter, chapter 7, medical anthropology is heteroglossic, the socially distributed product of a multiplicity of perspectives and voices. This is necessarily so, he argues, for "[d]isease and human suffering cannot be comprehended from a single perspective" (p. 62). His purpose is not to eliminate the medical model but to carve out a distinct approach for an interpretive anthropology. If, as he suggests, "'[m]edical anthropology' is a kind of oxymoron" (p. 176), an impossible combination of positivist and interpretive epistemologies, the cyborg monster is nevertheless essential to cross-cultural understanding. The course of future research remains open.

Though Good adheres to matters having to do with illness and healing, the implications of his engagement with biological reductionism in its medical stronghold will reverberate across the spectrum of anthropology. Several elements of his argument have close analogs in other areas of the discipline, but the vigor with which he deploys them in the face of the dominant medical and belief/behavior models is exciting.

Like medical anthropology, the Lewis Henry Morgan Lectures as an on-going series are socially distributed, heteroglossic and subjunctivizing. Any attempt to discern an overall direction in such a series is always provisional. Nevertheless, it is worth noting some of the parallels between this work and the last two volumes in the series, Stanley Tambiah's *Magic, Science, Religion, and the Scope of Rationality* and Marilyn Strathern's *After Nature: English Kinship in the Late Twentieth Century*. With Tambiah, Good emphasizes the historical character and cultural embeddedness of science and rationality. With Strathern, Good denies that society and culture are constructed out of elements external to themselves. As kinship, according to Strathern, is not constructed upon the facts of biological connection so, for Good, illness, suffering, and healing cannot be reduced to the biology of organisms.

ANTHONY T. CARTER, *Editor*
The Lewis Henry Morgan Lectures

Preface

This book consists of the Lewis Henry Morgan Lectures, which were delivered during March 1990 at the University of Rochester, and substantially revised and expanded during the subsequent two years. Having honored me by the invitation to deliver the lectures, members of the Department of Anthropology increased my debt beyond measure by their hospitality during the two weeks of my visit. I owe special gratitude to Professor Al Harris, who ably organized the Morgan Lectures for many years, and to Professor Tony Carter, who has now taken on that responsibility. To the faculty, graduate students, and others in the University community who were my hosts and engaged me in discussion, I offer my sincere thanks.

This book represents an effort to work through a set of ideas with which I have struggled for more than twenty years. During 1964–65, I spent a year as an undergraduate student at the University of Nigeria. I returned with a sense of the profound inadequacy of describing the world of my Ibo and Yoruba classmates in a manner that gave privilege to my own views of reality. It was that experience that led me to the comparative study of religion, and then to the study of anthropology. It was also that experience that provided the intuitive grounding for my intellectual engagement with symbolic anthropology at the University of Chicago.

When I turned my attention to medicine, eventually taking a teaching position in the Department of Psychiatry at the University of California, Davis, I began to confront the epistemological questions implicit in the position I intuitively held. Can we seriously contemplate an epistemological – and ethical – stance that does not privilege the knowledge claims of biomedicine and the biomedical sciences? If we accept such claims, what are the consequences for how we represent illness and healing in other cultural traditions? How do our analyses subtly reproduce and legitimize our own common-sense knowledge of medicine and the social world in which we live? On the other hand, if we deny the foundational claims of biomedicine, what alternative ways of thinking and writing are available to us?

This set of questions lies at the heart of much of what I have written during the past fifteen years. And it is this set of issues which I address in as coherent a fashion as I am able in this book. I attempt to show that our views of language,

xv

meaning, and knowledge are subtly present in nearly all that we write in anthropology, and that medical anthropology is a key site in our discipline to address some of the most difficult – and exciting – issues that we face today.

Perhaps not surprisingly, the book turned out to be different than it would have been had I written it a decade earlier, when I first jotted down an outline for a similar text. The ensuing years have seen important developments in interpretive studies, on the one hand, and the rise of diverse forms of critical analysis, on the other, all influencing how we think and write today. In the course of preparing the lectures and elaborating the manuscript, I found myself struggling to reformulate many of the issues about which I have previously written. It is my hope that the text may provoke a similar struggle for at least some of those who read it.

This book includes the core of the lectures, augmented by several additional chapters. Chapters 1, 3, and 5 were presented as the first three Morgan Lectures, and have been revised for this text. Chapters 2, 4, and 6 have been added to fill out the argument. Chapter 7 grew out of my reflections for the concluding lecture, but is largely rewritten.

Given the history of this project, I want to acknowledge a number of individuals who have contributed to my thinking and to this book in particular. Present throughout this text are the voices of several of my teachers: Wilfred Cantwell Smith, who taught the comparative study of religions at Harvard Divinity School; Raymond Fogelson, who first introduced me to medical anthropology and provided enormous support during my graduate years; Clifford Geertz, whose seminar on the theory of culture at the University of Chicago put me to work on many of the issues addressed here; Victor Turner, whose energy and ideas about social drama, narrative, and experience inspired a generation of Chicago students; and Lloyd Fallers, a gentle scholar and my advisor, who died while I was in the field.

Present also are the voices of my colleagues at Harvard, the graduate students and post-doctoral fellows with whom I have been privileged to work, a small group of visiting scholars from Tanzania and Kenya who read and commented on the text, and a larger group of colleagues in the field with whom I have discussed these issues over the years. At Harvard, Leon Eisenberg, Stanley Tambiah, Bob and Sarah LeVine, Nur Yalman, Dan Goodenough, and Allan Brandt deserve special thanks. Students (and former students) who have taken my graduate seminars on theory in medical anthropology have discussed many of the issues of this book with me, quietly criticizing my formulations and influencing me immeasurably. Though I am certain to omit names that deserve mention, Terry O'Nell, Paul Brodwin, Eric Jacobson, Lawrence Cohen, Paul Farmer, Jim Kim, Anne Becker, Linda Hunt, Lindsay French, Michael Nathan, Julia Paley, and David Attyah are among them. Of special importance have been conversations with fellows in the Harvard program, including Peter Guarnaccia, Janis Jenkins, Tom Csordas, Cheryl Mattingly, Linda Garro, David Napier, and Bob Desjarlais; the latter three made extensive comments on parts of the text. Among my colleagues, Allan Young, Charles Leslie, Ronald Frankenberg, Amélie Rorty,

Steve Fjellman, Gilles Bibeau, Ellen Corin, Vincent Crapanzano, Mariella Pandolfi, Debra Gordon, Margaret Lock, Mitzi Goheen, Hank Herrera, Ayala Gabriel, Don Pollock, Unni Wikan, Atwood Gaines, and Rick Shweder have each made unique contributions to this manuscript and to the ideas developed here. To all of these friends and colleagues, my thanks.

I owe special appreciation to Martha MacLeish Fuller for help in preparing the manuscript and proof-reading the text.

It is difficult to convey the extent to which my thinking on the issues addressed in this book has been influenced by my friend and colleague Arthur Kleinman. Since 1970 we have been engaged in dialogue about matters that concern both of us deeply. Arthur's own work and our many conversations have stimulated my thinking and tested my ideas, and his editorial comments on the text have improved its quality. No expression of my appreciation is adequate.

Finally, I acknowledge with gratitude the constant presence in this book of my wife and colleague, Mary-Jo DelVecchio Good. Mary-Jo has collaborated with me on all of the research discussed in the following pages; the data are hers as much as mine, and many of the interpretations derive from her insights and are reflected in our joint publications. The ideas I discuss here have evolved in a conversation with her that has lasted more than twenty-five years. Whatever depth and insight I am able to muster in this text grow out of that conversation. Mary-Jo sustained and encouraged me throughout the preparation of the Morgan Lectures and has read and commented on every page of this manuscript. It is to her that I dedicate this book.

1

Medical anthropology and the problem of belief

Part of the special delight of being invited to give the Morgan Lectures was the opportunity it afforded me to read the work of Lewis Henry Morgan and be reacquainted with his life. Though largely remembered for his masterful ethnography of the Iroquois and his technical kinship writing, Morgan was no stranger to what we might now call applied anthropology. For Morgan, scholarship and activism were closely linked. During the 1840s, when the rapacious Ogden Land Company sought to deprive the Seneca of their land – as Morgan wrote, "[they] pursued and hunted . . . [the Seneca] with a degree of wickedness hardly to be paralleled in the history of human avarice . . . " (quoted in L. White 1959: 4) – Morgan rallied local citizens to the cause of the Indians, and carried the fight to the United States Congress. In recognition for his service, he was adopted by the Seneca, made a member of the Hawk clan, and given the name Tayadaowuhkuh, or "one Lying Across," or "Bridging the Gap," "referring to him as a bridge over the differences . . . between the Indian and the white man."

Morgan's commitment to utilize his knowledge of the Seneca in their behalf has special meaning for medical anthropology. But it is not simply his activism that lends relevance to his work. Morgan played a crucial role in carving out kinship as an analytic domain, and the conceptual problems he faced were similar in intriguing ways to those which face medical anthropologists. Robert Trautmann, in his fine book on Morgan's "invention of kinship" (1987), notes that it may sound odd today to speak of the "discovery" of kinship, since aspects of family and kin relations are everywhere present and part of everyday experience. In reality, Trautmann argues, precisely this everyday quality of kin relations made them resistant to analysis.

> . . . the provisions of the kinship system are everywhere attributed to some immanent order, whether of Nature or of God or some other, which gives it the transparency of that which constitutes "the way things are." Like the air we breathe, it is all around us and we cannot see it. Kinship had to be discovered, and it was discovered through the discordant, noncommonsensical kinship of the cultural other. (Trautmann 1987: 3)

For Morgan, a practicing lawyer, it was his finding, to his great astonishment, that the Seneca attribute descent and prescribe the inheritance of property and office

1

so differently than we do – that is through females only – that served to "denaturalize" kinship as a domain and "make it available to consciousness" (Trautmann 1987: 4). And it was based upon this recognition that Morgan designated kinship as a *cultural domain*, an aspect of human societies having coherence and structure and thus a domain for systematic research and analysis.

Those of us who would turn anthropological attention to disease and illness face an analogous problem. The elements of observation are readily at hand – in our own encounters with fevers and pains, chronic medical conditions, or life-threatening diseases, and in our experience of the suffering of others. And although we commonly recognize personal and cultural differences in beliefs about disease or in what medical sociologists have called "illness behavior," the sense that disease itself is a cultural domain is strongly counter-intuitive. Disease is paradigmatically biological; it is what we mean by Nature and its impingement on our lives. Our anthropological research thus divides rather easily into two types, with medicine, public health, and human ecology providing models for the study of disease and its place in biological systems, and social and cultural studies investigating human adaptation and responses to disease. It takes a strong act of consciousness to denaturalize disease and contemplate it as a cultural domain.

From the perspective of the late twentieth century, it is difficult to appreciate fully the conceptual problem which Morgan faced in the study of kinship and the human family. It is easy today to be relativist when we consider aesthetics or philosophy or child-rearing in other societies, recognizing that others may have more profound or more interesting ways of understanding the world and organizing social life than we do. Kin systems are part of this social order, and with the important exception of our assumptions about the prohibition of incest, diversity of family relations seems only appropriate, given the distinctive forms of life in which they are embedded. For the Victorians, quite the opposite was true. The Victorians felt the family to be closely linked to the natural order, both biological and moral. Other forms of accounting kin and forming families were felt to be unnatural, abhorrently so.

If we contemplate for a moment our own views of medicine, we may recognize more easily what Morgan faced in his efforts to rethink the human family. We all know, of course, that medical knowledge has advanced rapidly over the past century, that it is progressing at a nearly unimaginable speed today. And we have little doubt that the medical sciences tell us with increasing accuracy about the human genome or the cellular contributions to disease – that is, about human biology, about Nature. This knowledge has yielded ever more powerful therapeutics and resulted in longer and healthier lives. As a consequence, we face a moral imperative to share that knowledge, to provide public health information to those whose beliefs serve them poorly as a basis for healthy behavior, in particular to provide broad public health education for societies with high rates of infant mortality, infectious diseases, and other scourges prominent in populations which have undergone neither the demographic nor educational revolution.

Our views of medicine serve as an apt analogy to Morgan's understanding about the achievements of Victorian society and the family as a dimension of it. Societies are progressive. Change results from increasing knowledge of the order of Nature and increasing conformity of society to that knowledge. Progress occurs through accumulating practical and scientific knowledge, or as Morgan wrote, "man commenced at the bottom of the scale and worked his way up to civilization through the slow accumulations of experimental knowledge" (in Trautmann 1987: 173). For the Victorians, their system of family relations was felt to be such an achievement, a highly evolved realization of the natural order. We in the twentieth century conceive medicine to be a similar achievement.

Morgan was thus confronted with a difficult interpretive dilemma when he found that the Iroquois, whom he so admired, conceived family relations in a manner considered immoral and abhorrent by his contemporaries. His response, ultimately, was to reconceptualize kinship – not simply as a part of Nature, but as a social and cultural domain – and it is in this sense that he "invented" kinship. In developing his analysis, Morgan distinguished "descriptive" kin terms, cultural categories which correctly reflect natural blood relationships, from "classificatory" terms, which do not, thus shaping a debate which has been carried on in kinship studies since that time.

In the course of these pages it will become clear that similar issues are central to the comparative study of illness and medical knowledge. In particular, it is difficult to avoid a strong conviction that our own system of knowledge reflects the natural order, that it is a progressive system that has emerged through the cumulative results of experimental efforts, and that our own biological categories are natural and "descriptive" rather than essentially cultural and "classificatory." These deeply felt assumptions authorize our system of medical knowledge and, at the same time, produce profound difficulties for comparative societal analysis. Just such difficulties lie at the heart of the conceptual problems of medical anthropology. Although evolutionist thinking about kinship systems is hard for us to intuit, making Morgan seem very much a nineteenth-century figure, thinking of systems of medical knowledge as analogies to kin systems makes it clear that the issues raised by Morgan are alive today. Our convictions about the truth claims of medical science rest uneasily with our recognition of our own historicity and our desire to respect competing knowledge claims of members of other societies or status groups. Indeed, the confrontation between the natural sciences and historicism – the view that all knowledge is unavoidably relative to historical context – has been the central issue of philosophy, the sociology of knowledge, and historical studies of science for much of this century. Within anthropology today, I would argue that medical anthropology is the primary site in which these issues are being addressed and investigated.

While studies in medical anthropology share many philosophical issues with kinship studies, including such epistemological dilemmas, they also open onto quite distinctive domains. It was Morgan's great contribution to recognize the extent to which premodern societies are organized in terms of kinship rather than property relations, thus placing kinship studies at the heart of all studies of social organization. While this analysis is also relevant to social and cultural studies of medical systems, medical anthropology has unique concerns with issues of biology and culture, with human suffering and ritual efforts to manage disorder and personal threat, and thus with the investigation of human experience and the existential grounds of culture. These, as well as the philosophical issues at stake in cross-cultural studies of disease and health care, will be central to the discussion to follow.

In the 1960s, it was something of an embarrassment to be identified as a medical anthropologist. Medical anthropology was largely a practice discipline in those days, shaped by a group of pioneering anthropologists – Benjamin Paul, George Foster, Charles Erasmus, Hazel Weidman, and others – committed to putting anthropology at the service of improving the public health of societies in the Third World. Social theory was largely peripheral to this discipline, and given the splendid debates among structuralists, ethnoscientists, symbolic anthro-pologists, linguists, and ethnolinguists, all committed to rethinking cultural studies, medical anthropology seemed a kind of poor cousin. Since that time there has been an explosion of interest and activities in this field. In 1957, Ben Paul assembled the names of 49 American anthropologists with experience in public health; today there are more than 1,700 members of the Society for Medical Anthropology. More importantly for its place in the field, the diverse issues that concern medical and psychiatric anthropologists have moved ever closer to the center of the discipline, and have become ever more prominent in the social sciences and humanities at large. Discussions of culture and representation have increasingly turned to the analysis of illness representations, from popular medical knowledge to social representations of diseases such as AIDS (see Farmer and B. Good 1991 for a review). Medical institutions have become key sites for the analysis of power and domination, and feminist studies have drawn on medical phenomena to explore the gendered representation of women's bodies, birthing and reproduction, and the relation of these to changes in the division of labor.[1] Theoretical and applied work, though still in tension, increasingly nourish one another, and vigorous theoretical debates have developed, which have relevance throughout anthropology. Indeed, as I will argue, current concerns in medical anthropology today and the phenomena to which it attends have the potential to play a special role in revivifying aspects of our larger discipline.

Over the last decade, my own work – much of it carried out in collaboration with my wife, Mary-Jo DelVecchio Good – has addressed the theoretical and substantive issues in medical anthropology in ways which frame the questions addressed in the Morgan Lectures. First, I have attempted to situate medical anthropology in relation to a set of philosophical debates about the nature of language, subjectivity, and knowledge.[2] I have argued that our philosophical presuppositions, whether explicit or implicit, play an important role in formulating the research program in our field. And I have tried to demonstrate that medical anthropology provides an extremely interesting vantage from which to address these very debates.

More specifically, I have explored the idea that a view of scientific language as largely transparent to the natural world, a kind of "mirror of nature," which has been an important line of argument in philosophy since the Enlightenment, has deep affinities with biomedicine's "folk epistemology" and holds a special attraction for the medical behavioral sciences. I have argued, however, that this conception of language and knowledge, referred to in our writings as the "empiricist theory of medical language,"[3] serves poorly for either cross-cultural research or for our studies of American science and medicine. Those who employ it are led to formulate problems in terms of belief and behavior, and often reproduce our common-sense views of the individual and society. After years of teaching and carrying out research in medical settings, I am more convinced than ever that the language of medicine is hardly a simple mirror of the empirical world. It is a rich *cultural language*, linked to a highly specialized version of reality and system of social relations, and when employed in medical care, it joins deep moral concerns with its more obvious technical functions.

In place of a medical social science focused on belief and behavior, a number of medical anthropologists have pursued theoretical and analytic studies more in keeping with this view of medical language, giving special attention to illness meanings and experience. My own work has advanced a view of illness as a "syndrome of experience," "a set of words, experiences, and feelings which typically 'run together' for members of a society" (B. Good 1977: 27). Drawing on research on popular illness categories in Iran and from American medical clinics, our work has explored the diverse interpretive practices through which illness realities are constructed, authorized, and contested in personal lives and social institutions. In this view, what philosopher Ernst Cassirer called "the formative principles" by which life worlds are constituted and organized become a predominant focus of attention.[4] Such a perspective requires an understanding of language and experience counter to that in much of the medical social sciences, and frames a quite different set of issues.

Medical anthropology has thus come to be a site for joining debate of critical social, political, existential, and epistemological issues. To use a metaphor suggested to me by Amélie Rorty, medical anthropology has become our discipline's "London," a metropole where diverse voices engage in substantial matters of the day. Many of the central concerns of anthropology are clearly present in the issues we face – the role of the biological sciences as both instrumental reason and soteriology in contemporary civilization; the efficacy of symbolic practices in the constitution of experience and the production and reproduction of social worlds; the human body as both the creative source of experience and the site of domination; and efforts to place renewed understanding of human experience at the heart of our discipline. The Morgan Lectures, and their elaboration in this text, were conceived as a contribution to this larger project.

The view of medical anthropology I have briefly outlined here has been criticized from several perspectives in recent years. For example, in an essay published in *Current Anthropology* in 1988, Carole Browner, Bernard Ortiz de Montellano, and Arthur Rubel argue that the excitement generated by medical anthropology in the early 1970s and its hope for "uniting theory and practice in a new health science at once cumulative, comparative, integrative, and methodologically sound" has gone largely unfulfilled. Instead, they argue, medical anthropology has followed a "particularistic, fragmented, disjointed, and largely conventional source." Citing specifically the work of Allan Young, Byron and Mary-Jo Good, and Arthur Kleinman, they go on: "This is because most medical anthropologists are mainly interested in issues of meaning and in the symbolic and epistemological dimensions of sickness, healing, and health . . . " (p. 681). They conclude their indictment (p. 682) with a quote from Professor Joseph Loudon, a physician and anthropologist:

> A supposedly empirical discipline which gets unduly concerned about epistemological worries is in danger of losing its way. . . . there are certainly some aspects of social anthropology [including at least some areas of ethnomedicine] where external categories of more or less universal reference are available which, if used with reasonable caution, make possible comparative analysis over time and space. . . .

Following this critique, Browner and her colleagues outline a research program for medical anthropology, counter to the "meaning-centered" approach, that focuses on "cross-cultural comparative studies of human physiological processes," which are "essentially the same species-wide" and can serve as external referents necessary to prevent cross-cultural research from degenerating into pure relativism.

This essay represents a current debate within medical anthropology. It should be clear already, however, that it points toward much more fundamental issues. At stake is not only the question of the place of biology in the program of medical anthropology, a question I take very seriously, but a critique developed within medical anthropology over the past decade of biomedicine and the research paradigm of the behavioral sciences of medicine. At stake also are various debates in anthropology today about how we conduct cultural studies and ultimately about what kind of human science anthropology should be. And lying beneath these debates are opposing views of how historicism – the view that "human understanding is always a 'captive' of its historical situation" (D'Amico 1989: x) – can come to terms with the natural sciences, particularly in cross-cultural research. With all due respect to Professor Loudon, a medical anthropology that ignores epistemological worries is certain to reproduce important dimensions of conventional knowledge in an unexamined fashion.

The chapters of this book will explore several specific dimensions of the larger project I outlined above, all addressing the nature of language, subjectivity and social process in cross-cultural studies of illness and human suffering. I begin with an examination of the concept "belief" in anthropology. Specifically, I will argue that "belief" is a key analytic term within the empiricist paradigm, and that this concept is linked to a set of philosophic assumptions in a way that is far from obvious. I hope to show that the emergence of "belief" as a central analytic category in anthropology was a fateful development, and that use of the term continues to both reflect and reproduce a set of conceptual difficulties within modernist anthropology. If by the end of this chapter, I can raise serious questions for my readers about that favorite collection of odd job words of Anglo-Americans – "believe," "belief," "beliefs," "belief systems" – my first goal will have been achieved.

In the pages that follow, I explore several dimensions of an alternative theoretical framework for the comparative study of illness and medical practices. In particular, I discuss issues which have little prominence in an anthropology framed in terms of belief: the anthropology of experience and what we can learn from studies of human suffering; studies of interpretation and its constituting role in social process; and critical analyses of medical discourse and the institutional and societal relations in which they are embedded. The overall text of this book, as of the Morgan Lectures upon which it is based, is thus organized not around a particular piece of ethnographic work – although I will present data from research in Iran, Turkey, and American medicine – but is designed to explore a set of theoretical issues in the field.

Science, salvation, and belief: an anthropological response to fundamentalist epistemologies

I begin with "an anthropological response to fundamentalist epistemologies" because of my intuition that there is – quite ironically – a close relationship between science, including medicine, and religious fundamentalism, a relationship that turns, in part, on our concept "belief." For fundamentalist Christians, salvation is often seen to follow from belief, and mission work is conceived as an effort to convince the natives to give up false beliefs and take on a set of beliefs that will produce a new life and ultimate salvation. Ironically, quite a-religious scientists and policy makers see a similar benefit from correct belief.[5] Educate the public about the hazards of drug use, our current Enlightenment theory goes, heralded from the White House and the office of the drug czar, get them to believe the right thing and the problem will be licked. Educate the patient, medical journals advise clinicians, and solve the problems of noncompliance that plague the treatment of chronic disease. Investigate public beliefs about vaccinations or risky health behaviors using the Health Belief Model, a generation of health psychologists has told us, get people to believe the right thing and our public health problems will be solved. Salvation from drugs and from preventable illness will follow from correct belief.

Wilfred Cantwell Smith, a comparative historian of religion and theologian, argues that the fundamentalist conception of belief is a recent Christian heresy (Smith 1977, 1979). I want to explore the hypothesis that anthropology has shared this heresy with religious fundamentalists, that "belief" has a distinctive cultural history within anthropology and that the conceptualization of culture as "belief" is far from a trivial matter.

A quick review of the history of medical anthropology will convince the reader that "belief" has played a particularly important analytic role in this subdiscipline, as it has in the medical behavioral sciences and in public health (see chapter 2 for more details). Why is there this deep attachment to analyzing others' under-standings of illness and its treatment as medical "beliefs" and practices, and why is there such urgency expressed about correcting beliefs when mistaken? To begin to address this issue, I first describe in a bit more detail the general theoretical paradigm that frames what I have referred to as the "empiricist theory of medical knowledge." I will indicate its relationship to the intellectualist tradition in anthropology and to debates about rationality and relativism, showing how the language of belief functions within the rationalist tradition. At the end of this chapter, I review recent criticisms that have shaken the foundations of this paradigm, criticisms that suggest the need for an alternative direction in the field. This discussion will serve to frame the constructive chapters that follow.

The language of clinical medicine is a highly technical language of the bio-sciences, grounded in a natural science view of the relation between language, biology, and experience (B. Good and M. Good 1981). As George Engel (1977) and a host of medical reformers have shown, the "medical model" typically employed in clinical practice and research assumes that diseases are universal biological or psychophysiological entities, resulting from somatic lesions or dysfunctions.[6] These produce "signs" or physiological abnormalities that can be measured by clinical and laboratory procedures, as well as "symptoms" or expressions of the experience of distress, communicated as an ordered set of complaints. The primary tasks of clinical medicine are thus diagnosis – that is, the interpretation of the patient's symptoms by relating them to their functional and structural sources in the body and to underlying disease entities – and rational treatment aimed at intervention in the disease mechanisms. All subspecialties of clinical medicine thus share a distinctive medical "hermeneutic," an implicit understanding of medical interpretation. While patients' symptoms may be coded in cultural language, the primary interpretive task of the clinician is to decode patients' symbolic expressions in terms of their underlying somatic referents. Disordered experience, communicated in the language of culture, is interpreted in light of disordered physiology and yields medical diagnoses.

Medical knowledge, in this paradigm, is constituted through its depiction of empirical biological reality. Disease entities are resident in the physical body; whether grossly apparent, as the wildly reproducing cells of a cancer, or subtly evident through their effects, as in the disordered thoughts and feelings of schizophrenia or major depression, diseases are biological, universal, and ultimately transcend social and cultural context. Their distribution varies by social and ecological context, all medical scientists agree, but medical knowledge does not. Medical theories reflect the facts of nature, and the validity and rationality of medical discourse is dependent upon the causal–functional integration of biological systems.

One central goal of the pages that follow is to develop an alternative way of thinking about medicine and medical knowledge, a theoretical frame that challenges this common-sense view while still accounting for our conviction that medical knowledge is progressing, and one that serves us better as a basis for cross-cultural comparisons. To do so, it is important to recognize the epistemological assumptions of this common-sense view, and to appreciate its power.

The empiricist theory of medical language is grounded in what philosopher Charles Taylor calls "the polemical, no-nonsense nominalism" of Enlightenment theories of language and meaning.[7] For seventeenth-century philosophers such as Hobbes and Locke, the development of a language for science required a demystification of language itself, showing it to be a pliant instrument of rationality and thought, as well as the emergence of a disenchanted view of the natural world. The development of such a natural philosophy and the attendant theory of language required the separation of "the order of words" from "the order of things," in Foucault's terms (1970), the freeing of the order of language and symbols from a world of hierarchical planes of being and correspondences present in Renaissance cosmology. What we must seek, Francis Bacon argued, is not to identify ideas or meanings in the universe, but "to build an adequate representation of things" (Taylor 1985a: 249). Thus, theories of language became the battle ground between the religious orthodoxy, who conceived "nature" as reflecting God's creative presence and language as a source of divine revelation, and those who viewed the world as natural and language as conventional and instrumental.[8]

What emerged was a conception of language in which *representation* and *designation* are exceedingly important attributes. Such a position was bound to a view of knowledge as the holding of a correct representation of some aspect of the world, and an understanding of the knowing subject as an individual who holds an accurate representation of the natural world, derived from sense experience and represented in thought. Meaning, in this paradigm, is constituted through the referential linking of elements in language and those in the natural world, and the meaningfulness of a proposition – including, for example, a patient's complaint or a doctor's diagnosis – is almost solely dependent upon "how the world is, as a matter of empirical fact, constituted" (Harrison 1972: 33). Although this view has been widely criticized by now, it continues to have broad influence in philosophy, psychology (in particular cognitive psychology and artificial intelligence research), in the natural sciences, and in Western folk psychology. It is associated with an understanding of agency as instrumental action, and with utilitarian theories of society, social relations, and culture as precipitates of individual, goal-directed action (Sahlins 1976a).[9]

This broad perspective has the status of a kind of "folk epistemology" for medical practice in hospitals and clinics of contemporary biomedicine. A person's complaint is meaningful if it reflects a physiological condition; if no such empirical referent can be found, the very meaningfulness of the complaint is called into question. Such complaints (for example of chronic pain)[10] are often held to reflect patients' beliefs or psychological states, that is subjective opinions and experiences which may have no grounds in disordered physiology and thus in objective reality. "Real pathology," on the other hand, reflects disordered physiology. Contemporary technical medicine provides objective knowledge of such pathology, represented as a straight-forward and transparent reflection of the natural order revealed through the dense semiotic system of physical findings, laboratory results, and the visual products of contemporary imaging techniques. And "rational behavior" is that which is oriented in relation to such objective knowledge.

At this point in the argument, I sometimes feel I have painted myself into a corner. How can such a view be disputed? This is precisely what we mean by medical *knowledge*, and we should all be grateful that medicine has progressed as far as it has in identifying disease mechanisms and rational therapies. In later chapters, especially in chapter 3 where I examine how medical students come to inhabit this specialized world of medical knowledge, I argue that the empiricist theory hides as much as it reveals about the nature of everyday clinical practice and the forms of knowledge that guide it, and I develop an alternative approach to conceptualizing the nature of medical language. In the remainder of this chapter, however, I want to examine the extent to which the medical social sciences and some forms of anthropology share with medicine this empiricist theory of knowledge and outline some of the difficulties that arise for cross-cultural studies because of this.

Rationality and the empiricist paradigm in anthropology

The empiricist paradigm is most clearly represented by the intellectualist tradition in anthropology, which was prominent in Britain at the turn of the century and reemerged under the banner of Neo-Tylorianism in an important set of debates about the nature of rationality during the 1970s.[11] Although I can only briefly address some aspects of this debate, even a cursory examination will indicate how the rationalist position flows out of the "Enlightenment" tradition of anthropology, demonstrate the critical role of "belief" in this paradigm, and suggest why it has had such power within medical anthropology.

A central issue in the rationality debate has been discussion of the problem of "apparently irrational beliefs" (for example Sperber 1985: ch. 2). How do we make sense of cultural views of the world that are not in accord with contemporary natural sciences, it is often asked. Do we argue that members of traditional cultures live in wholly different worlds, and their statements are true in their worlds, not ours, or even that they cannot be translated intelligibly into our language? Advocates of a typical rationalist position hold that such relativism is essentially incoherent, and have often argued either that seemingly irrational statements must be understood symbolically rather than literally or that they represent a kind of "proto-science," an effort to explain events in the world in an orderly fashion that is a functional equivalent of modern science. The crucial interpretive problem, for this tradition, is how to answer a question stated explicitly by Lukes (1970: 194): "When I come across a set of beliefs which appear *prima facie* irrational, what should be my attitude toward them?" Given our claims that other forms of thought are rational, how do we make sense of beliefs that are obviously false?

For much of this debate, Evans-Pritchard's *Witchcraft, Oracles and Magic among the Azande* (1937) serves as the primary source. This book was the first and is arguably still the most important modernist text in medical anthropology. It has had enduring influence because of the wealth of the ethnography and the richness of its interpretation of witchcraft as an explanation for illness and misfortune. Which anthropologist can think of cultural responses to misfortune without conjuring the image of Evans-Pritchard's young lad stubbing his toe and blaming witchcraft for its failure to heal, or of the granary collapsing? To these misfortunes, the Zande explanation was clear. "Every Zande knows that termites eat the supports [of the granaries] in course of time and that even the hardest woods decay after years of service," Evans-Pritchard reports. But "why should these particular people have been sitting under this particular granary at the particular moment when it collapsed?" Thus, although practical reasons explain the immediate causes of illness and misfortune, the Azande turn to witchcraft to answer the "why me?" question, to find an underlying cause in the moral universe and a response that is socially embedded and morally satisfying.

The Azande text has been the key for the rationality debate for another reason. Evans-Pritchard in this text was explicitly empiricist, and his work provided examples that serve as paradigmatic challenges to relativism. Take, for example, his analysis of the Zande autopsy to investigate witchcraft, which appears as a substance in the intestine of a witch. Since witchcraft is inherited by kin, an autopsy may be performed on a deceased kinsman to determine whether others bear the unwanted substance. Evans-Pritchard (1937: 42) describes the scene:

> Two gashes are made in the belly and one end of the intestines is placed in a cleft branch and they are wound round it. After the other end has been severed from the body another man takes it and unwinds the intestines as he walks away from the man holding the cleft branch. The old men walk alongside the entrails as they are stretched in the air and examine them for witchcraft-substance. The intestines are usually replaced in the belly when the examination is finished and the corpse is buried. I have been told that if no witchcraft-substance were discovered in a man's belly his kinsmen might strike his accusers in the face with his intestines or might dry them in the sun and afterwards take them to court and there boast of their victory.

Evans-Pritchard's (1937: 63) interpretation of this dramatic scene is telling.

> It is an inevitable conclusion from Zande descriptions of witchcraft that it is not an objective reality. The physiological condition which is said to be the seat of witchcraft, and which I believe to be nothing more than food passing through the small intestine, is

an objective condition, but the qualities they attribute to it and the rest of their beliefs about it are mystical. Witches, as Azande conceive them, cannot exist.

He goes on immediately to argue that although mistaken, the Zande views serve as a natural philosophy and embrace a system of values which regulate human conduct. They are, however, mystical. "Mystical notions," he argues in the book's introduction (p. 12), are those that attribute to phenomena "supra-sensible qualities," "which are not derived from observation" and "which they do not possess." "Common-sense notions" attribute to phenomena only what can be observed in them or logically inferred from observation. Though they may be mistaken, they do not assert forces that cannot be observed. Both are distinct from "scientific notions." "Our body of scientific knowledge and Logic," he says (p. 12), "are the sole arbiters of what are mystical, common-sense, and scientific notions."

Evans-Pritchard assumes in this account that the meaning of Zande "medical discourse" – whether of witchcraft, oracles, or "leechcraft" – is constituted by its referential relationship to the natural order as reflected in empirical experience. Analysis in the rationality literature follows from this assumption; it frames Zande beliefs as propositions, then questions the verifiability and the deductive validity of their inferences. Since we know that witches cannot exist empirically, it is argued, the rationality of Zande thought is called into doubt. It follows that the anthropologist must therefore organize analysis in response to the following kinds of questions. How can a set of beliefs and institutions which are so obviously false (propositionally) be maintained for such long periods of time by persons who in much of their lives are so reasonable? How could they possibly believe that, and why haven't their beliefs progressed, that is come to represent the natural world more correctly? Do such beliefs imply that the Zande have a different "mentality" or different psychological or logical processes than we? Do they simply divide up the common-sense and religious domains differently than do we (as Evans-Pritchard responded to Lévy-Bruhl)? Are some societies simply organized around views that are reasonable but wrong?

Not altogether obvious in Evans-Pritchard's text is the juxtaposition of "belief" and "knowledge." The book is devoted largely to Zande mystical notions – witchcraft and sorcery – and ritual behaviors, such as resort to the poison oracle. One chapter, however, entitled "Leechcraft," is devoted to their common-sense notions of sickness. The language of "belief" and "knowledge" mirror this distinction. The book begins: "Azande *believe* that some people are witches and can injure them in virtue of an inherent quality . . . They *believe* also that sorcerers may do them ill by performing magic rites with bad medicines . . . Against both they employ diviners, oracles, and medicines. The relations between these *beliefs* and rites are the subject of this book" (p. 21; my emphasis). On the other hand, the Leechcraft chapter argues: "Azande *know* diseases by their major symptoms" (p. 482). "The very fact of naming diseases and differentiating them from one another by their symptoms shows observation and common-sense inferences" (pp. 494–495). Thus, the book is organized around a distinction between those ideas that accord with objective reality – and, I might add, with the medical practice of deriving diagnoses from symptoms – and those that do not; the language of knowledge is used to describe the former, the language of belief the latter. Evans-Pritchard's text transcends its empiricist formulation, in particular because of the subtlety of its analysis of Zande reasoning and the location of witchcraft in Zande social relations, but it makes explicit many of the assumptions found more generally in the rationality tradition and shared by much of the medical social sciences.

If Evans-Pritchard's work on the Azande is the classic modernist text on witchcraft and illness, Jeanne Favret-Saada's *Deadly Words. Witchcraft in the Bocage* (1980), first published in French in 1977, is surely the classic post-modernist ethnography on the topic. Favret-Saada's ethnography is a first-person account of her effort to investigate witchcraft in rural France. In the early months of her work, villagers referred her to a few well known healers who were often interviewed by the press, but the peasants themselves refused to discuss the matter with her. Witchcraft? Only fools believe in that!

> "Take an ethnographer," she begins (1980: 4). "She has spent more than thirty months in the Bocage in Mayenne, studying witchcraft . . . 'Tell us about the witches', she is asked again and again when she gets back to the city. Just as one might say: tell us tales about ogres or wolves, about Little Red Riding Hood. Frighten us, but make it clear that it's only a story; or that they are just peasants: credulous, backward and marginal . . .
>
> "No wonder that country people in the West are not in any hurry to step forward and be taken for idiots in the way that public opinion would have them be . . . "

The book is an account of how she eventually found her way into the discourse of witchcraft. She was taken ill, beset with accidents, and sought the aid of a healer in the region, an unwitcher. She began to interview a man and his family, whom she had met when the man was a patient in a mental hospital. As they told her the details of his illness and who they suspected might be responsible, she realized that they saw her as a healer and now expected her to act on their behalf. Why else would she ask about such matters so explicitly? Only the powerful would dare to ask such questions.[12] Simply by asking about their difficulties, she was seen to be entering into their struggle with an enemy wishing them harm, a life and death struggle in which she was now an advocate for their interests. Witchcraft, she came to see, was a battle of powerful wills, a fight to the death, a fight through the medium of spoken words. One could only talk about witchcraft from an engaged position – as one bewitched, as a suspected witch, or as one willing to serve as unwitcher. To engage in talk was to enter the struggle.

In Favret-Saada's account, the language of belief, the position of the ethnographer, and assumptions about the relation of culture and reality are radically different than in Evans-Pritchard's text. Science for Favret-Saada is not the arbiter between the empirically real and the mystical, as for Evans-Pritchard, but one of several "official theories of misfortune," backed by powerful social agencies: the School, the Church, the Medical Association. Language is not a set of neutral propositions about the world, which the ethnographer judges to be more or less empirically valid, but the medium through which vicious and life-threatening power struggles are engaged. The world of illness and witchcraft only opens to the ethnographer as she enters the discourse. And much of the text turns on ironic reflections on "belief" – the peasants' claims not to believe in witchcraft, even as they seek the help of the unwitcher; the mocking view of the authorities about those who do believe; and Favret-Saada's juxtaposition of the meaning of belief in her text and in that of Evans-Pritchard. For many ethnographers, as for the French press, the question is whether the peasants really believe in witchcraft, and if so, how they can hold such beliefs in today's world. But for those attacked by a sorcerer, for those peasants – and Favret-Saada herself – whose very lives were at stake, *belief* in witchcraft is not the question. How to protect oneself, how to ward off the evil attacks producing illness and misfortune, is the only significant issue to be addressed.

Much has changed in the world of anthropology between that of 1935 colonialist Africa and contemporary post-colonialist ethnography. Evans-Pritchard's confident positioning of himself as observer and arbiter of the rationality of the native discourse is largely unavailable to us today. And throughout the history and sociology of science, the confident recording of science's progress in discovering the facts of nature has also given way. I will return to these issues as the discussion proceeds, but the juxtaposition of Evans-Pritchard's and Favret-Saada's texts brings into focus the role of "belief" as an analytic category in the history of anthropology and in the study of such phenomena as witchcraft, provoking several questions. Why has the discussion of others' beliefs come to be invoked increasingly with irony? What is the role of belief in the empiricist paradigm, and why has that position begun to give way? Where does the disjunction between "belief" and "knowledge," which I noted in *Witchcraft, Oracles, and Magic* and which serves as the basis for Favret-Saada's irony, come from? Why "belief," and what is at stake here?

The problem of belief in anthropology

Rodney Needham's *Belief, Language and Experience*, published in 1972, is the classic examination of the philosophy of belief by an anthropologist. Needham explores in great detail assumptions about belief as mental state, asking whether philosophers have formulated this with adequate clarity to allow us to use the term in cross-cultural research, and asking whether members of other societies indeed experience what we call "belief." After an extraordinary review, he concludes both that philosophers have failed to clarify "the supposed capacity for belief" and are unlikely to do so, and that evidence suggests the term may well not have counterparts in the ethnopsychological language of many societies. Needham's analysis suggests that Evans-Pritchard's claim that the Azande believe some people are witches may be a less straightforward description of the mental states of Zande individuals than we usually presume. For the moment, however, I want to focus on another dimension of belief as anthropologists have used the term in cultural analysis.

Mary Steedly, an anthropologist who worked with the Karobatak people in Sumatra, tells how when she was beginning fieldwork she was often asked a question, which she understood to mean "do you believe in spirits?"[13] It was one of those embarrassing questions anthropologists struggle to answer, since she didn't, personally, but respected and wanted to learn about the understandings of persons in the village in which she worked. After stumbling to answer the question for some months, she discovered her questioners were asking "Do you trust spirits? Do you believe what they say? Do you maintain a relationship with them?" Any sensible person believes in their existence; that isn't even a meaningful question. The real question is how one chooses to relate to them.

Anthropologists often talk with members of other societies about some aspect of their world which does not exist in ours and which we are comfortable asserting is not part of empirical reality. How is it that "belief" has come to be the language through which we discuss such matters – the Zande witches, or the three humors wind, bile, and phlegm in Ayurvedic medicine, or the four humors of seventeenth-century European and American medicine? Moreover, why have we in Western civilization given such importance to beliefs, such importance that wars in Christendom are fought over beliefs, that church schisms and persecutions and martyrdom revolve around correct belief? How is it that belief came to be so central to anthropological analysis, and what is implied by the juxtaposition of belief and knowledge?

By far the richest discussion of the history of the concept belief is to be found in the writing of Wilfred Cantwell Smith, the historian of religion, whose lectures when I was a graduate student set me to thinking about these matters. In two books completed during the late 1970s, Smith explores the relation between "belief" and "faith" historically and across religious traditions. He sets out not to compare beliefs among religions, but to examine the place of belief itself in Buddhist, Hindu, Islamic, and Christian history. Through careful historical and linguistic analysis, he comes to the startling conclusion that "the idea that believing is religiously important turns out to be a modern idea," and that the meaning of the English words "to believe" and "belief" have changed so dramatically in the past three centuries that they wreak profound havoc in our ability to understand our own historical tradition and the religious faith of others.

The word "belief" has a long history in the English language; over the course it has so changed that its earlier meanings are only dimly felt today (Smith 1977: 41–46; 1979: 105–127). In Old English, the words which evolved into modern "believe" (*geleofan, gelefan, geliefan*) meant "to belove," "to hold dear," "to cherish," "to regard as lief." They were the equivalent of what the German word *belieben* means today (*mein lieber Freund* is "my dear or cherished friend"), and show the same root as the Latin *libet*, "it pleases," or *libido*, "pleasure." This meaning survives in the Modern English archaism "lief" and the past participle "beloved." In medieval texts, "leve," "love," and "beleue" are virtual equivalents. In Chaucer's *Canterbury Tales*, the words "accepted my bileve" mean simply "accept my loyalty; receive me as one who submits himself to you." Thus Smith argues that "belief in God" originally means "a loyal pledging of oneself to God, a decision and commitment to live one's life in His service" (1977: 42). Its counterpart in the medieval language of the Church was "I renounce the Devil," belief and renunciation being parallel and contrasting actions, rather than states of mind.

Smith (1977: 44) sums up his argument about the change of the religious meaning of "belief" in our history as follows:

> The affirmation "I believe in God" used to mean: "Given the reality of God as a fact of the universe, I hereby pledge to Him my heart and soul. I committedly opt to live in loyalty to Him. I offer my life to be judged by Him trusting His mercy." Today the statement may be taken by some as meaning: "Given the uncertainty as to whether there be a God or not, as a fact of modern life, I announce that my opinion is 'yes'. I judge God to be existent."

Smith argues that this change in the language of belief can be traced in the grammar and semantics of English literature and philosophy, as well as popular usage. Three changes – in the object of the verb, the subject of the verb, and the relation of belief and knowledge – serve as indicators of the changing semantics of the verb "to believe." First, Smith finds that grammatically, the object of the verb "to believe" shifted from a person (whom one trusted or had faith in), to a person and his word (his virtue accruing to the trustworthiness of his word), to a proposition. This latter shift began to occur by the end of the seventeenth century, with Locke, for example, who characterized "belief" along with "assent" and "opinion" as "the admitting or receiving any proposition for true, upon arguments or proofs that are found to persuade us . . . without certain knowledge . . . " (Smith 1977: 48), and was firmly represented by the mid-nineteenth century in John Stuart Mill's philosophy. In the twentieth century we have seen a further shift as beliefs have come to mean "presuppositions," as in "belief systems."

A second shift has occurred in the subject of the verb "to believe," from an almost exclusive use of the first person – "I believe" – to the predominant use of the third person, "he believes" or "they believe." In anthropology, the impersonal "it is believed that" parallels the discussion of culture as belief system or system of thought. This change in subject subtly shifts the nature of the speech act involved – from existential to descriptive – and alters the authorization of the speaker, as I will discuss in a moment with reference to the use of belief as an analytic category in anthropology.

Third, Smith observes that an important and often unrecognized change has occurred in the relation of belief to truth and knowledge, as these are historically conceived. Bacon wrote in 1625 of "the belief of truth," which he defined as the "enjoyment of it," in contrast to the inquiry or wooing of truth and the knowledge or presence of truth. Belief maintains its sense here of holding dear, of appropriating to oneself that which is recognized as true. By the nineteenth century, however, "to believe" had come to connote doubt, and today it suggests outright error or falsehood. Knowledge requires both certitude and correctness; belief implies uncertainty, error, or both. Thus, I can report that a student of mine *believes* Lewis Henry Morgan to have been a professor of the anthropology department in the University of Rochester, but anyone who has studied Morgan's life *knows* that this was never so. Smith's favorite illustration of the juxtaposition of belief and knowledge is an entry in the Random House dictionary which defined "belief" as "an opinion or conviction," and at once illustrates this with "*the belief that the earth is flat*"! Indeed, it is virtually unacceptable usage to say that members of some society "believe" the earth is round; if this is part of their world view, then it is knowledge, not belief!

Smith goes on to argue that our failure to recognize this shift in meaning has led to mistranslation of texts in the Christian tradition and ultimately to "the heresy of believing," the deeply mistaken view that belief in this modern sense is the essence of the religious life rather than faith. *Credo*, in the Latin, is literally "I set my heart" (from Latin *cordis* or heart [as in cordial] and *-do* or *-dere*, to put). *Credo in unum Deum* was correctly translated in the sixteenth century as "I believe in one God," when it meant "I formally pledge my allegiance to God," Whom we of course all acknowledge to be present in the world. Today, it is a mistranslation, suggesting that the Credo consists of propositions the veracity of which we assert. This is historically inaccurate and profoundly misrepresents the traditional ritual acclamation. Equally importantly, for the comparativist, the misplaced focus on beliefs as the primary dimension of religious life has led to mistranslations and misunderstandings of other religious traditions, and in Smith's view, to the great failure to explore the *faith* of others in their historical and communal contexts, even to make faith a central category in comparative research.

Smith's argument about the importance of placing the study of faith rather than beliefs at the center of comparative and historical studies of religion has important implications for the study of illness experience, some of which will become apparent in later chapters. My interest at this time, however, is the place of "belief" in the history of anthropology, and what the use of the term tells us about the anthropological project. In what way does Smith's analysis of belief relate to the use of the term in anthropological writing? What is the history of believing in anthropology? How is the use of "belief" related to the epistemological assumptions of anthropologists?

From my initial explorations, it would appear that the term "belief" as it is employed in anthropology does indeed connote error or falsehood, although it is seldom explicitly asserted. A quick scan of the typical volumes on an anthropologist's shelf will provide many examples. My own favorite, paralleling Smith's discovery in the Random House Dictionary, comes from Ward Goodenough's little book, *Culture, Language and Society* (1981). In a discussion of "propositions" and the nature of reasoning cross-culturally, he provides the following example from the German ethnologist Girschner, to illustrate the "reasonableness" of members of other cultures.

> Consider, for example, the following comment by a Micronesian navigator, defending his *belief* that the sun goes around the earth (Girschner, 1913 . . .)
>
> I am well aware of the foreigner's claim that the earth moves and the sun stands still, as someone once told us; but this we cannot *believe*, for how else could it happen that in the morning and evening the sun burns less hot than in the day? It must be because the sun has been cooled when it emerges from the water and toward setting it again approaches the water. And furthermore, how can it be possible that the sun remains still when we are yet able to observe that in the course of the year it changes its position in relation to the stars? [emphasis added] (Goodenough 1981: 69).

Quite reasonable, even if mistaken: that is how the beliefs of others seem to be.

The juxtaposition of belief and knowledge is most evident in the intellectualist writing of turn-of-the-century British social anthropology. An example from a classic text in medical anthropology will be particularly instructive. W. H. R. Rivers' *Medicine, Magic and Religion* was published in 1924, the first major comparative study of medical systems by an anthropologist–physician.[14] The book is designed to show how concepts of disease vary cross-culturally, but focuses largely on beliefs about causation of disease. Rivers uses "believe" largely in the third person or impersonally; the object of belief is almost exclusively propositions; and these propositions are, from Rivers' point of view, counter-factual. For example, he writes (1924: 29):

> Thus, in Murray Island, in Torres Straits, disease is believed to occur by the action of certain men who, through their possession of objects called *zogo* and their knowledge of the appropriate rites, have the power of inflicting disease. Thus, one *zogo* is believed to make people lean and hungry and at the same time to produce dysentery; another will produce constipation, and a third insanity.

His attitude is made clear several pages later, when he discusses the rationality of such beliefs. "From our modern standpoint we are able to see that these ideas are wrong. But the important point is that, however wrong may be the beliefs of the Papuan and Melanesian concerning the causation of disease, their practices are the logical consequence of those beliefs." This view is conveyed more subtly, however, and with far more profound implications at the end of the book. The conclusion is devoted to illuminating the role of belief in the practice of Western medicine. Whereas in earlier chapters of the book, the word "believe," along with "ascribe," "regard," and "attribute," appears on nearly every page of discussion of the medical concepts of others, the word "believe" does not appear in the final fourteen pages of the book. Here the word "knowledge," and cognates "recognize," "realize," "acknowledge," and "awareness," are used to describe Western medicine. Rivers could not have more clearly stated his judgment.

This juxtaposition of what others believe to what we know is not only true of intellectualist writers such as Tylor, Frazer, and Rivers. Close reading of the

Evans-Pritchard text I have been discussing shows that he uses "belief" and its cognates to far greater analytic advantage than his predecessors, focusing on the coherence of a set of ideas. "All their beliefs hang together," he writes (1937: 194), "and were a Zande to give up faith in witch-doctorhood he would have to surrender equally his belief in witchcraft and oracles." The study of folk "logics" is an important part of the repertoire of cultural analysis, and Evans-Pritchard was a master of this genre. Nonetheless, his analysis framed culture as beliefs, and these were juxtaposed to knowledge – grossly in the introduction of the book, then in a subtle and nuanced way throughout this classic text.

The subtle or explicit representation of belief and knowledge as disjunct continues to be found in anthropological writing up to the present time. It is most explicit in rationalist writing and subsequent discussions of relativism. A final example from Dan Sperber's book *On Anthropological Knowledge* (1985), which proposes to "outline an epistemology of anthropology" (p. 7), will illustrate. The central chapter in the book is entitled "Apparently Irrational Beliefs." It begins with an extract from Sperber's field diary during his research in Ethiopia, when an old man, Filate, comes in a state of great excitement to tell Sperber that he has learned of a dragon – "Its heart is made of gold, it has one horn on the nape of its neck. It is golden all over. It does not live far, two days' walk at most . . . " – and asks him if he will kill it. Since Sperber had respect and affection for old Filate, and since Filate was too poor to drink and was not senile, Sperber was left to puzzle how such a person could actually believe in dragons and about how to reconcile his respect for Filate with "the knowledge that such a belief is absurd."

Sperber's analysis of this problem leads him directly to the usual arguments about the nature of rationality. How are we as anthropologists to interpret cultural beliefs – be they about dragons or the role of witchcraft in causing illness – that are "apparently irrational," that is, not in accord with how we know the empirical world to be? Are such beliefs to be taken as literal or "symbolic"? If they represent literal claims about the nature of the empirical world, why have such systems not given way in the face of empirical experience? In Evans-Pritchard's words, why do the Azande practitioners not "perceive the futility of their magic" (1937: 475)? And what is the alternative? A strong relativist claim that the Azande world and ours are incommensurable, that so different are they that we cannot translate between our world and theirs? Sperber follows through these arguments; he ridicules the view that the mind "actively creat[es] its universe" (Mary Douglas 1975: xviii), as deriving from a "hermeneutico-psychedelic subculture" (Sperber 1985: 38), and develops a detailed analysis of different types of propositional beliefs. In the end, he concludes that old Filate's belief was only "semi-propositional" and was "not factual," that is, that it was not a kind of belief intended to really represent the way the world is and not clear enough to be stated in propositional terms that could be falsifiable. Thus his solution is that the old man really didn't believe in the dragon after all, that it was only a kind of fantasy to entertain himself and ultimately the anthropologist.

My intent is not to join the rationality debate and the technical issues it raises here, although these questions serve as the stimulus for many of the concerns of this book, nor to speculate on old Filate's motives. Here my intention is to raise meta-level questions about the role of "belief" in anthropology. How does it happen that the "apparently irrational beliefs" provide the paradigmatic problem for a central tradition in anthropology? Any human science, historical or anthropological, must deal with problems of translation, of differing world views and understandings of reality, of course. But how does it happen that "irrational beliefs" becomes the central, paradigmatic issue?

Surprisingly, there seems to be little analysis of the history of the concept "belief" in anthropology.[15] It is constantly employed, a kind of Wittgensteinian "odd job word," but often used with little self-consciousness.[16] The word almost never appears in indexes, even when it is employed throughout a text, and thus its use is not easy to trace. It is beyond the scope of this discussion to attempt such a history, but a brief review of anthropological texts suggests several hypotheses.

First, the juxtaposition of "belief" and "knowledge" and the use of "belief" to denote (or at least connote) counter-factual assertions has a long history in both anthropology and philosophy. This is contrary to what might be expected for both disciplines – for anthropology, because our primary goal has been to make understandable other societies in a non-judgmental way; for philosophy, because much of modern epistemology is designed to investigate the grounds for true belief.

Second, belief as an analytic category in anthropology appears to be most closely associated with religion and with discussions of the so-called folk sciences. "Belief" is most closely associated, that is, with cultural accounts either of the unknowable or of mistaken understandings of the "natural world," where science can distinguish knowledge from belief. In medical anthropology, analysis of "beliefs" is most prominent in cultural accounts of those conditions (such as infectious diseases) for which biological theories have greatest authority, and least prominent for those forms of illness (for example psychopathology) for which biological explanations are most open to challenge.

Third, the term belief, though present throughout anthropological writing, appears with quite varied frequency and analytic meaning in different theoretical paradigms. For example, it seems far less central in American anthropology, with its background in nineteenth-century German historicist theorizing, than in British social anthropology, in particular in the rationality literature.

Fourth, the representation of others' culture as "beliefs" authorizes the position and knowledge of the anthropological observer. Though differing in content, anthropological characterizations of others' beliefs played a similar role in validating the position of the anthropologist as the description of native religious beliefs did for missionaries. However, the rising concern about the position of the anthropologist vis-à-vis members of the societies he or she studies has produced a "crisis" in ethnographic writing (Marcus and Fischer 1986: 8) and a generalized epistemological hypochondria,[17] and this change in the relationship of anthropologist to the "Other" can be traced in the increasingly self-conscious and ironic uses of the term "belief."[18]

Fifth, despite such post-modern hypochondria in some regions of the contemporary social sciences, the term "belief" and its counterparts continue to be important odd job words not only in the cognitive sciences, where culture is closely linked with states of the mind, but in fields such as the medical social sciences, where the conflict between historicist interpretations and the claims of the natural sciences is most intense. Examination of the concept thus has special relevance for medical anthropology.

These are rather crude hypotheses, which will require further research to elaborate and to verify or reject. However, they reflect my conviction that it was fateful for anthropology when belief emerged as a central category for the analysis of culture. This formation of anthropological discourse was linked to the philosophical climate within which anthropology emerged, a climate in which empiricist theories and sharp conflicts between the natural sciences and religion were prominent. It was also rooted in anthropologists' traditional relations to those they studied, framed by the superiority of European and American science and industrial development and by the colonialist context of research. Given the semantics of the term, that is the *meaning* "belief" had taken on by the late nineteenth century and continues to have in the twentieth century, the analysis of culture as belief thus both reflected and helped reproduce an underlying epistemology and a prevailing structure of power relations.

A shaking of the foundations

Anthropology's greatest contribution to twentieth-century sociology of knowledge has been the insistence that human knowledge is culturally shaped and constituted in relation to distinctive forms of life and social organization. In medical anthropology, this historicist vision runs headlong into the powerful realist claims of modern biology. Enlightenment convictions about the advance of medical knowledge run deep, and although faith in medical institutions has given way to some extent, medicine is a domain in which "a salvational view of science" (Geertz 1988: 146) still has great force.[19] No wonder that discussions of "the problem of irrational beliefs" so often cite medical examples.[20]

Nonetheless, the foundations for a comparative, cross-cultural study of illness, healing and medical knowledge which is based in the empiricist paradigm have been profoundly shaken in recent years. Geertz concludes his chapter on Evans-Pritchard in *Works and Lives* (1988), noting that the confidence that shines through Evans-Pritchard's writing, as well as through Lévi-Strauss's *Tristes Tropiques* (1955), is simply not available to ethnographers today. Our relationships with those we study have changed profoundly, and our confidence in our own view of reality, even in the claims of the natural sciences to simply represent the empirical world, has been seriously undermined. This change is represented by increasingly ironic reflections on terms such as "rationality" and "belief" in anthropology, feminist studies, and the sociology of science, and by the proliferation of new approaches in medical anthropology.

Several aspects of the empiricist paradigm relevant to comparative medical studies have become especially problematic, pushing our field in new directions. First, positivist approaches to epistemology and the empiricist theory of language have come under sustained criticism in philosophy, the history and sociology of science, and anthropology. Whichever authors one invokes – Thomas Kuhn, Michel Foucault, Paul Feyerabend, Hilary Putnam, Richard Rorty, or a generation that grew up with these figures – older theories of the relationship between language and empirical reality now seem dated. Rationality and relativism no longer neatly divide the field. Increasingly, social scientists and philosophers have joined in investigating how language activities and social practices actively contribute to the construction of scientific knowledge.[21]

In this philosophical climate, medical anthropologists face the task of investigating how cultures with their unique forms of social practice – "illness behavior," the activities of diagnostic and healing specialists, healing rites – formulate reality in distinctive ways, and how knowledge claims and the meaningfulness of language are organized in relation to these distinctive forms of reality. Claims that biomedicine provides straightforward, objective depictions of the natural order, an empirical order of biological universals, external to culture, no longer seem tenable and must be submitted to critical analysis. And for this, the empiricist theory of medical language with its focus on representation will not do; it must give way to alternatives.

Second, the normative dimensions of the empiricist paradigm seem increasingly unacceptable. It is not that any of us doubt that the biological sciences have made astounding advances in understanding human physiology, but we are no longer prepared to view the history of medicine as a straightforward recording of the continuous discovery of the facts of nature. Given the rapidity of change of scientific knowledge, as well as subaltern and feminist critiques of science and its authority, claims to "facticity" have been seriously undermined. The role of science as arbiter between knowledge and belief is thus placed into question. Critical analysis has replaced celebration as the idiom of the history and sociology of science.

It is a special irony, worth noting, that Evans-Pritchard and Rivers both used the archaic term "leechcraft" to distinguish the empirical aspects of a society's medical knowledge from its mystical beliefs. From today's vantage, leeching seems hardly more empirical than mystical, and it is a reminder of the hazard of using categories from today's rapidly changing medical knowledge as a basis for judging the empirical validity of claims of others.

For medical anthropology, the inadequacy of using contemporary clinical practices and biomedical knowledge as the norm for comparative studies can be illustrated in several ways. The analysis of healing activities of other societies as "protoscience" or primitive forms of current subspecialties – as primitive surgery or folk psychotherapy – is now largely discounted, at least when made explicit. On the other hand, comparative studies organized in terms of categories and practices current in biomedicine – for example, cross-cultural analyses of "diagnosis" understood to be the interpretation of physical symptoms of the individual who is ill – are more common. Such analyses are, however, as likely to be misleading as revealing (see B. Good and M. Good 1981). "Diagnosticians" in many societies seldom inquire about symptoms, and the sufferer is often not even present when diagnostic inquiries are made. Instead, the social field or the spiritual world is often the subject of "diagnostic" inquiry. Thus, grounding cross-cultural analysis on practices current in contemporary biomedicine may produce findings more artifact than real. Perhaps even more important, given the rich cultural frames for conceiving human suffering in many of the societies we study, holding up our own biological language of illness and care as the norm seems profoundly inadequate.

Third, the place of the ethnographer as objective, scientific observer – both in research and in ethnographic texts – seems less and less available to us today. Evans-Pritchard could assume such a position in his writings on the Azande only by ignoring his own relation to the colonial authorities. Favret-Saada (1980: 10) suggests that even Evans-Pritchard, while conducting field research, could situate himself outside of Zande witchcraft discourse – beyond possible charges of being a witch himself, for example – only because the Azande granted him the title "Prince without portfolio," which served as a kind of exemption from the claims of the discourse and thus protected him. Whatever the case for Evans-Pritchard and witchcraft, the position of today's anthropologist is increasingly contested. When carrying out research in Iran in the 1970s, we could only enter religious discourse as potential converts, participate in political discourse by assuming some position in relation to the Shah's struggle for legitimacy as well as the religious and secular resistance to his rule, or engage in medical discourse as potential actors. In medical anthropology, arbitrating between belief and knowledge suggests positioning ourselves within what Favret-Saada calls "the official theories of misfortune," backed as they are by powerful social agencies. Finding a stance both as researcher and in the ethnographic text is thus increasingly difficult. The position implied by the language of belief is often untenable.

Finally, a variety of more technical analyses of belief suggests problems with the empiricist program, challenging the utility of "belief" as an analytic category, even questioning the existence in other societies of "beliefs" in our sense of the word.[22] A view of culture as propositional, mentalistic, voluntaristic, and individualistic – for example, of medical beliefs as rational propositions about the world, held in the minds (or brains) of individuals, and subject to voluntary control – is an elaboration of a particular folk psychology; such a view reproduces an ideology of individualism that matches poorly with much of what we know about the real world. When invoked in studies of "stress" or "care-seeking," for example, rational behavior and the "responsibility" of individuals is privileged at the expense of social constraints and intersubjectivity.[23] Finally, the myth that we can deduce beliefs from "sincere assertions," from statements people make to us about what they really think, presumed in much of the philosophical literature, ignores what is obvious to anthropologists – that all discourse is pragmatically located in social relationships, that all assertions about illness experience are located in linguistic practices and most typically embedded in narratives about life and suffering.[24]

Thus, despite powerful authorization by biomedicine and the biological sciences, the empiricist program in medical anthropology is deeply problematic. I will be arguing in the following pages that how we situate ourselves in relation to the underlying theoretical issues at stake here is extremely important for how we conceive a program for medical anthropology. How we situate our research in relation to biomedical categories and claims, the nature of authority we grant to biological and medical knowledge, the problems we see as central to the field, and the way we define the project in which we are engaged are all strongly influenced by our stance on these issues. More than this, I am convinced that medical anthropology is one of the primary sites within anthropology where alternative responses to the confrontation between historicism and the natural sciences are being worked out.

Although I have focused largely on epistemological issues in this first chapter, I want to foreshadow the argument to come by noting that all medicine joins rational and deeply irrational elements, combining an attention to the material body with a concern for the moral dimensions of sickness and suffering. In his Marett Lecture in 1950, Evans-Pritchard argued that "social anthropology is a kind of historiography" that "studies societies as moral systems . . . " In all societies, even in the modern world with overarching moral orders no longer intact, serious illness leads men and women to confront moral dimensions of life. It is after all a central task of "the work of culture" to transform human misery into suffering, and to counter sickness with healing.[25] Biomedicine, as other forms of healing, is of special interest because it combines the empirical or natural sciences with this primal task. It is thus both the privilege and the obligation of medical anthropology to bring renewed attention to human experience, to suffering, to meaning and interpretation, to the role of narratives and historicity, as well as to the role of social formations and institutions, as we explore a central aspect of what it means to be human across cultures.

2

Illness representations in medical anthropology: a reading of the field

In their extended essay on the perceived breakdown of coherent conceptual paradigms in anthropology today, Marcus and Fischer argue that our post-colonial self-awareness and a broad loss of faith in totalizing theoretical visions has provoked a "crisis in representation," which has in turn served as "the intellectual stimulus for the contemporary vitality of experimental writing in anthropology" (1986: 8). Little wonder there should be such a crisis. Despite our attachment to those with whom we have carried out research and our dedication to represent their interests and point of view in our writings, we find ourselves part of a discipline whose history is strewn with cultural representations which now seem profoundly ethnocentric, often clearly aligned with colonial regimes and those in power, explicitly gendered, and at times racist. Our embarrassment with this history is compounded by the fact that many of our informants and articulate intellectuals in the societies we study now read not only our own books and articles, but those of our predecessors as well. Their criticism of anthropology's legacy and of our own work gives the lie to our claims to speak for others, to represent them as they would represent themselves. Anthropological discussions of the past decade have thus become increasingly concerned with the nature of ethnographic representation, with our objectification and portrayal of "the Other," with the place of the author and those represented in the ethnographic text, and with the "authorization" of our portrayals and our claims to ethnographic knowledge.

Medical anthropology has had its own form of critical self-analysis in the past decade, arising not only from these general developments in anthropology and the human sciences but from characteristics specific to cross-cultural studies of illness, healing, medicine, and health care institutions. Medical anthropologists can hardly fail to acknowledge links between colonialism and early anthropological writing on medical "beliefs and practices," which resulted in the use of highly pejorative analytic terms for what Rivers called "medicine, magic and religion." But criticism of that early work has often been part of medical anthropology's specific form of "cultural critique." From its inception, anthropological

25

writing on "traditional medicine" has been linked to criticisms of biomedical theories as well as physicians, public health specialists, and medicine as practiced in our own society. The first explicitly "medical" anthropology, the applied work of anthropologists involved in international public health in the 1950s, was formulated not only to enhance the efforts of public health practitioners but as a critique of their cultural naiveté.[1] Members of societies toward which such efforts were directed are not "empty vessels," waiting to be filled with whatever health knowledge is being advocated by health educators, Polgar wrote in a classic essay outlining the fallacies typical of public health programs (Polgar 1963; cf. B. Paul 1959). Their "habits and beliefs" constitute elements in an elaborate "cultural system" (Paul 1955: 15), which the public health specialist would do well to understand before advocating new habits and ideas. As Benjamin Paul wrote, "If you wish to help a community improve its health, you must learn to think like the people of that community" (1955: 1). Early studies of folk illnesses and popular concepts of disease among members of American subcultures had a similar aim of criticizing physicians for their failure to understand the cultural forms through which such persons understood and responded to their illness (for example Rubel 1960, 1964; Clark 1959; Snow 1974).

These early studies led to more fully developed research on the great and little traditions of medicine and healing in India and China, elsewhere in Asia, and in Latin America, Africa, and the Middle East. The Wenner-Gren conference on "Asian Medical Systems," which resulted in the book edited by Charles Leslie (1976a), and the Fogarty International Center conference on "Medicine in Chinese Cultures," resulting in a book by that title edited by Kleinman et al. (1976), were key moments in the emergence of the comparative study of health care systems. While maintaining an element of critique of the cultural naiveté of physicians and public health specialists, the scholarship in this tradition has developed a distinctly anthropological analysis of health care systems, showing biomedicine to be one system among many and extending the challenge to biomedicine's hegemonic claims more generally.

Even more than criticizing medical practitioners for their failure to understand the richness of the medical ideas of their patients or the health care systems of those with whom they worked, studies of healing systems in traditional societies have often been designed explicitly or implicitly to demonstrate the inadequacies of "Western" medical ideologies and health care institutions. In the conclusion to one of the first full ethnographies of an ethnomedical system, Fabrega and Silver (1973: 218–223) outlined thirty-three propositions "that appear to underlie and guide the curing process" of the "Western Biomedical System" and the "Zinacanteco System" (in the Chiapas region of Mexico), set forth as diametrically opposed systems. Western medicine understands the body as a complex biological machine, while the Zinacanteco see the body as a holistic integrated aspect of the person and social relations. Our treatments are mechanical and impersonal, our healers characterized by distance, coolness, formal relations, and the use of abstract concepts; their curing makes use of emotionally charged symbols, and the treatment relationship is characterized by closeness, shared meaning, warmth, informality, and everyday language. Western curing is aimed exclusively at the mechanical body, while Zinacanteco procedures are directed at social relations and supernatural agents. In this study and many which have followed, healing in other societies is found to have qualities increasingly absent from our own medicine. In many instances, a romanticized vision of the other is juxtaposed to a caricatured image of ourselves. Cross-cultural studies of healing have thus served to advance and extend a cultural critique of biomedicine and of North American and European societies more generally. In particular, they reproduce themes about the alienation of medicine from intimate social relations, the increasing bureaucratization and professionalization of the experience of illness, and the fragmentation of our soteriological vision, themes having wide currency both in medicine and broader social criticism.

A more political critique of medicine and international health emerged in the 1960s. Activists and scholars within anthropology, as well as members of American ethnic communities and Third World physicians and scholars, criticized the implicit acceptance by applied anthropologists and medical social scientists of the medical profession's Enlightenment claims that lack of knowledge and maladaptive behavior are the sources of ill health. Anthropology's concentration on folk beliefs and folk illnesses often excluded analytic attention to the distribution of health care, to social inequities and industrial policies which burden minority communities and the poor with ill health, to international policies that produce underdevelopment in the health arena, to barriers to health services that originate in medical practice rather than among the folk. The field thus ultimately failed to give adequate attention to macro-social and historical features of health care systems. Political economy criticisms such as these emerged in the 1960s and have continued with increasing vigor into the present, producing a growing body of scholarship.

I will be describing more recent developments in the critical studies of bio-medicine later in this chapter. However, it is not simply the critique of our own forms of healing through glimpsing ourselves in the mirror of the other, nor criticisms of the political economy of health that gives vitality to medical anthro-pology. Criticism of medicine, whatever form it takes, is nearly always linked for North American anthropologists to a commitment to helping bring the benefits of public health and medical services to non-Western societies or to cultural minorities and the poor in our own society. The duality of the anthropologist's role as critic and participant has provided an ironic cast to that commitment. Foucault's analyses of medicine and psychiatry as primary "disciplinary" institutions in modern society, as agencies which extend surveillance and control of the state into the most intimate domains of life, stand in stark contrast to the evident need for the most basic health services in much of the world. Sociological critiques of the doctor–patient relationship, and feminist accounts of how medical knowledge encodes dominant significations of gender and of women, stand side by side with accounts of terrible and needless maternal mortality in many societies, of deaths which could easily be prevented by extending health services. Historical and cultural analyses of tuberculosis, cancer, schizophrenia, venereal diseases, and AIDS all reveal both dramatic advances in knowledge and therapeutic efficacy and an encoding of dominant cultural ideologies at the core of medicine and its practices. Critical analyses of medicine and its reproduction of dominant power relations are thus often juxtaposed uneasily with anthropologists' commitment to extending the presence and benefits of medicine and efforts to promote humane practice. This juxtaposition and the dual role of many anthropologists as critics of and committed participants in the work of medicine provide a special quality to medical anthropology's cultural critique.

Debates concerning how to write about and analyze the "illness represen-tations" of others, however, reflect not only an ambivalence about the extension of medicine's power and the anthropologist's contribution to that process, but an underlying epistemological ambivalence as well. Any analysis of local medical culture – of the illness representations of individuals or the forms of medical knowledge of a given society or subculture or therapeutic tradition – requires the anthropologist to take an epistemological stance concerning the knowledge claims made by our informants. This forces medical anthropologists to deal with difficult questions implicit in the choice of analytic strategy. How do we represent the claims to knowledge of healers in another society, given the authority of bio-medical knowledge? How do we situate our analyses of diverse traditions of medical knowledge and practice – of Ayurveda in India or traditional Chinese medicine, or African ritual traditions of healing, or that of Catholic charismatics in North America – in relation to medicine? How do we maintain a conviction that popular medical cultures represent genuine local knowledge, given the corrosive authority of biomedical science and the obvious efficacy of its preventive and therapeutic measures? The issue is not simply that of the "efficacy of traditional healing." Questions of the efficacy of clinical medicine, especially as practiced in much of the world, are often quite distinct from the truth claims of biomedical science, and the same is even more true for other forms of healing. The question is rather how we situate our analyses of cultural representations of illness, encoded in popular or folk therapeutic traditions or in individual understandings and practices, in relation to the truth claims of biomedicine.

These epistemological questions point further to a series of empirical and theoretical questions about the relation of culture and illness. How do we conceptualize illness as the object of cross-cultural research? To what extent is it to be considered "external to culture," an object in the natural world about which peoples have more or less correct representations, "beliefs" that contrast with empirical knowledge? To what extent is "disease," in Kleinman's early definition of the term, distinct from "illness"? Is cultural representation a part of the object itself, biology cultural at its core, and what specifically would such a claim entail? How are social relations manifest and reproduced in illness representations and disease itself? How do we write analytically about the extremely diverse representations of illness in popular culture, specialized therapeutic traditions, and medical science? And how do we frame programs of research for the field consistent with our views on these issues?

Responses to questions such as these, to what I described in the first chapter as the contradictions between the historicist perspective of anthropology and the universalist claims of biomedical science, and more generally to the problem of how we analyze cultural representations of social and biological "objects," have provided a special theoretical vitality to current debates in medical anthropology. In this chapter I reflect on the history of medical anthropology, in particular anthropology's analysis of illness representations and the emergence of something akin to paradigmatic disputes within medical anthropology during the past decade, as a venue for taking stock of such issues. A discussion of the primary theoretical frames that have been articulated may bring into focus issues that provide the impetus for the constructive chapters of this book.

Epistemological claims in early studies of illness representations: rationalist and relativist theories

The earliest anthropological writings on culture and medicine share much of the embarrassing evolutionary language of other parts of the field. Conventional histories of medical anthropology (for example Wellin 1977) outline a heritage that includes the writing of W. H. R. Rivers, Forrest Clements, historian Erwin Ackerknecht, and others for whom terms like "primitive," "magical," "mystical," "pre-logical," "proto-scientific," and "folk" are all common adjectives for "medical beliefs" among "natives." For those who wrote within what I have called the empiricist tradition, especially British intellectualist writers, illness representations could be ranked according to a hierarchy of increasing rationality. Through the 1940s, medical beliefs and practices of non-Western peoples were often interpreted as early stages of medical knowledge, a kind of proto-science elaborated in primitive theories of disease causation, primitive surgical practices, and primitive knowledge of pharmacological properties of plants and minerals. The historical evolution of human knowledge, whether from magic to religion to science, as Rivers argued, or from primitive or proto-scientific theories of disease causation to those of contemporary biomedicine, served as the frame for contrasting primitive or folk beliefs with scientific knowledge. Clements' monograph, *Primitive Concepts of Disease* (1932), followed an extreme "culture-trait" approach: a classification of five theories of disease causation was provided (sorcery, breach of taboo, intrusion by a disease object, intrusion by a spirit, and soul loss), and the geographical and historic distribution of these cultural elements was mapped (cf. Wellin 1977: 50–51). Ackerknecht, a physician and historian who acknowledged the influence of the British functionalists as well as Ruth Benedict, rejected any analysis of trait distribution. Medicine is a cultural configuration, he held, a functionally integrated system of cultural beliefs and practices, and must be analyzed within cultural context. Nonetheless, Ackerknecht held firm to his empiricist convictions. Medical categories such as "surgery" or the "autopsy" served as the basis for historical comparisons, and Ackerknecht held that primitive medicine as a system "is primarily magico-religious, utilizing a few rational elements, while [our modern-Western] medicine is predominantly rational and scientific employing a few magic elements" (1946: 467; quoted in Wellin 1977: 52). Identifying the empirical knowledge (its "rational elements") in such primitive systems, characterizing "beliefs" about disease causation and treatment, and providing a history of the emergence from primitive medicine of more accurate representations of the natural world of disease thus served as the larger research program. Although the "modern medicine" contemporary to these writers was characterized as a social and cultural institution, thus contributing to a later sociology of medicine, the scientific understandings of disease which were current for these writers served to distinguish the primitive from the modern and belief from knowledge.

Quite independent of later critiques of evolutionary and colonialist aspects of the analytic language employed, however, elements of what I have described as an "epistemological ambivalence" were present even in this early work. In particular, the analysis of a society's medical beliefs and activities as an integrated body of ideas and a coherent social institution raised serious questions for the identification of isolated rational or proto-scientific elements embedded within a primarily magico-religious system. An example from the physician anthropologist W. H. R. Rivers will illustrate. In a short paper read at the Seventeenth International Congress of Medicine in London on August 7, 1913, Rivers (1913: 39–42) described his observation of a native practitioner on the Solomon Islands (where he was a member of the Percy Sladen Trust Expedition) who provided "abdominal massage" which was carried out "so far as I could tell, just as it would have been by a European expert."

> On questioning the woman who was the subject of the treatment, it seemed that she was suffering from chronic constipation, and if the matter had not been gone into more fully, it might have been supposed that the Solomon Islanders treated this disease according to the most modern scientific therapeutics. Further inquiries, however, brought out the fact that the manipulations we had observed had had as their object the destruction of an octopus which, according to the native pathology, was the cause of the woman's troubles. She was held to be suffering from a disease called *nggaseri* caused by the presence of an octopus in the body. On inquiring into prognosis, we were told of a belief that the tentacles of the octopus tended to pass upwards and that, when they reached the head of the patient, a fatal result ensued. The object of the treatment was to kill the octopus, and in the case we observed treatment had already been carried out for several days, and the octopus, which had at first been very large, had now become small and was expected soon to disappear altogether. This result, however, was not ascribed so much to the mechanical action of the manipulations as to the formulae and other features of the treatment which accompanied the passage. (Rivers 1913: 39)

Rivers went on to indicate the questions raised by this case for his analysis.

> A few years ago I should have had no hesitation in regarding this Melanesian practice as an example of the growth of a rational therapeutic measure out of a magical or

religious rite. I should have supposed that these practices of the Solomon Islanders were designed originally to extract the octopus . . . from the body, and that it would only be necessary to slough off what we regard as the superstitious aspect of the practice to have a true therapeutical measure. I should have regarded the Melanesian practice as one which has preserved for us a stage in the process of evolution whereby medicine evolved out of magic, and as a matter of fact, I believe that the vast majority of my anthropological colleagues, at any rate in this country, would still be fully satisfied with this view. Many students of anthropology, however, are now coming to see that human institutions have not had so simple a history as this view implies . . . (Rivers 1913: 40)

As he proceeds with his brief analysis, Rivers does not spell out the obvious question facing the cross-cultural researcher – whether he was observing "massage" at all, whether an activity understood in so different terms by its practitioners can be analyzed as an early version of "the true therapeutical practice," that is, the practice of British massage therapists of Rivers' day. Rivers instead raises the hypothesis of historical diffusion of this practice as an alternative to his usual evolutionary formulation. Nonetheless, in this small piece, he acknowledges the difficulties with "so simple a history," that is with projecting the relation of belief to knowledge backwards into evolutionary history, and calls for a recovery of the actual history of ideas. Along with Ackerknecht, he recognizes that any given idea or practice has meaning in relation to medicine conceived as a larger "social institution" (1913: 41) and that this poses serious problems for the very definition of terms of analysis. Thus, even among the classic empiricist writers, difficulties with using contemporary categories of disease or therapeutic practice as the basis for investigating variations in cultural beliefs were recognized.

The primary alternative to the empiricist writers of the first half of this century was developed by American anthropologists in the Boasian tradition. Interestingly, the data that served as the basis for a relativist alternative were drawn from psychiatry rather than from infectious diseases and medical or surgical interventions – a pattern that has continued in much anthropological writing to the present. In a small paper entitled "Anthropology and the Abnormal," published in the *Journal of General Psychology* (1934), Ruth Benedict elaborated a critique of current theories of psychopathology. In particular, she sought to show that "confusion" follows from viewing psychological abnormality in terms of "social inadequacy" or in relation to "definite fixed symptoms" (p. 76), rather than in relation to a culture's values and definitions of normalcy. The essay begins with the observation that anthropological studies show that "mannerisms like the ways of showing anger, or joy, or grief in any society," or "major human drives like those of sex" "prove to be far more variable than experience in any one culture would suggest." This finding raises difficulties for "the customary modern normal–abnormal categories and our conclusions regarding them" (p. 59). Indeed, she argues, "it does not matter what kind of 'abnormality' we choose for illustration, those which indicate extreme instability, or those which are more in the nature of character traits like sadism or delusions of grandeur or of persecution, there are well-described cultures in which these abnormals function at ease and with honor, and apparently without danger or difficulty to the society" (p. 60). Benedict then provides a series of examples – of "trance and catalepsy" developed among shamans, of homosexuality as a "major means to the good life" in Plato's *Republic*, and of quite dramatic cases in which "an abnormality of our culture is the cornerstone of their social structure." Civilizations thus select from among "the whole potential range of human behavior" some forms of personality, some modes of behavior and experience, which they idealize and stamp with the approval of morality, while others are viewed as abnormal, deviant, or immoral. From this she drew conclusions that have continued to be influential in psychological anthropology and cross-cultural psychiatry:

> Most of those organizations of personality that seem to us most incontrovertibly abnormal have been used by different civilizations in the very foundations of their institutional life. Conversely the most valued traits of our normal individuals have been looked on in differently organized cultures as aberrant. . . . The very eyes with which we see the problem are conditioned by the long traditional habits of our own society. (Benedict 1934: 73)

Problems of social functioning are thus not the sources but the result of definitions of abnormality, and "symptoms" are both defined as such and culturally elaborated as forms of behavior available to "unstable individuals."

Benedict's claim here went beyond the general argument that cultural conventions define forms of emotional expression or behavior or personality types as normal or abnormal. Within the tradition of Boasian anthropology, Benedict was responding to positivist psychology of the day with the argument that psychopathology or psychiatric disease is constituted in cultural forms that can only be interpreted in relation to the larger cultural pattern of a particular society. Boasian anthropology, as Stocking (1968) has shown, was closely related to the German historicist writing of the late nineteenth and early twentieth centuries, with its criticisms of positivism in both the human and natural sciences, its interests in subjective culture, and its concern with historically emergent cultural configurations, holism, vitalism and systems theory.[2] Viewed from the perspective of this intellectual tradition, Benedict was articulating several claims about the nature of psychopathology. First, psychological distress is a form of social reality specific to a particular culture and language, not simply a disease or cluster of symptoms or psychological deficit interpreted in local terms. Psychiatric illness cannot be separated from a particular cultural context, and is therefore subject to Sapir's classic comments on the nature of social reality:

> . . . the "real world" is to a large extent unconsciously built up on the language habits of the group. No two languages are ever sufficiently similar to be considered as representing the same social reality. The worlds in which different societies live are distinct worlds, not merely the same world with different labels attached. (Sapir 1949 [1929]: 69)

Sapir differed with Benedict on several points. He held that the "true locus of culture" is to be found in "the interactions of specific individuals and, on the subjective side, in the world of meanings which each one of these individuals may unconsciously abstract for himself from his participation in these interactions" (Sapir 1949 [1932]: 515), rather than in "society."[3] And he down-played the tyranny of normalcy as a primary cause of maladjustment and pathology.[4] However, Benedict's formulation of psychiatric illness as a culturally specific form of reality, rather than a set of universal diseases "with different labels attached," is consistent with Sapir's overall position and with the historicist critique of positivist psychology.

Second, Benedict was making the more specific point that any social institution or behavior cannot be interpreted as an isolable trait, but only in relation to a cultural configuration. Elsewhere she indicated one source of her theories when she commented explicitly upon the *Gestalt* psychologists' writings about the need to study sense-perception in relation to "the subjective framework" and the "wholeness properties" rather than as "objective fragments." "The whole determines its parts, not only their relation but their very nature. Between two wholes there is a discontinuity in kind, and any understanding must take into account their different natures, over and above a recognition of the similar elements that have entered into the two" (Benedict 1934: 57). Her 1923 dissertation on the Guardian Spirit trait in American Indian cultures concluded that this "trait" became a fundamentally different cultural object when it entered into a particular cultural *Gestalt*, and she carried this conviction to her analysis of all forms of behavior, including abnormality or psychopathology.

Third, Benedict was arguing that normality and abnormality are ethical concepts, variants of "the concept of the good" (p. 73). And as "we do not any longer make the mistake of deriving the morality of our own locality and decade directly from the inevitable constitution of human nature," so we should also recognize the essential relativity of concepts of abnormality. Benedict drew her reflections on these issues to a close with a specific hypothesis.

> The categories of borderline behavior which we derive from the study of the neuroses and psychoses of our civilization are categories of prevailing local types of instability. They give much information about the stresses and strains of Western civilization, but no final picture of inevitable human behavior. Any conclusions about such behavior must await the collection by trained observers of psychiatric data from other cultures. . . . It is as it is in ethics: all our local conventions of moral behavior and of immoral are without absolute validity, and yet it is quite possible that a modicum of what is considered right and what wrong could be disentangled that is shared by the whole human race. When data are available in psychiatry, this minimum definition of abnormal human tendencies will be probably quite unlike our culturally conditioned, highly elaborated psychoses such as those that are described, for instance, under the terms of schizophrenia and manic-depressive. (Benedict 1934: 79)

This hypothesis has served to orient a lively research literature that continues in medical and psychiatric anthropology and cross-cultural psychiatry to this day. One line of discussion elaborated Benedict's argument that the shamans of many societies would be considered seriously disordered in our own society.[5] A small set of papers argued that shamans are persons suffering schizophrenia but are in a cultural environment which provides them validation and a meaningful role. These papers often use the term "schizophrenia" in a quite confused way, and the hypothesis has been largely abandoned. Others, however, have followed her lead in exploring the cultural elaboration of trance and possession, and with the new interest in "dissociation" in American psychiatry, the study of the relation of these to pathologies of dissociation in our own society is once again quite active.[6]

A second line of empirical research has investigated the extent to which psychopathology varies across cultures. On the one hand, under the broad rubric of "culture-bound disorders," some have explored Benedict's hypothesis that societies develop quite specific and highly elaborated forms of psychopathology.[7] On the other, a set of studies have investigated variations in the phenomenology and course of schizophrenia, depression, manic-depressive illness, and anxiety disorders.[8] A third line of discussion and research has extended Benedict's hypothesis that each culture labels some forms of behavior as deviant and treats these as illness, and that such labelling has important consequences for those so identified. Early forms of the "social labeling" hypothesis treated the Soviet incarceration of political dissidents under the label "schizophrenic" as a prototype for all mental illness, and were rightly rejected. However, "social response" theorists have developed an extremely important literature on how society's institutionalized responses to "primary deviance" (including, for example, an initial psychotic episode) are crucial in shaping the life course of sufferers and the course and prognosis of psychopathology. Indeed, studies of the role of social and cultural processes in determining whether an episode of major mental illness will become chronic and deeply debilitating are some of the most important in psychiatric anthropology and social psychiatry today.[9]

Benedict's initial formulation has thus been followed by an extremely productive program of theorizing and empirical research, and the "collection by trained observers of psychiatric data from other cultures" has proceeded much further apace than in many areas in the field. For purposes of examining the history of theorizing about culture and illness representations, however, several points are worth noting. Benedict and those who have followed her lead have developed an alternative form of cultural critique to that provided in the rationalist tradition. Her response to positivist psychologists was not simply that they and their medical colleagues have failed to understand cultural beliefs that motivate behavior, beliefs which are coherent and rational in their own way. (Benedict used the term "belief" in her 1934 essay only once [p. 59], and that to refer to our own "false sense of the inevitability" of "custom and belief" that has become standardized across two continents.) Her challenge was more fundamental. Illness is relative to the cultural and ethical forms of a particular society. Any truly scientific psychology must recognize the cultural relativity of pathology, rather than simply assume that our own illness forms are part of human nature and therefore universal. Embedded in this formulation was the claim that illness representations or understandings of abnormality are not simply more or less accurate theories of a phenomenon external to culture, but that such representations constitute the very phenomenon itself. Pathology is an essentially cultural object, in this formulation, and representations are part of the very essence of the object. It is this basic formulation that sets off these early relativist writings from their rationalist counterparts.

There were, however, problems in Benedict's formulation that have continued to confuse discussions in medical and psychiatric anthropology. Benedict's hypotheses about the extent of cultural variation in the "neuroses and psychoses," in particular for those described "under the terms of schizophrenia and manic-depressive," have not stood up to empirical investigation. In particular, her argument that even the psychoses are part of the arc of human behavior that is considered normal and is valued highly in some societies, confuses "temperament" – characteristics such as individualism or aggressiveness or suspiciousness – with major pathology, and discounts the severity of major mental illness and the devastation it wreaks in the lives of individuals and families. Her understanding of psychopathology as essentially a problem of "adjustment," which reflected theorizing of her day, no longer seems tenable. Furthermore, while her use of psychiatric labels such as "paranoid" and "megalomaniac" to characterize whole cultures was intended to indicate that our own labels for pathology are culture-bound and relative, her rhetorical move led to an essential pathologizing of the cultures about which she wrote. Terms derived from clinical descriptions of individuals were applied to societies, producing enormous difficulties that emerged in the culture and personality literature and discredited much of the work of psychological anthropologists.

In spite of these basic difficulties, Benedict's formulation of the cultural mapping of the "borderline" between the normal and abnormal, her discussion of the power of social response to amplify pathology, and her basic contention that abnormality and pathology are inseparable from cultural interpretation continue to have relevance for many of the issues in our field. And her fundamental claim that pathology itself is inseparable from culture is one which continues to challenge empiricist theories about the relation of cultural representation and disease.

The juxtaposition of early rationalist and relativist writings in anthropology, typified by the British intellectualist Rivers and the American cultural anthropologist Benedict, highlights a faultline that runs through the literature on culture and illness, a faultline in epistemological stance, in form of cultural critique of medicine, and in overall conceptions of a program for anthropological studies of illness. Understanding the history of these positions clarifies what is at stake in many of the debates in the field and provides a foundation for theoretical and methodological discussions which will follow. An uncritical description of the field in these terms, however, would serve to perpetuate some of the least enlightening debates in medical, psychiatric and psychological anthropology. In particular, the juxtaposition of the analysis of psychopathology in relativist terms – as culturally defined abnormality, with culture-bound disorders as the prototype

– over against the analysis of "medical" disorders, in particular infectious diseases, in rationalist terms has served the field poorly (see B. Good 1992b for a fuller discussion). Although these positions are still evident in writing and research, this division of the field no longer accords with what we know about psychiatric, infectious, or chronic medical disorders. It also no longer represents the primary theoretical positions that have evolved in the field since the early 1970s. And as I discussed in the first chapter, the stark juxtaposition of rationalism and relativism no longer maps the important epistemological positions in anthropology, philosophy, or the sociology of science, though they continue to be evoked in arguments.

In the remainder of this chapter, I will outline four theoretical positions that have evolved in the field, in particular since the late 1970s, provoking lively and at times heated debates. My goal is by no means a complete review of the field. It is rather to use the rubric "illness representations" to draw attention to epistemological presuppositions implicit in and often hidden by these debates. Reflections on these issues will lay the ground for the chapters that follow.

Current debates concerning illness representations: four orienting approaches in medical anthropology

Reviews in the *Biennial* (and *Annual*) *Review of Anthropology* by Scotch in 1963, Fabrega in 1972, and Colson and Selby in 1974 map the emergence by the early 1970s of a growing literature on "ethnomedicine" and of research in "medical ecology and epidemiology." Less than a decade later, Allan Young (1982) remarked in the *Annual Review of Anthropology* on the enormous growth in the field in the few intervening years – on the appearance of specialized collections, anthologies, theoretical works, ethnographies, textbooks, book series, and new journals. He then provided a reading of theoretical developments in the field during these years. The flourishing of academic work resulted from a decade of studies of "medical systems," which produced a growing body of ethnographic data on the complex forms of medical knowledge and therapeutic traditions in much of the world.[10] It also reflects the beginnings of an extraordinary specialization within medical anthropology, and the development of a theoretical literature articulating an autonomous anthropological account of illness, therapeutics, and medical knowledge.

The development of medical anthropology as a domain of anthropological theorizing during these years is especially noteworthy. Kleinman's *Patients and Healers in the Context of Culture* (1980), coupled with the publication of the new journal *Culture, Medicine and Psychiatry* beginning in 1977, marked a coming of age of theorizing in medical anthropology, and writing in the field became increasingly explicit about the philosophical and methodological issues at stake. Thus, when Young reviewed the field in 1982, he could write a critical account of theoretical positions that had developed in the previous decade. This represented a qualitative change in the status of the field.

Quickly setting aside approaches originally developed for analysis of other domains (such as religion and ritual) and those borrowing methodological and conceptual categories from the largely positivist medical behavioral sciences, Young outlined an emerging theoretical distinction between what he called an "anthropology of illness" and an "anthropology of sickness." He provided a critical reading of what he labeled "the explanatory model of illness approach" and called for elaboration of an alternative position "which gives primacy to the social relations which produce the forms and distributions of sickness in society" (1982: 268). Although I believe that in labeling meaning-centered analyses "EM theorizing" Young seriously misrepresented that tradition, his paper contributed to the emergence of clearly articulated theoretical positions in the field. His review both acknowledged the emergence of a rich theoretical discourse in medical anthropology and helped advance a critical analysis of the concepts and strategies employed.

Given the growth of the field, it is no longer possible to provide a review of the whole field in a single essay or chapter.[11] It is even impossible in the space of a few pages to provide a full account of the theoretical developments of the past decade. A brief discussion of four approaches to the study of "illness representations," however, may help make sense of the problems we face in developing a genuinely anthropological account of illness and provide an assessment of current debates about the nature of medical knowledge. In particular, comparison of the place of language in each of these "paradigms" and of the vision of a program for medical anthropology implicit in each reveals significant differences in epistemological stance and in the conception of comparative studies.

Illness representations as folk beliefs: the persistence of the empiricist tradition

The medical behavioral sciences – medical psychology, the sociology of illness behavior, applied behavioral sciences in public health, epidemiology – have been important features of North American medical research and education for several decades, and have grown rapidly over the past fifteen years, contributing to the criticism of what is broadly referred to as "the medical model." In large measure, however, these writings rely on belief and behavior models firmly rooted in a positivist or empiricist paradigm which they share with biomedicine. The language of belief is ubiquitous, and although biomedicine is criticized for its failure to attend to social and psychological variables, medical knowledge is largely assumed to be normative. The individual actor – subject to environmental stresses, site of disease, source of rational and irrational illness behavior – is analytically primary. And applications are largely directed at educating individuals to modify irrational behavior – to reduce risk factors, comply with medical regimens, seek care appropriately.

Throughout its history, medical anthropology has engaged in a critique not only of biomedicine but of the positivist medical behavioral sciences as well. Responses to illness that differ from that assumed rational from the physician's point of view are not simply the result of lack of information or "superstitions," anthropologists have argued. They are grounded in culture, a system of beliefs and practices which however variant from biomedicine has its own logical structure – a cultural logic – and serves adaptive functions that often go unnoticed. Thus culture is asserted as a central feature of human response to illness, a feature largely ignored by the medical behavioral sciences, and this assertion has served as the source of a wide-ranging anthropological critique.

In labeling this section "The persistence of the empiricist tradition," I mean to suggest that in spite of the criticism of the medical behavioral sciences, a strong current of anthropological theorizing continues to reproduce much of the underlying epistemological framework of the biosciences. I have argued that the rationalist tradition, represented by W. H. R. Rivers, had a powerful presence in medical anthropology. Although they criticized naive public health specialists, applied medical anthropologists of the 1950s drew on a language of belief and behavior that placed them clearly within this tradition. Since the mid-1970s, applied work in medical anthropology has become far more specialized than could have been imagined by the pioneers in this area, and some of the most interesting and critical writing has come from those engaged directly in international health settings. My argument, however, is that important elements of the empiricist paradigm continue to exert great influence in the field. They are present in the common-sense view of medical anthropology as the study of beliefs and practices associated with illness by persons from diverse cultures, as well as in the models used to facilitate collaboration among anthropologists, clinicians, epidemiologists, and others in applied settings. They are present subtly in studies of lay health beliefs and care-seeking. And they have been articulated quite explicitly in recent formulations of medical anthropology in "biocultural" or "ecological" terms. It is my goal here to summarize three of the key elements in the empiricist paradigm and to outline a critique that opens to newer directions in the field.

There is a danger that some may read my analysis and critique of the current empiricist paradigm in medical anthropology as a criticism of applied or multi-disciplinary work in the health sciences or of studies that take biology and ecology seriously. Others may feel that discussions of theory are largely irrelevant to such work. Let me be clear. I am by no means equating anthropology applied to clinical or public health settings with the empiricist tradition or any other; fortunately, excellent work, drawing on quite diverse traditions, is being done in such settings.[12] And I agree with Rubel, who has long argued (for example, Rubel and Hass 1990: 119) that we need to turn from "mentalistic" studies of folk illnesses to research that incorporates an understanding of biology and focuses on major health problems of populations. My contention, however, is that the theoretical difficulties of the empiricist paradigm have extremely important implications for research as well as for efforts to apply our insights in health care settings. Analysis of these difficulties is thus relevant to our understanding of the relation of biology and culture, to methodological discussions, and to practical work in clinical settings, health education, and international public health.

What I am calling here the common-sense or empiricist approach in the medical social sciences has three essential elements: the analysis of illness representations as health beliefs, a view of culture as adaptation, and an analytic primacy of the rational, value-maximizing individual. It is my argument that taken together these constitute a form of "utility theory," in Sahlins' (1976a) terms, which reproduces conventional understandings of society even while introducing culture into the medical paradigm.

First, the analysis of culture as "belief" figures prominently not only in the medical behavioral sciences, but in much of medical anthropology as well. From research and interventions based in the "Health Belief Model," developed by social psychologists working with public health specialists in the 1950s, to the sociology of "lay health beliefs" to anthropological studies of ethnomedicine, classically defined as "those beliefs and practices relating to disease which are the products of indigenous cultural development" (Hughes 1968), "belief" serves as an unexamined proxy for "culture." While all anthropologists today find Rivers' colonialist language offensive, it is still common to find his formulation of the field prominently quoted:

> The practices of these peoples in relation to disease are not a medley of disconnected and meaningless customs, but are inspired by definite ideas concerning the causation of disease. Their modes of treatment follow directly from their ideas concerning etiology and pathology. From our modern standpoint we are able to see that these ideas are wrong. But the important point is that, however wrong may be the beliefs of the Papuan and Melanesian concerning the causation of disease, their practices are a logical consequence of those beliefs. (W. H. R. Rivers 1924 [quoted, for example, in Welsch 1983: 32])[13]

It seems almost natural that a section on culture and medicine in a new undergraduate textbook on applied anthropology (*Applying Cultural Anthropology*, written by Podolefsky and Brown [1991]) would be entitled "Belief, Ritual, and Curing," even though analysis of beliefs has little place in the four essays in this section and none of the other ten sections of the book bear the label belief in their titles.

"Belief" typically marks the boundaries between lay or popular medical culture and scientific knowledge, as I discussed in the first chapter. To take examples almost at random, a recent public health study of "knowledge regarding AIDS" in Kinshasa, Zaire, summarized its findings as follows:

> Awareness of AIDS is almost universal, and the vast majority *know* the four main modes of transmission. Almost half *believed* in transmission by mosquitoes and in a vaccine or cure for AIDS. The majority of male respondents *knew* of condoms, but negative attitudes toward condom use are widespread, and few respondents perceived them to play a central role in combatting AIDS. (Bertrand et al. 1991; emphasis added)[14]

The findings from this research are potentially quite important. However, as formulated in this report, lay beliefs are false propositions, juxtaposed to medical knowledge, and the clear implication is that correcting false beliefs is a first priority of public health.

Or again, in a quite good ethnographic account of the response of local people on a Papua New Guinea island to the opening of a government first aid post, Lepowsky (1990: 1049) poses the question for her research as follows: "What happens when Western medicine is introduced to people who believe that virtually all serious illness and death are due to sorcery, witchcraft or taboo violation?" She goes on to describe the "belief system" on Vanatinai, juxtaposing the medicine of the aid post orderly with that of traditional beliefs, and shows that even when credit is given to the efficacy of penicillin, people stressed "the supernatural potency of my American pills," and "the belief in the personal and supernatural causation of this life-threatening illness (by sorcery) had remained the same" (p. 1059).[15] In these and many other studies, traditional medical culture is routinely analyzed as a set of beliefs, explicitly or implicitly juxtaposed to medical knowledge, and a central question for the research is how "traditional medical beliefs" (which are obviously false) can hold out in the face of bio-medicine's efficacy and claims to rationality.

Analyses of traditional medicine as belief systems, such as these, are often linked quite closely to a second element in the empiricist paradigm, a view of "medical systems as sociocultural adaptive strategies," as Foster and Anderson subtitled their chapter on medical systems (1978: 33). While few would accept the explicit and sometimes crudely stated functionalism of this book today, their view of medical systems as adaptive is often unchallenged. They write: "just as we can speak of biological adaptive strategies that underlie human evolution, so too can we speak of *sociocultural adaptive strategies that bring into being medical systems*, the culturally based behavior and belief forms that arise in response to the threats posed by disease" (p. 33; emphasis added).

Medical anthropology was formulated in terms of human ecology and biological adaptation by Alland in an influential paper in the *American Anthropologist* in 1966 and in a monograph in 1970.[16] This formulation served as a response to a narrow rendering of ethnomedicine in cognitive terms, that is as folk beliefs, and placed studies of medical systems in a dialogue with a growing literature on human biology, social ecology, the history of infectious diseases, and the epidemiological consequences of particular behaviors. It thus brought biology more clearly into medical anthropology.

Ironically, the ecological paradigm reproduces the view of ethnomedicine as belief system which it set out to criticize. Alland outlined the program for the ecological approach explicitly within the evolutionary models of cultural ecology, in particular the neofunctionalist theories of Vayda and Rappaport, and many of the "biocultural" approaches in medical anthropology accept this framework uncritically. For example, in their text *Medical Anthropology in Ecological Perspective*, McElroy and Townsend (1985) distinguish genetic adaptations, individual physiological adaptations through a life course, and "the use of cultural information shared by a social group and transmitted through learning to each generation" (p. 73). These "cultural customs, beliefs, and taboos," which constitute the medical system, have direct as well as unintended adaptive effects. Traditional medical "beliefs and behaviors" are thus analyzed as cultural traits that enhance a population's adaptation to their ecological environment.[17] Culture, from this perspective, is conceived as a set of adaptive responses to diseases, which are here interpreted as analytically prior to and independent of culture, and medical systems are the sum or result of cumulative individual strategic responses, "strategies that bring into being medical systems" (Foster and Anderson 1978: 33).[18]

Analysis of specific forms of illness behavior which give theoretical primacy to individuals and to their adaptive "strategies" or "choices" constitutes a third element of the rationalist paradigm in the medical behavioral sciences. Paradigmatic of this approach have been studies of care-seeking strategies. Early anthropological studies of care-seeking drew on the medical sociology literature on "illness behavior" and the "lay referral system" (Freidson 1961, 1970), as well as on the social psychology literature on the Health Belief Model. All were a response, in a sense, to naive medical and public health questions about why people do not go to the doctor (as they obviously should) when they get sick. A brief examination of the health belief and illness behavior models provides a clear indication of the assumptions of the rationalist paradigm.[19]

The Health Belief Model (HBM) was developed in the 1950s by a group of social psychologists influenced by Kurt Lewin, in response to efforts by members of the Public Health Service to increase utilization of widely available preventive measures for diseases such as tuberculosis – and later, rheumatic fever, polio, and influenza (Rosenstock 1974). In close accordance with various behaviorist theories of motivation and decision making, the model predicted that behavior depends largely upon the value placed by the individual on a particular goal, and upon the individual's estimate of the likelihood of an action resulting in the goal (Maiman and Becker 1974). More specifically, the model hypothesized that perceived susceptibility to a disease and perceived severity of that disease, combined with perceived benefits of preventive actions minus perceived barriers to taking those actions, explained the likelihood of an individual taking preventive health measures, complying with prescribed regimens, or utilizing medical services.

In spite of continued reliance on HBM theories in health education, the leading figures of this field, Janz and Becker, concluded their 1984 review with a pessimistic evaluation of the approach: "Given the numerous survey-research findings of the HBM now available, it is unlikely that additional work of this type will yield important new information" (p. 45). Why was this the case? Why has HBM research failed to cast light on the most significant cultural differences in illness behavior and rates of morbidity and mortality? In part, I believe, its limitations result from the HBM's narrow conception of culture and human action.

The theory of culture assumed by HBM researchers has two characteristics.

First, HBM theories are explicit versions of what Sahlins (1976a: 101–102) calls "subjective utilitarianism." Its actor is a universal Economic Man, proceeding rationally toward the goal of positive health, a preference only slightly modified by health beliefs. Actors weigh the costs and benefits of particular behaviors, engaging in a kind of "threat-benefit analysis," then act freely on their perceptions to maximize their capital. As Sahlins notes, in such utilitarian theories culture is "taken as an environment or means at the disposition of the 'manipulating individual,' and also a sedimented result of his self-interested actions" (1976a: 102). Although purportedly Lewinian in its focus on the perceptions of individuals, the theory analyzes the structure of health beliefs and thus health culture only to the extent that they contribute to the rational calculus of the care-seeker who is ultimately free to make voluntary choices.

Second, HBM theories have a narrow and classically empiricist theory of culture as health beliefs. Developed specifically to help public health specialists convince people to act more rationally – to use preventive services, obey doctors' orders, or utilize medical services "appropriately" – such theories evaluate health beliefs for their proximity to empirically correct knowledge concerning the seriousness of particular disorders or the efficacy of particular behaviors or therapies. The wealth of meanings associated with illness in local cultures is thus reduced to a set of propositions held by individual actors, which are in turn evaluated in relation to biomedical knowledge.

The Health Belief Model thus presumes a quite explicit theory of culture. Lay medical culture is the precipitate of rational, adaptive behaviors of individuals, and it takes the form of more or less accurate beliefs which are held in individual minds. Thus, in the HBM research, the analysis of culture is made doubly subservient, relativized to the privileged perspective of current medical knowledge, and placed in the service of a utilitarian theory of illness behavior.

A second example is closer to much anthropological work. David Mechanic (1982: 1; cf. Mechanic 1986) outlines a basic model of illness behavior that could easily be translated into a research program current in much of medical anthropology.

> Illness behavior . . . describes the manner in which persons monitor their bodies, define and interpret their symptoms, take remedial actions, and utilize the health care system. People differentially perceive, evaluate, and respond to illness, and such behaviors have enormous influence on the extent to which illness interferes with usual life routines, the chronicity of the condition, the attainment of appropriate care, and the co-operation of the patient in the treatment of the condition.

This model holds, essentially, that the individual experiences bodily sensations, appraises these (or makes illness attributions) using available illness representations (or explanatory models), then makes treatment choices in consultation with members of a lay referral network. It would seem that this model is reasonably value-free and could accommodate and highlight differences among cultures. But is this the case?

In a study by Lin and his colleagues (1978), which examined care-seeking pathways followed to mental health services by Anglo, Chinese, and American Indian patients in Vancouver, only one of the three ethnic groups studied fit easily in this model. Individuals from the Anglo-Saxon and middle European sample experienced symptoms, consulted family members, reviewed available resources, and chose mental health or social service resources, following a pattern very close to that outlined by the illness behavior model. The two other groups studied, however, fit the model less easily. For the ethnic Chinese, there were early and prolonged efforts by the family to manage problems in each episode without encouraging the sufferer to seek professional care. Many were isolated in the home and allowed few contacts. Remarkably advanced psychiatric symptoms were often present before any outside care was sought. Medical interventions eventually occurred, although involvement with legal and social agencies was rare. Clearly, the sick individual was not the source of decision making, and the family was much more than a "lay referral network." Indeed those who are sick have little freedom of action, and the family organizes the entire care-seeking and therapy management, which often consists largely of seclusion. The American Indian patients, however, were even further from the seemingly neutral model of illness behavior. These patients were most commonly found among Vancouver's homeless mentally ill, with neither a family to organize care-seeking choices, nor the ability to actively organize their own care. They were often transferred between social service agencies and police, who became the major groups responsible for "care-seeking decisions" rather than the patients themselves.

This study raises significant questions about what may seem to be the most culturally-sensitive models of the medical behavioral sciences. The ability of the individual to appraise symptoms, review available resources, then make voluntary choices is simply a myth for many in our society and in other societies. The model of the rational, autonomous care-seeker (or even the therapy management group) organizing treatment choices to maximize perceived benefits to the sufferer is hardly a value-free model. It is rather a model of how members of our society are thought to act, an ideological model which reproduces conventional under-standings and serves best when used to study middle-class Americans who have health insurance and are seeking care for relatively minor problems. When the sampling domain is adequately delimited, the illness behavior model (as the health belief model) accounts for much of the variance in care-seeking behavior. It does tell us why some people choose to seek care for some problems, not others. However, it does so only by excluding those persons who have the least control over their lives, by treating as external to the model the most important structural conditions which constrain care-seeking, by ignoring much of what happens during the management of chronic and critical illness, particularly in tertiary care settings, and by defining culture as the instrumental beliefs of individuals.

Anthropological studies of the past two decades have sought to overcome the limitations of these models. In the process, they have transformed the sociological conception of care-seeking into a tool for rich ethnographic investigations, and sparked an important debate about the differential contributions of subjective culture (or belief) and objective or macrostructural contributions to care-seeking. Anthropological research in this field began with Romanucci-Ross's (1969) analysis of care-seeking as a "hierarchy of resort" to traditional, contact culture (Christian), or European curative practices on the Admiralty Islands. As studies of pluralistic health care systems developed in the 1970s, many focused on how "choice points" are organized in relation to diverse medical traditions and healers (Kunstadter 1976), how culture shapes the "health seeking process" and the ends sought through treatment (Chrisman 1977; Kleinman 1980; Nichter 1980), and how "therapy management" (Janzen 1978b, 1987) and referral are organized. Particularly elegant were studies of "natural decision making," based explicitly in the theory and methods of cognitive science, which developed formal models for "the nature of the information considered and . . . the nature of how it is processed" as members of a society confront illness and take action, rather than correlating characteristics of patients or diseases with types of care sought (J. Young 1978, 1981; Young and Garro 1982; cf. Garro 1986b). Critical studies within medical anthropology, however, pointed to limitations implicit in the care-seeking literature. Health decisions are far more constrained by objective social factors and macro-level structures of inequality, many have argued, than by subjective "beliefs" or cognitive factors.[20] For example, Janzen (1978a) called for placing such research in relation to macro-social structures, and Morsy (1978, 1980, 1990) has argued strongly that narrow attention to culture and perception ("socio-culturalism," she calls this) has led to the neglect of both local and global power relations which constrain many aspects of the care-seeking process. This debate has generated not only theoretical discussions but empirical studies designed explicitly to investigate the relative role of beliefs about the nature of an illness and such structural factors as availability and cost of treatment in determining choice of therapies (J. Young 1981; Young and Garro 1982; Sargent 1989).

These studies provide both an elaboration and a useful critique of much of the literature on care-seeking in sociology and social psychology. What I believe deserves thought, however, is why anthropologists so readily frame their ethno-medical research as an investigation of the choices individuals make in seeking care and how such analyses are framed. On close examination, even much of the anthropological literature shares with psychological and sociological studies an image of the rational, value-maximizing individual responding adaptively to disease, selecting among a stable set of choices and motivated by a set of meanings external to the subject.[21] This is an image which is consonant with the ecological view that gives analytic priority to those "sociocultural adaptive strategies that bring [ethnomedical systems] into being" (Foster and Anderson 1978: 33), as well as with the rationalist tradition of analyzing illness represen-tations as folk beliefs. It is the convergence of the rationalist theories of medical beliefs, ecological theories of ethnomedical systems as essentially adaptive, and the analytic primacy of "choice" in studies of illness behavior that constitutes what I have called the "common-sense" or empiricist paradigm in medical anthropology. The very common-sense quality of this paradigm hints at its role in reproducing conventional knowledge about the role of the individual in society (cf. A. Young 1980) and suggests several reasons why this perspective faces theoretical, practical, and empirical difficulties.

First, as I argued in chapter 1, analysis of illness representations as folk beliefs is grounded in Enlightenment theories of language and meaning, and shares the difficulties of such theories. Disease is often taken to be a natural object, more or less accurately represented in folk and scientific thought. Disease is thus an object separate from human consciousness, conceived, as Cassirer writes of positivist theorizing, as given *"tout fait*, in its existence as in its structure, and . . . for the human mind [*esprit*] it is only a matter of taking possession of that reality. That which exists and subsists 'outside' of us must be, as it were, 'transported' into consciousness, changed into something internal without, however, adding anything new in the process" (Cassirer 1944: 18, quoted in Sahlins 1976a: 62). Folk thought, from this perspective, is "inspired by definite ideas" of disease causation, as Rivers held, and is a way of making sense of the world akin to science (Horton 1967). But Rivers' proviso that "from our modern standpoint we are able to see that these ideas are wrong" always haunts such rationalist accounts, provoking a crisis of representation for anthropologists even as it provides a clear program for the health educators.

The analysis of folk beliefs as "information" or even "explanation" also suggests a political and psychological neutrality contradicted by the recent literature on illness representations.[22] Popular metaphors of warfare and machismo help structure explanations of AIDS and the immune system, but whether in science or health education, these figures also "serve as a powerful *patriarchal* instrument by re-inforcing assumptions about who gets sick or ill – the weak, the submissive and the un-manly" (Warwick, Aggleton, and Homans 1988: 220, summarizing Rodmell 1987; see also Clatts and Mutchler 1989). Respected epidemiological accounts of the origins of AIDS often disguise "accusation" as information, for example representing Haitians in racist and culturally stereotyping terms as a means of providing common-sense explanations of the appearance of the disease in Haiti (Farmer 1990a, 1992; Murray and Payne 1989). Political and psychological meanings projected onto disease are thus turned onto the sufferer. No wonder Sontag (1989: 94) calls for the metaphors of AIDS "to be exposed, criticized, belabored, used up."

Ironically, Sontag's desire to do away with metaphors, to "use them up," reproduces the Enlightenment ideal of a culture-free representation of disease, of disease as objective reality, the biosciences as providing neutral and realistic representations, and folk culture as rife with dangerous and ultimately mistaken metaphors.[23] Surely it is important to "expose" the stigmatizing aspects of both scientific and popular accounts of disease and participate in the work of refiguring disease, gender, and the human body. But for the anthropologist, replacing mistaken folk culture with the "value-free information of science" seems a deeply inadequate goal for either cultural analysis or committed action.

The development of alternative approaches for analyzing disease and its representation has thus emerged as central to medical anthropology.

A second central difficulty with ecological theories of medical systems and many studies of illness behavior is the analytic primacy given to individual choice and the implication that illness representations and ethnomedical systems are ultimately derived from the rational, instrumental activities of individuals. Such theories are forms of utilitarianism and, as I suggested in my discussion of the health belief model, are subject to Sahlins' critique of the analysis of culture as "practical reason" (Sahlins 1976a).

Sahlins traces a conflict present in anthropology since the nineteenth century between utilitarianism and what he considers to be a truly anthropological account of culture and social action, a conflict he argues revolves around "whether the cultural order is to be conceived as the codification of man's actual purposeful and pragmatic action; or whether, conversely, human action in the world is to be understood as mediated by the cultural design, which gives order at once to practical experience, customary practice, and the relationship between the two" (p. 55). Utilitarianism, he argues, is characterized by a logic which he finds exemplified in Lewis Henry Morgan's analysis of culture: "The general line of force of the argument, *the orientation of logical effect*, is from natural constraint to behavioral practice, and from behavioral practice to cultural institution: circumstance → practice → organization and codification (institution)" (pp. 60–61).

And so it is with utilitarian theories in medical anthropology. Diseases provoke individual and social responses, and these are codified as ethnomedical systems. In the ecological paradigm, a variant of "naturalistic or ecological" utilitarianism, culture is conceived as "the human mode of adaptation," and "explanation consists of determining the material or biological virtues of given cultural traits" (Sahlins 1976a: 101). Culture is thus absorbed into nature, and cultural analysis consists of demonstrating its adaptive efficacy.[24] Rational choice paradigms are variants of "subjective utilitarianism," a complementary perspective, and are "concerned with the purposeful activity of individuals in pursuit of their own interests and their own satisfactions" (p. 102). Though culture provides a "relativized set of preferences," ultimately "only the actors (and their interest taken a priori as *theirs*) are real; culture is the epiphenomenon of their intentions" (p. 102).

The critique of subjective utilitarianism is more appropriate to many studies of illness behavior in health psychology and medical sociology than to most anthropological studies of care-seeking, and by no means equally relevant to all strands of the diverse anthropological literature. Indeed, as I have said, many anthropologists who have written on care-seeking would explicitly reject the relevance of Sahlins' characterization of utilitarianism to their own work, and some have developed positions around a critique of standard empiricist accounts. This is certainly true of those who have focused exclusively on the relation of a sufferer's structural position in society to choice of care, rather than on individual experience and motives (Morsy 1978, 1980). It is also true of those in the cognitive tradition who have developed "descriptive" rather than "normative" decision models (Garro 1986b: 176–177). For example, James Young (1981: 10) argued that rather than developing decision models that produce "optimal choices – those having highest utility, lowest costs, or greatest benefits," ethnographic research should attempt to model options actually considered and "real-world decision processes," which thus best account for actual behavior.

My question remains why anthropologists have so readily assumed that the study of care-seeking choices provides an obvious entree into describing a medical system, and why individual decision makers, guided by their personal beliefs, are so often the primary focus of investigation and analysis. Although the anthropological literature on care-seeking is now quite diverse in methodology and theoretical orientation, utilitarian assumptions often appear in the common-sense reasoning in this literature. This is troubling. The analytic conjunction of the utilitarian actor, instrumental beliefs that organize the rational calculus of care-seeking, and ethnomedical systems as the sum of strategic actions is uncomfortably consonant with neo-classical economic theories of the utilitarian actor, the market place, and the economic system as precipitate of value-maximizing strategies. Little wonder common-sense theorizing is commonsense.

Sahlins concludes his critique of utilitarianism with an affirmation of an alternative vision of cultural forms.

> All these types of practical reason have . . . in common an impoverished conception of human symboling. For all of them, the cultural scheme is the *sign* of other "realities," hence in the end obeisant in its own arrangement to other laws and logics. None of them has been able to exploit fully the anthropological discovery that the creation of meaning is the distinguishing and constituting quality of men – the "human essence" of an older discourse – such that by processes of differential valuation and signification, relations among men, as well as between themselves and nature, are organized. (1976a: 102)

It is precisely the challenge of overcoming an impoverished conception of human symboling, of meaning made servant to the biosciences and to practical reason, that has given vitality to much of the theoretical discourse in medical anthropology during the past decade. And it is the elaboration of an alternative vision of cultural forms, of their intersubjective quality and their role in constituting our relationship to and knowledge of human biology, which I attempt to set out in these pages.

The empiricist tradition in medical anthropology has largely moved from common-sense theorizing to technically elaborated ecological and biocultural models. However, the greatest energy in the past decade has come from the development of positions critical of the empiricist approach and the emergence of a complex conversation among theoretical traditions. In the remaining pages of this chapter, I review three such positions, focusing again on the underlying theories of language and representation, thus setting the stage for the development of one such alternative for the field.

*Illness representations as cognitive models: the view from cognitive
anthropology*

In the late 1950s and early 1960s, a small group of anthropologists, influenced by
the emergence of the cognitive sciences in psychology, outlined a program for
anthropology under the banner of "ethnoscience," "ethnosemantics," or "the
new ethnology." The goal of investigating how language and culture structure
perception and thus the apparent order in the natural and social world had its roots
in Boasian anthropology, particularly in the writings of Sapir, Whorf, and
Hallowell.[25] And the analytic language of investigating "folk models" was already
present in cultural anthropology. However, linguistic anthropologists such as
Goodenough (1956), Frake (1962), and Sturtevant (1964) set out to place cultural
studies on a more scientific footing, one in which the structure of language and the
structure of cognition jointly served as a basis for understanding culture and
the structure of the cultural world as perceived by members of a society.
Goodenough in particular called for the study of culture as shared knowledge, as
the investigation of what people "must know in order to act as they do, make the
things they make, and interpret their experience in the distinctive way they do"
(Quinn and Holland 1987: 4). Goodenough's mandate focused on the identification of generative cultural models that account for what members of a society
say and do. The effort to use replicable methods to "specify the cognitive
organization of such ideational complexes and to link this organization to what
is known about the way human beings think" (Quinn and Holland 1987: 4) has
characterized over thirty years of studies in this field.

A modest thread running through cognitive studies in anthropology has been an
interest in disease classification, ethnotheories of illness and healing, and the
structure of illness narratives. In some cases, such studies have been conducted by
medical anthropologists working in the cognitive tradition; in others, the medical
domain has simply provided cognitivists an opportunity to investigate the nature
of cultural models. Together with cognitive studies in medical psychology
(Skelton, Croyle, and Eisler 1991), cognitive anthropologists have developed a
distinctive theory of illness representations that contributes to current analytic discourse.

The earliest studies in the field were focused almost exclusively on categorization. Frake's classic study of the diagnosis of disease among the Subanun of
Mindanao (1961) provided a model for eliciting and analyzing a disease taxonomy
in terms of diagnostic categories and the symptoms that serve as distinctive
features of each. The study was conducted without reference to biomedical
categories; Frake sought a purely "emic" understanding of Subanun categories of
skin disorders and of diagnosis as a "pivotal cognitive step" in attaching a name
to an instance of "being sick" (1961: 132). Horacio Fabrega, a medical anthropologist and psychiatrist, elaborated Frake's techniques in the context of a larger
investigation of the Zinacanteco ethnomedical system in Chiapas, Mexico. In a

series of studies, Fabrega and his colleagues used ethnosemantic techniques to identify native illness categories and the symptoms presumed to be the distinctive features of each, and to compare the knowledge structure and judgments of lay persons and healers (Fabrega 1970; Fabrega and Silver 1973). They then went on to compare Zinacanteco and biomedical categories (of skin disorders) as alternative systems of mapping symptoms onto disease names (Fabrega and Silver 1973: 135–140).

Undertaken in a context in which ethnomedical research had focused largely on describing exotic folk illnesses and providing generalized descriptions of health beliefs and practices, these early studies were a significant step toward the detailed investigation of everyday medical knowledge. However, in retrospect, their limitations are apparent. Their definitions of the domain of medical knowledge were extremely limited, and their analytic framework was narrowly referential, focusing almost exclusively on taxonomy. In large measure they thus reproduced the empiricist view of language as designating or pointing to objects in the world (cf. B. Good 1977; B. Good and M. Good 1981, 1982). Furthermore, they specified symptoms as the defining characteristics of diseases, although acknowledging that causation is often more closely linked to treatment than are symptoms. Thus, even when integrated into broader ethnographic studies, such as Fabrega and Silver's ethnography, the early ethnosemantic studies made claims about the scientific representation of folk knowledge that were overstated and unrealistic.[26]

A second generation of ethnosemantic studies of medical knowledge is represented by the work of Young and Garro (J. Young 1981; J. Young and Garro 1982). They investigated the structure of folk medical knowledge in a Mexican village, now however using a variety of relevant "criterial attributes" (including cause and severity) in addition to symptoms to model illness beliefs. This analysis was linked to a formal study of decision making. Four criteria – seriousness, type of illness, faith in the effectiveness of folk versus medical treatment for a given type of illness, and expense of treatment – were found relevant for distinguishing among illness categories in the choice of treatment from various folk or biomedical sources. By investigating decision making in individual cases of illness, they were able to develop a model that accounted for over 90 percent of treatment choices. This research went considerably beyond earlier studies by investigating knowledge of particular events, rather than only generalized medical knowledge, and by demonstrating the relevance of both medical beliefs and structural constraints on treatment choices. However, it continued to focus on criterial models and decision trees, which were giving way to new interests in schema theory in cognitive psychology.

By the early 1980s, cognitive anthropologists began to turn from "feature models" to various "schema" or "prototype" models to represent cultural knowledge. Drawing specifically on research on medical beliefs, D'Andrade (1976) voiced his dissatisfaction with earlier approaches:

the attributes of disease with which informants are most concerned and which they use in making inferences about diseases are not the defining or distinctive features, but the connotative attributes of "seriousness," "curability," and the like. For example, what people know about cancer is not what defines a cell as cancerous, but rather that having cancer is often fatal and painful.[27] (1976: 177–178)

Increasingly, anthropologists sought ways to represent the "ethnotheories" that organize cultural worlds rather than lexical items that demarcate objects in that world. For example, Geoffrey White (1982a) reviewed methodological advances from taxonomic to propositional and inferential models for the study of "cultural knowledge of 'mental disorder'," suggesting that cognitivists and symbolic anthropologists join in studying the implicit "theories" of disease and ethno-psychological theories of social behavior in common-sense thinking about illness, rather than limiting attention to classification (1982a: 86). Clement's essay in the same volume is particularly illustrative of the transition to new approaches. Having used ethnosemantic techniques for eliciting data on Samoan concepts of mental disorders, she argued for reconceptualizing analysis in terms of "folk knowledge": "*folk* knowledge is viewed as an aspect of the group. Folk representations, the means through which folk knowledge is expressed, are . . . products of the institutionalized patterns of information processing and knowledge distribution with the group" (Clement 1982: 194). She thus sought to reanalyze her data in terms of cultural representations produced and reproduced in rituals, healing activities, and processes of social change, rather than solely in terms of individual classificatory schemes.

In efforts to move beyond feature models to a broader understanding of folk knowledge, psychologists' theories of "scripts," "prototypes," or "schemas" proved useful (see Casson 1983, Quinn and Holland 1987, and D'Andrade 1922 for reviews). Essentially, it was argued that culture provides simplified representations of the world – of cultural objects, of action sequences, of propositional relations – which generate statements and judgments that individuals make, organize behavior and life plans, and thus serve as the building blocks of cultural knowledge. During the 1980s, researchers attempted to demonstrate that simplified models of a wide variety of cultural domains – from Trobriand litigation (Hutchins 1980) to Ifaluk emotions (Lutz 1988) to marriage in the United States (Quinn 1987) – could account for much of the natural discourse and behavior associated with these domains.

Cognitive studies in medical and psychological anthropology during the past decade have focused largely on describing the ethnotheories or cultural models for emotions, psychological functioning, and illness in various societies. In nearly all of this work, it is assumed that simplified cultural models can be deduced which make sense of the cultural data elicited in these domains. Studies of cultural models have been undertaken not only to investigate folk models or common-sense reasoning, but to analyze the knowledge generated by the medical sciences or professional psychology as well.[28] Lutz (1985), for example, explored the meaning of "depression" among the Ifaluk people of the South Pacific. However, her investigation begins with an analysis of how Western ethnopsychology frames our understanding of depression by distinguishing "thought disorders" from "affective disorders" in a fashion that makes little sense for the Ifaluk. Similarly, Geoffrey White (1982b) shows that rather than simply studying how emotional problems are "somatized" in Asian societies, Western processes of "psychologization" and the very distinction of somatic from psychological need to be investigated in relation to our own ethnotheories of the person.

In a more specifically medical set of studies, Linda Garro (1986a, 1988, 1990) has investigated models of illness held by members of an Ojibway Indian community in Manitoba. In a study of explanations of high blood pressure, she criticizes previous research that represents illness models as "static," research which "does not represent the knowledge that generates [informants'] statements and that allows individuals to assimilate new information and make inferences" (1988: 89). Second, she argues that little research in medical anthropology has been able to identify and explain intracultural consensus and variation. Using open-ended explanatory model interviews to generate statements about high blood pressure, then analyzing true-false responses by informants confronted with such statements, Garro was able to identify "four key concepts of the prototypical model for blood that rises," stated in propositional form. She demonstrates that this prototype can be used to generate the majority of statements about high blood pressure among Ojibway informants, and also to identify individuals who hold idiosyncratic models not consistent with the "shared" cultural model.[29]

Cognitive studies of illness representations thus serve as an increasingly powerful critique of many generalized accounts of health beliefs and assumptions that "cultural beliefs" are consensual. They have provided clear analyses of the ethnotheories and prototypical schema associated with various domains of medical knowledge, and sought to investigate the nature of cultural consensus and variation. They increasingly combine formal methods of elicitation with analyses of natural discourse, and studies of illness or care-seeking narratives (Garro 1992; Price 1987) have again brought cognitive anthropologists into conversation with symbolic anthropologists. In some cases, implications of studies of cognitive models and "everyday reasoning" have been applied to problems of health education (Patel, Eisemon, and Arocha 1988).

Nonetheless, cognitive studies of "illness beliefs" or "cultural knowledge" – the terms are often used interchangeably – continue to share some of the criticisms of studies of folk beliefs outlined in the previous section. Although the analytic category "knowledge" has become more prominent and "belief" less, "knowledge" continues to refer largely to "what an individual needs to know" to be a competent member of a society. The epistemological issues at stake in claims to study folk "knowledge" have been largely ignored, and the individual mind (or brain) is seen as the primary locus of culture and meaning. Illness representations are thus largely understood in mentalistic terms, abstracted from "embodied knowledge," affect, and social and historical forces that shape illness meanings. Illness models are studied in formal, semantic terms, with little attention to their pragmatic and performative dimensions or to the civilizational traditions that provide their intellectual context. Indeed, it is troubling to note that despite similarity in forms of cultural analysis between cognitivists and studies of medical semiotics in pluralistic medical systems (for example Staiano 1986; Ohnuki-Tierney 1981, 1984), cognitive studies have drawn very little on the larger tradition of civilizational analysis. As a result, studies of particular cultural domains often tell us remarkably little about the societies being studied.[30] Furthermore, as Keesing, a critic from within the tradition, notes, early cognitive anthropology was "naively reductionistic in its tacit premise that cultural rules generate behavior" and that "cultural rules generate social systems as well as behavior." He concludes, "Cognitive anthropology remains, I think, curiously innocent of social theory" (Keesing 1987: 387). This innocence of social theory, combined with the theoretical centrality of the individual thinker and actor in the cognitive tradition, opens the tradition to critical analysis of the sort outlined for empiricist theories.

Illness representations as culturally constituted realities: the "meaning-centered" tradition

Arthur Kleinman's work, beginning in the late 1970s, marked the emergence of a new approach to medical anthropology as a systematic and theoretically grounded field of inquiry within the larger discipline. At a time when ethnomedical systems were increasingly defined in ecological and adaptive terms, Kleinman designated the medical system a "cultural system" and thus a distinctive field of anthropological inquiry. His work combined an interest in complex medical systems, following in the Leslie tradition, detailed ethnographic analyses of illness and healing in Chinese cultures, theoretical development linked to symbolic, interpretive, and social constructivist writing, and an interest in applied medical anthropology. Kleinman's writing, editing, and advocacy for anthropological studies in medicine and psychiatry sparked – and paralleled – a burst of theoretical developments in the field; together these stimulated the emergence of both interpretive approaches and critiques of those approaches during the 1980s. Because the following chapters of this book are devoted to elaborating an interpretive approach to the field, conversant with critical analyses, here I will simply sketch out central themes of the interpretive tradition and its relation to the analysis of illness representations.

Whereas many writers in the empiricist tradition have treated disease as a part of nature, external to culture, and cognitive anthropologists have generally been indifferent to the epistemological status of disease, interpretive anthropologists have placed the relation of culture and illness at the center of analytic interest. Kleinman's work on explanatory models has often been misread. Eliciting and providing accounts of explanatory models of illness are certainly a means of analyzing patients' understandings of their condition, and serve as an entree to teaching clinicians to elicit the "native's point of view" during their clinical work

(Kleinman, Eisenberg, and Good 1978). Explanatory models are also cultural models which serve cognitive functions akin to those analyzed by cognitive anthropologists (Kleinman 1974).[31] But the more fundamental claim from the meaning-centered tradition has been that *disease is not an entity but an explanatory model*. Disease belongs to culture, in particular to the specialized culture of medicine. And culture is not only a means of representing disease, but is essential to its very constitution as a human reality (Kleinman 1973b; B. Good and M. Good 1981). Complex human phenomena are framed as "disease," and by this means become the objects of medical practices (see chapter 3). Disease thus has its ontological grounding in the order of meaning and human understanding (A. Young 1976). Indeed it is the mistaken belief that our categories belong to nature, that disease as we know it is natural and therefore above or beyond (or deeper than) culture, that represents a "category fallacy" (Kleinman 1977). This paradoxical claim has served as source for much of the theorizing and empirical research in the interpretive tradition.

First, it has served as the basis for exploring the relation of biology and culture and for studies of the cultural shaping of the phenomenology and course of illness. In epistemological terms, the claim that disease is an explanatory model was not an idealist counter to biological reductionism, but a constructivist argument that sickness is constituted and only knowable through interpretive activities. Rather than either reifying or denying the significance of biology, the interpretive paradigm has taken a strongly interactionist and perspectivist position. Biology, social practices and meaning interact in the organization of illness as social object and lived experience. Multiple interpretive frames and discourses are brought to bear on any illness event, and in Bakhtin's words, each offers "a concrete heterological opinion on the world."[32] Interpretations of the nature of an illness always bear the history of the discourse that shapes its interpretation, and are always contested in settings of local power relations (Kuipers 1989; Mishler 1986a; Kleinman 1986; B. Good and Kleinman 1985; B. Good, M. Good, and Moradi 1985). Empirical research has thus been directed both at how various forms of therapeutic practice construct the objects of medical knowledge – as "clinical realities" – as well as at how cultural interpretations interact with biology or psychophysiology and social relations to produce distinctive forms of illness. Studies of biomedicine have indicated surprising diversity in the construction of clinical realities across subspecialties within a given society (Hahn and Gaines 1985), and even greater diversity across national boundaries (for example Lock 1980; Maretzki 1989; M. Good, Hunt, Munakata, and Kobayashi 1993).

Culture, Kleinman argued early on (1973b), provides a symbolic bridge between intersubjective meanings and the human body. What is the nature and actual extent of culture's efficacy? In empirical terms, how variant are the symptoms and course of diseases? Research in this tradition suggests that cultural "idioms of distress" (Nichter 1981) organize illness experience and behavior quite differently across societies, that culture may provide "final common ethnobehavioral pathways" (Carr and Vitaliano 1985) and even construct unique disorders. In particular, profound individual and cross-cultural differences in the course and prognosis of major chronic diseases have been shown to be produced by cultural meanings, social response, and the social relations in which they are embedded (for example Waxler 1977a; Jenkins 1991). The role of therapeutic practices both in the "clinical construction of reality" and in producing healing efficacy has also been investigated. In particular, rhetorical practices associated with healing activities have been shown to have powerful effects in a number of empirical studies (Csordas 1983, 1988; Csordas and Kleinman 1990; Finkler 1983; Gaines 1979, 1982; Kapferer 1983; Kleinman and Sung 1979; Laderman 1987, 1991; Roseman 1988). Thus, rather than focusing on representation *per se*, this tradition has investigated how meaning and interpretive practices interact with social, psychological, and physiological processes to produce distinctive forms of illness and illness trajectories.

Second, during the past two decades, medical anthropologists interested in meaning and interpretation have engaged in wide-ranging investigations of symbolic structures and processes associated with illness in popular culture and various therapeutic traditions. Rather than focusing narrowly on health beliefs or on distinctive features and cognitive models, such studies have provided interpretive accounts from many theoretical points of view – cultural studies of classical non-Western medical systems (Lock 1980; Ohnuki-Tierney 1984; Nichter 1989), semiotic and historical studies (Zimmerman 1987; Devisch 1990; Bibeau 1981), interpretive ethnographies of North American and European bio-medicine (M. Good et al. 1990; Hahn and Gaines 1985; Lock and Gordon 1988), and studies of metaphor (Kirmayer 1988) and semantic networks (B. Good 1977). In contrast with the cognitive tradition, these studies have often been civilizational in scope and self-consciously theoretical, whether in relation to semiotics, hermeneutics, phenomenology, narrative analysis, or critical interpretive studies.

The analyses of "semantic networks" in Iranian and American medical culture, which I undertook along with Mary-Jo Good (B. Good 1977; M. Good 1980; B. Good and M. Good 1980, 1981, 1992; B. Good, M. Good, and Moradi 1985), should be read in this context. We developed the approach as an effort to interpret complaints of "heart distress" in a small town in Iran, as well as to understand how Greek medicine, which originated in a civilization and era far removed from twentieth-century Iran, seemed so tightly knit to the everyday lifeworld of the community in which we worked (cf. B. Good and M. Good 1992). We went on to use the approach for investigating the meaning of symptoms in American medical clinics and for exploring a number of the core symbolic domains of American medicine.[33]

Semantic network analysis provided a means of systematically recording the domains of meaning associated with core symbols and symptoms in a medical lexicon, domains which reflect and provoke forms of experience and social relations, and which constitute illness as a "syndrome of meaning and experience." Although the term semantic network has not had a uniform meaning or method, ethnographic research designed to map out the symbolic pathways associated with key medical terms, illness categories, symptoms, and medical practices has been an important aspect of empirical studies in the meaning-centered tradition.[34] This research suggests that networks of associative meanings link illness to fundamental cultural values of a civilization, that such networks have longevity and resilience, and that new diseases (such as AIDS) or medical categories acquire meaning in relation to existing semantic networks that are often out of explicit conscious view of members of the society (for example Farmer 1992: 59ff.; Murray and Payne 1989). This research also suggests that semantic networks are not simple precipitates of social practices or explanatory models, though they are routinely reproduced through such practices. But semantic networks are deep cultural associations (such as that between obesity and "self control") that appear to members of a society simply as part of nature or an invariant of the social world and may therefore be part of hegemonic structures (cf. B. Good and M. Good 1981). Explanatory models in diverse fields such as behavioral medicine or obstetrics or immunology are often generated to rationalize or explain associations which are observed to be part of the natural order.

Third, in the past several years, interpretive studies have focused increasingly on embodied experience as the grounds and problematic of illness representations. Sickness is present in the human body, and sufferers often face difficulties similar to the ethnographer in representing its experience. Anthropologists in the interpretive tradition have had a special concern to produce "experience-near" accounts which render the body present, while criticizing purely cognitive renderings of illness. Some have used phenomenology explicitly to study the medium and structure of experience, conceiving the body as subject of knowledge and experience and meaning as prior to representation. History and social relations leave their "traces" in the body, and as Pandolfi (1990: 255) writes, "this body becomes a phenomenological memoir that opens a new way of interpreting distress and suffering and illness." Studies of "embodiment" (Csordas 1990; Gordon 1990; Pandolfi 1990) and the "phenomenology" of illness experience (Corin 1990; Frank 1986; Ots 1990; Wikan 1991; see also case studies in Kleinman and Good 1985 and M. Good et al. 1992) have thus become increasingly important ways of investigating the relation of meaning and experience as intersubjective phenomena. The difficulties of adequately representing suffering and experience in our ethnographic accounts, the problematic relation of experience to cultural forms such as narratives, and efforts to understand the grounding of such experience in local moral worlds are problems of current concern in this tradition (e.g. Kleinman and Kleinman 1991; B. Good 1992a; Das 1993; Mattingly 1989).

Interpretive studies in medical anthropology have been criticized from several sides – as unduly theoretical and irrelevant to most applied work, as attending too little to human biology, as lacking in the scientific rigor of epidemiology or cognitive studies, or as too "clinical" and too closely aligned with the interests of medicine. More importantly, some have charged that those who have analyzed how illness realities are constituted through interpretive and representational processes have too often treated such realities as consensual and failed to provide a "critical" stance vis-à-vis illness representations and medical knowledge. Rhodes (1990: 164), for example, argues that "critical perspectives tend to emerge out of the cultural analysis of biomedicine" but that interpretive anthropologists have often failed to pursue such perspectives.

What I have described here as the interpretive paradigm was initially grounded in the studies of Asian medical systems and theoretically in symbolic or cultural analysis in American anthropology. Given the emergence of practice theories and wide-ranging forms of critical analysis, it is little surprise that some formulations in this tradition now seem dated or that the very term "meaning-centered" now seems best placed in quotes. However, the interpretive paradigm continues to maintain a distinctive perspective on language and representation, drawing on the historicist tradition and contemporary theorists such as Charles Taylor, Hilary Putnam, and Paul Ricoeur. Although this tradition stands in tension with Marxist or critical theories of culture and representation, I will be arguing that this tension is the source of much of the creative work in our field today.

The elaboration of a program of critical studies in medical anthropology represents a fourth orienting approach in the field, one which has developed in an on-going conversation with interpretive approaches, and it is to that approach which I now turn.

Illness representations as mystification: views from "critical" medical anthropology

A self-consciously "critical" approach to medical anthropology has developed in the past decade, both in conversation with and reaction to interpretive approaches to the field.[35] In part, this tradition reflects a growing interest in anthropology at large in more fully integrating history and historical analyses of colonialism, political economy, and "subaltern studies" of various forms into ethnographic analysis and writing. Again, I can only highlight several themes in this literature.

First, medical anthropology has begun to develop an important set of studies of how political and economic forces of both global and societal scope are present in the local health conditions and medical institutions studied by ethnographers. Such studies are an effort to understand "health issues in light of the larger political and economic forces that pattern interpersonal relationships, shape social behavior, generate social meanings, and condition collective experience," in Singer's (1990: 181) words. There is a long tradition in the medical social sciences and in "social medicine" of investigating the distribution of health services, the role of power in health care relationships and transactions (Waitzkin 1991), and the social institutions and inequities responsible for the distribution of morbidity and mortality – what Kleinman refers to as "the social production of disease" in contrast to the "cultural construction of illness," and what McKinlay (1986) calls the "manufacture of illness" (cf. Waitzkin and Waterman 1974). In recent years, medical anthropologists have drawn explicitly on dependency theory and other traditions of political economy theorizing to advance such research within anthropology (see Morgan 1987 and Morsy 1990 for reviews). Some have joined public health, ecological models, and political economic perspectives to investigate the "political ecology" of disease, in particular in the context of "Third World underdevelopment" (Morsy 1990: 27; cf. Turshen 1977, 1984, and Onoge 1975). Nearly all anthropologists today struggle to bring their understanding of historical and macrosocietal forces to bear on their ethnographic analyses of illness episodes and local worlds of health care (see Janzen 1978a, 1978b for early statements of this concern). And Marxist medical anthropologists have had a special interest in critical studies of medicine in capitalist and socialist societies.

Second, anthropologists in this tradition have attempted to develop a critical or neo-Marxist approach to the analysis of illness representations and medical knowledge. Often quoted is Keesing's critique of interpretive anthropology: "cultures do not simply constitute webs of significance, systems of meaning that orient humans to one another and their world. They constitute ideologies, disguising human political and economic realities. . . . Cultures are webs of mystification as well as significance" (Keesing 1987: 161). Theories of illness representations as mystification, in particular as mystifications of underlying social relations or relations of power, often draw on two sources: Gramsci's analysis of hegemony, and Foucault's "genealogy" of power. Gramsci's writing on hegemony focuses attention sharply on the role of cultural forms in rendering existing social relations common-sense, a part of ordinary reality, natural. For Gramsci, hegemony asserts itself subtly, leading to

> the permeation throughout civil society . . . of an entire system of values, attitudes, beliefs, morality, etc., that is in one way or another supportive of the established order and the class interests that dominate it. . . . to the extent that this prevailing consciousness is internalized by the broad masses, it becomes part of "common sense." . . . For hegemony to assert itself successfully in any society, therefore, it must operate in a dualistic manner: as a "general conception of life" for the masses and as a "scholastic programme."[36] (Greer, cited in Martin 1987: 23)

A critical medical anthropology forcefully poses the question of when illness representations are actually misrepresentations which serve the interests of those in power, be they colonial powers, elites within a society, dominant economic arrangements, the medical profession, or empowered men. Critical analysis investigates both the mystification of the social origins of disease wrought by technical terminology and metaphors diffused throughout medical language, as well as the "social conditions of knowledge production" (A. Young 1982: 277). Forms of suffering derived from class relations may be defined as illness, medicalized, "constructed as dehistoricized objects-in-themselves" (A. Young 1982: 275; cf. Taussig 1980, Frankenberg 1988a) and brought under the authority of the medical profession and the state. For example, symptoms of hunger or diseases that result from poverty, whether among the North American poor or the impoverished cane cutters of Brazil, are often medicalized, treated as a condition of individual bodies – "diarrhea," "TB," "nerves," or "stress" – rather than as a collective social and political concern (Scheper-Hughes 1988). The transform-ation of political problems into medical concerns is often akin to "neutralizing" critical consciousness, and is thus in keeping with the interests of the hegemonic class (Taussig 1980; Scheper-Hughes and Lock 1987; Lock and Scheper-Hughes 1990). Analysis of illness representations, from this perspective, requires a critical unmasking of the dominant interests, an exposing of the mechanisms by which they are supported by authorized discourse: making clear what is mis-represented in illness.

Following from the analysis of illness representations as hegemonic, and counter to a resultant tendency to represent those who suffer oppression as passive, a body of scholarship has elaborated Foucault's assertion that "where there is power, there is resistance" (Foucault 1978: 95–96). Most influential has been Scott's analysis of the "everyday forms of resistance" among Malay peasants (Scott 1985) and his more recent study of the "arts of resistance" evident in the "hidden transcripts" of the oppressed (Scott 1990). For medical anthropologists, the term resistance has served to bring attention to cultural forms and activities which resist the increasing medicalization of our lives and thus of the encroach-ment of hegemonic cultural forms. A key text in this work was Emily Martin's (1987) study of the metaphors associated with reproduction in obstetrics and gynecology and in middle-class and working-class women's understandings of menstruation, birthing, and menopause. Martin attempted to show how the metaphors found throughout medical writing draw on images from commodity capitalism to represent women's reproduction and their status as reproducers. She investigated the hypothesis that working-class women have been more able to resist those metaphors than have middle-class women. A growing feminist literature has followed her lead and is now analyzing medical and scientific discourses about women and their bodies (for instance Jacobus, Keller, and Shuttleworth 1990).

The concept of resistance has also been used to analyze forms of illness experi-ence more commonly studied as "possession," "hysteria," or "somatization." For example, Ong (1987, 1988) examines how violent episodes of spirit possession on the shop floors of multinational factories in Malaysia express peasant women's reactions to changes in their identity and to demeaning work conditions. Possession episodes not only serve as part of a complex negotiation of selfhood and reality, but resist the work of the factory by bringing production to a halt. Similarly, Lock (1990) has analyzed how the complaints of *nevra* of Greek women in Montreal "give voice to oppression," in particular in relation to their work in the garment industry, but at the same time "reinforce differences" and place these women in "a dangerous, liminal position" (cf. Dunk 1989; Van Schaik 1988). A "critical" analysis, in this tradition, is thus one that renders explicit the social and political meanings covertly articulated in the language and action of illness or possession.

At its best, the critical medical anthropology literature has served to advance

Allan Young's 1982 challenge to medical anthropology to develop "a position which gives primacy to the social relations which produce the forms and distribution of sickness in society." When combined with "thick description" and close analysis of meanings, such studies illuminate the many voices engaged in the struggle to respond to sickness and its threats and reveal how oppressive global and societal forces are present in small details of living and dying.[37] Not surprisingly, however, a great deal of the literature explicitly identified as "critical" is long on critique, long on program, and short on real historical and ethnographic analysis. Not surprising, I say, because the combining of macrosocietal and historical analysis with ethnographic writing is one of the most challenging problems of the discipline (Marcus and Fischer 1986: ch. 4). Not surprising also because rather dated Marxist analytic concepts – including the notion of cultural representation as "mystification" – are sometimes used in this literature with little critical awareness.[38] All too often explicit use of the term "critical" has served primarily to index and authorize the moral and political stance of the writer, rather than to further research and analysis. The juxtaposition of "critical" to "clinical" as positions in the field, and the implicit or explicit equation of "clinical" and "interpretive," is one example in which polemic has largely replaced analysis, in my opinion, and has been particularly misleading.

An important theme in the "critical" medical anthropology literature has been a set of pointed criticisms of those anthropologists who advocate introducing clinically relevant concepts from the social sciences into medical practice. Taussig sounded this theme early, warning that "there lurks the danger that the experts will avail themselves of the knowledge only to make the science of human management all the more powerful and coercive" (1980: 12), and the call to "disengage" from the "interests of conventional biomedicine" (Scheper-Hughes 1990: 192) has been sounded time and again (for example Singer 1989a, 1990; Baer 1986; Morgan 1990). Those who hope to encourage a more humane practice of medicine through their teaching and research activities within medical settings may be accused of liberal naiveté with some justification, given the current economics of medical practice in the United States and the enormous power of medicine to reproduce itself as a cultural institution. However, the criticisms leveled against those committed to making social science relevant to medicine deserve careful examination.

Criticisms of clinical applications of anthropology are often implicitly or explicitly based on an understanding of the clinical encounter as a "combat zone of disputes over power and over definitions" (Taussig 1980: 9). As Singer (1989a: 1198) writes, "we have accounts of the gathering of intelligence, the mobilizing of allies, the formulating of strategies, and the pressing of demands; in short, a narrative of struggle and combat in the very heart of physician-controlled territory." The likening of power relations in the clinical encounter to a "war" between doctor and patient seems to reflect Foucault's suggestion in "Truth and Power" (although the reference has not been made explicit), when he writes: "isn't power simply a form of warlike domination? Shouldn't one therefore conceive all problems of power in terms of relations of war?" (Foucault 1980: 123). Surely there are occasions when physicians, some even knowingly, "wage war" on the poor, acting as agents of the state and corporate interests, duping the poor with scientific labels and placebo drugs which only serve to mystify, or even worse carrying out medical experimentation disguised by lies or silence. But equally sure am I that these occasions serve badly as the analytic prototype for understanding medical practice. Were this true, why should Navarro (for example 1989) or Himmelstein and Woolhandler (1986) be so concerned about the inequities in the distribution of medical services? And why should the sick, including we anthropologists (who usually have access to the best technical health services in the world), be so desperate for good quality medical care, even to be treated in a humane and caring fashion?

What is perhaps most surprising and worthy of research is not simply that the sick sometimes respond to physicians' power with individual or collective resistance, but that they respond in this fashion so seldom. Power differences among participants in medical or healing encounters are often enormous, certainly among the greatest that we routinely experience in contemporary American society. Yet these differences have seldom produced real resistance. Instead, access to power and the ability to employ it on behalf of the sufferer is universally required if one is to be considered a healer (Glick 1967).

Pappas (1990) distinguishes nicely between "power," "domination," and "exploitation" as present in medical institutions and relationships. However, when he – and many other "critical" medical anthropologists – analyzes "the doctor-patient interaction," these essential distinctions are often quickly lost, and all inequities of power and knowledge are reduced to "exploitation."[39] Medicine is not all war or exploitation, strident claims notwithstanding. It is also a conversation, a dance,[40] a search for significance, the application of simple techniques that save lives and alleviate pain, and a complex technological imagination of immortality. It is a commodity desperately desired and fought for, perhaps even a basic "human right," even as it is a fundamental form of human relating. All medical anthropologists should join the struggle for more equitable distribution of health resources and services and for more humane medical practice, even as we pursue critical analyses of medical institutions and the abuses of medical power. Attacks on clinically relevant writing in our field have done all too little to forward these goals.

Activists within the critical tradition have outlined a program of engaged activities, many of which anthropologists from all theoretical positions will support. Furthermore, the role for anthropologists in clinical teaching – as in community or public health activities – deserves continued debate. However, setting "clinical" over against "critical" is surely mischievous, confusing the point of application or the audience of a particular essay with a theoretical paradigm. Taussig 1980) might well be considered making "clinical" recommendations when he advocated using clinical transactions to unmask rather than mystify the structural sources of disease, and Waitzkin's (1991) recent analysis of clinical discourse is an attempt to draw clinically relevant conclusions from a Marxist analysis. Anthropologists of all theoretical persuasions work in clinical, public health, and policy arenas, as well as carrying out basic research. The claim that "clinical" approaches stand in contradiction to "critical" perspectives thus detracts from efforts to confront the limitations of our research paradigms and ignores the contradictions involved in any practical engagement. It is a claim, I believe, which should be firmly rejected.

A more fundamental theoretical problem faces those who write of illness and its representation within the critical tradition, as commonly formulated. For anthropologists, interpreting the culture of another as "mystification" or "false consciousness" raises difficulties not unlike those associated with the rationalist analyses of culture as "superstition": it risks making actors to be dupes – of a hegemonic system, in this case – even as it authorizes the perspective of the observer over against the claims of those we study. When analyzed as mystification, knowledge claims of others are made subject to the analyst's epistemological judgments, with some version of a distinction between science and ideology replacing Evans-Pritchard's contrast of scientific and mystical notions. We (the scientists) know what lies beneath that which is hidden or mystified by naive ethnomedical theories, even if the peasants do not. Studies of "everyday forms of resistance" provide a richer frame for critical analysis, but the "romance of resistance," as Abu-Lughod (1990) points out, often disguises a similar delegitimation of the literal claims of women and men that they are suffering from physical pain or possessing spirits.

Richard Bernstein has criticized phenomenologists such as Alfred Schutz for their failure to comprehend the constitution of the lifeworld in social and historical terms. He argues that Schutz's commitment to analyze the common-sense world makes it impossible for him to understand "false consciousness" (whether conceived in Marxist or Freudian terms), because he is "ignoring or glossing over the complex mechanisms of resistance, defense, or self-deception by which individuals fail to find 'understandable' what may in fact be their genuine in-order-to motives" (1976: 164). However, he goes on to affirm the importance of a more radical phenomenology.

> If one of the characteristics of ideology or false consciousness is that it systematically *mis-takes* what is relative to a specific historical context for a permanent feature of the human condition, it might even be argued that a thoroughgoing phenomenological analysis is truly radical and critical. Indeed, phenomenology would enable us to see through the variety of ideological distortions that affect our understanding of social and political reality. (Bernstein 1976: 168)

Efforts to develop a critical phenomenology provide a meeting ground for critical and interpretive anthropologists, posing questions not yet adequately addressed. How might we develop theories that give actors "credit for resisting in a variety of creative ways the power of those who control so much of their lives, without either misattributing to them forms of consciousness or politics that are not part of their experience . . . or devaluing their practices as prepolitical, primitive, or even misguided?" Abu-Lughod asks (1990: 47). How can we recognize the presence of the social and historical within human consciousness, recognize forms of self-deception and distortion, without devaluing local claims to knowledge? How can we write about illness in a manner that heightens our understanding of the realities of lived experience and still speaks to the larger social and historical processes of which the actors are only dimly aware? These are questions that face both critical and interpretive anthropologists as we move into the 1990s. They are questions which follow from critical theorizing of the past decade, but which require a rethinking of an epistemology that too easily transforms the meaning of illness and local forms of medical knowledge into mystification.

Emerging issues, recurring problems

When cultures and tongues had interanimated each other, language became altogether different; its very quality altered: instead of a Ptolemaic linguistic world, unified, singular, and closed, there appeared a Galilean universe made of a multiplicity of tongues, mutually animating each other. (Bakhtin, quoted in Todorov 1984: 15)

Russian literary critic Mikhail Bakhtin's image of "a multiplicity of tongues, mutually animating each other," is an apt image for the medical anthropology of the past two decades. No longer do medical anthropologists speak with a single voice concerning "health beliefs and cultural logics." Even as multiplicity is increasingly present in the medical settings in which we work, so too are there now a plethora of voices in the field of medical anthropology. And so it should be. The theoretical positions I have outlined continue to develop in conversations "mutually animating" one another. Individual anthropologists cross theoretical perspectives, depending on the audience and issues they address, and new positions that transcend or reshape these are emerging. Lock and Scheper-Hughes (1990), for example, call for a "critical-interpretive approach." Arthur and Joan Kleinman (1991) explore the language of resistance to investigate the experience of chronic pain (cf. Littlewood 1992). Kaufman (1988) draws on phenomenology to interpret the experience of disability in a collection on Gramsci. And Mary-Jo Good investigates the "political economy of hope" in analyzing differences in oncological practice and investments in technology in North America and other societies (M. Good 1990; M. Good et al. 1992).

The image of "heteroglossia" over against a discourse which is "unified, singular, and closed" not only describes the current state of the field, but is an image of how we necessarily proceed. Disease and human suffering cannot be comprehended from a single perspective. Science and its objects, the demands of therapeutic practice, and personal and social threats of illness cannot be comprehended from a unified or singular perspective. A multiplicity of tongues are needed to engage the objects of our discipline and to fashion an anthropological – scientific, political, moral, aesthetic, or philosophical – response.

The accounts of the relation of language to illness vary sharply among the four orienting perspectives I have reviewed here. In the empiricist approach, language is portrayed as depicting illness and as shaping the rational calculus of action. For cognitive anthropologists, language is viewed as the stuff of individual cognition, more or less widely shared, and as organizing individual perception. The interpretive tradition focuses on language as civilizational and intersubjective, as active and constituting, as opening to significance, while critical writers describe medical language as hiding, mystifying, and manipulating. Each of these perspectives represents a significant aspect of reality, and none has a corner on valid forms of cultural critique.

It is not my goal, however, to minimize what is at stake in debates among adherents of these perspectives, nor to suggest that these differences represent a dialectic to be resolved through some grand synthesis. The biomedical sciences and empiricist medical social sciences pose hard questions for advocates of any form of historicism or cultural relativism, and our inherited language is saturated with oppositions – between culture and biology, mind and matter, belief and knowledge – that subtly reproduce a history of opinion on these questions. Cognitivists pose difficult questions about the reliability of our data and thus of the conclusions of nearly all cultural accounts, in whatever tradition. And critical theories have rightly challenged hidden assumptions of much cultural analysis, enriching our analytic vocabulary immeasurably during the past decade. At the same time, each of these positions takes epistemological stances I have argued have troubling implications for medical anthropologists. Even current critical theorists maintain implicit distinctions between science and ideology that reproduce many of the difficulties of an older rationalist tradition.

I have argued that for medical anthropologists, these epistemological issues are not a matter of "mere" theoretical or philosophical interest, but a central concern for how we relate in writing and in action to those whose cultures and societies we study. How we conceive the authority of biomedical science is crucial to how we interact as anthropologists with those with whom we work. Thus, to fashion an epistemologically coherent position, one which makes sense of the claims of human biology and medicine and still acknowledges the validity of local knowledge in matters of sickness and suffering, is crucial for medical anthropology. Basic theoretical work is a central challenge to the discipline.

In this book, I attempt to articulate a position from within the interpretive tradition, conversant with critical theory, and to address a number of core issues that our discipline currently faces. The development of critical studies of how illness comes to meaning, of how reality (not simply beliefs about it) is organized and experienced in matters of sickness and care, is thus on the agenda. So too is the development of a "critical phenomenology": an approach which can provide a critical analysis of illness experience without the self-authorizing language of mystification or false consciousness remains to be written. Along with all of anthropology, we face the difficulty of joining political economy and interpretive perspectives, of integrating historical and global perspectives with rich cultural analysis in our ethnographic writing. And the development of a rigorous and

systematic program of comparative studies of sickness, one which provides a
critical anthropological analysis of biomedical categories but addresses the
genuine concern of Browner and her colleagues (1988) about the units for
comparison, is especially significant.

I have suggested that much of the inherited language of belief and behavior, so
readily assumed by the medical behavioral sciences, serves poorly for addressing
these issues. I have also reviewed the limitations of current paradigms developed
as critical responses to that language. The following chapters represent an attempt
to probe the tensions among these positions, to clarify the deep paradoxes that
frame all of our work, and to develop one path we might follow for the
comparative study of illness and forms of medical knowledge. It is by no means
comprehensive or exclusive. However, it suggests issues which must be addressed
if the field is to move forward.

3

How medicine constructs its objects

In a discussion among several second year Harvard medical students in which I was participating, one young woman described how she felt her medical education was changing her.

> Medical school is really weird. It is a forced emotional experience. We handle cadavers, have feces lab where we examine our own feces, go to [a mental hospital where we get locked up] with screaming patients. These are total experiences, like an occult thing or boot camp.
>
> . . . it's *not* just an extension of college. College was also a total experience, but you could get by with less direct engagement, and still learn things. Here you have to *interact* with the information. When you dissect a brain you have to interact with these things and with your own feelings. Look at what you're playing with.
>
> I feel like I'm changing my brain every day, molding it in a specific way – a very specific way.

How medical students learn medicine, how they "change their brains every day," how they "interact with their information," offers insight into the highly specialized world of American clinical medicine. Analysis of this process will serve as entree to a set of claims about the relation of culture, illness, and medical knowledge which I want to develop in the remaining chapters of this book. I begin with a discussion of how medicine constructs the "objects" to which clinicians attend, arguing that *medicine formulates the human body and disease in a culturally distinctive fashion,* using students' descriptions of how they learn and how they change as a basis for insight into this process. The discussion of biomedicine in this chapter will provide a basis for exploring how medical anthropologists can compare disease and its formulation across cultures – in professional and folk practice, in popular interpretive schemes, and in the experience of those who fall ill.

The quotation is drawn from notes I took while participating in a conversation among a group of Harvard medical students. These and other data for this chapter come from interview transcripts and field notes, and are part of a study of Harvard Medical School which I have been conducting in collaboration with Mary-Jo Good and with the help of two of our students, Eric Jacobson and Karen

Stephenson. For more than four years, we interviewed a cohort of approximately fifty students, selected primarily from the graduating class of 1990, talking with them about their personal and educational experiences. In addition, we interviewed faculty and administrators about the curricular reform – Harvard's New Pathway to General Medical Education – and about their experiences teaching in both the traditional or "classic" curriculum and the New Pathway.[1] I also attended several of the basic science classes as an anthropological participant and observer. The research is designed to allow comparisons of the experiences and socialization of students in the three curricula – the New Pathway, the "Classic" curriculum, and the Health Science Technology program – which were run simultaneously for students in the classes which entered in 1985 and 1986. The focus of discussion in this chapter, however, will not be on differences across these curricular groups. Instead I will examine practices and experiences common to students in all three curricula, many of which are viewed as so ordinary as to merit little attention.

In the first of the Morgan Lectures and the introductory chapter of this book, I argued that a prominent paradigm in the medical behavioral sciences is organized around the comparative study of beliefs about disease and suggested what I am convinced are fundamental problems with this perspective. I introduced the suggestion in conclusion to that lecture that we take as our analytic focus the "formative processes" through which illness is shaped as personal and social reality, examining how these vary across cultures and in different sites within a given culture. Competing analyses of the social, political, and cultural nature of such formative processes, their relation to human biology, and their reflection in "illness representations" has led to much of the energy in medical anthropology in the past decade.

In this chapter, I examine the construction of illness as an object of diagnostic and therapeutic activity within American clinical medicine. I begin the constructive chapters of this book with this issue in part to counter the assumption, underlying the empiricist paradigm, that the primary unit for analysis should be diseases or physiological processes that are "*external categories* of more or less universal reference," in Loudon's terms (1976: 38). I want to argue, paradoxically perhaps, that *biology is not external to but very much within culture*, and to discuss how clinical medicine constructs persons, patients, bodies, diseases, and human physiology. I use the phrase "how medicine constructs its objects" not primarily to criticize medicine or physicians for the "objectification" or "commoditization" of health or personal suffering (cf. Nichter and Nordstrom 1989), at least not at this moment, but to focus on those distinctive "formative processes" through which medicine formulates or constitutes that dimension of the world to which medical knowledge refers.

Lest I be taken for making absurd relativist claims – inviting a medical version of Dr. Samuel Johnson's refutation of idealism, when he kicked a stone and proclaimed, "I refute it thusly!" – let me be clear. When, after 1949, the Chinese came to interpret schistosomiasis as a problem of society rather than of individuals, they shifted the object of medical attention and launched a mass campaign to harness the people's knowledge and energy to wiping out the snails in the Chinese waterways, rather than attending exclusively to individuals with liver flukes (see Horn 1972 for a popular account of this campaign). When family therapists argue that poorly controlled juvenile diabetes or anorexia nervosa is a symptom of family pathology, they are attempting to redefine the object of medical knowledge (Minuchin, Rosman, and Baker 1978). The Zande autopsy and an American medical autopsy attend to different dimensions of the body, and based on their findings organize social reality in quite dissimilar ways. And when the Dean of Harvard Medical School suggests, as he has in recent years, that medical education may soon have to undergo radical changes as disease comes increasingly to be seen in molecular terms, redefining disease categories and physiological processes, he is pointing to a change in the landscape of medicine almost as radical as the change Foucault documented for French medicine between the eighteenth and nineteenth centuries. My interest is thus in exploring how the objects of medical attention are constituted in contemporary American clinical practice. This formulation is of course not unique; Foucault (1972) examined the changes in medicine's objects historically, and others have addressed the issue from the perspectives of culture, gender, and political economy. Here, however, I want to approach the issue in phenomenological terms, analyzing how the medical world gets built up as a distinctive form of reality for those who are learning to be physicians.

I first introduce philosopher Ernst Cassirer's theory of symbolic forms as an entry point for analyzing the formative practices specific to contemporary clinical medicine. I then examine data from the medical school study to discuss how medicine formulates sickness in strikingly materialist terms. In conclusion, I will suggest that despite this materialist shaping of illness by clinical medicine, moral and "soteriological" issues (that is, those referring to suffering and salvation) are fused with the medical and at times erupt as the central issues of medical practice.

Medicine as symbolic form

I have referred several times to the formative processes through which illness realities are formulated. I take this term – "formative" – from the work of Ernst Cassirer, the idealist philosopher of culture, whose three volumes on *The Philosophy of Symbolic Forms* appeared in German in the 1920s. Cassirer situated his work in the context of Kant's response to Hume, that is, in relation to the debate about whether knowledge derives from the empirical world impressing itself on the human mind via the senses, or whether such basic dimensions of human knowledge as space, time, and causality derive a priori from characteristics of the human mind. Cassirer followed Kant in discrediting what he called the "naive *copy theory* of knowledge," a view of the sign as "nothing but a repetition of a determinate and finished . . . content" (1955a: 107). However, rather than following Kant in attempting to discover the qualities of the mind that make order of random sense perceptions, Cassirer instead argued that culture or symbolic forms mediate and organize distinctive forms of reality.

> If all culture is manifested in the creation of specific image-worlds, of specific symbolic forms, the aim of philosophy is not to go behind all these creations, but rather to understand and elucidate their *basic formative principle*. It is solely through awareness of this principle that the content of life acquires its true form. (1955a: 113; my emphasis)

These basic "formative principles" are at work in language and myth, in religion, art, history, and science. All of these constitute distinctive "image-worlds," he says, "which do not merely reflect the empirically given, but which rather produce it in accordance with an independent principle. Each of these functions creates its own symbolic forms . . . each of them designates a particular approach, in which and through which it constitutes its own aspect of 'reality'" (1955a: 78). For Cassirer, culture was conceived as thoroughly historicized, as embodied in these distinctive symbolic forms and modes of human activity. Cultural forms such as science and art were not conceived as "simple *structures* which we can insert into a given world," that is not as glasses that provide a coloring to the world as we view it, but as "*functions* by means of which a particular form is given to reality" (1955a: 91).

> the content of the concept of culture . . . can be apprehended only in "action." Only in so far as aesthetic imagination and perception exist as a specific pursuit, is there a sphere of aesthetic objects – and the same applies to all those other energies of the spirit by which a definite universe of objects takes on form. (1955a: 80)

Thus the objects of science, of religion and mythology, and of aesthetics presuppose forms of imagination, perception, and activity, and together these constitute what Cassirer called "symbolic forms." The "objects" of medicine are similar in kind.

I have introduced Cassirer's ideas here to begin to suggest that we think of medicine as a symbolic form through which reality is formulated and organized in a distinctive manner. We need not adhere to Cassirer's idealist philosophy to draw upon his insights. Indeed, what he analyzed in the 1920s as "formative principles" or "fundamental forms and directions of human activity" might be seen as the central focus of a variety of theories in the contemporary social sciences. Compare, for example, Foucault's notion of medical discourses as consisting "not of signs (signifying elements referring to contents or representations) but as practices that systematically form the objects of which they speak" (1972: 49). Theories of social and discursive practices – in anthropology, the sociology of science, and philosophy – have taken us far beyond where the social sciences were when Cassirer wrote, making evident the absence of political, economic, and institutional structures in his theory.[2] Yet Cassirer's analysis of science, religion, and art as symbolic forms, as both modes of experience and kinds of knowledge, as forms of activity that articulate and reveal the world of experience, and his conception of the phenomenology of human culture as situated in the midst of

The Role of Culture

Foucault argument

activity and as "apprehending and elucidating [the formative] principles" (1955a: 114) is extremely suggestive for our studies of medicine.

It supports the notion, first of all, that we should focus on the generative processes, the formative practices through which illness and other dimensions of medical reality are formulated. Rather than belief and behavior, the focus is thus on interpretive activities through which fundamental dimensions of reality are confronted, experienced, and elaborated. Healing activities shape the objects of therapy – whether some aspect of the medicalized body, hungry spirits, or bad fate – and seek to transform those objects through therapeutic activities. Comparative research can thus investigate these formative practices across cultures, the nature of realities they recognize and formulate, the way, that is, they apprehend and act on reality, and their efficacy in transforming it.

This is not the place to discuss the matter in detail, but an approach that begins with attention to interpretive practices and their formative or generative role in the construction of medical reality suggests comparisons with Foucault's investigations of sexuality, madness, and disease in terms of discursive practices. In fact, it is interesting to read Foucault in light of Cassirer's Neo-Kantian program. Foucault's early writings – his so-called "archaeological" studies of medical discourse (Foucault 1970, 1972, 1973) – can be read as making the remarkable idealist claim that social institutions are the product of the episteme, the underlying epistemological structure, of a medical discourse. Furthermore, Foucault's focus on the shaping of perception – the "gaze" – by a medical discourse and the construction of medical objects through discursive practices has parallels to Cassirer's program. Foucault explicitly denies, however, the role of the subject or the constituting role of consciousness. In this, he seems to be rejecting Kant's claims about the role of consciousness in shaping knowledge, arguing for the mediating role of discourse in a manner that both shares similarities and reflects sharp differences with Cassirer's argument about the mediating role of symbolic formations. Perhaps because he was a historian, Foucault could picture discursive practices in the absence of active practitioners, the gaze in the absence of the perceiving subject, or as Dreyfus and Rabinow (1982: 187) write, "intentionality without a subject, a strategy without a strategist." This analytic move paralleled the disappearance of the author and a narrow attention to the text in French literary criticism. For Foucault, it served to advance a program of analysis of technologies of power rather than intentionality of subjects. However, Foucault's corpus excludes the centrality of experience and in large measure the dialogical qualities of discourse. For the anthropologist, this inattention to the lived experience of the subject is ultimately untenable, I believe. It contradicts the centrality of persons and of intersubjective experience in the field research of the anthropologist. And for all its attention to "the body" as the object of social practices, Foucault's work largely excludes attention to the body as source of experience and understanding. As my analysis proceeds, I will be arguing that if we are to understand how medicine constructs its objects, we will need to join together critical studies of practices and the analysis of embodied experience.[3]

Second, the view outlined here suggests that we ask what the central generative principles are for *medicine as a symbolic formation*. I will spell this out as the chapter proceeds, but I suggest that we ask what are the core organizing activities of medicine as a symbolic formation, as Cassirer asks for science, religion, and art.[4] And I suggest we consider in this light the role of medicine in mediating physiology and soteriology. Illness combines physical and existential dimensions, bodily infirmity and human suffering. However materialist and grounded in the natural sciences, medicine as a form of activity joins the material to the moral domain. Weber (1946: 267–301) held that civilizations are organized around a soteriological vision – an understanding of the nature of suffering, and means of transforming or transcending suffering and achieving salvation. In contemporary Western civilization, medicine is at the core of our soteriological vision.

These theoretical reflections provide the frame for the title of this chapter, "how medicine constructs its objects," and for an examination of how the medical world and its objects are built up for those learning medicine.

Entering the body, constructing disease

For over sixteen years, now, I have been teaching social medicine and anthropology in medical schools, attempting to conceptualize the nature of illness and medical care in social and cultural terms, trying to make ideas as diverse as hermeneutics and phenomenology relevant to medical students and clinicians. Over and over again I have been struck by the enormous power of the idea within medicine that disease is fundamentally, even exclusively, biological. Not that experiential or behavioral matters are ignored, certainly not by good clinicians, but these are matters separate from the real object of medical practice. The fundamental reality is human biology, real medicine, and the relevant knowledge is staggering in scope and complexity. It requires an extraordinary effort to make one's way into this system of knowledge, and for the medical student, the consequences of learning this special route are profound. From the first day of classes, medical students look ahead to the day they will have responsibility for a patient, will have to coax a diagnosis from an obscure presentation, oversee treatment, and bear responsibility for the consequences. The amount of information presented is massive, and all of it seems important. As the nervous joke goes among first and second year students, if a patient comes to you with a problem, you can't say, "oh, I'm sorry, I didn't go to class that day!"[5]

Early in the course of our study of Harvard Medical School, we came increasingly to understand that learning medicine is not simply the incorporation of new cognitive knowledge, or even learning new approaches to problem-solving and new skills. It is a process of coming to inhabit a new world. I mean this not only in the obvious sense of coming to feel at home in the laboratories or the clinics and hospitals, but in a deeper, experience-near sense. At times when I left a tutorial in immunology or pathology to go to an anthropology seminar, I would feel that I

The argued (handwritten margin note)

had switched culture as dramatically as if I had suddenly been whisked from the small town in Iran where we carried out our research back into Harvard's William James Hall. Not only was the language as different as Turkish and English, but the dimensions of the world that were beginning to appear – intricate details of the human body, of pathology and medical treatment – were more profoundly different from my everyday world than nearly any of those I have experienced in other field research. Thus we began to realize what an opportunity we had to investigate how the world of medicine gets built up as a distinctive world of experience, a world filled with objects that simply are not a part of our everyday world. Learning medicine is developing knowledge of this distinctive lifeworld and requires an entry into a distinctive reality system.

In Dan Sperber's chapter on irrational beliefs, which I discussed in my analysis of the anthropology of belief, he ridicules relativist approaches to the study of cognitive development. Such an approach, he argues, would "[imply] that the first stage of cognitive development consists not in acquiring knowledge in an essentially predetermined cognizable world, but, rather, in establishing in which world knowledge is to be acquired" (1985: 41). It is my contention that learning medicine is grounded precisely in "establishing in which world knowledge is to be acquired," and that studying how people learn offers insights into some of the formative practices through which medicine constructs that world. For medical students, the body and pathology are constituted as distinctively "medical" during their education. Entry into the world of medicine is accomplished not only by learning the language and knowledge base of medicine, but by learning quite fundamental practices through which medical practitioners engage and formulate reality in a specifically "medical" way. These include specialized ways of "seeing," "writing," and "speaking."

Seeing

Medical education begins in the new Harvard curriculum with an eight week course called "The Human Body," integrating anatomy, histology, and radiology, designed to provide an introduction to the "basic principles governing the organization of the human body from the molecular to the organismic level" (Harvard Medical School Tutor Guide 1987). Students attend lectures on anatomy and histology, and participate in case-based tutorials, histology lab, and gross anatomy labs, coordinated with radiology presentations. All are designed to provide entry into the body and the basic sciences. The teachers in the preclinical years (often called the "precynical years") are renowned laboratory scientists, and it is made abundantly clear that learning medicine during these first two years is above all learning the biomedical sciences. (Lest this seem obvious, a French physician friend described how his education began with the study of "semiology," that is signs and symptoms, how they present, their classification, and the diseases they indicate. Only toward the end of his training did they begin to look at the basic sciences.)

Medical education begins by entry into the human body. Viewed through the microscope, entered physically in the gross anatomy lab, seen with astounding clarity via contemporary radiologic imaging, or presented by master scientists, the body is revealed in infinite, hierarchical detail. Students begin a process of gaining intimacy with the body – attempting to understand its gross organization and structure three-dimensionally, examining tissue from gross function to molecular structure; students are as geographers moving from gross topography to the detail of microecology. The body is the object of attending and skilled manipulating, and, as one student said, "it is a world of its own that has for me virtually limitless possibilities for learning." Within the lifeworld of medicine, the body is newly constituted as a medical body, quite distinct from the bodies with which we interact in everyday life, and the intimacy with that body reflects a distinctive perspective, an organized set of perceptions and emotional responses that emerge with the emergence of the body as a site of medical knowledge.[6]

The anatomy lab is one critical site of this emergence.[7] It is a ritual space in which the human body is opened to exploration and learning, and in which the subjects of that learning engage in reshaping their experiential world. One student described the experience as being like an Outward Bound exercise or like combat.

> You take people, you take them completely out of context from their normal life, subject them to a whole new set of rules and have them do a lot of things you never thought you could do. And then when you take that back into your life in general and realize you're capable of that is when you realize you've grown so much.

Several steps are important in the phenomenological reconstruction of the body and its experience in this setting. The anatomy laboratory is demarcated as a separate order, having distinctive moral norms. Within this redefined context, the human body is given new meaning, and a new manner of interacting with that body is appropriate. Intrusions from ordinary reality into this space are experienced as "violation."

> I can remember a person who I think was an applicant, who was spending a day with one of the students kind of getting a feel for the experience. And she came in and just hung out in the anatomy lab. And I felt very violated in some funny way. I felt like she was an intruder . . . that without being properly introduced and given a context, I didn't want to be seen doing these coarse things in such a cavalier way by that person . . .

Students describe a variety of changes in their perception that occur within this demarcated space. In normal reality, the body surfaces – the skin, the hands, the eyes, the face, the clothing – convey personhood. The interior of a person is his or her thoughts, experiences, personality. In the laboratory, the hands, the feet, the head remain bound, and the torso and limbs are the object of sustained attention. As the skin is drawn back, a different "interior" emerges.

> Emotionally a leg has such a different meaning after you get the skin off. It doesn't mean at all what it meant before. And now the skin, which is our way of relating to other people – I mean, touching skin is . . . getting close to people – how that is such a tiny part of what's going on, it's like the peel of an orange, it's just one tiny little aspect. And as soon as you get that off, you're in this whole other world.

This "whole other world" becomes the paramount reality in the anatomy lab. It is a world with which the physician-to-be develops a tremendous intimacy. It is a biological world, a physical world, a complex three-dimensional space.

In anatomy, the body is revealed as having natural compartments. Sundering the natural structures is another kind of violation. One of the most shocking moments in anatomy lab was the day we entered to find the body prepared for dissecting the genitalia, the body sawn in half above the waist, then bisected between the legs. Students described their shock not at close examination of the genitalia, nor simply at the body being taken apart, but rather at the dismemberment, and at dismemberment that crossed natural boundaries. Dissection follows planes of tissue. Here the plane that cut the body was straight and hard, cutting across natural layers of tissue in an unnatural fashion. The majority of the time is spent trying to separate natural surfaces, to distinguish the boundaries of gross forms and identify tiny nerves, veins, lymph glands, and to match these to the anatomical atlas. These are gradually broken down and examined not only in relation to each other but in finer and finer detail, revealing the natural body.

Students are quite aware that they are learning an alternative way of seeing, that it is a way of seeing that they can usually "turn on and turn off," but that they are learning to "think anatomically" in a way that is central to the medical gaze. During anatomy, this way of seeing is not neatly contained in the laboratory or limited to the appropriate contexts for the medical perspective. While participating in anatomy as an observer, I would occasionally be walking along a street and find myself a body amidst bodies, rather than a person amidst persons. I found myself attending to anatomical features of persons I passed, rather than perceiving them as persons with social characteristics or imagined lives. Students describe vivid experiences of this sort. For example, a student doing a special rotation in pathology, which included routine autopsies, told me of perceptual shifts similar to those of students first doing anatomy dissections.

> I'll find myself in conversation . . . I'll all of a sudden start to think about, you know, if I took the scalpel and made a cut [on you] right here, what would that look like [he said laughing]. . . . very often that happens. And that's a frightening thing. You say: why are you thinking that way? You know, you're sitting here having a discussion with a person who's alive, and yet you're thinking about the procedures that you use when you're doing an autopsy.

My point here is not that anatomy is a "dehumanizing" experience, but simply that it is one significant contribution to the reconstruction of the person appropriate to the medical gaze, identified as a body, a case, a patient, or a cadaver. The person is a cultural construct, a complex and culturally shaped way of experiencing self and other, and cultural "work" is required to reconstitute the person who is the object of medical attention. This reconstruction of the person is essential to a student becoming a competent physician.

A central metaphor for medical education is that it is like "learning a foreign language." During orientation a biochemist remarked, "learning medicine is like

learning a language, and biochemistry has become the lingua franca of medicine."
The metaphor is commonly referred to by students and faculty alike. On the
surface, the meaning is clear. There is a huge vocabulary to be learned, a working
vocabulary as large as most foreign languages, and competence in medicine
depends on learning to speak and read the language (or perhaps a family of
languages). Much time in the early years of medical education is devoted to
developing fluency in this language, and the student skits which second year
students write and perform to satirize their experience are devoted to extensive
celebration and ridiculing of the technical language of medicine.

There is, however, a subtext. Learning the language of medicine consists not of
learning new words for the common-sense world, but the construction of a new
world altogether. As one student said,

> Some of it is just learning names, but learning names is, now you get into linguistics or
> semiotics or something, because learning new names for things is to learn new things
> about them. If you know the names of every tree you look at trees differently. Otherwise
> they're trees. As soon as you know all the names for them they just become something
> different. That's kind of what we're doing . . .

This student's visual metaphor, of "looking" at things differently, is an apt
image for the first two years of medical school. I was constantly impressed by how
visual the teaching of human biology was. Anatomy required a training of the
eyes, to see structure where none was obvious. Only with experience did gross
muscle masses become apparent and recognizable. Veins and arteries, nerves,
lymphatic vessels, and connective tissue were largely indistinguishable from one
another until weeks into gross anatomy. With practice, however, the intricate
structure of the human body became manifest. Histology and pathology required
similar training of the vision. Whether examining the color pictures of a histology
atlas or viewing slides through a microscope, shapes, colors, and lines all appeared
as confusion to the untrained eye. With experience, epithelial cells became
distinguishable from connective tissue, cells characteristic of the liver or kidneys
recognizable. Distinguishing among a welter of types of blood cells, identifying
types of pathological process, or recognizing organelles that constitute the inner
structures of cells took more time. Learning to make sense of the confusion that
appears through the microscope was largely a matter of learning to see.

This visual quality seems true not only of teaching the medical sciences, but of
the conduct of biological science itself. If mathematical relationships govern
astronomy or physics, three-dimensional images remain central in biology. The
discovery of the double helix shape of DNA – its tangible spiraling form – was
central to modern genetics, and investigating the actual shapes of polypeptide
chains is central to understanding how proteins interact, how biochemical
reactions occur.[8] Modern imaging techniques give a powerful sense of authority
to biological reality. Look in the microscope, you can see it. Electron microscopy
reveals histological concepts as literal. Look for yourself – there it is!

Learning to see is linked to learning biology's natural hierarchical order.

Students dissect a knee joint, examine an atlas of its structure, then view hyaline cartilage under the microscope and micrographs of the internal structures of these cells. The next day they see a patient with osteoarthritis, a disease of the cartilage. The message is powerful. There are worlds within worlds, each subsumed by the other. Tissue with distinctive functioning is revealed to consist of specialized cells, these to have highly specialized organelles, inner structures that are now understood as bounded environments for specialized biochemical processes, these revealed at the molecular level. And disease processes can be traced from surface appearance to deeper, more basic levels. As one student said as we discussed this matter:

> There were times when it was really striking. For instance, when we tried to explain psychology, behavior, based on neurology and then we thought about how neurology, the structure of the brain, well if it was influenced by genetics, then if you think about what a gene is, a gene really comes from a protein. So that if some disorder, like schizophrenia, is genetic, then there must be a protein. And that's something really concrete. I never thought that if something was genetic that there would be something that concrete and real that you could track down. That if a drug had an effect, drugs just don't have an effect magically, [but] because it's a molecule and interacts with other molecules in a person to have an effect. It binds to a receptor or it interferes with a membrane . . . That's really exciting when you see those insights.

This natural hierarchy is replicated as the implicit order of teaching. I began noticing slides in the basic science lectures – and of course no medical school lecture can be given without slides – often follow a predictable pattern. A slide showing the epidemiology of a disease will be followed by a clinical slide of a patient, and that by a pathological specimen. Then a slide of low magnification cell structure is followed by an electron micrograph, and from this level to diagrams of molecular structure and genetic expression. A slide at one level is often followed by one just above or just below in this hierarchy, and each level reveals the more basic structure of the next higher order.

I am reminded of the historian Arthur Lovejoy's marvelous analysis of "the great chain of being" as an idea in Western civilization (Lovejoy 1936). For nearly 2,000 years, he argued, the Platonic view juxtaposing the world of being over against the world of becoming held sway. The world of being was represented as an ontological hierarchy, from the material world of substance outward to the divine order. In large measure, this order was historicized during the Romantic age, then gave way, Lovejoy argued. One has a sense in the contemporary medical sciences of the enduring power of the idea of hierarchical orders, each encompassing the other, a timeless rational structure that gives order and sense to everyday existence. Unlike in the Platonic, medieval and renaissance view, however, ultimacy resides in depth, downward to levels that generate surface phenomena. And such deeper structures are not social or divine but ever more fundamental orders of material reality.

Thus the first two years of medical education provide a powerful interpretation of reality, anchored in the experience of the student. Surface phenomena of signs, symptoms, and experience are shown to be understandable with reference to underlying mechanisms at an ontologically prior level. Even broadly incorporative biopsychosocial models, articulated in the language of systems theory, represent biology at the center, social relations outward at the periphery (see, for example, Engel 1977). Those diseases for which a clear understanding of the mechanisms has been achieved provide the prototypes of medical knowledge, suggesting that all disease is of this kind, if only we understood. Myasthenia gravis, a quite rare neurological disorder, has a central place in neurobiology courses, because it is accounted for by a disorder of antibodies to the acetylcholine receptor. Diseases with known, specific mechanisms are taught as prototypes. The message is clear. The architecture of knowledge is in place; we only need to fill in the missing structural links.

This means of interpreting reality is both powerful, illuminating many disease phenomena and providing the basis for therapeutics, and at the same time profoundly ideological and often misleading. We think almost by reflex of behavior residing in our genes, the origins of disease in the individual medicalized body. Were we equally convinced that social organization and social relations were deep or central, the ontological source of the great chain of being, it would seem incomprehensible to continue to search for genetic differences for school accomplishments in children or to continue to ignore the social origins of infant mortality or violent deaths among our youth, and the study of neuroplasticity, that is the role of social experience in forming our neurological system, for example, might be more central than it is.[9] However, my goal at the moment is not to critique the medical perspective but to indicate its tremendous power and to suggest some of the formative activities by which it is authorized and elaborated.

Writing and speaking

If learning to see in a new way is fundamental to the construction of the objects of medicine during the first two years of medical education, learning to write and speak are critical during the early years of clinical training. These are the years when paper cases are left behind, when after years of both wanting to see real patients and wondering if they would ever know enough to take responsibility for someone who is ill, the students finally enter the world of the hospital and join teams of interns, residents, and attending physicians who care for the sick. It is during this time that they learn to construct sick persons as patients, perceived, analyzed, and presented as appropriate for medical treatment. Learning to write up a patient correctly is crucial to this process in some quite subtle ways.

I asked a third year student what experiences made him feel like he was gaining competency during his pediatrics rotation. "Write-ups," he said, laughing. "I got better at doing write-ups. They got less painful to do. Progress notes . . . learning to write in the new way." "A very important part of medicine?" I asked. "Very important part. Learning to talk in the right way, another part. Like learning to communicate." I asked him to tell me about learning to write.

> One thing about medicine I actually admire is [that] there really is an ideal of clarity . . . and [logical presentation]. The ideal write-up has sort of all the facts that argue in favor, and all the facts that argue against, and conclusions drawn from those . . . drawn together in sort of a summarizing formulation about what you think is going on and then a plan of attack. I mean, something very satisfying about that. Of course the real world doesn't lend itself to that, so you distort the real world a little bit to make it fit that nice pattern.

He compared learning to do this to learning to read a book and write a character study of one of the figures in the book, during grammar school. After doing many of them, you come to read a book with this new job in mind, he said. It is similar in medicine.

> . . . You begin to approach the patient now with a write-up in mind, [he said], and so you have all these categories that you need to get filled. Because if you don't do that, you go in, you interact, . . . you talk, . . . you go back and you realize that you left out this, this, this and you need to go back. And when you go in with the write-up mentally emblazoned in your mind, you're thinking in terms of those categories.

He went on to describe the standard categories of a medical interview – chief complaint, history of present illness, review of symptoms, past medical history, family and social history, and physical exam. But these interview categories are those of the written document. The write-up is not a mere record of a verbal exchange. It is itself a formative practice, a practice that shapes talk as much as it reflects it, a means of constructing a person as a patient, a document, and a project.

Writing authorizes the medical student as it constructs the patient.

> . . . you do a write-up, you sign it, you date it. It's an official hospital document. It goes in their chart. *Everyone* reads it. . . . So there's that feeling of like, "oh my god, people are going to read this." There's also a feeling of "I finally belong here. I mean, I feel totally inadequate and incompetent, but I am now a third year medical student, and I'm supposed to be here."
>
> . . . To a large extent, you're authorized through your writing. That's sort of what justifies everything else, is you are actually now communicating important information, and that entitles you to poke and prod, . . . spiritually, verbally, and physically. And there's a sense now [that] you've been empowered somehow to perform this role . . . you interview with more authority when you're going to be writing up the interview. There's a sense where you're not just a voyeur. You're producing a document, so this is not just for your kicks. This is for real. . . . Now you have a project. Now you have to sort of turn on the burners because you have to do something with this person. They become yours in the sense that you're going to present them at rounds, and you're going to be evaluated on how well you work them up and you're going to . . . you see what I mean? Suddenly now they're a commodity in a certain sense that you have to process and present.[10]

Thus, writing is multifaceted. It authorizes the medical student, justifies the interaction with the patient. It organizes the conversation with the patient, the whole process of working up the patient. It is written for an audience: other physicians who will not only make decisions based on the document, but judge the student based on its writing. And it is a critical dimension of formulating the patient as a project for treatment

> . . . basically what you're supposed to do is take a walking, talking, confusing, disorganized (as we all are) human being, with an array of symptoms that are experienced, not diagnosed and take it all in, put it in the Cuisinart and puree it into this sort of form that everyone can quickly extrapolate from. They don't want to hear the story of the person. They want to hear the edited version . . .

I asked him about the editing out of patients' stories.

> You're not there to just talk with people and learn about their lives and nurture them. You're not there for that. You're a professional and you're trained in interpreting phenomenological descriptions of behavior into physiologic and pathophysiologic processes. So there's the sense of if you try to tell the people really the story of someone, they'd be angry; they'd be annoyed at you because you're missing the point. That's indulgence, sort of. You can have that if you want that when you're in the room with the patient. But don't present that to me. What you need to present to me is the stuff we're going to work on.

Another student described how when she was first learning medical interviewing, "I felt that it was a great privilege for me to hear some intimate details of their lives," and she would spend time listening to what patients wanted to talk about. By the fourth year, however, she said "you start to develop this sense of 'well, I have a job to do here and I'm doing something for you, so I'm going to just do it as efficiently as I can'."

I have quoted from these interviews at some length because they describe one of the central formative practices of medicine, writing, which opens onto a family of other such activities. Writing both reflects and shapes conversations with patients. It provides the categories and structures of those conversations, and it represents a structure of relevance that justifies the systematic discounting of the patient's narrative. It organizes the patient as a document, a project to be worked on. It is written for a specific audience. And it serves as the basis for another set of practices, which I will briefly discuss under the heading "speaking."[11]

There is an enormous social science literature on doctor–patient communications. In our interviews, however, medical students indicate relatively little concern about this domain of talk. In part this is because it constitutes a surprisingly small amount of time. Several students estimated for me that on a medicine service, with very sick patients, outside of the new patients whom they admit, they often spend at little as twenty minutes a day in one-to-one conversation with patients. ("So what," I asked one student, "is a day all about then?" "It's about numbers and lab values and rounds and teaching," she responded.) But the medical students' lack of concern about their conversations with patients is also a result of their perception that the central speech acts in medical practice are not interviewing patients but presenting patients. About presentations of patients we have many, many stories from students.

One student described his early clinical experience: I think the main thing . . . you learn [is] kind of the daily rhythm, which is rounds in the morning, work rounds, what are work rounds, what are attending rounds, what are visit rounds. . . . [He went on] . . . a big part of rounds is presenting cases, and in some ways that's probably the biggest thing medical students learn . . . Doing case presentations is probably the main thing you concentrate on . . . [for] the medical student, their one chance to be in the lime light is when they present, and it's also probably the area where you're most likely to either gain the respect or . . . the annoyance of your colleagues, and especially your superiors . . .

Case presentations are a genre of stories, through which persons are formulated as patients and as medical problems.[12] The presentations are stereotyped in format, but vary in length depending on the context. One student reported: "Morning rounds, you give short stories, bullets. Attending rounds you give longer stories. Presenting admissions you give even longer stories. . . . And in teaching experiences there are illustrative stories. That's a whole other kind of story."

Virtually every student remembers the pain of telling a story poorly and enraging a resident or attending. "It was probably my first patient," one student told of an early experience on surgery, "and I started to go into this whole thing about why the person's here, what we found on the physical exam, and of course none of this was what [the chief resident] wanted to hear. It was like he wanted a two second blurb on this person on how they were doing. . . . He just jumped down my throat. He said, 'All right, what are you doing? Why are you wasting my time? Just get to the important stuff.' When I didn't know what the important stuff was, he got even more mad . . . "

Learning what "the important stuff" is and how to present it in a persuasive way is central to becoming a physician. It requires that one know enough about the patient's condition, the disease processes, the diagnostic possibilities, and the appropriate treatments to sort through a huge chart filled with information and present the critical issues in a few minutes. And it requires the ability to tell a good story, organized chronologically, tracing origins and consequences of the disease process, or outlining a diagnostic puzzle.

I've been told a number of times by house officers, my supervisors, or teachers . . . that you should be sort of leading up to something which is your differential diagnosis, and that you should tell the story of this patient such that you'll persuade your audience of your final, most likely diagnosis, or of your differential, and why you've included certain diseases and excluded others.

Interest in the story reflects the interest in the case. "My intern always used to say," another student said laughing, "a good case is one where you don't make the diagnosis for an hour. A great case is where you don't make the diagnosis for a day. But if it takes a week to make a diagnosis, now that's what they call a 'fascinoma'." This student had had the rare opportunity for a medical student of having admitted two of the most interesting cases seen on the Medicine service at the Massachusetts General Hospital for some time, and had been invited to present both of them at the Morbidity and Mortality rounds. Because he is a natural performer, his presentations were a smash hit and probably the most memorable experiences of his clerkship years.

Students become quickly aware of the performance dimension. They rehearse presentations, learn to give them without notes, even to make up details if they do not remember them exactly, and are very aware of the response. If the performance is not successful, the team members start fidgeting, rolling their eyes, tapping a pencil, or simply tune out. "When you take up too much time, you kind of ruin everything for everyone. You hold up the team, you mess up the rhythm for the rest of the day . . . " And this is the single most important source for criticism or approval which students experience in the early stages of clinical training. "It's not how much time you spend with your patients or how caring you are with them or how good a rapport you establish with them, or how amazing your knowledge of pathophysiology or whatever," to quote a student, but your presentation of cases.

Current literary criticism rejects the view that narratives are simply pure reflections of experience, just "a story of what happened."[13] Some theorists argue that they are mere conventional fictions. I am suggesting something much more than this. Stories are one means of organizing and interpreting experience, of projecting idealized and anticipated experiences, a distinctive way of formulating reality and idealized ways of interacting with it. I will be returning to this theme in talking about illness narratives (see chapter 6). However, my point here is that presenting cases is not merely a way of depicting reality but a way of constructing it. It is one of a set of closely linked formative practices through which disease is organized and responded to in contemporary American teaching hospitals. Case presentations represent disease as the object of medical practice. The "story" presented is a story of disease processes, localized spatially in tissue lesions and disordered physiology and temporally in abstract, medicalized time (Frankenberg 1988c). The person, the subject of suffering, is represented as the site of disease rather than as a narrative agent. The patient is formulated as a medical project, and given the extreme pressures of time, case presentations are designed to exclude all except that which will aid in diagnostic and therapeutic decisions. Get to the point, students are told. What's the real story here? What do we have to do? What is done is what we mean by medical care – the identification of pathology, and the application of medical therapies. One result is the inattention to the lifeworld of the patient, now widely documented in the medical social science literature (for example Mishler 1986a; Kleinman 1988b). Another result, however, is what we know as routine, rational medical practice.

With time, I could analyze other practices which medical students must learn. They learn to represent illness and physiological functioning as numbers and lab values, to engage in a distinctive form of clinical reasoning, to do procedures. They learn to enter into appropriate relations with other physicians, to negotiate among diverse and conflicting interests and claims. All of these are important interpretive practices, and they are closely interdependent. Taken together, they constitute a complex "language game," in Wittgenstein's terms, that produces a "way of life." I have focused on writing and speaking here because they quickly recede into the background, outside the purview of curricular reforms. And I have drawn them to our attention because they often seem to be mere reflections on a preconstituted world rather than key practices in its shaping.

Though I refer to these practices in Wittgenstein's analogy as part of a language game, it should be clear that they are deadly serious and have consequences in the material world. I asked a student whether the switch from basic science reasoning to clinical reasoning was a very important change between the basic science years and the clinical years.

> I don't think it's really all that different than the cases we had in tutorial, but I think what's utterly different is that you're not just reading a case or a story about someone having an operation . . . you go in the hospital and you find yourself being part of [actual] decisions to open up people's bodies and take veins from one place and stick them in another place or cut out hunks of their intestines, or whatever, that can never be put back, I mean just doing huge things to people when often times it's not known 100 percent that the person even has that problem but no one can think of anything more likely, and they are kind of in dire straits and something needs to be done.

The student was reflecting two things. First, what I have been calling formative practices – writing charts, presenting cases, speaking with patients – are what Austin (1962) called "speech acts"; they are annunciations that have tremendous consequences in the real world. They are not simply forms of literary representation, ways of thinking about the world. They are powerful ways of acting. They lead to further actions, medical procedures, technical interventions, the use of pharmacological agents. Thus when I speak about "the medical construction of the body through various interpretive practices," I am describing acts which quite literally shape and reshape the body.

Second, at the end of his comments, this student was reflecting an awareness of the conventionality and arbitrariness of many of those actions. A resident says, "Well, we're going to give this kid a fourteen-day course of antibiotics." But how do we know that it shouldn't be ten days or twenty days, the student asked himself. There's no data about this, it's just what we do. But this is true not only of such benign interventions. He also felt it to be true of the most dangerous, risky or experimental procedures. Having rotated from a neurology service that now had several of his previous patients who had had intraoperative myocardial infarctions or strokes shortly after the surgery, he saw the potential ill effects of such interventions; "cutting off someone's nose to spite their face," he called it.

> . . . it often seems like as medical students we kind of slide into doing these kind of things which can have just unimaginably great consequences for patients and we just sort of do it because we've incrementally learned about the biology and the science and the pathology and the pharmacology and we kind of inch into it and suddenly there we are saying, "I'll write the orders that such and such be done to this patient."

During their first year of clinical activities – the third year of medical school – students often become acutely aware of the arbitrariness of many of the specific activities in which they engage, as well as of the powerful forces that support conformity. They see treatments that have poor outcomes as well as those that provide benefit. They see some residents or attending physicians doing procedures they think should not be done or behaving miserably toward patients. At the same time, they recognize they are not senior enough to judge what should be done, and they feel deeply the pressure to show solidarity, not to question the actions of those up the hierarchy. They seldom recognize, however, the relationship between their perceptions of arbitrariness and hierarchy.

Students learn the formative practices I have been describing in an extra-ordinary "totalizing" institutional setting. Their whole lives – their waking lives as well as much of their sleep – are spent in the hospital. They are constantly examined, especially during teaching rounds, and observed – by interns, residents, attendings. Their actions are judged in written evaluations, which have important consequences for what residency programs they may get into.[14] When inter-viewing students about this aspect of their experience, I often think of Foucault's image of the "panopticon," a circular prison allowing inmates in its cells to be scrutinized by the guard in a tower in the central courtyard at any moment, an image Foucault took from Bentham to describe those modern institutions which combine observation, disciplinary control, and teaching (Foucault 1977: 195–228). Hospitals are of course not prisons, and medical students resent lack of attention and supervision even more than they dislike the constant evaluation. But they quickly discover they are part of a formalized hierarchy, and those more powerful dispense rewards – the right to learn new procedures, teaching time, a few extra hours of sleep, and positive evaluations – as well as punishment. They "have total control over your self-esteem," one student said, particularly through their public praise or belittling of students. They can also require students to spend their time doing trivial and uninteresting work – "scut" – rather than offering opportunities for learning a new skill.

The regulatory procedures that students experience as giving others "total control" over them are not designed simply to control patients and practitioners, as Foucault's analysis often seems to suggest. They are designed first to control and manage error. As Bosk (1979) described in his classic treatment of a surgical residency, clinical teachers face the dilemma of needing to allow students to work at the limits of their competence and therefore make errors, in order to promote learning. But since errors potentially have such grave consequences, all practices must be carefully regulated. This regulation serves not only to reduce arbitrary practice on the part of students, but to control the practices and the interpretations of members at each level of the hierarchy. Adherence to a set of standards defines "competence," and competent practice is governed by a strong set of moral norms (cf. M. Good 1985).

These norms control not only practices, but acceptable definitions of reality as well. For the student, the house staff and attendings provide the "only reference to reality that you have," as one said. When they seem trustworthy, students find it easier to feel that the perceived arbitrariness derives from their own lack of knowledge. The student I was quoting above said that for him, the attending physician, the individual in charge of the service, plays a key role in validating the whole system. They can serve as "guardian angels," in his words.

> . . . my impression is if you really respect that person, then you tend to feel a lot more comfortable with the whole system, and the arbitrary aspects and the times when people seem to be acting by convention versus from proven data or whatever don't make you feel as uncomfortable. But if the guy at the top is someone who you don't respect or something for whatever reason, which has only happened to me once, you really start to, I think, at least for me, feel very kind of ill at ease with the whole kind of enterprise.

Hierarchy and the control of the arbitrary are thus intimately related. "Standards of practice," defined and enforced hierarchically, place sharp limits on the actual arbitrariness of clinical activities, while they validate the sense of their rightness. Medical education thus authorizes clinical practices and their objects; at the same time, these practices construct the objects of medical attention and reproduce the power relations in which they are embedded.

Medical practice and the soteriological

In focusing on the formative dimensions of medical practice, I have resisted providing a conventional critique. What I have described indicates some of the powerful, experience-based practices by which medicine formulates sickness from a materialist and individualizing perspective. Disease is resident in the individual body, and the goal of treatment is to understand surface phenomena with reference to a deeper ontological order, to link symptoms and signs to physiological structure or functioning and to intervene at that level. Disease has a natural course; the story of the disease is one without a personalized agent. The narrative and phenomenological structure of illness experience, and the person who is agent of suffering, are relevant to routine clinical practices only insofar as they reveal the pathophysiological order, enabling the physician to formulate and document the case as a medical project. The clinical narrative – that is, the case as presented in rounds – and associated clinical stories most often conceive the patient as person and actor only so far as patients are seen as morally responsible for their diseases – the despised alcoholic's esophageal bleed – or as willing agents in conforming to recommended treatments.[15]

This picture, which follows directly from the analysis I have outlined, provides the stuff of conventional critiques of contemporary medicine. It has a large measure of truth. It is also, however, a kind of caricature and always only partial. The sketch I have presented of clinical practice is most true for a tertiary care hospital setting, where the task is to treat severe, usually acute, medical problems and discharge the patient as quickly as possible. It is also more true for medical students than for experienced clinicians. The elemental practices of clinical work absorb the attention of the student, who must learn the simplest procedures, forms of reasoning, and ways of speaking and acting, while these quickly fade into the background for the skilled clinician, allowing for a different kind of attending – at least ideally – to the person who is ill. It is for this reason, however, that our research on how medical students learn lays bare those elemental practices and shows them to provide the skeleton of medical activity and medical knowledge.

This sketch is also partial because every medical school strives to teach students a set of practices complementing the standard diagnostic and therapeutic activities. Courses in social medicine or the medical humanities and behavioral sciences teach students to attend to patient narratives and experience, to evaluate ethical issues in medical practice, and to consider the social context of illness and care. Forms of interviewing and assessing patients appropriate to such perspectives are also taught. In some curricula these issues receive scant attention; in some, such as the Patient–Doctor course of Harvard's New Pathway curriculum, a great deal of effort is devoted to teaching these complementary practices and the knowledge associated with this view of sickness and care. However, social and behavioral issues are always a tiny part of medical curricula, and in the clerkship years, these so-called "psychosocial" dimensions of medicine are almost always marginalized, absorbed within the standard work-up, set aside for exceptional cases, or discounted entirely.[16]

Conventional criticisms of medical practice seem particularly inadequate, however, because they fail to recognize how fundamentally the materialist and individualist vision is instantiated within the simplest, constituting practices of medicine. They also fail to recognize the constant presence of what I have earlier referred to as the "soteriological." I began with the argument that soteriological concerns suffuse medical care – they are always present within it – and at times irrupt into awareness or cause a breakdown in routinized practice. I suggested that the juxtaposition of the rational–technical or physiological with the existential or soteriological is essential to our understanding medicine as a symbolic formation. Let me give an example.

A third year medical student, a young woman, told me the following story during one of our interviews, in answer to my question about what makes an "interesting" case.

We had one patient that had steroid psychosis, or I think that's probably what it was finally in the end, we decided, some kind of psychosis. He was an AIDS patient. It was actually a really frightening case because he at one point, this was the most . . . timid man, really very calm and fearful sort of person who turned into just an aggressive, sort of animalistic kind of person, whether it was due to the steroids he was getting or whether it had something to do with HIV encephalitis or whatever. It could have been various things, he just had (short laugh) a really frightening shift of personality. At one point he had pulled out his I.V. and there was blood all over the bathroom and he was threatening people that he was going to scratch them or bite them and give them AIDS, and it was really very . . .

BG: *Was it explicit?*

Yeah, "you're going to get it, you're next!" This was while we were on call one night so I was there, and it was really very scary.

BG: *He was acting out all of the unspoken fears.*

Yeah, very much. I mean he was totally uninhibited, I mean I'm sure that he was expressing a lot of fear of dying . . . while this was happening he was essentially saying all the things that he could never say normally. Just screaming at the top of his lungs, "I'm going to die. I'm dying and I don't know why I'm here. Why are you doing this for me? You know I'm dying." And the whole thing feeling like he wanted to do some kind of damage on other people, like someone should pay for how horrible life is treating him, which are all some pretty real issues but which of course never have been addressed with him since that's just not what happens. So he basically was restrained for a lot of days and his steroids were stopped and he calmed down after a number of days, but he was seriously that way for two or three days. So that case was brought up, but mostly not because everyone considered it interesting, although I did (laughing), but because there wasn't any other cases really going on so we ended up discussing that, but really by default because there wasn't anything else that wasn't run of the mill.

I asked how the case had been discussed, whether the dramatic episode she had described and its implications became central to the discussion. "That was actually really interesting," she said. There was a discussion of what could have caused a psychotic reaction, but the resident who presented it never described the details, never opened the issue of how frightening it was: " . . . it was sort of the macho kind of thing like, (take charge, deep voice) 'patient had an acute psychotic break and we just took care of that,' the fearless resident."

The hospital is not only the site of the construction and treatment of the medicalized body, but the site of moral drama. This case is a reminder of the nature of that drama – of human suffering and fear, of the confrontation with illness and death on the part of both the sick and those charged with their care, and of efforts to contain and manage the drama. Surely what is evident in this case is the irruption of the fundamentally moral dimension of illness into this rational–technical sphere. What is remarkable is the use of routine medical procedures to manage the rupture of the common-sense reality of the hospital rather than to open them to moral reflection. Order was restored. The medical definition of the event was maintained through physical force and the interpretation of the rupture by routine speaking practices. One has a sense here of what Habermas calls the "colonization of the lifeworld," the shaping of the experiential world of our moral lives by instrumental rationality, highly routinized procedures, and both technical and technological management.[17]

But again, this hardly seems the whole story. Medical practice can never fully contain the moral and the soteriological. Indeed, events such as these, which are not so uncommon, really, reveal the foundations of medical practice. This is, in a sense, what medical practice is all about. From early on, many medical students speak of a kind of "passion" required for doctoring. Not only do they seek a specialty that will maintain their intellectual excitement, but many describe their desire for a passionate engagement with the primal forces of sickness and suffering, a passionate struggle on behalf of their patients. It is an attitude for which students long, although they are ambivalent about its demands. It is an attitude all too often lost in years of training and practice, but it remains present as a dimension of all healing.

One could read Foucault's descriptions of the hospital and medical practice, as well as much medical anthropology, with little sense of the moral and soteriological core of the experience that is present, present for the ill and their families, present as an underlying assumption of those who enter the profession, present among physicians and their patients confronting life-threatening conditions, and present too within the routinized practices through which objects of medical care are constructed so that they can be treated medically. I have suggested that it is precisely the conjoining of the physiological and soteriological that is central to the constitution of medicine as a modern institution, or in Cassirer's terms, a symbolic formation. Medical knowledge is not only a medium of perception, a "gaze," as one might take from Foucault. It is a medium of experience, a mode of engagement with the world. It is a dialogical medium, one of encounter, interpretation, conflict, and at times transformation.

I also suggested in the introduction that medicine plays a very particular soteriological function in modern societies, characterized as they are by materialist individualism. You will recall Weber's wonderful description of the central role of ideas of redemption or salvation in the organization of civilizations, ideas organized around "an image of the world" and "a stand in the face of the world." "'From what' and 'for what' one wished to be redeemed and, let us not forget, 'could be' redeemed, depended upon one's image of the world," he wrote.

> One could wish to be saved from political and social servitude and lifted into a Messianic realm in the future of this world; or one could wish to be saved from being defiled by ritual impurity and hope for the pure beauty of psychic and bodily existence. One could wish to escape being incarcerated in an impure body and hope for a purely spiritual existence. (Weber 1946: 280)

And he goes on with other possibilities cultures have explored. What I am suggesting is that medicine is deeply implicated in our contemporary image of what constitutes the suffering from which we and others hope to be delivered and our culture's vision of the means of redemption. In a civilization deeply committed to biological individualism, one in which spirit is ever more a residual category (Comaroff 1985: 181), the maintenance of human life and the reduction of physical suffering have become paramount. Health replaces salvation, as Foucault wrote in his conclusion to *The Birth of the Clinic*.

> This is because medicine offers modern man the obstinate, yet reassuring face of his finitude; in it, death is endlessly repeated, but it is also exorcised; and although it ceaselessly reminds man of the limit that he bears within him, it also speaks to him of that technical world that is the armed, positive, full form of his finitude. (Foucault 1973: 198).

Sickness, death, and finitude are found in the corpse, in the human body. And salvation, or at least some partial representation of it, is present in the technical efficacy of medicine.

Lest I be understood as romanticizing medicine, I remind you of the terrible costs of such a narrowly biological view of the human person, of such devotion to maintaining biological life. The abortion debate no longer turns on discussion of the presence of the spirit or soul in the fetus, or even on what constitutes personhood, but narrowly on a politicized commitment to "life." Infant mortality rates have come to be seen as almost the sole criterion of the success of international public health programs. And in this country we spend an astounding proportion of our health care dollars on the last several weeks of life, so great is our commitment and our technological capacity for extending life.

At the same time, this soteriological resonance of medicine makes understandable aspects of clinical practice neglected or obscured by many standard sociological or anthropological analyses. Physicians and students tack back and forth between engagement in clinical practices and moral reflection. The language of hope, given narrative shape in clinical discussions around cancer or other life-threatening illnesses, takes on a transcendent quality (M. Good et al. 1990). Caring, exemplified by our idealized vision of medicine, is at the center of our moral discourse. Indeed, medicine is the central site for the discussion of many of the most important value issues in contemporary society. Perhaps this soteriological quality of medicine explains our outrage when physicians fail to live up to these moral standards.

My goal in this chapter has been to suggest some ways of thinking about medicine as a "symbolic form," a symbolically mediated mode of apprehending and acting on the world. I have provided a brief analysis of American clinical medicine as a set of distinctive interpretive practices. Such an approach suggests methods for comparative research – for comparing types of medical practices across societies, and for analyzing modes of interpretation that give rise cross-culturally to extremely diverse forms of illness realities and their management. I have tried to develop this analysis in a way consistent with an epistemological position counter to that which I criticized in the first chapter. I turn next to a discussion of the semiotic structures that mediate knowledge and experience of sickness, before moving on to the investigation of the social and cultural shaping of illness as a mode of human experience.

4

Semiotics and the study of medical reality

Throughout his work, Cassirer asserted that symbolic forms are "organs of reality," that they are formative of what we apprehend as real and available to human knowing and acting. In *Language and Myth* (1946: 8), he wrote:

> ... the special symbolic forms are not imitations, but *organs* of reality, since it is solely by their agency that anything real becomes an object for intellectual apprehension and as such is made visible to us. The question as to what reality is apart from these forms, and what are its independent attributes, becomes irrelevant here.

In this chapter I continue my reflection on medicine as a symbolic form through a discussion of medical semiotics. The argument that human biology or disease is "very much within culture" and best understood as a symbolic form is strongly counter-intuitive, unless we interpret this as a rather trivial recognition that all consciousness and therefore knowledge is symbolic or meaningful. Cassirer made a much stronger claim, however, when he argued that science, aesthetics, and religion are each distinctive forms of knowledge, and that mythology, for example, is a special form of reality (rather than a psychological or symbolic distortion) and a mode of apprehending the world (1955b). Cassirer's philosophical position is closely akin to the historicist theory of culture that emerged in the Boasian tradition, sharing a concern for how historically evolving cultural forms mediate experience and knowledge. This tradition provides a basis for an analytic strategy that views biomedicine as one form of knowledge among many, rather than as a depiction of the biological world that can serve as the norm for judging all other accounts.

My interest in thinking through the relevance of Cassirer and this tradition for medical anthropology begins with my conviction of the importance to our field of a number of the central themes of Cassirer's work – "the multiplicity of worlds, the speciousness of 'the given,' the creative power of the understanding, the variety and formative function of symbols," as Goodman (1978: 1) summarizes them in the opening sentences of his book *Ways of Worldmaking*. I argued in the last chapter for the primacy of social practices in the constitution of medical reality. In this chapter, I want to address the structure of the symbolic more directly.

Cassirer argued throughout his corpus that symbolic forms are not merely more or less accurate or vivid reflections of reality, but that they actively constitute the diverse worlds in which we experience and have knowledge of reality.[1] Reality is to be found within manifold human experience, and it is through the study of symbolic forms that we have access to distinctive ways of knowing and thus to what is knowable of reality. Such a view required Cassirer to investigate the nature of reality formulated in the various symbolic forms, as well as the underlying role of "the symbolic" (*das Symbolische*) in its apprehension. In particular, it required a distinctive analysis of the "sign." As Cassirer (1955b: 23) wrote:

> An essential element of the correspondence between the diverse cultural forms is that the sign exerts an active, creative force in all of them – myth and language, artistic configuration, and the formation of theoretical concepts of the world and its relationships. Humboldt says that man puts language *between* himself and the nature which inwardly and outwardly acts upon him, that he surrounds himself with a world of words in order to assimilate and elaborate the world of objects . . .

This "active, creative force" of the sign and its role in assimilating and elaborating a "world of objects" is the subject of much of Cassirer's philosophy of culture.[2] This view of symbolizing also provides a framework for developing an anthropological understanding of diverse forms of medicine and their role in the assimilation and elaboration of the world of medical objects.

Any theory that argues that culture and social practices produce distinctive ways of apprehending reality, distinctive forms of knowledge, runs up against the problem of translatability (see Tambiah 1990: ch. 6 for a discussion). If the natural world, outside of culture, does not provide the basis for translation across cultures, as held by the empiricist tradition, how do we answer the charge that cultures must then be ultimately incommensurable and translation impossible? For the anthropologist, the problem of how we translate across medical systems – for example, between biomedicine and another form of medical knowledge – is a central and quite practical fact of life. In this chapter, I will explore the contribution of methods from a broadly conceived "semiotic" analysis to the comparative study of medical knowledge, arguing for the necessity of a critical, anthropological form of hermeneutics.

Problems of translating across medical worlds and forms of medical knowledge

Edwin Ardener (1982: 2–4) provides an intriguing discussion of the work of Benjamin Whorf relevant to the approach I will be taking. Whorf is of course among the most criticized of Boasian anthropologists for his relativist claims that language determines experience and therefore produces separate cultural worlds. Ardener points out that Whorf's rather idealist intuitions about language came to him as he faced quite material problems. Whorf was a fire-insurance assessor; in his work he observed that the disposing of flammable objects in a hazardous fashion often resulted from underlying linguistic classifications. "Empty gasoline drums" exploded because they were classified "empty" (of gasoline) rather than "full" (of fumes), encouraging people to smoke cigarettes near them. "Spun limestone" and "scrap lead" from condensers (both highly combustible) were disposed near fires, because they were classed as "stone" and "lead." As Ardener notes, "Physical explosions ([Whorf] appeared to say) were produced by a careless mixture of categories as well as of chemicals . . . It is the *material* nature of Whorf's basic problem that contains the interesting antidote to his own, and other people's flight into debates on cultural reality" (1982: 3–4). Ardener concludes from his discussion that much of the debate about language, reality, and relativism is specious.

> . . . when issues are big enough there is no recourse but to firmly universalistic principles. Yet cross-cultural (or subcultural) misunderstanding on supposedly trivial issues (whatever the possibilities on greater ones) is a very real problem at the level of close interactions between individuals, so much so that it is itself a human universal, and whether we like it or not language looms very large in these situations. (Ardener 1982: 3)

Misunderstandings which occur "at the level of close interactions between individuals," where "language looms very large," have provided the source for many of medical anthropology's insights into culturally discrepant lifeworlds. Physicians and their patients categorize signs and symptoms differently; in Whorf's (1956: 213) terms, they "cut nature up, organize it into concepts, and ascribe significances" in a fashion appropriate to their own speech community and their own existential concerns. Because categories and lifeworlds differ between patients and physicians, medical conversations are filled with interruptions, misinterpretations, and failures of understanding – a finding reported commonly in the medical social sciences and experienced by nearly anyone who has visited a physician. International public health specialists face constant difficulties in translating between medical concepts and local illness categories for related reasons. Again, these are revealed in the midst of quite pragmatic activities. For example, Lincoln Chen (1986) reported that a child survival project in Matlab, Bangladesh succeeded in convincing only 22 percent of eligible mothers to accept tetanus vaccinations, even though neonatal tetanus accounted for 26 percent of infant mortality in the region and the biological efficacy of vaccinating pregnant women is 100 percent. Some others, it seemed, feared the vaccination would harm the fetus; others confused vaccination and injectable contraception. However, a prominent confusion concerning the efficacy of the vaccination to prevent neonatal tetanus arose from cultural differences in how nature is "cut up" and categorized quite akin to those described by Whorf. Chen (1986: 1263) summarizes: "The three local Bengali terms for describing tetanus – *alga*, *dhanostonkar*, and *takuria* – also apply to neonatal syndromes that resemble tetanus, so clients perceived the vaccine as being only about 50 percent effective in eradicating *alga*, *dhanostonkar*, and *takuria*." Because "tetanus" and local illness categories differ in the phenomena they denote, the translation of claims about the efficacy of the tetanus vaccine was unsuccessful.

Similar difficulties are reported by researchers who attempt to translate even quite basic questionnaires or symptom checklists for use in a culture other than that in which they were developed. For example, translation of a simple question from a World Health Organization psychiatric screening instrument, "Do you sleep badly?", was found by a researcher in Ethiopia (Kortmann 1990: 386) to elicit only examples of sleep which had been disturbed as a result of nightmares or sleepwalking. Early morning awakening and inability to fall back to sleep, or difficulty falling asleep, were not included as meanings of the translation. As a consequence, the questionnaire failed to elicit evidence of key markers of major depression, which was one of the primary goals of the instrument. "Headaches" are differentiated in Puerto Rican Spanish from "brain aches," a distinction unavailable in English (Abad and Boyce 1979), making translation of apparently quite simple questionnaire items difficult. And the rich somatic vocabulary available in many languages (see Ebigbo 1982 for an example from Ibo culture in Nigeria) simply has no meaningful translation into American popular or medical language. No wonder that controversy continues around all efforts to operationalize higher order categories such as dementia, schizophrenia, depression, or somatization, although few doubt their universality as human phenomena.

These difficulties, all manifest at the "close level of individual interactions," seem as expectable to the anthropologist as differences between American and Eskimo categories of snow or English and Nuer classifications of markings on cattle, and the examples can easily be multiplied. However, though important for sorting out sources of cross-cultural misunderstanding, they offer little challenge to the biomedical paradigm and are hardly surprising to clinicians. All are examples of differences in categorization; they illustrate how culture mediates the process of "designation," of distinguishing among phenomena perceived in the natural world and ordering them through systems of classification. They are thus easy to subsume within biomedical "hermeneutics," that is, within the typical interpretive practices of clinical medicine which map signs and symptoms onto their biological and physiological referents. For the clinician or the public health specialist, recognition of the role of culture in this process is often a step forward. For the anthropologist, it is only a hint of more profound ways in which symbolic relations mediate knowledge and reality. Close attention to such phenomena leads quickly to a more fundamental challenge to empiricist hermeneutics and to those approaches in the medical social sciences that conceive culture to have its effects primarily at the level of designation and classification.

Careful scrutiny of "cross-cultural (or subcultural) misunderstandings" provides the anthropologist entree to more subtle and far-reaching ways in which symbolic forms and their distinctive semiotic processes serve as an "organ of reality." In the following pages I examine several examples that illustrate the interdependence of semiotic structures and interpretive practices, the "cosmological" and "performative" axes in Tambiah's (1977) terms, examples that suggest how an anthropological hermeneutic can offer a challenge to the bio-medical. The discussion is not intended to suggest that comparative studies in terms of "higher order categories" (such as particular disease categories) are impossible, but by entering the discussion at a more microscopic level to indicate both the difficulties and prospects of comparative research.

"Relational semiotics" and the meaning of symptoms: interpreting a clinical case

While we were teaching a seminar on social and cultural aspects of medicine some years ago, one required of all first year residents in a family medicine program, Mary-Jo and I required each participant to videotape an interview with a patient in which the physician elicited the patient's explanatory model and the meaning of the presenting symptoms. One resident interviewed a twenty-two year old woman who came complaining of rectal bleeding. She had previously been seen by another physician in the clinic; that physician had now graduated from the program, and this was the first visit of the young woman with the resident from our seminar. He used her visit as an opportunity to elicit a general personal and family history from her, as well as to deal with her primary medical problem. The transcript of the interview serves as the basis for the analysis.[3]

The physician met briefly with the young woman, who came accompanied by a girl friend, learned that her primary concern was rectal bleeding, and asked if she would be willing to have their meeting recorded. She agreed, the videotape was started, and the clinical encounter went forward. The physician quickly reviewed the young woman's medical history and her previous experience in the clinic, then asked about the severity and the history of her rectal bleeding. She provided a brief narrative about its origins – she first noted a bit of bleeding near the time she had suffered a sports injury – and her previous examination for the problem, during which the physician assured her there was no cause for alarm. She described how the bleeding had increased, how the blood now made her stools appear black and tarry, how she experienced pain like a "hook" sticking into her, and her concern that she might have a growth. She responded to the physician's questions that she sometimes felt nauseous, like something foul was draining into her, and that she had tried treating the problem by "eating lots of vegetables and fruit," avoiding "preservatives in food and meat," and taking hot baths. By these means she had succeeded in controlling the problem for some time. However, the bleeding had again gotten worse, and a friend of hers who had suffered a similar problem urged her not to wait before seeking treatment. This friend had gone to a special hospital, "because she's a Jehovah Witness and she wouldn't have any problem with the blood issue there . . . " She had had surgery, and now "has to go to the bathroom out of a sack"; she recommended that her young friend see a physician before the problem progressed. Thus, she had now come to have the problem checked.

A cursory reading of the transcript of the interview suggests little in the way of misunderstanding or the interruptions which are often apparent in medical interviews (see Mishler 1986a. and Fisher and Todd 1983 for examples). The physician encouraged the young woman to describe the problem that brought her to the clinic, to discuss her concern about the bleeding, and to tell her story of the history of the illness. He assured her that he would provide a physical examination and order any required tests. Then, given the leisure of time, he invited her to tell him more about her personal and family history as a way of "getting to know her better." She talked about belonging to Jehovah's Witnesses, told of her convictions in a way that seemed to allow her to "witness" to the physician, and discussed her objections to blood transfusions. She was encouraged to elaborate her narrative and was given the opportunity to discuss her religious views quite fully.

A more careful reading of the text indicates that a typical biomedical hermeneutics organized the physician's interpretation of the young woman's discourse. The interview followed the typical categories of a medical interview (and of course a medical chart). The physician elicited the "chief complaint," an appropriate "history of present illness," a brief "review of systems" relevant to the presenting problem, a short "past medical history," and a relatively elaborate "family and social history." The encounter concluded with a physical exam. More than this, the physician's questions indicate a standard – and quite appropriate – concern about the physiological "reference" of the presenting complaints, that is the source and cause of bleeding. Did her description of the symptom indicate an intestinal bleed, caused perhaps from a cancer or some other condition, or external bleeding from an anal fissure or hemorrhoids? What had been the course and history of the condition, and what tests were appropriate to its diagnosis? In addition, given the seminar requirement that he elicit an explanatory model, the resident sought to learn what the patient believed was causing her illness, interrupting her narrative briefly to ask if she feared that the bleeding was caused by cancer, and whether she was deeply concerned by it. From the medical perspective, the interview and the patient's discussion of her symptoms were unremarkable, although they were more elaborate than usual and the resident was unusually unhurried, empathetic, and competent.

An anthropological reading of the text of the interview, however, indicates that the primary symptom – rectal blood – was incorporated in a complex set of semiotic relationships in no way limited to the referential relation of sign to its physiological source. The text is pervaded with symbolic oppositions, and blood appears as a mediator between opposing domains in a manner familiar from several decades of structuralist interpretations of myth, ritual, and other symbol systems. An anthropological hermeneutics suggests an interpretation of the patient's symptoms that was far from apparent to the physician, revealing a discrepancy in medical realities at a deeper level than an initial reading suggests.

In response to the physician's question about the meaning of "the blood issue" which she had mentioned, the young woman described her understanding of the

Jehovah's Witnesses' views of blood and transfusions. Her account was part exegesis, part witness, and part personal narrative.

> Jehovah's Witnesses don't take blood, because the blood is, uh, the Bible refers to the blood as the life [*Uh hm*],[4] and we're not to take anybody's life into our own bodies [*I see*], and it's no different if a doctor tells you not to drink alcohol, if you don't, if it doesn't pass over your lips, and they take it and put it into an I.V., it's no different, you're still disobeying the doctor's orders, and the same goes with drinkin' blood. You wouldn't slice somebody's throat and drink it, so you don't stick it in your veins [*Uh hunh*], and Biblically it's in Leviticus in . . . ["chapter 17," her friend interjected].
>
> I've got a card that I show my doctors, you know, I had that put on my medical records in case of an emergency where a doctor might feel in his opinion that I'd lose my life if I didn't have a blood transfusion. It's on my records here at the medical center, . . . and then there's also a booklet that I can give my doctor, . . . if I'm going to go in for surgery and he doesn't understand it, then there's a whole bunch of information on blood, how it's uh, really it's a filthy product, because it's takin' somebody else's, you know, stuff into your body. It does a lot of things. You can even die from takin' blood transfusion [*Uh hunh*] so . . .
> *So you feel uhh you mentioned that blood is a filthy product?*
> Uhn hunh. It's unclean. [*Uh huh*] Uh huh. People don't even handle it when they're, when they go through the purification process, whatever it is, I'm not exactly sure what it is, but I know that they don't handle it because it even makes their skin break out just to touch it. [*Uh huh*] And uh for people to die from taking it into their body, it's something foreign. The only thing the way we're set up, we won't live with anything foreign in our bodies, except for a woman when she's giving birth to a child, that's the only foreign thing that really lives in the body. [*Uh huh*] Outside of that, . . . after you leave your paren— your mother's body, you're, you're a different person, the blood's not the same, uhm, it's an individual [*Uh hm*].

In this explication, the young woman introduced a set of symbolic oppositions that provided the context for her understanding of her bleeding (see figure 1). Blood is, in the Bible's terms, "life"; it is the essence of an "individual," and with its loss "I'd lose my life," as she said. On the other hand, transfusable blood or blood from another person taken into oneself is "foreign"; it is a "filthy product," "unclean," requiring "purification," and ultimately something "you can even die from."

The physician acknowledged the importance of her religion, and then went on to ask her to talk briefly about her personal and family history. She described her relationship with her family.

"blood as the life"	"you can even die"
"it's an individual"	"it's something foreign"
	"filthy product"
	"unclean"
	requires "purification"

Figure 1 Opposing domains of the meaning of "blood"

Well, we're close. My parents got divorced, and we went through all kinds of problems. When Satan can break up that family life, then he's accomplished his purpose, and things don't go too well after that, an' I resorted to drugs, an' my parents, they went their separate ways, you know, thinkin' about age, lookin' forward to death, not havin' a hope in view, of better conditions, they, they went through some problems too, drugs, an', uhh, you know, different things, prostitution, an' when you have pressures like that it creates, it helps, it promotes the diseases that are in your body, and my mother had to have some operations 'cause of cancer, an' my, I saw my father age a lot. But it's, since I found the truth, I've been st–, I've studied the Bible for a year with Jehovah's Witnesses, an' then I was baptized this last week. Then my life's taken a change, an' now I communicate better with my family, now because I can talk about that hope, an', uh, you know I have uh, I have respect for them now [*Um hm*] um, because they're my parents. They don't always do what's right, but . . .

Here the opposing domains of blood as the essence of life and blood as filthy, impure, foreign product are extended to her life narrative and that of her family (figure 2). A life in which Satan has his way, one "looking forward to death, not having a hope in view," is juxtaposed to the baptismal new life of "hope" and "truth." In one, divorce, drugs, prostitution, and fear of death are present, and these "promote the diseases that are in your body." In her own life history, the young woman describes passing through this old life into the new through her study of the Bible and the transforming rite of baptism. As a result, she has laid claim to the truth, to hope, and consequently a new relationship with her family.

She went on to extend these themes explicitly to disease, cancer in particular, and to the physical environment (figure 3). She described the "tumors and cancer" her mother suffered, and surgery in which she had had "her female organs removed."

I have a feeling that that is probably going to run in my family because we're farmers, we raise potatoes and beans, an' they used D.D.T. right out there in the fields where they'd be dustin', drinkin' the water out of the irrigation ditches, eatin' those potatoes, an' (*sure*) an' there was nothing wrong with it then. They didn't tell people that it was, uh, caused cancer, so . . .

Others in her family had also suffered from tumors – her great-grandmother, her great-grandfather:

The baptismal life	*The old life of Satan*
"I found the truth"	"looking forward to death"
"I was baptized"	
"I can talk about that hope"	"not having a hope in view"
"communicate better with my family"	divorce
"I have respect for . . . my parents"	"Satan can break up that family"
	"drugs," "prostitution"
	"diseases that are in your body"
	"cancer," aging

Figure 2 Opposing domains in personal and family history

my great-grandfather had a tumor in his head, took a drink of water out of one of those drinkin' fountains that was inside of a concrete wall, raised up, hit his head, an' he died before he hit the ground (*Un hunh*), an' so it's just things like that. I think that's common to mankind, these days, you know, sickness and death (*Uh huh*), you know, an' uh, it's just something that's normal for this abnormal system . . .
So you think the system we live under is pretty abnormal?
 Oh certainly, the environment, we've brought this all on ourselves, pollution, like today, I can't hardly breathe out there (*Uh huh*) for the pollution, an' that throws nature off (*sure*), the balance of nature. . . . it's too much toxins for the body to handle . . .

The physician asked her to draw these issues back to her current problem, raising implicitly the (referential) question of whether her primary concern was that she may have a hidden cancer. Her response, however, summarized the opposing categories that provided the meaning of her symptom.

Well, . . . we've all got our problems, you know, . . . we're all livin' here. There's no way to be immune to, you know, being here with all . . . the filthy environments. You've just gotta take care of yourself the best you can (*Um hm*). I look after my parents. You know, I see if they've got what they need, . . . I try to supply them with fresh fruits and vegetables, I try to encourage my father to do that, you know, he's got a garden out in his back yard, now . . . I can't govern what they do in their lives, you know. All I can do is just hope for, hope that they, their hearts will be right (*Um hm*).

In these passages of the dialogue, the relevance of the young woman's initial comments about treating herself with fresh fruits and vegetables and avoiding additives is made clear. She elaborated the opposing domains she was suggesting in relation to personal health and the environment (figure 3). We have polluted our earthly environment, our food and water, thrown off the balance of nature. This has resulted in cancers and tumors and increasing illness. In "these days," "sickness and death" are "common to mankind." We can take care of ourselves the best we can, but our ultimate hope – for ourselves, for our family members – lies elsewhere.

When the physician attempted to shift the interview at this point, asking if there were any other medical problems she wished to discuss, she briefly described other concerns within the symbolic context now well described. She mentioned a discussion she had had with a previous physician about "superfluous hair" that

Nature and the body in balance   "This abnormal system"
"balance of nature"   "filthy environment"
"fresh fruits and vegetables"   "pollution," "toxins," "D.D.T."
"a garden"

                                    "sickness and death"
                                    "tumors"
                                    "a hormone imbalance that is part of the system"
                                    "superfluous hair"

Figure 3 Opposing domains in the body and the physical environment

might indicate "a hormone imbalance that is part of the system," and her reluctance to take hormonal medications. The physician inquired, from his reading of the chart, about her hay fever and asthma. She described how her asthma is affected by allergens and more generally by the pollution in the air which she takes into her body. In these comments, the analogy of the human body to the physical environment and the role of violations of each in producing imbalance and pathology are made explicit.

Near the conclusion of the interview, the physician remarked on the young woman's concerns about "these violations of your body." She responded by elaborating the larger cosmological frame for her concerns.

I don't think I worry about it too much (*Um hm*). It's this, it's not going to go on too much longer. If it were to go on like this, um, if it was to be left up to mankind, he'd destroy himself, an' that's not gonna happen. The Bible tells us that. So I feel confident in that, in that aspect, because I have a hope of better conditions. Something that we're gonna live right through.

. . . Secular history proves the Bible, in general, in the first place. There's a king, . . . Was it Sennacharib? An', uh, he was going to attack Jehovah's people at that time, . . . he was marching on Jerusalem, an' they camped over in this valley, and the Bible account is that one angel wiped out a hundred and eighty five thousand men. That was a literal happening, an' when he went out in the morning, he saw all those dead bodies around. The Bible tells us that Jehovah's gonna, the Day of Jehovah, that's God's name (*Um hm*), . . . that's what's gonna happen, that . . . his large army is going to wipe out the wickedness, an' that the earth is going to be here, an' the meek-hearted ones are the ones that are gonna be left over in it, an' that there's gonna be a resurrection of the righteous and the unrighteous (*Um hm*), that uh people who were victims of this environment who wanted to do better but because the food caused them to be a little on the insane side, or hyperactive, or death molded their lives because they didn't feel that they had enough time to do things the right way, uh those people who, who their hearts are really right, an' only God can read hearts (*Um hm*), they're gonna be the ones resurrected, an' they'll have a chance to live in a perfect system here, on earth, where there won't be this pollution. The people who are destroying the earth are gonna be done away with – it talks about in the Bible how they're gonna have to be torn away from the earth –
How do you see yourself on this earth, in some of the terms you're describing? . . .
I'm part of Jehovah's family (*Uh huh*). I have become a part, a member of his family (*Um hm*), an' only Jehovah's Witnesses, only Jehovah's people, unless you happen to die before the tribulation, an' the tribulation is when God, Revelation talks about the scarlet colored wild beast an' the harlot that rides that beast, well the beginning of the last days started in 1914, where the sign was world war (*Um hm*), an' World War I began in 1914, and since then wars and rumors of war. While the scarlet colored wild beast is, represents the nations (*Um hm*), and the prostitute or the harlot that rides that beast is false religion. What they've done is taken the truth and twisted it. . . . They preach sects (*Sex?*), you know, sects "s-e-c-t", they, it's uh twisting the truth, and that's where the prostitute comes from, because it's prostituted the truth. . . . if you take a close look at history, all these wars have been religious wars. . . . Well, Witnesses, they don't kill their brother, they pay their taxes because the Bible says "give Caesar's things to Caesar, an' God's things to God," (*Um hm*), and so, that's it, you know, . . .

Finally, here, the opposing symbolic domains, throughout her discourse, are shown to emerge from a historical soteriology and cosmology (see figure 4). The narrative this young woman provides is temporally sequential and historical, but history is represented as the framework for a contest between the Old Kingdom and the New Kingdom, which will be resolved finally on the Day of Jehovah. Humanity lives today in a period of struggle between the end of the old and the emergence of the new, an overlap of an age of wickedness and a new age of righteousness, and Jehovah's Witnesses belong to and bear witness to the new kingdom of God. This overlapping age began in 1914, according to the patient's account, and will continue through a period of great tribulation until the Day of Jehovah, when God with his army will "wipe out the wickedness." In "these days," sickness and death are common to mankind. Mankind is polluting and destroying the earth, overturning nature; cancer and tumors, insanity, hyperactivity, and lives "molded by death," are a part of the human condition. The nations, at war with one another, are likened to the scarlet beast. Sectarian religion is akin to the harlot that rides upon the beast and prostitutes the truth. In these times, Jehovah's people live as representatives of the New Kingdom among the old. They belong to Jehovah's family, living in hope and awaiting the great resurrection when, along with those whose hearts are known by God to be right, they will experience God's salvation and will "have a chance to live in a perfect system here, on earth . . . "

The primary symptom which this young woman brought to her physician – rectal bleeding – had meaning not only in relation to the physiological origins of the blood, but in relation to a larger field of symbols which she described in her conversation with the physician. This semiotic domain is susceptible to a structuralist reading. Lévi-Strauss (for example, 1963, 1969) elaborated a basic insight of structuralist linguistics that meaning is constituted through distinction, through the dividing of a conceptual or empirical domain by opposing significations, related in a larger system. In his preface to Jakobson's *Six Lectures on Sound and Meaning*, Lévi-Strauss (1985: ch. 9) recalls how many years earlier

New Kingdom	Old Kingdom
New Earth	Wickedness
Resurrection of the righteous and the unrighteous	"The people who are destroying the earth are going to be done away with"
"a chance to live in a perfect system here, on earth"	"torn away from the earth"
Free from "pollution"	Insanity, hyperactivity
	Lives molded by death
Jehovah's people	Sects, prostitute the truth
Jehovah's family	Those who "kill their brother"
Those who "give Caesar's things to Caesar, and God's things to God"	

Figure 4 Cosmological domains: the Old Kingdom and the New Earth

Jakobson's lectures had stimulated his own thinking about mythology. Phonemes, Jakobson had argued, are "meaningless units that are opposed within a system, where they create meanings precisely because of this opposition" (Lévi-Strauss 1985: 185); similarly, Lévi-Strauss argued, signs confer meaning through their relational qualities, that is through their opposition to other signs and their place in a system of semiotic relations. Lévi-Strauss turned this insight to the analysis of cultural forms, loosing a flood of research and creative work throughout the social sciences and humanities. In particular, he demonstrated that the most fundamental contradictions and dilemmas of the human condition – life and death, fertility and barrenness, purity and impurity, good and evil – are creatively rendered, represented, and resolved in mythology, ritual activities, and other cultural forms. From this perspective, healing rituals mediate health and sickness, life and death, hope and despair; they transform the status of the sufferer by first identifying the sickness as belonging to one cluster of symbolic domains, then ritually moving the sufferer across the mysterious margins to a new identity grounded in opposing symbolic domains (Yalman 1964; Kapferer 1983). Symptoms are given meaning within a cultural system relationally, by the position they occupy within complex symbolic codes, and traditional forms of healing may have efficacy through such symbolic codes and the experiences they evoke.

In the text of the conversation of the young Jehovah's Witness patient which I have been analyzing, the meaning of the symptom "rectal bleeding" emerges in relation to such a symbolic code. "Blood" occupies a mediating role between opposing domains. The blood of the individual is pure, the essence of life, while foreign blood is filthy and can cause death. Baptism, traditionally rendered as being "washed in the blood of the Lamb," mediates between the old life and the new, between a life of wickedness, of drugs, divorce, and prostitution, and a life of truth, hope, and respect for family and government. We live on an earth in which the natural balance has been upset by pollution, toxins, and filth, and the "sickness and death" associated with this despoiled earth – insanity, hyperactivity, hormonal imbalance and superfluous hair, and tumors and cancer – can only be redressed by efforts to eat fresh fruits and vegetables. Ultimately, the age of wickedness will be brought to an end by the shedding of blood, by a great slaughter of the wicked on the Day of Jehovah. A New Earth will come into being, the resurrection of the body will overcome sickness and suffering, and humanity will live as Jehovah's family.

I am of course not arguing that the physician should have attended primarily to the meaning of symptoms in these terms. The patient came to the clinic to learn the source of her bleeding, and the physician responded with an appropriate elicitation of the medical history and a physical examination. From the text and the videotape of this encounter, however, it seems likely that her rectal bleeding had more profound meanings for this young woman. She had been baptized only a week before. Her bleeding belonged symbolically to her old life, a life she associated with the breakup of her family, with drugs and prostitution, and with tumors and cancer. It seems reasonable that her effort to resolve this long-standing medical problem was an attempt to separate herself from the meanings associated with this powerful symbol and to move forward with her new life. One can easily imagine a scenario – for example, if she had continued to express serious concerns about the bleeding even after the problem was diagnosed as an insignificant result of hemorrhoidal bleeding – in which the interpretation I have proposed would serve as entree to a therapeutic response to the intrusion of the old life into the new.

It is also worth noting that although the physician was attempting to elicit an explanatory model, a rather different cultural form was present in the discourse. The physician sought her perception of the cause of the bleeding, asking persistently about her fears of cancer; he elicited her image of its pathophysiology and underlying cause, her past treatment efforts, and expectations for the future. All of these were present in her response. However, unity was given to the discourse not by this logic, the rational explanation of the cause, nor primarily by the narrative structure of her life history, but by a set of semiotic relations present in the discourse, relations which emerge from a historical narrative of Jehovah's activities in this world. It was this structure that was "formative" of the discourse and of the "object" of her medical experience.

Finally, the interpretation that emerges from analysis of the discrepancy of the meaning of "blood" for the young woman and her physician provides a first illustration of the claim that medicine as a symbolic form serves as an "organ of reality." "Blood" is a substantially different reality in the medical and religious discourses, and one does not have primacy over the other. The presence of the blood and the appropriate medical response depended primarily upon the physiological site of its origins. The meaning of the blood and therefore of the symptom, however, indeed the very nature of "blood" was for this young woman not separable from the place of blood in her religious discourse. In this discourse, its meaning is relational, and the relations are given only by the larger semiotic or mythic structure, as conveyed by the religious mythology of the Jehovah's Witnesses community.

The mythic structure provides the sufferer a frame for interacting with the social and physical environment and organizes it as a special form of reality. It is not, however, fully determinate of the personal meanings of the symptom. As Lévi-Strauss concludes his preface to Jakobson's lectures:

> ... a myth never offers a determined meaning to those who listen to it. A myth proposes a grid, definable only by its rules of construction. For the participants in the culture to which the myth belongs, this grid confers a meaning not on the myth itself but on everything else: that is, on the images of the world, of the society, and of its history, of which the members of the group are more or less aware, as well as on the images of the questions with which these various objects confront the participants. (Lévi-Strauss 1985: 145–146)

The religious reality of which blood was a part and the questions with which this cultural object confronted the young woman grew out of the position of blood in the semiotic system. The blood also, however, had a significant place in her life history, which she interpreted by means of the "mythic" structure. The bleeding she experienced thus mediated domains of experience, life history, and social relationships even as it mediated opposing fields of signs.

In this first example, I have examined a discrepancy between medical and religious formulations of reality – within a single culture, and in relation to a clear, physiological symptom. These two formulations are drawn from quite distinct social worlds and produce quite different interpretations of "blood," interpretations legitimized by different communities and institutional forces. However, the interaction between physician and patient and the differences in their understandings resulted in no overt conflict. The physician took a neutral, supportive stance toward this patient's "beliefs," and the interpretive discrepancies were quite subtle. And an anthropological analysis can explicate the differences between interpretations with relatively little epistemological worry. In the second case, to which I now turn, a more serious problem of anthropological interpretation arises. I examine a concept in Islamic medicine that seems to have no ready translation into biomedicine and its scientific referents. However, in this instance we can begin to see the role of a classical "scientific" concept in reproducing and rendering legitimate relations of power and inequality in the Islamic world. Here anthropological hermeneutics takes on a critical cast.

Hot and cold, raw, cooked, and rotten: the problem of digestion in Islamic medicine

Several decades of research on humoral medical systems – classical Greek medicine, Islamic and popular Hispanic traditions, Ayurveda, Chinese medicine – have had to face problems of translatability or commensurability of the kind widely discussed in philosophy in recent years.[5] Humoral medical systems conceive the universe as made of basic opposing qualities – hot and cold, wet and dry, in the Greek system – and physiological functioning as a set of interactions among basic constituent "humors" – blood, phlegm, yellow bile, and black bile, in the Greek and Islamic case. Historical and anthropological studies have made us familiar with classical traditions of humoral medicine, enabling us to discuss with little difficulty humoral classifications of illnesses or herbal remedies (as hot and cold) and associated therapeutic practices.[6] However, when pressed to spell out specific relations between humoral and biomedical categories, we are forced upon problems of cross-cultural misunderstanding of the sort to which Ardener referred in the essay I quoted at the opening of this chapter. For example, Browner and her colleagues (1988: 687) describe the two classificatory terms for uteroactive medicinal plants in highland Oaxaca, Mexico – plants which are "warming" and "irritating" – and the ethnophysiological concepts upon which these are based. However, when attempting to determine "the extent to which the phenomena described can be understood in terms of bioscientific concepts and methods," they conclude that the practical constraints on the translatability of the two concepts are quite different. "Whether or not these plants actually 'warm' (that is, change the quality of) the blood or body is not currently amenable to empirical validation using standard bioscientific methods. Empirical assessment of the remedies' 'irritating' effects using bioscientific techniques is more productive" (Browner et al. 1988: 687). They go on to show that those plants classified as "irritants" in the ethnomedical system do indeed contain uteroactive chemicals. However, the implications for the empiricist program of the non-translatability of the concept "warming," a category basic to the humoral tradition, is passed over without comment.

Finding biomedical equivalents of "warming" is a problem I will not be able to solve in the following discussion. "Warming" and "cooling" in classical Greek and Islamic medicine or in popular humoral traditions indeed seem untranslatable, although with time in a culture the categories increasingly make intuitive sense. However, beginning precisely with the acknowledgement that these categories are not "amenable to empirical validation using standard bioscientific methods," I want to explore what more we have to say once we recognize the limits of translatability.

The adjectives "hot" (*isdi*) and "cold" (*soğukh*) or "cool" (*serin*)[7] were constantly employed in popular reasoning about health and illness and in medical advice given by folk practitioners in the Turkish-speaking town in East Azerbaijan, Iran, when Mary-Jo and I carried out our research in the 1970s.[8] A neighbor of mine, a shopkeeper in his 50s, regularly replied to my salutations and inquiry "how are you?" with "*badan isdidi*," "my body is hot." I soon began attending to the temperature of my friends' hands when I greeted them. Illnesses were classified hot or cold, foods and herbal medicines as heating and cooling, and individuals and classes of persons were known to have a distinctive "temperament" (*tabi'i*) as more or less hot or cold. Gender, age, individual temperament, and type of illness were all taken into consideration when selecting a herbal remedy for a particular illness or when deciding what foods someone who was ill should avoid. I once heard two traditional women trying to determine the proper herbal remedy for the granddaughter of one of the women. The child had a stomach problem they believed was caused by problems of the liver. Because the child was a girl (and therefore of cool temperament), one of the women argued they should use cardamom, a hot remedy. The other woman argued that a hot drug would further heat the child's liver, causing her to have a skin rash. She suggested the child should be given a cool herb known to be good for stomach problems.

Humoral concepts also provided the basis for special diets followed at particular stages of life. For example, during their first forty days after the delivery of a child, women in the town were known to be weak and cool and thus vulnerable to cool illnesses. A special diet of hot foods, such as pistachios and eggs, was given to post-partum mothers to strengthen their bodies and combat coldness. It was often debated whether women who delivered baby girls should be given a concoction of honey, flour, and butter (known as *khurmagi*) to increase their bodily heat and ensure that the next child born would be a boy.[9] And so the discussions went. Hot and cold were simply part of everyday cognition and reasoning about diet and matters of health, illness and therapeutics, as well as about the emotions and social life.

While doing our research we tried to make rudimentary translations of the humoral system, to attach key terms to our own conceptual system and match these up to our experience in order to make sense of what we heard. It was not so difficult. Bodies are hot with fever and often cool when suffering an upset stomach. The elderly feel the need of heat more than the young. Many of the foods classed "hot" were high in energy, our friends told us, though some especially difficult to digest foods, such as animal fat, are cool. Despite this intuitive sense, much of what we learned remained quite fragmentary until we returned from research and went back to the classic Islamic and Greek medical texts. Reading these helped provide a systematic context for data that had seemed fragmentary. However, it also made clear the difficulties of the kind of common-sense translations we were making. Heat as a cosmological principle does not map neatly onto either common-sense experience or concepts from contemporary science. How then are we to deal with "misunderstandings" of this sort? In order to address this issue, I will take an anthropological excursion through several conceptual issues in Islamic medicine that provide the requisite context for understanding terms from popular medical culture in Iran, before returning to the problem of translatability.

"Heat" is a core concept in both classical Greek and Islamic physiology and medicine. To understand the concept, it is necessary to recognize that "heating" serves as a model of transformation that is central to theories of digestion. These provide the foundation for normal physiology, pathophysiology, and popular theories of illness in a way that is seldom recognized in either the historical literature or anthropological writing on humoral medicine.[10]

A central intellectual problem for Greek and Islamic medical theorists was the transformation of the "natural" into the "vital." Key to the growth, development, and health of the human body is the transformation of natural, raw aliment into the vital tissue constituent of each organ of the body.[11] Thus, scholarly discussion of the "nutritive" functions or digestion provided a key opportunity for speculation on this problem. In both the Greek and Islamic texts, the process of nutritive transformation is conceived through the master metaphors of cooking and fermentation (as of wine). The morbid inverse of the process is conceived as rotting and as souring or spoiling. These provide the underlying structure for nearly all normal and abnormal physiological processes and were understood in relation to the observed transformative powers of heat.

In the classic texts of Galen and Islamic theorists such as Ibn Sina (Avicenna), digestion is conceived as follows. When food is eaten, it undergoes "heating" or "cooking" first in the stomach and then in the liver, where it is transformed into the four humors. Blood is the primary product of the liver and travels from there to all organs of the body. One part of the blood travels to the heart, where it undergoes further cooking and is combined with the breath, thus being

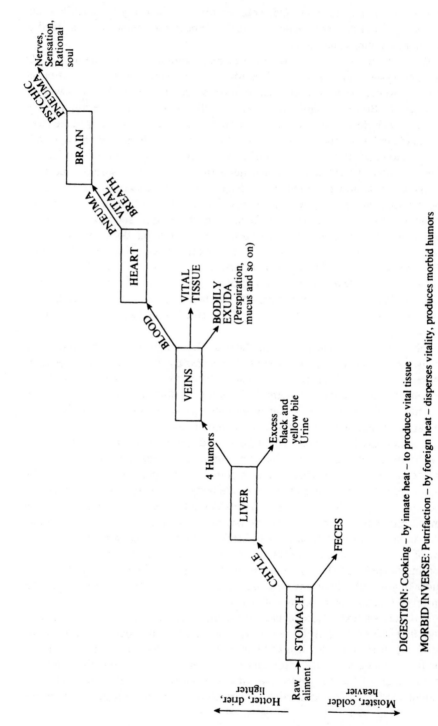

DIGESTION: Cooking – by innate heat – to produce vital tissue

MORBID INVERSE: Putrifaction – by foreign heat – disperses vitality, produces morbid humors

Figure 5 Digestion in classic Greco-Islamic medicine

transformed into the "vital breath." This vital breath or *pneuma*[12] travels through the arteries to each part of the body, where it interacts with the blood and "true assimilation" occurs, nourishing the organs (Ibn Sina, *Canon*: 113). The liver thus produces the "dense part" of the humors, the heart the "rarefied part," and the breath produces life. (See figure 5 for a schematic diagram of this process.)

The "cooking" begins in the stomach, surrounded as it is by the hot organs: the liver and spleen, the omentum (abdominal wall) and the heart (Ibn Sina, *Canon*: 88) . The stomach sorts out the indigestible material and transforms the raw food into "chyle," "a fluid or humor, preconcocted and already elaborated, but still needing its concoction to be completed" (Galen, *Usefulness*, I: 205).[13] However, it is in the liver that the most important digestion, the transformation of the food into blood, takes place. This process is typically described as "cooking" or as "fermentation." Al-Ruhawi, the medieval Islamic writer of the "Practical Ethics of the Physician," likens the liver to an "earthenware pot put on the hearth" (*Ethics*: 51). Galen (*Usefulness*, i: 204) compares the liver to a bakery:

> Just as city porters carry the wheat cleaned in the storehouse to some public bakery of the city where it will be baked and made fit for nourishment, so these veins carry the nutriment already elaborated in the stomach up to a place for concoction common to the whole animal, a place which we call the liver.

Elsewhere Galen likens the process of digestion to the fermentation of wine:

> Let us, then compare the chyle to wine just pressed from the grapes and poured into casks, and still working, settling, fermenting, and bubbling with innate heat. The heavy, earthy part of its residues, which I think is called the dregs, is sinking to the bottom of the vessels and the other, light, airy part floats. This latter part is called the flower and forms on the top of light wines in particular, whereas the dregs are more abundant in heavy wines. In making this comparison, think of the chyle sent up from the stomach to the liver as bubbling and fermenting like new wine from the heat of the viscus and beginning to change into useful blood; consider too that in this effervescence the thick, muddy residue is being carried downward and the fine thin residue is coming like foam to the top and floating on the surface of the blood. (*Usefulness*, I: 205–206)

The outcome of the "cooking" or "fermenting" is the production of blood. Bile is produced as a hot, light (dry) by-product which rises to the top as "foam" on the cooking blood or as the foamy "flower" on the fermenting wine. Black bile, the atrabilious humor, is the cold, heavy (moist) by-product, compared to the sediment or dregs, the earthy residue of fermentation. The degree of heat and extent of cooking are the primary determinants of the product of the transformation. Here Ibn Sina introduces the notion of over-heating and burning (or "oxidation"), to which we will refer in a moment.

> One must not forget that the most fundamental agents in the formation of the humours are heat and cold. When the heat is equable, blood forms; when heat is in excess, bilious humour forms; when in great excess, so that oxidation occurs, atrabilious humour forms. When the cold is equable, serous humour forms; when cold is in excess, so that congelation becomes dominant, atrabilious humour forms. (Ibn Sina, *Canon*: 90)

Thus the liver produces the humors, which are the basic agents of nutrition and constituents of the body. The two most important of these are the blood (sanguineous humor) and the phlegm (serous humor). Blood is the prime agent of nutrition; however, as it leaves the liver, "it is still charged in abundance with a thin, watery fluid which Hippocrates calls the vehicle of the nutriment . . . " (Galen, *Usefulness*, I: 207). Phlegm maintains the necessary moisture in the body; it provides nourishment for the organs of serous temperament, such as the brain; and it is "imperfectly matured blood" which may be transformed into blood through the action of innate heat (from cold and moist to hot and moist).

A portion of the blood, according to classical theory, passes through the vena cava directly to the right auricle of the heart. Here it is further cooked by innate heat of the heart, becoming hotter, thinner, lighter, purer, more "spirituous." It then passes to the right ventricle and on to the left ventricle: some through the lungs, which it nourishes; some through the thin, slightly porous membrane separating right and left ventricles. In the left ventricle, the blood receives a final cooking, and is united with the vital breath or *pneuma*, and the thin, spirituous blood, highly charged with life-giving *pneuma*, is sent into the arteries to carry out its nutritive function. Some of the vital *pneuma* proceeds to the arteries at the base of the brain, where it is further transformed into psychic *pneuma*. This *pneuma* serves the rational soul; it is sent out through the nerves, enabling them to provide sensation to all parts of the body.

The nutritive function is thus imaged as a series of stages of "cooking" that transform raw aliment into the humors, into blood, into a hot, attenuated blood, highly charged with vital *pneuma*, and finally into living tissue. At each stage the products of the coction are hotter and lighter, rising toward the realm of air and fire, ultimately in the direction of spirit and intellect as the rarefied blood is combined with the vital *pneuma*.[14] Proceeding in the opposite direction, a residue is produced at each stage that becomes an excrementitious discharge. Feces are produced from the concocting in the stomach; excess black and yellow bile are discarded from the cooking in the liver; urine from digestion in the liver and the nutrition of the kidneys. And all other exuda – perspiration, ear wax, saliva and mucus, eye sordes, nails, and hair – are produced in the final stage of transformation of aliment into living tissue.[15]

The classical tradition conceived a morbid physiological process that was imaged as "rotting," "putrification," or "stagnation" and that was the structural inverse of the process of cooking or fermenting of the aliment. This physiological process was considered the primary cause of disease. These metaphors were thus critical for medical reasoning. Ibn Sina describes the sources of disease as follows.

Our bodies are exposed to injury from two directions – one exterior and one interior. The interior source of injury is the dissipation of the moisture from which we are created, and this dissipation proceeds in an orderly manner. The second source is the putrefactive breakdown and metamorphosis of the humour, into a form such that the fermentive phenomena of life are no longer able to proceed.

The second source of injury differs from the first in that dryness is here introduced in virtue of *depravity* of humour; and this dryness continues neutralizing the moisture of the body until the "form" ceases to have a capacity for life.

Finally, the putrefactive breakdown disperses the vitality, because it first destroys the moisture and then disperses it, and simply dry ash is left behind. (Ibn Sina, *Canon*: 359)

Similarly, the great Islamic renaissance scholar Ibn Khaldun (*Muqaddimah*: vol. II, 375), describes how incompletely digested food rots and remains in the stomach, liver, or veins, where it produces a false heat. He compares the process in the body to "food that is left over and eventually becomes putrefied, and [to] dung that has become putrefied. Heat develops in it and takes its course." This heat is a primary source of fevers.

"Putrefactive decomposition," according to Ibn Sina, sets in when the innate heat of the body becomes "feeble," reducing the ability of the body to "effect digestion and maturation." Because the innate heat – "the intermediary between the natural faculties and the humours" – is weak, "stagnation sets in and foreign heat now finds the humours no longer opposed to its action" (Ibn Sina, *Canon*: 270). Rotting is caused by alien heat or "heat from a foreign source" which "unites with the moisture of the humours and alters their temperament in such a manner that it will no longer respond to the temperament of the natural breath" (Ibn Sina, *Canon*: 240).

"Stagnation" is often used in the *Canon of Medicine* almost interchangeably with "oxidation," that is burning or cooking at too high a heat. Either excessive heating, or occasionally excessive cooling, can reduce the humor to "ash." The process is compared to the charring of wood. "Thus, wood is first charred and finally becomes a white ash. Heat applied to a moist body makes it black; applied to a dry body it makes it white. Cold applied to a moist body makes it white, and applied to a dry body makes it black" (Ibn Sina, *Canon*: 84).

Both putrification and oxidation transform the humor into "morbid" humors, which contrast with the "sweet," healthy form. Each form of morbid humor has a distinctive color and taste, enabling the physician to identify it when it appears in the blood, feces, or urine or as a bad taste in the mouth of a patient.

Several causes are elaborated for the process of decomposition and the production of morbid humors. If food is not properly digested in the stomach, it may rot and stagnate. This may result from the consumption of too much food, especially cold food (al-Ruhawi, *Ethics*: 37, 51; Ibn Sina, *Canon*: 398). If additional food is eaten before previous food has been digested, the mixture may be passed to the liver before it is all turned to chyle, and "the unassimilated nourishment . . . becomes putrefied" (Ibn Khaldun, *Muqaddimah*: vol. II, 375). Morbid processes may also arise from drinking impure water. Rain water may become putrescent, if not boiled, and water that stands in marshy ground may become mixed with decomposing earth (Ibn Sina, *Canon*: 225–226). In addition, air may become putrid. This is particularly serious because air nourishes the vital breath or spirit: "It is the air that gives energy to the spirit and thus strengthens the influence of the natural heat upon digestion" (Ibn Khaldun, *Muqaddimah*: vol. II,

375; cf. vol. II, 136–137). For Ibn Khaldun, this provides one mechanism for the decline of civilizations. As population density increases, the air in the cities becomes putrid, and great epidemics result (*Muqaddimah*: vol. II, 136–137).[16]

The process of digestion – the metamorphosis of food into blood and tissue through cooking produced by innate heat – and the opposite or negative transform of digestion – the rotting of food or the humors to produce morbid humors, which are inassimilable and which disperse the moisture of the body – provided the basic structure for all physiological theory in classical Galenic–Islamic medicine. It also provided the theory upon which clinical diagnostics and therapeutics was based. Disease caused by the presence of a morbid humor is treated by evacuation of the abnormal matter. This may be accomplished through blood-letting, cupping with bleeding, leeches, purgation, emesis, cupping, enemas, sweating, and other less important therapeutic techniques.[17] Clinical medicine is the art of differentiating the normal from the abnormal (through attention to the temperament of the individual), of identifying abnormalities as signs of intemperament or evidence of morbid humors, and of prescribing medication or therapies for righting the intemperament or evacuating the morbid humors. From these simple structural principles, a great complexity of theorizing, observation, classification, and therapeutics was developed. And this theoretical tradition and the therapeutics that embraced these principles served as the basis for professional and popular medicine for a remarkable period of history across diverse civilizations (Temkin 1973).

At the beginning of this section, I posed the question of the translatability of the concept "warm" in humoral medicine, suggesting that it has no single reference "external to culture" which serves as the source of its meaningfulness and correspondence to a concept in our own medical theories. It should now be clear that translation of this simple term requires an excursion into a highly elaborate scientific and semiotic tradition, where "warming" is revealed as a central metaphor generative of much of the theorizing in Galenic–Islamic medicine. Interpretation of a single concept or lexical item thus involves comparisons of conceptual systems, the practices that enact and reproduce that system, and the "objects" produced by these activities, rather than a search for symbolic elements that map onto the same material referent. I am not suggesting that a concept from humoral medicine has no empirical relation to the material world – my Iranian neighbor who monitored his "temperature" attended closely to body sensations, while the classical pharmaceutical scholars were deeply interested in the empirical effects of a wide range of medicinal elements. The empirical relation cannot, however, be extracted from the conceptual structure that organized observation and experience and a set of scientific and clinical practices. It belongs to a system of knowing as well as a body of knowledge.

"Warm" and "cool," along with cooking as a metaphor of mediation and transformation, were central to Galenic–Islamic medical theorizing, and any translation of "warm" as a quality of herbal remedies must take this theoretical context into account. The opposition of "hot" and "cold" was also present, however, in the representation of social relations and in speculation about their cosmological foundations, and these also bear on the translatability of the concept. G. E. R. Lloyd's phrase "polarity and analogy" (Lloyd 1966) may serve as an entree to a brief discussion of how this opposition was extended to understanding the social world and the cosmos, and the implications of such metaphoric extensions for interpreting a form of medical knowledge.

"Polarity" was common to symbolic systems and scholarly argumentation from the Presocratics through the classics of Islamic science and cosmological writing. In one of the earliest contemporary accounts of symbolic dualism, Lloyd (1966; cf. 1973) described the wealth of opposing symbolic categories found in Greek cosmological writing, science, and religion, and the role in scientific reasoning of these oppositions and the analogical correspondences conceived to exist among them. According to Lloyd, Aristotle attributed the general doctrine that "most human things go in pairs" to Alcmaeon, whose theory he compares with the Table of Opposites of the Pythagoreans. "One group of Pythagoreans apparently referred to ten definite pairs of opposite principles: limited and unlimited, odd and even, one and plurality, right and left, male and female, at rest and moving, straight and curved, light and darkness, good and evil, square and oblong (*Metaph.* A 5 986a 22ff.)" (Lloyd 1966: 16). Many of the detailed theories relating physiological, psychological, and cosmological phenomena among the Greeks – Presocratics, Aristotle, Hippocrates, Galen – applied and elaborated these oppositions. For example, a group of theoretical debates concerning the differentiation of the sexes at birth was largely limited to rationalizing the presumed correlation of male, right, and hot, in contrast to female, left, and cold (Lloyd 1973: 171–176). Aristotle undertook animal dissections to disprove previous writers' views that the sex of a child is determined by its position on the right or left side of the mother's womb (males on the right, females on the left). Having concluded this theory was empirically invalid,[18] he nonetheless granted that "to suppose that the cause of male and female is heat and cold, or the secretion (*apokrisis*, that is, seed) which comes from the right or the left side of the body, *is not unreasonable* (*echei tina logon*)" (Lloyd 1973: 175). In this set of polar oppositions, those elements associated with the "right" were considered superior. The Pythagoreans associated the right with limit and good, the left with the unlimited and evil. Some Hippocratic writers explained differences between male and female as deriving from oppositions associated with right and left, superior and inferior. And Aristotle stated explicitly "that right is the origin of locomotion, and is better and nobler than its opposite, and he uses this theory quite extensively in accounting for such facts as the position of various organs in the body" (Lloyd 1973: 178–179). Needless to say, this semiotic structure rendered gender relations as inherent in the very syntax of knowledge and as given in the natural order, as I will note in a moment.

Greek forms of polarity and analogy were reproduced and elaborated in classical Islamic medicine, as well as astrology, numerology, cosmology, and other "sciences,"[19] and in popular medical treatises. However, elements from the

"Unani" or Greek tradition were combined with distinctively Islamic convictions (intense monotheism, Qur'anic cosmology, historical narratives of God's revelation), Sufism, the Middle Eastern Hermetic or wisdom (*hikmat*) tradition, and local cultural forms to create a uniquely Islamic discourse. For example, cosmologists joined Ptolemaic and Plotinian theories with Qur'anic elements. The cosmos was conceived as a united hierarchy of being, from the heavenly spheres that know "neither generation nor corruption nor change nor transformation nor augmentation nor diminution . . . "[20] to the sublunary world of generation and decay. Both man and jinns belonged to the sublunary world (though man's soul or rational faculty transcends corporeality), while the angels belong to the heavenly spheres. Humans and jinns thus interact routinely in much of the Islamic world, and jinns are ubiquitous as causes of illness, objects of therapeutics, or as possessing "winds" (see, for example, Safa 1988).

The classical symbolic oppositions and their correspondences were also joined to religious law and integrated into representations of the social order. For example, the Islamic polarity of the religiously "pure" and "impure" was joined to other symbolic oppositions (male/female, right/left), and popular medical treatises provided physiological explanations for the designation of bodily "residues" as impure (*najes*). Al-Suyutti's *Tibb-ul-Nabbi* (p. 171) notes, "The waste products of the digestion which occurs in the heart and in the bladder are the growth of hair. Religious Law orders these hairs to be plucked in the case of the armpits and to be shaved in the case of the pubes." Social categories – gender, age, physical and psychological temperament, race, and national character – were all represented as having distinctive natural qualities and temperaments. For example, al-Ruhawi (*Ethics*: 48) wrote that "in the age of children, there is great heat due to the proximity of its period to the beginning of existence – to the seminal fluid, blood, and soul – all of which are hot . . . In old age, there is coldness because of remoteness from the origins previously mentioned."[21] As I described in the opening paragraphs of this section, these associations continue to serve as the grammar for social classification in popular discourse in Iran today.

I have outlined this analysis of the structure of Galenic–Islamic medical knowledge in some detail to indicate the difficulties facing translation as conceived within the empiricist paradigm. Key terms in the humoral tradition are not given meaning by "an external category of more or less universal reference," and a program of research designed to determine the relation of such terms to bioscientific concepts by investigating how both map onto things in the "mind independent world" (Putnam 1981: 72) faces grave difficulties. This is not to suggest that there are no empirical correlates of humoral concepts; as I have argued several times, both pharmaceutical research in Safavid Iran and popular therapeutics in Maragheh in recent years relied upon empirical observation and experience. However, translations that depend upon "external categories" face problems similar to those Putnam finds for the "similitude theory of reference": "The trouble is not that correspondences between words or concepts and other entities don't exist, but that too many correspondences exist. To pick out just one correspondence between words or mental signs and mind-independent things we would have already to have referential access to the mind-independent things" (Putnam 1981: 72–73).

Putnam goes on to argue that his rejection of the correspondence theory of meaning does not signal his acceptance of the "incommensurability thesis" of Feyerabend and Kuhn.

> The incommensurability thesis is the thesis that terms used in another culture, say, the term "temperature" as used by a seventeenth-century scientist, cannot be equated in meaning or reference with any terms or expressions *we* possess. As Kuhn put it, scientists with different paradigms inhabit "different worlds". . . . The rejoinder this time is that if this thesis were really true then we could not translate other languages – or even past stages of our own language – at all. And if we cannot interpret organisms' noises at all, then we have no grounds for regarding them as *thinkers, speakers,* or even *persons.* (Putnam 1981: 114)

Here, one can only respond with Ardener that "when the issues are big enough there is no recourse but to firmly universalistic principles" (1982: 3). For the anthropologist, however, the problem of misunderstanding "at the level of close interactions" is not solved simply by adhering to maxims of "interpretive charity" advanced by Putnam and Davidson. Davidson holds with Putnam that the fact that we can converse with and translate the statements of members of another culture is adequate reason to reject the notion of "incommensurability." He goes on to state this as a methodological proposal.

> In the case of language, the basic strategy must be to assume that by and large a speaker we do not yet understand is consistent and correct in his beliefs – according to our own standards of course. Following this strategy makes it possible to pair up sentences the speaker utters with sentences of our own that we hold true under like circumstances. When this is done systematically, the result is a method of translation. (Davidson 1980: 238–239)

As a warning that places boundaries on claims of cognitive relativism, this philosophical move seems reasonable.[22] As a practical approach for the comparative study of medical systems, however, Davidson's proposal (cf. Davidson 1974) is wholly inadequate. The data I have presented to this point allow several methodological conclusions about how we can interpret concepts such as the hot and cold of humoral systems without resort to either empiricist hermeneutics or a simple matching up of pairs of sentences.

First, I argued in chapter 3 that the comparative study of medical systems and medical knowledge should begin with attention to the interpretive practices formative of the medical lifeworld. I began with medical practices because of my conviction that meaning and reference can only be understood – and translated – in the context of practical activities and engaged sense-making. In contrast to the analysis of "behavior," often conceived as an individual's actions that are motivated and organized by his or her beliefs, medical "practices" are best understood as elementary forms of social activity from which individual functioning springs.[23] An anthropological hermeneutics requires not merely a mapping of symbolic elements from one system to another or a pairing up of sentences, but a comparison of the situated practices through which knowledge is produced and elaborated.

Second, in this chapter, I have evoked a rather broad conception of "semiotics" to argue that translation requires the interpretation of symbolic elements in relation to a field of signs. Structuralist analyses have made it plain that cultural symbols attain their meaning and significance relationally – that is through their opposition and correspondence to other symbols. But binary oppositions are only one example of a more general set of symbolic relationships. Symbols can only have their meaning through their relation to other symbols and in the context of a larger symbolic order. Cassirer outlined a theoretical frame for such a position, in particular in his espousal of the "functional" (or relational) rather than "substantivist" character of numbers in mathematics and of scientific knowledge more generally.[24] It follows that any serious analysis of a given concept within a particular system of medical knowledge requires an understanding of that concept in a field of symbolic relations. Such analysis leads directly to questions about the larger cosmological scheme framing these relations and the "*episteme*" that governs what kinds of symbolic relations will be counted as knowledge for members of the society being studied. The naturalistic tendency to map symptom to physiological site, complaint to the bedrock of biology, obscures the relational meaning of elements in all medical systems – or simply reproduces symbolic relations that emerge from our own empiricist semiology.

It should also be clear, however, that a system of medical knowledge and the practices through which it is reproduced, elaborated, and applied are interrelated in ways far more complex than those suggested by belief and behavior models. In his study of variation and change in male initiation rituals and the "tradition of knowledge which they sustain" in a New Guinea society, Fredrik Barth (1987) demonstrates that accounting for the creative modification of that tradition depends on a recognition of the "metapremise" that ritual knowledge is hidden and esoteric, and on a detailed understanding of the social forms of the ritual practice, and the ends to be accomplished by ritual activity. "That which is created is not a text, a 'work' of art or science, but a transformation of a group of young persons into men who think and feel about – sense – nature and themselves in certain ways and with certain imagery" (Barth 1987: 79). I suggested in my analysis of Galenic–Islamic medicine that the semiotic structure of humoral medicine was closely associated with distinctive medical and scientific practices, but did not attempt to demonstrate this in detail. I want only to note here that Unani medicine functioned both as a speculative science and as a therapeutic or clinical practice (among professional, folk, and popular practitioners), and although sharing a formal symbolic structure, these two forms of activity presumed quite different ends. For the scholars, that which was created *was* a text, a work of science, and the norms of adhering to the classic tradition while reconciling Greek and Islamic elements served as the meta-premise for scientific practice. For medical practitioners, on the other hand, that which is created is the transformation of an individual sufferer or a community, and the therapeutic imperative provides quite different premises for practice. The translation of concepts such as "hot" and "cold" in the humoral system thus requires analysis of both semiotics and practices, scientific and therapeutic, and the interrelations among these.

A third methodological implication to be drawn from the analyses here is that translation depends on our understanding not only the symbolic forms of medical knowledge and the formative practices with which they are associated, but the modes of experience they mediate. I have alluded briefly to this issue in my discussion (in chapter 3) of "seeing" as a form of medical practice, a basis for knowledge claims, and a mode of experience in contemporary biomedicine. I also described briefly the forms of experience made relevant by humoral medicine – both for practitioners engaged in diagnostic work, and for the interpretation of bodily experience by lay persons. Chapters 5 and 6 will return to the analysis of intersubjective experience in greater detail, indicating how social and symbolic forms provide members of a society access to distinctive modes of experience. However, it is important to follow Cassirer again in noting that the symbolic forms mediate the "sensuous" or "sensate" (*Sinnliches*) and the "sense" (*Bedeutung*, meaning) it embodies, and that the two are closely linked in our experience and knowledge of aspects of reality (Hamburg 1949: 84). Interpretation thus requires an implicit or explicit phenomenology.

Finally, my discussion of Galenic–Islamic medicine gave some indication of how medical knowledge serves simultaneously as a theory of the human body and as a basis for reflection on and reproduction of social relations. The symbolic oppositions from Greek medicine and cosmology provide a kind of grammar for some aspects of social relations in Islamic societies such as Iran today. Relations of hot/cold, wet/dry, and right/left, further linked to the Islamic pure/impure opposition, are assumed in discussions of gender and age, as well as in commentaries on the effects of some rituals or on the closeness of social relationships. (For example, funerals are said to cool the passions, sermons and Moharram rites to heat the passions and arouse righteous indignation and resolve [M. Good and B. Good 1989].) My analysis of these relations, however, has not drawn Durkheimian conclusions (that symbolic structures reflect more fundamental structures of society) nor has it been an attempt to emulate the highly abstract analyses of Lévi-Strauss.[25] Islamic medicine was always Greek medicine – *Tibb Unani* – and was only one of several competing and overlapping conceptual systems drawn upon in the representation of social relations in Iranian society. Indeed, these oppositions are limited in their cultural elaboration and emotional intensity (in contrast with the Moharram narratives, for example), and studies of such oppositions only begin to tell us how Greek medicine is integrated into local cultural worlds in Islamic societies. We have argued elsewhere that studies of semantic networks provide a better means of investigating how the language and practices of Greek medicine could be used to articulate very local meanings and social relations (B. Good 1977; B. Good and M. Good 1982, 1992). It is important, however, to recognize explicitly the extent to which gender relations were rendered natural through Galenic–Islamic medicine, indexed as a reflection of biology and cosmology, inherent in the very syntax of knowledge.

Symbolic oppositions from Islamic medicine served not only to reflect on social relations, but to render them legitimate and thus reproduce relations of power and inequality (see B. Good and M. Good 1992 for a discussion). More than a generation of feminist scholarship has shown how the correspondence of the male/female opposition to others which index superiority/inferiority relations (right/left, hot/cold, pure/impure) serves to reproduce gender hierarchy and legitimize everyday practices that instantiate hierarchy.[26] "Hot" and "cold" were essential to Greek biological reasoning on the differentiation of male and female – on conception, the relation of semen and menses, and the intellectual superiority of men. Lloyd notes that Aristotle's view that "males are hotter than females depends first on the notion that semen and menses are the end-products of strictly comparable processes, and . . . on the quite arbitrary assumption that semen is the *natural* product of the process of concoction, and the menses are an *impure* residue" (Lloyd 1966: 59).[27] These views were maintained in the Galenic corpus, in Islamic science, and in popular medical culture in Islamic societies. For example, Delaney (1987) argues that even in Turkey, where hot/cold distinctions are hardly recognized, fundamental conceptions of male–female relations and sexual honor and shame refer ultimately to theories of procreation and the cultural biology of reproduction.[28] Men provide the generative seed, women the field within which the seed grows. Men's honor resides in shielding their wives from access to other men, thus ensuring the legitimacy of their children. And male and female stand in a hierarchical relationship, closely related to the classical Islamic cosmology.

> In this cosmological system the material, unregenerate, and eventually perishable aspects of life and women associated with it are devalued in relation to and encompassed by the creativity and spiritual essence of men and God. . . . As the world is dependent on and encompassed by God, so too are women dependent on and encompassed by men (Delaney 1987: 44)

Thus, she argues, the honor/shame complex "is a distinctive system in which power, sex, and the sacred are interrelated and seen to be rooted in the verities of biology. The 'truth' of biology is, in this case, the particular (and peculiar) theory of monogenesis" (Delaney 1987: 45).

The biology of "monogenesis," which holds that men's seed alone provides the creative source for the "fathering" of children, differs from that of Galen, who held that embryos are the joint product of fluid from testis and ovary (see M. Good 1980 for a fuller analysis). However, the monogenetic theory of procreation is widespread in the Islamic world, and is widely accepted as a part of Greco-Islamic physiology. "Hot" and "cold" thus serve as the basis for social knowledge, and power, sex, and the sacred are naturalized and seen to be rooted in the "verities of biology." Because Greek medicine was introduced into societies in which such gender relations were long established, however, one might also argue that the acceptance of this tradition and the conviction of its efficacy arose not merely from the physiological effects of its therapeutics. Greco-Islamic biology was widely felt to be veridical, and in its popular medical form to have cultural authority, in part because it provided a model that linked power, sex, gender relations, and the sacred.

I began this analysis of Islamic medicine with the observation that "misunderstanding" is almost certain to result from efforts to translate the humoral concept "hot," especially if we attempt to relate it to a comparable biomedical concept. I have attempted to show that a repair of understanding in this case will not be accomplished by testing the empirical validity of the concept but only by a classic hermeneutic strategy. Only by moving recursively from text to context, situating the concept "hot" in a semiotic field, a set of medical and speculative practices, domains of intersubjective experience made available by these practices, and the larger field of social relations can we provide a coherent interpretation of the concept. Medical knowledge cannot be abstracted from a symbolic formation and a set of social relations. Medical knowledge is at the same time social knowledge. The comparative study of forms of medical knowledge thus requires a critical hermeneutics of the kind outlined here. And such an approach raises a host of researchable questions quite different from those made apparent by the empiricist program.

5

The body, illness experience, and the lifeworld: a phenomenological account of chronic pain

In his book *Objective Knowledge*, Karl Popper (1972: 106) outlines a "three-world" theory, which serves as the basis for his epistemological arguments:

> we may distinguish the following three worlds or universes: first the world of physical objects or physical states; secondly, the world of states of consciousness, or mental states, or perhaps behavioral dispositions to act; and thirdly, the world of *objective contents of thought*, especially of scientific and poetic thoughts and of works of art.

What I have described as biomedicine's "folk epistemology" is consistent with such an ordering of reality. Disease is located in the body as a physical object or physiological state, and whatever the subjective state of individual minds of physicians and patients, medical knowledge consists of an objective representation of the diseased body. I have argued for an anthropological alternative to such an analysis of medical knowledge, based on a critical examination of how medical practices and ontologies shape the objects of medical attention. However, the difficulties with the objectivist account are more immediately evident when we look closely at illness and its experience. For the person who is sick, as for the clinician, the disease is experienced as present in the body. But for the sufferer, the body is not simply a physical object or physiological state but an essential part of the self. The body is subject, the very grounds of subjectivity or experience in the world, and the body as "physical object" cannot be neatly distinguished from "states of consciousness." Consciousness itself is inseparable from the conscious body. The diseased body is therefore not simply the object of cognition and knowledge, of representation in mental states and the works of medical science. It is at the same time a disordered agent of experience.

In a biographical account of his experience of major depression, *Darkness Visible: A Memoir of Madness*, William Styron writes of how he first began to notice the onset of his illness. "It was not really alarming at first," he writes (1990: 42), "but I did notice that my surroundings took on a different tone at certain times: the shadows of nightfall seemed more somber, my mornings were less buoyant, walks in the woods became less zestful . . . " Changes there were, certainly, in the body as physiological state, however much neuroscientists may still disagree about just which changes are decisive for melancholia or major depressive episodes. But for Styron, it was the world that first seemed to change. With hindsight, he came to interpret those changes as part of the process of the illness, but the body as physical object and as agent of experience did not belong to separate worlds. The illness was present in the lived body. It was experienced as a change in the lifeworld.

For some medical conditions, the objectivist rendering of the body has served medicine reasonably well. For other processes to which medicine attends – birth, or chronic illness, for example – the abstracting of a world of physical objects and physiological processes from social and meaningful phenomena ("birthing," "illness") has led to a rational but highly distorted form of medical practice. For yet other conditions, such as chronic pain, the distinction between the world of physical objects and mental states so obscures understanding as to render the phenomenon largely unintelligible. Chronic pain challenges a central tenet of biomedicine – that objective knowledge of the human body and of disease are possible apart from subjective experience (M. Good et al. 1992). The folk distinction between the world of objective reality and that of subjective experience also raises havoc in the management of pain in the "social body" and the "body politic," where policies concerning compensation or disability payments break down over debates about how to provide objective markers of pain.[1] The integration of human experience into accounts of disease is thus a constant challenge for medical discourse and policy debates.

When one turns to the human sciences for guidance, remarkably little is to be found. The literature on illness representations is voluminous – in history, literary studies, the social sciences, and the medical humanities, whether analyzed as beliefs or cultural models or illness narratives or mystified social relations. But detailed, ethnographic accounts of illness experience, or a well wrought theoretical vocabulary for the study of illness as human experience, are largely absent. We know intuitively that ritual practices of mourning and experiences of grief have important differences both within and across cultures, quite different trajectories and rhythms, and that the two answer to quite different analyses. But although the study of funeral rituals is extensive, it is nearly impossible to find experience-near accounts of grief.[2] The same is remarkably true for the study of illness. Although descriptions of healing rituals are plentiful, the difficulty of finding full, rich accounts of the experience of important forms of illness is startling. More than that we hardly know what such studies should look like. Indeed the assumption that experience is subjective, belonging to the "dark grottoes of the mind," and therefore ultimately unknowable, undermines any effort to develop comparative studies of particular forms of human experience.

In medical anthropology, this is an issue we can no longer neglect. Research that attends only to semiotic structures or social processes seems to miss the essence of what gives illness its mystery and human suffering its potency. Even more importantly, however, any truly anthropological account of illness cannot afford to attend only to objective disease and to cultural representation, with subjective experience bracketed as a kind of black box. A primary claim that I have been developing in these pages is that medical knowledge is socially and culturally variant, and that in part this is true because illness itself, the object of medical knowledge, is socially and culturally variant. An understanding of what this could mean, the development of a theoretical frame to account for findings of enormous variation in the course and prognosis of such profoundly debilitating diseases as schizophrenia, and the development of categories and methods for investigating how illness varies across cultures all require serious attention to what Arthur and Joan Kleinman (1991) have recently called the "ethnography of experience."

This chapter is written as a contribution to the development of a theory of illness experience. Rather than the body as site of domination or the object of medical practice, my primary attention in this chapter will be focused on the body as creative source of experience. The relations among embodied experience, intersubjective meaning, narratives that reflect and rework illness experience, and the social practices that mediate illness behavior are central to my account. More specifically, this chapter is a methodological exercise. It is an effort to provide an account of illness experience drawing on the phenomenological analyses of Alfred Schutz. A single case study of an individual suffering chronic pain serves as the primary data. My hypothesis is that as Styron describes in his memoir, serious illness, along with grief and other extreme experiences, provokes a shift in the embodied experience of the lifeworld, leading to what literary theorist Elaine Scarry (1985) calls "the unmaking of the world." I argue that we can specify in phenomenological terms several features of this process, which may prove useful in future comparative studies. I argue that social structures and practices mediate and further shape the "unmaking" of the lifeworld, requiring us to pursue a "critical" phenomenology. And I explore the hypothesis that narrative, the imaginative linking of experiences and events into a meaningful story or plot, is one of the primary reciprocal processes of both personal and social efforts to counter this dissolution and to reconstitute the world.

Data for my discussion are drawn from several studies on chronic pain carried out with my colleagues at Harvard Medical School.[3] I begin with an analysis of the text of a single, four hour interview with a twenty-eight year old man suffering from chronic pain, and develop the themes of my analysis in relation to this case. I discuss the case in three parts: the "narrative," the "phenomenology," and the "symbolization."[4]

The narrative: the origin myth and a life history of pain

"Doctor, is it possible that an experience in childhood can cause pain like this?" I was greeted at the door to my office in the Medical School by a sixty-four year old man bringing his twenty-eight year old son for an interview. The older man was tall and fairly thin, had a sagging face, and showed sadness and concern. The son looked even younger than his twenty-eight years, walked rather stiffly, his face frozen and expressionless, perhaps, it appeared, the result of medications. I deflected the question, though it remained among us, asked them to join me and sit down, explained that I was an anthropology professor, not a physician or a therapist, and invited the younger man, whom I'll call Brian, to participate in the study. He agreed readily, and with his permission, I invited his father to remain for the interview.

What followed was a remarkable story of a life of pain – a pain with a haunting origin myth, a pain that radically shaped the lifeworld of a young man, a pain for which he struggled to find meaning and a language for expression. After asking a few brief questions about his background, I asked Brian to tell me about his pain, to tell me the story about when it began and how he had tried to treat it. The narrative that evolved represented an effort to give shape to the pain, to name its origins in time and space, to construct a biography that made sense of a life of suffering.

He had a clear name for his pain – "I describe it as TMJ" – and a moment of diagnosis – the fall of 1984, November, recognized by a general physician who noticed snapping and clicking in his jaw when he opened and closed his mouth. But the description of his pain and its history quickly eluded ordered characterization, spilling out into his life.

> . . . I always seemed to have these things happening to me. I'd encounter dizzy spells and not know why I'd had them. . . . I was depressed and would just always be seeing counselors, would always be in a therapist's office for one reason or another. Then, [I had] the headaches, the dizzy sensations, sometimes had nausea that accompanies it. . . . it erupts in different places in your body. It comes in my head, then I have pains in my chest, . . . it starts radiating and going into your joints and going, traveling around inside your body, it's like a heat . . . it's a burning type of a heat, and ah wrenching, and you feel it traveling along and then it . . .

But when did it all begin? "it might have . . . begun in adolescence, although it became more pronounced, as uh, as I got older . . . " But did you seek treatment for it in high school? "I hadn't even thought of it or interpreted it as a physical problem." As psychological? " . . . even before I entered high school I think I was seeing therapists, and even when I was a child I was seeing therapists." So you have a long history with psychological counselors? " . . . a very long history . . . " Since the time your father mentioned, since you were two? "Yeah."

There are no secrets here, no mysteries to find voice for the first time. A generation of therapists have heard the story. But it remains primeval, mysterious.

> at about that time, Mother had become gravely ill and she wasn't able to take care of me, and Father didn't feel in a place where he could do . . . a good job of it either. He didn't want to have relatives come on the scene and take care of me. So, there was a . . . an . . . institution . . . an orphanage of some sort. . . . So I spent a period of three months when I was two years of age and . . . it might have just come in right at that time . . . that stripped me of any parental attachment. And ah . . . it was very traumatic. I have no conscious memory of it, but . . . something that damaged my feelings in the process.

And so a story took shape. The mother of this small child had hepatitis and was hospitalized. His father chose not to leave him in the care of the family members, but to the care of an orphanage he trusted. The infant emerged three months later completely changed, a "zombie," he says. Brian was considered to be of above average intelligence in his childhood, but he was extremely sensitive and suffered spells of anxiety, of panic.

During adolescence Brian began to have pain – increasingly intense pain, "chronic headaches, radiating pains in and around my head, in the ear canal, and my throat." He had spasms in his mouth and felt he was being choked. His depression and spells of anxiety continued; he would get anxious, dizzy, feel the terror of losing control. And then, "over a long period of time the depression sets in, the chronic malaise and fatigue." He has been treated with both anti-depressant and anti-anxiety medications, and was taking both at the time of the interview. The mysterious events within the walls of the orphanage, hidden from view and prior to symbolized memory, are inscribed in his personal history as well as his body, evoking terror unmitigated by medication or psychotherapy.

Overlapping this narrative, a second unfolds. In 1984, three successive physicians, treating him for congestion and pain in his ears and head, heard a clicking and popping sound in his jaw, suggested he might be suffering from "temporomandibular joint disorder" or TMJ, and recommended restorative dentistry. An ENT specialist explained his problem as "a malfunction of the jaw." Thus began a reinterpretation of all of his pain. "I was still a little bit skeptical about the whole thing." But when the third consecutive physician mentioned the problem, "I said well, now, there's just no way of ducking it anymore." As a consequence, "I began to think that this is something that may have a physical basis in my jaw and that I'd better start looking into . . . actually see where it leads me, and the whole idea was . . . one of hope, I guess, because now I had pinpointed something and defined it in a way. I can say that it's in my head, but it's not all in my head."

Since that time, his life has been ordered in part by relationships with a succession of medical specialists. He has been to several dentists, who focused on the problem of misalignment of his jaw and treated him with occlusal devices. He spent over a year in treatment with a physical therapist, who undertook deep tissue massage of his entire body. Most recently he had gone to a surgeon for further evaluation. He has had periods of respite and hope, when treatments seemed to be having some benefit, but each has been short-lived. The latest set of x-rays and evaluation found no abnormality requiring surgery, and the surgeon recommended relaxation, meditation, and exercise. "And how did this strike you?" I asked.

> Well, it sort of was an answer I may have been able to give myself actually. I didn't need to see a specialist for that. . . . it's back to an ambiguity again. And then it goes back into my conflict about my body. Is it my body? Is it my thinking process that activates physical stresses? Or am I, or is it the other way around? It's all that uncertainty that . . .

"No magic bullet," I said.
Yeah, no magic bullet. Every time I look for one, I seem to encounter just another
... maze or morass of things ...

Two narrative structures, attempts to authorize the self, follow patterns all
too recognizable to those who study chronic pain in Western culture. Soma is
juxtaposed to Psyche. The body as object of treatment and source of hope is
juxtaposed to life history as the source of suffering and psyche the object of
therapy. These life stories represent competing narratives or plots, competing
efforts to, as Paul Ricoeur (1981a: 278) says, "extract a configuration from a
succession." All narratives, as theorists from Aristotle to Kenneth Burke to
Hayden White have shown, are stories about lived experience.[5] They describe
events along with their meaning for persons who live in and through them. They
"emplot" experience, revealing its underlying form. The two narratives that
emerged in Brian's account are attempts to link his lived experience to an underlying coherence, a story line, a meaning. And the story has a quality Ricoeur
(1981a: 277) calls "directedness," a teleology, a sense that the story is going somewhere. The narratives are aimed not only at describing the origins of suffering, but
at imaging its location and source and imagining a solution to the predicament.
When the imagined outcome of the story fails to materialize, however, when
suffering is not relieved, neither narrative gains authority, and the self is
threatened with dissolution.

The phenomenology: the shaping of a world of pain

Elaine Scarry, in her book *The Body in Pain: The Making and Unmaking of the
World* (1985), provides an arresting description of the nature of pain, based on
analyses of descriptions of torture. Acute pain resists language, she says. It is
expressed in cries and shrieks, in a presymbolic language, resisting entry into the
world of communication and meaning. It "shatters" language (p. 5); indeed,
"intense pain is world-destroying" (p. 29).

Unlike torture victims, for many pain patients, language is far from shattered in
a literal sense. Brian was frighteningly articulate, though language at times
seemed inadequate to express the subtle sentient quality of his suffering. As he
sat stiffly and quietly, he described so rich an inner world that I listened with
astonishment. At the same time, his pain has a "world-destroying" quality. It
shapes his world to itself, resists objectification and threatens the structure of his
everyday life.

"How would you describe what's going on inside of your body?" I asked.
Sometimes, if I had to visualize it, it would seem as though there there's a
ah ... ama, a demon, a monster, something very horro, horrible lurking around banging
the insides of my body, ripping it apart. And ah, I'm containing it, or I'm trying to
contain it, so that no one else can see it, so that no one else can be disturbed by it.
Because it's scaring the daylights out of me, and I'd assume that ... gee, if anybody had
to, had to look at this, that ah ... they'd avoid me like the plague. So I redouble my

efforts to . . . say . . . I'm gonna be perfectly contained about this whole thing. And
maybe the less I do, the less I make myself known, and the less I, I ah, I venture out or
. . . or display any, any initiative, then I won't let the, this junk out. It seems like there's
something very, very terrible happening. I have no control over it . . .

Through the haunting words and menacing images of his description, Brian
provides us access to a world of pain. It is a shocking world of monsters ripping
apart his body, a private world he fears to share with others, a world they could
not possibly understand, and yet a world absolute and inescapable for him, which
he wants desperately to construe as imaginary but cannot. At the same time,
through great determination, Brian has continued to go to work every day as a
claims processor in a private insurance company. He lives with his family, attends
meetings of a support group, visits physicians and therapists, attends classes at
night, and is a painter.

Worlds of experience

What do we mean by invoking the term "world" in this context, and how is it
related to an analysis of experience? Do we gain analytic power by speaking of the
world of the chronic pain sufferer? In what way can chronic pain be said to
"unmake" the world for the sufferer?

The term "world" as used throughout this analysis is derived from a long
history of phenomenologically oriented philosophers and social scientists – from
Husserl, Merleau-Ponty, and Sartre to Nelson Goodman, and from William James
to Alfred Schutz and various contemporary sociologists and anthropologists. For
Husserl, the "lifeworld," the *Lebenswelt*, is the world of our common, immediate,
lived experiences (see Cockelmans 1967). This world is often contrasted with the
objective world of the sciences, and many assume that the latter represents reality
in the strict sense of the word. Husserl and like-minded social scientists have
argued that rather than the lifeworld presupposing this scientific world, the
obverse is true. Science is grounded in the lifeworld. It assumes a particular
perspective, a particular attitude to be taken toward reality, and it constitutes
distinctive forms of knowledge, but it presupposes dimensions of experience and
its interpretation common to the lifeworld (see Brand 1967).

The scientific world is only one of several worlds or "subuniverses" in which
we live, worlds which include those of religious experience, of dreams and
fantasies, or music and art, and of the "common-sense" reality which is paramount
in much of our lives.[6] These are not simply forms of individual experience, but
diverse worlds, with distinctive objects, symbolic forms, social practices, and
modes of experience.

Merleau-Ponty followed Husserl in situating phenomenology between
empiricism and transcendental idealism. Phenomenology is a descriptive science,
he wrote, that "offers an account of space, time and the world as we 'live' them"
and "tries to give a direct description of our experience as it is . . . " (1962: vii).
The world is constituted prior to our entry into it; it is not a result of our thinking

– we are thrown into it. (And thus he pursues a critique of transcendental idealism.) It is an intersubjective world, a social and cultural world, a world that resists our desire to shape it to our own whims, a world of social and empirical facts and realities that cannot be wished away.

In *Phenomenology of Perception*, Merleau-Ponty (1962) elaborates an analysis of the body as the ultimate medium of experience and thus of our understanding of the phenomenal world.[7] Rather than beginning his analysis with the division between objective world and experiencing subject, he starts with the "preobjective," the existential beginnings of "the experience of perceiving in all its indeterminacy and richness" (Csordas 1990: 9; cf. Merleau-Ponty 1962: 207–242). He then examines the movement of perception from the body, the grounds of experience and intentionality, to the objects as constituted in perception. His analysis has served as the basis for recent discussions of embodiment, in philosophy and medical anthropology.[8] This phenomenological tradition suggests that in attempting to understand the experiential world of chronic pain, or to study illness experience cross-culturally, we must explore the organization of embodied sentience, of experience in all its sensual modalities, as well as the objects of experience. The rhythms and disruptions of experience presume a socially organized lifeworld, and a description of the contours of the social world as experienced requires attention not only to the cognitive shaping of experience, but to the sensual body as well.[9]

In Brian's description, bodily experience assumes enormous proportions. Arising from the jaw joint, the pain quickly eludes narrow characterization, as Brian describes the flood of sensations and the anxiety it engenders. Panic merges again into his description of pain.

> It goes into the head . . . the maxillary muscles . . . in the roof of my mouth would get all tightened up, and so I had to drink something warm to relax it. And it goes down here, and people would describe it as being choked or having this lump of . . . this sensation of being restricted all the way through here. [He gestured to his throat and chest.] And it starts going down. And then as your anxiety builds, . . . and you start feeling other things, and . . . sensations of heartburn and ah . . . sometimes, I get . . . dizzy along with that. I start to breathe more rapidly. . . . the scariest part of it is that I'm losing control . . . I attributed ah weakness in my leg to that and having stress in one leg more than the other . . . it's always my left hand that seems to be . . . have more pain in it than in the . . . these ah, muscle cramps that go down my ah left arm, and sometimes a numb sensation in my hand . . . Seems like at the worst moments, all my symptoms are ah prevalent . . . I have to do something. I've gotta get things done. I'm ah, I'm working and ah, why do I have to, have to have the allness of this type of, of affliction.

Pain becomes an "all," an experience of totality, not a single set of feelings but a dimension of all his perception. It flows out from the body into the social world, invading his work and infiltrating everyday activities.

The self is constituted in relation to a world, and it is not only through direct description of embodied experience but through the description of that lifeworld that we have access to the selves of others.[10] Persons suffering chronic illness or the "reality shock" of life-threatening conditions often describe their feeling that the world has changed.[11] Much of the taken-for-granted of common-sense reality is recognized as conventional. The mutuality of the world, the sense that the world we live in is common to those around us, gives way. Significance shifts; quite different things in life come to matter. The challenge that chronic or life-threatening illness poses for the sufferer's sense of reality, its threat to "unmake" or transform the world (Scarry 1985), suggests a method for investigating the phenomenology of illness experience.

Chronic pain and the unmaking of the "world of everyday life"

Alfred Schutz (1971), in his essay "On Multiple Realities," follows other phenomenologists in distinguishing the "world of everyday life" from other primary forms of reality – dreams, fantasies, the world of art, science, the world of religious experience. Each of these has distinctive characteristics, distinct forms of organizing experience and modes of acting, which Schutz attempted to identify and analyze. For example, he showed that "common-sense" reality is characterized by the natural attitude, one in which objects are taken-for-granted rather than submitted to critical attention, as in the scientific attitude. It is the world of our everyday activities and projects, rather than a world of theory or imagination. Each form of reality is a distinctive "province of meaning" and mode of experience. It is my contention that Schutz's categories of analysis of "common-sense reality" can provide the basis for inquiring into the world of chronic illness, examining how the everyday world is systematically subverted or "unmade." I would argue that we can use this method to further social and cultural analysis, whether we follow Whorf and Hallowell in investigating the shaping of perception by language and culture, or Mauss and Bourdieu in investigating the socially informed body and cultural practices.[12]

Schutz (1971) indicates six features of common-sense reality, aspects of the making of the everyday world akin to Cassirer's formative principles. For the body in pain, these formative processes are systematically deformed.

First, Schutz asserts that a specific "form of experiencing the self" is typical of common-sense reality. In the everyday world, the self is experienced as the "author" of its activities, as the "originator" of on-going actions, and thus as an "undivided total self." We act in the world through our bodies; our bodies are the subject of our actions, that through which we experience, comprehend and act upon the world. In contrast, Brian described his body as having become an object, distinct from or even alien to the experiencing and acting self.[13] He articulated several dimensions of this objectification.

The pain has agency. It is a demon, a monster, lurking within, banging the insides of his body. Pain is an "it" which "erupts in various places in your body," a force which streaks around the body, which Brian seldom feels able to control. At the same time, pain is a part of the subject, a "thing" of the body, a part of the self. As a consequence, the body itself becomes personified as an aversive agent.

It is invested with menacing autonomy. " . . . I think it's against me, that I have an enemy," Brian said of his body.

> [there are] those moment too when I think it's, . . . I'm outside myself, this whole thing I've got to deal with is ah, a decayed mass of tissue that's just not any good, and I, I'm almost looking at it that way again; as if my mind were separated . . . from my self, I guess. I don't feel integrated. I don't feel like a whole person . . .

In Brian's world, the body has special primacy. As he eloquently describes, his body and its pain absorbs the world into itself, floods out into the world and shapes not only his experience but the experienced world. Brian struggles to continue to work, but the "allness of this type of affliction" threatens to overwhelm him. His body dominates consciousness, undermining his sense of being an "undivided total self" who is the "author" of activities, threatening to unmake the everyday world. It is only through "tremendous effort" that he can attend to what is for most of us our paramount world. He is absorbed, that is to say, not with the relevance of career, relationships, or other of the orienting rhythms of social life in North America, but instead, his attention and preoccupations are absorbed by his pain.

Second, Schutz (1971: 218–222) argues that a "form of socialty" is typical of common-sense reality. One of the most fundamental assumptions of everyday life, according to Schutz, is that we live in the same world as persons around us, that the world we experience and inhabit is shared by others. For many persons with chronic illness, this assumption is called into doubt. Their world is experienced as different, as a realm which others cannot fully fathom. They feel alienated from others, separated from the everyday world of work and accomplishment.[14] "I feel left out," another patient told me. "TMJ has really like put a hold on my life." For many, medical activities come to dominate their lives, replacing their normal interactions, increasingly shaping their lives to the world of clinics and therapies and tests and medications, increasingly alienating them from the social relations and projects that have been central to their lives.

For the sufferer of pain, this sense of alienation from others is often particularly acute. Pain resists the objectification of standard medical testing; there are no pain meters, no biochemical assays for pain. It resists localization; most efforts to identify the site of the origin of chronic pain fail, despite all advances in imaging techniques, and nearly all surgical attempts to remove pain pathways are quickly undone by the body's efficient generation of new pathways.[15] Given the close link between the visible and the real in the clinical practices of medicine, resistance to imaging yields challenges to the reality of the condition and disaffirmation of the sufferer. Absolute certainty to the sufferer, pain remains ambiguous and unverifiable to others; it remains interior, resisting social validation (Scarry 1985: 4, 56).

Brian described his experience of the breakdown of a commonly shared reality. "People really can't understand the TMJ person at all. . . . They don't believe in you. They think you're just a little bit different and strange. Ahm, sort of ahm a misfit . . . inscrutable. . . . Maybe this is just something you're making up." Brian desperately wishes he could believe the pain were made up, that he could "explain it away, . . . say that it's all just imaginary, it's a figment, it really doesn't exist." He cannot do so. On the contrary, pain is the central reality, dominating experience and expression. Verbal objectification, communication of one's experience to others, and thus the extension of the self into the world are increasingly reduced to expressions of pain. But since others doubt the word, they doubt the world and its author. As a consequence, the self and the world of the pain sufferer are threatened with dissolution.

A third feature of the everyday world, Schutz argued (1971: 214–218), is the experience of having a "common time perspective," one we share with others. This is far more subtle than we often imagine, as becomes clear when persons discover they have life-threatening illness and begin to reassess time. Such persons often report experiencing time differently than those around them. Time is precious, it is short, not to be wasted, experienced with impatience.[16] For Brian, inner and outer time, what Schutz calls *duree* and cosmic time, seem out of synch. Even more terrifying, time itself seems to break down, to lose its ordering power.

> it's kind of strange when I come home at night and I lay down for fifteen minutes. I might drift off into sleep and I might not, but I'm sort of in an in between state and ah, . . . then I won't know whether half an hour has passed or a whole day, or ah three or four hours. Time becomes distorted.
> For me, . . . time . . . seems to be spreading out, almost like I can't say anything is happening now. I have no way of pigeon-holing a specific span of time which I can get a few things done. Seems like I'm usually losing track of it. I can't keep up with it. Or it's all, everything's caving in on me at once; the past, the present are coming together all at one time. . . . episodes that repeat over and over again: you know, physical episodes of pain that seem to repeat. I can remember a time in the past when you've had it, and you can't even distinguish now from then. You really get a very warped and distorted view of what time is. So, that's sort of, a very disturbing aspect of it.

Time caves in. Past and present lose their order. Pain slows personal time, while outer time speeds by and is lost. "I feel like the world is passing me by," another patient told me. An act of will is required to order time, and time filled with pain is experienced as lost. Thus as articulate as Brian is about the world of pain, it cannot be sustained by language. It is a world threatened by dissolution. Space and time are overwhelmed by pain, and the private world not only loses its relation to the world in which others live, its very organizing dimensions begin to break down. Pain threatens to unmake the world, and in turn to subvert the self.

Schutz identifies three other dimensions of the everyday world, which I will describe more briefly. Common-sense reality has a specific form of consciousness: "wide awakeness" and full, active attention (1971: 212–214). Pain, by contrast, is distracting, tiring, and pain medications fashion a change in consciousness. The everyday social world, Schutz argued, is organized in terms of our intentional projects (pp. 222–226). For many pain sufferers, everyday life goals are subverted by the prominence of pain, and the world of suffering and of medicine come to be the paramount reality, replacing the prior social world. And Schutz argued that the natural attitude is to suspend doubt in appearances; we "take the world and its objects for granted until counterproof imposes itself" (p. 228). In particular, we suspend awareness of our mortality and the resulting "fundamental anxiety" concerning our death. We live as though the present extends indefinitely. For those with chronic or life-threatening illness, this *epoche* or suspension of doubt often fails. Vulnerability – of the body, and of the self – is an ever present companion. Many describe an irrational sense of betrayal, the feeling that faith in their body and the taken-for-granted world have been stolen away. With the irruption of awareness of mortality comes the sense that the world itself is untrustworthy. Thus the world of everyday consciousness and experience is systematically subverted.

Although the conscious body is deeply implicated in the "unmaking" of the lifeworld, it would be a mistake to underestimate the extent to which the social and political body is also a source and medium of experience. If experience is intersubjective and evolves in dialogue with those in the social environment, this dialogue and the structures it mediates are also constitutive of experience. In the case of torture, as described by Scarry, the conscious world is unmade by the systematic procedures of the torturer, which seem designed with a phenomenological cunning. In the case of chronic pain, much of the social and political world in which the sufferer engages is designed specifically to provide care and alleviate suffering. However, the institutions of modern medicine are most often shaped to the task of the "remaking" of the lifeworld with all too little cunning. Indeed, the irrationalities of medicine as a social and political institution often contribute, both overtly and subtly, to the unmaking of the everyday world of the sufferer.

Chronic pain patients often become deeply involved in the health care system, as they persist in efforts to find relief and efficacious treatment. Their interactions with the medical system play a crucial role in shaping their experience. Of the thirty-two TMJ patients we interviewed, over 70 percent had been to ten or more different types of practitioners for treatment. For many of them, the health care system, along with the bureaucracy of insurance and welfare agencies, had come to occupy much of their time and activity. Their pain and feelings of self worth were often deeply affected by the consistent disaffirmation they encountered and their struggle for legitimacy (see Kaufman 1988). In some cases, they were also influenced in a primary way by the irrationalities of the reimbursement and disability systems to which they were subject.

A young woman in our research told me about one kind of downward spiral. Her pain forced her to take a leave from work, and she began a constant round of doctors and clinics. She tried to return to work, but her pain was so disabling that her physician recommended she take a leave. As a consequence, she lost her job; "that's when everything went away," she said, "and I haven't really been back since." "Now, actually we're going to . . . welfare, and social security, medicaid. That's enough to keep me busy, but still it's nothing like . . . working." She has continued to seek medical care, determined to find an effective treatment, go back to work, and get on with her life. Without insurance, however, she has gone from having a small savings to having unmanageable debts and relying on welfare. Despite her best efforts, to date she has not succeeded in being recognized as validly disabled and eligible for SSI payments. She is thus forced to seek medical care from practitioners who will wait for payment until she receives such insurance. She describes this experience as "very draining." It "looked like the hole kept getting bigger. It didn't get smaller, it just kept getting bigger and bigger, and then I knew I needed the treatment to try to help, but never did get any, never was nothing, not that much progress . . . " Thus, for this young woman, as for many chronic pain sufferers, conforming to the schedule of the health care system and attempting to negotiate the irrationality of the American welfare and insurance bureaucracies came to be a world of its own, replacing the everyday world which had preceded it. "It keeps me busy," as this young woman said, but it does so at the expense of the world of work and accomplishment. The "political body" of pain and its management serves as source and medium for her experience, shaping her activities and forming her world to its own.

The symbolization: the struggle for a name

If chronic pain and other forms of chronic illness threaten to systematically deconstruct or subvert the lifeworld, this dissolution is countered by a human response to find or fashion meaning, to reconstitute the world, or as Scarry (1985: 6) says, "to reverse the deobjectifying work of pain by forcing *pain itself* into avenues of objectification." Many medical activities, as well as traditional forms of healing, can be seen as devoted in part to such objectification and reconstituting of the threatened lifeworld. Diagnostic and therapeutic activities, as well as efforts to construct an effective narrative of suffering or to fashion meaningful careers in spite of illness, can be understood as efforts to counter the unmaking of the lifeworld. Diagnosis is an effort to depict the source of disease, to localize and objectify cause. It is also, however, an effort to "invoke" an effective response. Narrativization is a process of locating suffering in history, of placing events in a meaningful order in time. It also has the object of opening the future to a positive ending, of enabling the sufferer to imagine a means of overcoming adversity and the kinds of activities that would allow life experience to mirror the projected story.

One of the central efforts in healing is to symbolize the source of suffering, to find an image around which a narrative can take shape. In his classic account of the Dinka, Godfrey Lienhardt (1961) describes the response to those suddenly possessed. Ajak was a young man with an origin myth even more remarkable than that of Brian. He was born without testicles, and was about to be put into the river by his father; instead, the infant's father was prevailed upon by his mother to offer a white sheep in sacrifice to Divinity, whereupon first one, then the other testicle appeared. Ajak was suddenly possessed by a power. He ran wildly for twenty minutes, and finally collapsed, sprawling on the ground. Lienhardt describes the response (p. 59):

> Then a minor master of the fishing-spear came and, addressing what he said to the thrashing form of Ajak, asked whatever it was which troubled him to tell its name and say what it wanted. In his address he tried to elicit answers from several potential sources of possession, saying, "You, Power" (*yin jok*), "You, divinity" (*yin yath*), and "You, ghost" (*yin atiep*). No reply, however, came from Ajak, who continued to moan and roll about. The master of the fishing-spear then began to take to task the Power which troubled Ajak, as follows: "You Power (*jok*), why do you seize a man who is far away from his home? Why do you not seize him there at home where the cattle are? What can he do about it here? . . . "
>   Ajak mumbled unintelligibly; the spectators were clearly expecting something to speak through his mouth, and to tell us its name and business. They explained that in due course it would leave him (*pal*). When I asked what "it" was, I was told variously that it would be his (clan) divinity (*yath*), or the ghost of his father, or the free-divinity Deng, or "just a Power" (*jok epath*). Since it would not announce itself, how could one know?

The naming of the source of suffering, particularly for those in chronic pain, often resembles this mysterious scenario. What is your name? Why are you troubling him? the physicians seem to be asking. The response is often unintelligible. "It" refuses to speak. And if it will not announce itself, how can one know? The young man I have been describing was possessed of such an entity. The pain has resisted symbolization, refused to answer to a name, though many names have been proposed. "Childhood trauma," a generation of therapists have called out, and a narrative and treatments have been devised, but it refuses to answer. The name "TMJ" has been invoked, offering a moment of hope of localization and relief. But this too has failed. Brian recognizes the seductive quality of his longing for a somatic disease with a physical cure, because of his remarkable honesty. But too much is at stake to give up hope. To name the origin of the pain is to seize power to alleviate it, and the intensity of the pain demands urgency. To name the origin of the pain is also a critical step in the remaking of the world, in the authoring of an integrated self.

At the time when I undertook the interview, Brian stood at the threshold between symbolization and despair. He finds some relief in his art work, for him, it seems, a symbolic form of world making and self-objectification. When language fails as a medium of self-extension, he turns to surrealist painting.

> there are times when I, when a lot of things that are ineffable about what goes on internally, I can find expression in the art. A lot of bizarre things I can't verbalize come out in the images I [construct] . . . If I have a shrieking person inside me, someone that's yelling and screaming and trying to get out, sometimes I don't do it concretely. You know, I don't do it verbally. I do it by . . . it comes out in the [painting] . . .

Lienhardt provides a provocative analysis of the role of symbolization in healing. The Dinka "Powers," these possessing spirits, may be understood to represent complexes of Dinka experience, he suggests, which they understand to be the grounds of their experience.

> Without these powers or images or an alternative to them there would be for the Dinka no differentiation between experience of the self and of the world which acts upon it. Suffering, for example, could be merely "lived" or endured. With the imaging of the grounds of suffering in a particular Power, the Dinka can grasp its nature intellectually in a way which satisfies them, and thus to some extent transcend and dominate it in this act of knowledge. With this knowledge, this separation of a subject and an object in experience, there arises for them also the possibility of creating a form of experience they desire, and of freeing themselves symbolically from what they must otherwise passively endure. (1961: 170)

For Brian, the monsters and the demons contained in his body may be primordial forms of such images, visual images arising from the pre-objective imagination of one who expresses himself most clearly in the visual images of his art work, and thus forms of objectification of the grounds of his suffering. However, these remain latent sources of objectification. Unlike the experience of the Dinka, Brian's demons are not fully integrated into the intersubjective world, social beings which serve to join consciousness to the social world, subject to ritual action and thus forces for healing. Instead, he seeks relief through the identification of his suffering as the result of a physical lesion or a psychological trauma. Unfortunately, in the absence of a shared cultural myth, medical, dental, and psychiatric care too have failed to provide a successful symbolization of his disorder, one which is effective in moderating his suffering. As a consequence, Brian has clung to his art work as a form of imaginative self-extension, of projecting of consciousness into the world. He also adheres to his work, to a career which maintains his relation to the social order. These courageous activities have enabled him to cling tenuously to the everyday world.

The making and unmaking of the world[17]

In an essay on the French impressionist Cézanne, Merleau-Ponty described the painter's vision of the world, which, he said, "penetrates right to the root of things beneath the imposed order of humanity."

> We live in the midst of man-made objects, among tools, in houses, streets, cities, . . . We become used to thinking that all of this exists necessarily and unshakably. Cézanne's painting suspends these habits of thought . . . This is why Cézanne's people are strange, as if viewed by a creature of another species. . . . there is no wind in the landscape, no movement on the Lac d'Annecy; the frozen objects hesitate as at the beginning of the world. It is an unfamiliar world in which one is uncomfortable and which forbids all human effusiveness. If one looks at the work of other painters after seeing Cézanne's paintings, one feels somehow relaxed, just as conversations resumed after a period of mourning mask the absolute change and give back to the survivors their solidity. (Merleau-Ponty 1964: 16)

Merleau-Ponty compares Cézanne's perception of the world to that of mourners, which provides an eloquent commentary on the nature of the grief experience, even as it describes Cézanne's paintings. For the mourner, the world also appears unfamiliar; people are strange, the landscape unnatural, movement stops midstream. The mourner has an acute awareness of the conventionality of the objects we live among; nature appears alien. And then, at some time, the world gets put back together. Conversation resumes. For those who have suffered a serious loss, this is a long, tortuous process, requiring serious work, grief work, hardly a simple resumption of conversation. Indeed, with the appropriate ethnographic observation, one could show, I think, how mourning rituals in many societies are aimed precisely at rebuilding the conventional world, returning solidity to the social order of the survivors, returning the "houseness" to our houses, the "streetness" to our streets, masking the absolute change that has occurred.

Merleau-Ponty and other phenomenologists often drew upon studies of individuals with psychopathology or severe perceptual impairments – blindness, deafness, aphasia. As in the case accounts of neurologist Oliver Sacks (1985), an impairment of some neurological functions reveals hidden dimensions of taken-for-granted aspects of human perception and the perceived world. (Who would have guessed, for example, that a specific perceptual mechanism is necessary to prevent us from mistaking a wife for a hat, as Sacks showed?) It has been my contention that we can use this method in reverse, examining dimensions of perception and the perceived world as an approach to understanding illness and its experience. In particular, rather than simply trying to describe what illness "feels like," I have suggested we focus on how dimensions of the perceived world are "unmade," broken down or altered, as a result of serious illness, as well as on the restitutive processes of the "remaking" of the world.

"Sickness subjects man to the vital rhythms of his body," Merleau-Ponty wrote (1964: 172). As such, it breaks into the normal rhythms of life. Lived experience is organized in natural social rhythms, moving from activity to rest, from work to play, concentration to relaxation. Exclusive involvement in one or the other is a sign of pathology, or a moral flaw.[18] We have some sense from the anthropological literature of the social shaping of such rhythms, as social life moved from formal transactions to intimacy, from structure and hierarchy to ritual and *communitas*, from the everyday world to specialized worlds of religious experience or aesthetics or philosophical contemplation, and on a larger scale, from periods of order and quietude to eruptions of social dynamism or revolution. Sickness and pain submit experience to the body's vital rhythms, infusing everyday experience with its distorting presence, focusing our awareness on the body as object, alien to the experiencing self, the object of cultural practices. The normal personal and social rhythms of experience are often subverted, shaped to the body's demands.

They are often replaced, to some extent, by the new rhythms of treatment and care. Robert Murphy begins the prologue to his account of his own paralytic illness with a brief, vivid description of the night sounds on the neurological service, a floor of the hospital inhabited by the irreversibly ill. Its residents "are not transients," he writes (1987: 1), "here for one or two weeks, but habitués, denizens. Their confines are not alien to them – which makes the situation no less unpleasant – for the rhythms of their care are part of a familiar routine." At night, when guests from the outside world leave, "the reinstatement of the hospital regimen . . . allows the patients to fall back into well-worn paths, grown familiar through many hospitalizations. In a way, they are glad when their guests leave." This moment, immediately contrasted with Murphy's life as a professor before his illness, alerts the reader to a long process that will eventuate in the radical revision of the everyday rhythms of his life, providing a sense perhaps of a resolution that follows years of resistance to the encroachment of the medical establishment's routines into his world.

The experience of chronic pain – in the phenomenal, social, and political body of the sufferer – has special characteristics in the context of American culture and the American medical system.[19] Chronic pain lays bare the contradictions of our metaphors of mind and body (Kirmayer 1988). In Merleau-Ponty's terms, pain begins in the pre-objective body. But in the process of its perception, it heightens the distinction between subject and object, mind and body. As I described in chapter 3, our medical practices are designed to localize suffering in a discrete site in the body, a site which can be made visible and subjected to therapeutic procedures. Chronic pain resists such objectification, defeats medical practices aimed at its localization time and again. It is thus proclaimed subjective, a functional disorder of the subjective self, now held responsible for producing its own suffering. The resistance of pain to objectification, which Scarry identifies, is thus amplified by ideological and cultural practices. And as we have seen in the case of Brian, this juxtaposition of subject and object, mind and body, and the resistance of pain to be located in either is represented in narrative accounts, as well as in therapeutic strategies.

There is a structural correlate of this ambiguity. Because pain resists objectification, the treatment of chronic pain is conducted in a liminal zone of American medicine, in a set of wildly diverse institutions, pain centers, forms of therapies, and therapeutic ideologies. This is doubly true in the case of jaw joint disorders, because of their liminal position between medicine and dentistry. Chronic pain patients thus find themselves rejected by standard medical practice and referred to institutional settings which are then vilified as non-scientific, alternative, nonorthodox, and for which reimbursement is unavailable or only marginally legitimate. The resistance of the body to the treatment of pain is thus amplified in experience by the contradictions of the American health care system.

Over against both the phenomenological and social processes that unmake the everyday world for the chronic pain sufferer, I have argued that various restitutive processes can also be seen at work. I have focused on two linked interpretive practices which serve this end: "symbolization" and narrative. A word about each. I have several times described efforts to find a diagnosis as a form of symboliz- ation akin to "invoking" the origins of suffering rather than "depicting" them. I follow here a distinction made by philosopher Charles Taylor, whose work I discussed in the first chapter. The usual medical understanding of diagnosis follows an empiricist, referential view of language – that language more or less accurately depicts the objective world, that other functions of language are metaphorical or subjective and secondary. Taylor argues that from the view of language as intersubjective and constitutive of lifeworlds, a position he develops and defends (1985a, 1985b), the invocative function is often more primary than the describing or depictive functions of language. He takes as his example religious or mythical language, in which "the words are true/right because they have power, they invoke the deity, they really connect with what he is" (1985b: 286). In these terms, religious statements – that "God takes the form of a bull," for example – are not simply metaphors for something more real, some aspect of social structure or the means of production, but a way of invoking and formulating reality. Similarly, the symbolic naming of the sources of suffering serves to formulate the object of treatment and thus organize a set of social responses and therapeutic activities. Certainly in the treatment of chronic pain, but also in far more medical practice than we usually realize, I suspect, the defining of a particular medical problem as the source of sickness, which is to be addressed through treatment, is more like invoking than depicting. In the context of complex medical problems, any representation is partial at best. As the medical student I quoted in the second lecture said, "you distort the real world a little bit to make it fit that nice pattern." And it is standard in medical practice to use the patient's response to treatment as an indicator of the accuracy or correctness of the representation. But this is precisely using language to invoke. And if we assume that response to nearly all treatment – even routine pharmacological treatment – is far more multidimensional than a simple drug response, which placebo research has made patently obvious (for example Moerman 1983), it indicates the extent to which diagnosis and symbolization of the sources of suffering serve to invoke a mode of experience and form of reality as much as to represent or describe them. As Taylor concludes in a discussion of Frege, "you cannot understand how sentences relate to their truth-conditions . . . until you have understood the nature of the (social) activity, the form of life, in which they get so related" (C. Taylor 1985b: 292).

I have also focused on narrativization as a process through which the lifeworld is reconstituted. Although I have suggested that the inability to localize pain in a particular site in the body provokes a crisis of objectification and a special need for narrative, pain is not unique in requiring the work of narrative. Disease occurs, of course, not in the body, but in life. Localization of a disorder, at very best, tells little about why it occurs when or how it does. Disease occurs not only in the body – in the sense of an ontological order in the great chain of being – but in time, in place, in history, and in the context of lived experience and the social world. Its effect is on the body in the world! And for this reason, I have argued, narratives are central to the understanding of the experience of illness, to placing pain or epileptic seizures, as we will see, in relation to other events and experiences in life.

Cross-culturally, there are various prototypical illness narratives, filled with humoral pathologies, spiritual forces, efforts at ritual healing, and these stories contrast sharply with the American stories of pain. American pain narratives seem inevitably to derive from the contradictions of mind–body dualism, the highly complex and often delegitimizing language of stress, and the quest for affirmation that accompanies the search for relief. But the American pain stories, as with illness narratives across cultures, bring a certain coherence to events. As Roland Barthes wrote, narrative "ceaselessly substitutes meaning for the straightforward copy of the events recounted" (quoted in H. White 1981: 2).

It would be a mistake to fail to see how much is at stake in the telling of the story, in the effort to tell the correct story. Hayden White writes, "If we view narration and narrativity as the instruments by which the conflicting claims of the imaginary and the real are mediated, arbitrated, or resolved in discourse, we begin to comprehend both the appeal of narrative and the grounds for refusing it" (1981: 4–5). Narratives are the source of contested judgments. Contests such as choice of which treatment should be given, about whether any treatment is justified, about whether one should be reimbursed for medical care or given compensation for injury are adjudicated in terms of such narratives. And narratives are the basis for "moralizing judgments," as Hayden White says (1981: 2–3). A great many anthropological studies of illness have shown that sickness is universally experienced as a moral event, as a rupture of the moral order that invokes such "moralizing judgments."[20] And efforts to bring meaning to such events requires not only resort to theodicy, in Weber's terms, that is to answering "why me?" (with an implied "why me rather than him?"), but to the yet more fundamental soteriological issues. What is the nature of this suffering? What is the moral order that makes sense of it? What are the sources for hope to go forward in this context?

In sum, I am suggesting that we can bring method to the cross-cultural investigation of illness experience, method quite different than that suggested by the standard paradigms of the medical behavioral sciences. The unmaking and making of the world are social as well as perceptual processes that can be systematically investigated. They lead us quickly to phenomenological dimensions of illness experience, as well as to narrative and ritual dimensions of efforts to reconstitute the world unmade. They also reveal the practices and ideologies that encode structures of social relations and power, as these shape the rhythms of illness and therapies, and are thus subject to a critical phenomenology. And they open onto moral questions provoked by suffering. This chapter is only a small beginning, then, in suggesting directions for our investigation of experiential dimensions of human suffering.

6

The narrative representation of illness

In 1988, I spent the summer in Turkey with my wife Mary-Jo and a group of Turkish colleagues interviewing persons who had been identified as suffering seizure disorders by members of an epidemiological research team. The researchers were conducting a four nation study of the community prevalence of epilepsy, types of treatment and social disability associated with the disease, and the response of the condition to various medications, with the support of the Pharma International Division of Ciba Geigy. Our goal in collaborating with this project was to develop a set of anthropologically oriented case studies, drawn from a community sample (in contrast to more common clinical studies). The community base for the sample, the availability of neurological data on all individuals, and the link to an epidemiological study made this a special opportunity. We invited persons identified as suffering seizure disorders, along with their families, to tell us stories about their illness and to describe their illness experiences – to tell us about their seizures, their efforts to find effective treatment, the responses to their condition by persons in their community, and the effects of the illness on their lives.[1]

The larger project began with a public health concern. Figures indicate relatively low utilization of anti-convulsive medications in much of the Third World, although clinical evidence suggests that seizure disorders are prevalent.[2] Anecdotal data and a few published reports indicate that epilepsy is not only prevalent but highly stigmatized in many societies, that it produces significant psychosocial disability and often leads to physical injuries suffered during seizures.[3] At the same time, when competent medical care is provided, epilepsy is susceptible to fairly clear diagnosis and to medical therapies.[4] Why then is utilization of medications typically so low? Does it reflect poor medical treatment, misplaced expectations of complete cure, the rejection of drugs owing to side effects, the primacy of treatment by non-medical healers, or some other factors? Because surprisingly few anthropological studies have investigated these issues across cultures, we took the opportunity provided by the Ciba Geigy project to investigate the meaning and experience of seizures in a Turkish community.

Data from this study provide the opportunity for addressing not only problems

135

of medical care and public health, but for reflecting on theoretical and methodological questions central to this book as well. In the last chapter, I proposed that the narrativization of suffering serves to reconstitute the lifeworld "unmade" by chronic pain. In this chapter, I examine in more detail the role of narrative in the constitution of illness and illness experience. In particular, I am interested here in exploring how illness narratives are structured in cultural terms, and how these reflect or give form to distinctive modes of lived experience.

During our interviews in Turkey, many of the conversations we had – with those suffering seizures, with family members, persons in the community, and health care providers – were made up largely of stories. We were told stories of the sudden and shocking onset of seizures or fainting, of particularly dramatic episodes of seizures or extended loss of consciousness, of years of efforts in which families and individuals engaged in a quest to find a cure, of especially memorable interactions with physicians and with religious healers, and of experiences at work, with friends, and, for example, in marriage negotiations that were influenced by the illness. Analysis of these stories – the specific episodes embedded in these narratives, as well as the overall "story" of the illness in the lives of individual sufferers and families – allows us to examine in more detail the narrative construction of illness experience discussed only briefly in the last chapter.

The opening response to our initial question in the first household we visited was a story so vivid and so unexpected that it set the stage for much of what we learned in this project. We had traveled to a rather small, rural town some distance from Ankara on Turkey's central Anatolian plateau, and made our way to the home of Meliha Hanim,[5] a fifty-six year old woman identified in the epidemiological study as suffering primary generalized epilepsy. Two of my Turkish colleagues and I were welcomed into a lush garden courtyard by a warm gracious woman and her daughter-in-law. We sat down on cushions laid for us at the front of the house, shaded from the heat of the morning sun by vines and fruit trees. After introductions and an invitation to tell us her story – the woman had previously agreed to participate in the epidemiological project – we asked her simply how her illness had begun. The woman's daughter-in-law interrupted to answer the question.

> "My mother[-in-law]'s father had already married two women; he married twice. In addition to her mother, he took a third. Of course, in due time, problems arose in the household – like her step-mother wouldn't call her 'my child,' or her father 'my daughter.' So it was difficult for her. There were people who wanted to marry her, and her father wanted to force her to marry one of them. She didn't want to be given to that man. In fact, with my current father, my father-in-law, she eloped. After she went off, her father attacked her with a knife. He came to the house that they had gone to. When he was hitting the door like this [she gestured wildly], he was stabbing the door, he smashed the door open, he came in, and when she saw her father with a knife in his hand, she received a 'shock,' she was frightened, and from that day until today, she has been fainting. Whenever she is nervous, each time there is something upsetting. And also it happens at night."

"It generally happens at night," the older woman herself interjected.

"While sleeping?" my colleague asked.

"While sleeping. For instance, while sitting here, I suddenly fall back. It can happen anywhere – in the toilet, in the stable, at my neighbors, while sitting there, I fall back. I don't know how it happens."

A quite complicated story emerged. Meliha Hanim had been suffering from seizures – or "fainting," as she described the episodes – for nearly forty years. When she was a young woman, she resisted her father's wishes to marry a man he chose and instead eloped with her husband – or had been "kidnapped" by him: the terms are ambiguous in Turkish. A short time after they had gone off to live together, her father came to force her to return. When she heard him beating on the door and saw him going to the window, forgetting it was covered with bars, she fainted away in fright. Since that time she has had recurrent seizures.

According to the daughter-in-law, she loses consciousness, tears run down her face, she hiccups, and she jumps. Her husband later told us it is just as though she were asleep.[6] In addition, Meliha Hanim told us she sometimes sees visions during her fainting spells, visions of her father with the knife in his hand, the same knife with the black handle that he had when he tried to break into her house when she first fainted, and she has dreams of people being killed, dreams that she is being threatened.

Meliha Hanim reported a long history of seeking medical care, both from physicians and from religious healers. She herself has a "powerful hand," inherited from her mother, which she uses for healing infants. She has been to shrines and various hocas, both men and women who are religious healers.[7] As her husband later said, "I swear, the hoca in the nearby village built the second floor of his house with the money I gave him. I spent a lot of money, but found no remedy." Doctors haven't been much better. "They treat people like animals," the husband told us. It remains unclear from the family's account whether doctors ever established a firm diagnosis of epilepsy. Recently, a physician diagnosed her problem as hypertension, told her not to eat salt, and put her on medications for her blood pressure. Her husband told us the fainting had recently declined in frequency. She does not take anti-convulsive medications.

The conversations we held with Meliha Hanim, her husband, and her son and daughter-in-law were quite different than we anticipated and left us feeling confused – though with a sense that the questions were more interesting than we had anticipated. Were these "fainting" spells she suffered really caused by epilepsy, or were they psychogenic or hysterical seizures, perhaps some culture-specific form of dissociation? Were they caused by the initial psychological trauma, or were they caused by some other medical condition? The neurologists, relying on clinical evidence gathered using a detailed interview schedule – no EEGs were conducted – had judged Meliha Hanim to be suffering from primary generalized epilepsy, based on her long history of recurrent seizures and the description of the episodes. Was her use of the term "fainting" (bayilma) rather than epilepsy (*sar' a*) significant in any way? What is the meaning of "fainting" in Turkish culture?

As the interviews went on, it became evident that "fainting" is a cultural category often used to describe classical tonic–clonic seizures. However, the term is associated with a more general semantic domain that includes fainting occurring in times of acute distress or in the context of a life of suffering, and is less stigmatizing than the term "epilepsy." "Epilepsy" is used most often to report a physician's diagnosis or to discuss extremely severe cases such as those associated with mental retardation. In popular discussions, "epilepsy" is more closely associated with madness than is "fainting." Thus our discussions were most commonly about "fainting," even for those who also described their condition as "epilepsy," and the narrative structure, the stories of illness and the life stories associated with the condition, were organized around this more general domain. As a result, however, the stories were often quite ambiguous as to the nature of the illness, and it was often unclear whether the stories were "reports of experience" or were largely governed by a typical cultural form or narrative structure.

The same issue was raised in our attempts to elicit a "history" of the illness – again, a problem shared by physicians who attempt to elicit a clinical history. The stories we heard were life stories, and the temporal structure was organized around events of importance to individuals and families. The illness was "emplotted" within several typical narrative structures, one of which was represented by Meliha Hanim's story of a dramatic threat producing an episode of fainting, which then led to persistent fainting or seizures throughout life despite sometimes desperate and costly attempts to find relief. But were these stories reports of the way this illness, with its storm of electrical activity that either remains focalized in one part of the brain or generalizes throughout the brain, is provoked and inserts itself into the lives of sufferers, producing behavioral events reported by the narratives? Or did the cultural structure of the narrative dominate, producing a cultural fiction?

Our study was not designed in a fashion that would allow us to answer these questions explicitly. Neither, of course, are most clinical histories able to answer such questions. Clinicians may see a patient shortly after an initial fainting episode and follow that individual quite closely through their illness. However, very few of the individuals with whom we spoke in the Turkish study had such a history with physicians, and Turkish clinicians face many of the same difficulties I discuss here when they try to construct a clinical "history." These difficulties fall generally under the rubric of the "mimetic" question, relevant not only to clinical medicine, but being asked with increasing insistence today in the social sciences and humanities – in history, literary criticism, and psychology. What is the relationship between story and experience?[8] To what extent do stories report or depict events or experiences as they occurred? Conversely, to what extent do typical cultural narratives actually construct "events," give events or experience their sense, produce what we mean by an event or history of experience? Does a good history mirror events and experience, or does it select events and organize them in a culturally conventional fashion based on an underlying view of what is significant? To what extent is social life itself organized in narrative terms?

The past decade has seen the development and elaboration of a technical literature on this broad topic. Although a full discussion is well beyond the scope of this book, it is my general claim that these issues cannot be avoided in our analysis of the relation between culture and illness, and that this literature provides analytic tools that allow us to address problems in medical anthropology in a fresh way.

Narrativity, illness stories, and experience

Phenomenologically oriented anthropologists, particularly those in the Boasian tradition – Whorf, Hallowell, and Geertz, for example – have argued that experience is cultural to the core. The "behavioral environment of the self," in Hallowell's terms, that is the perceptual world in which we find ourselves and to which we are oriented, is organized through language and symbolic forms, as well as through social and institutional relations and practical activities in that world (Hallowell 1955). Our primary access to experience is thus through analysis of cultural forms. In broad outline, this understanding of the cultural saturation of experience is widely accepted in anthropology today.

Narrative studies re-problematize this relation between culture or symbolic forms and experience. We of course do not have direct access to the experience of others. We can inquire directly and explicitly, but we often learn most about experience through stories people tell about things that have happened to them or around them. Narrative is a form in which experience is represented and recounted, in which events are presented as having a meaningful and coherent order, in which activities and events are described along with the experiences associated with them and the significance that lends them their sense for the persons involved. But experience always far exceeds its description or narrativization. New questions will always elicit new reflections on subjective experiences, and any of us can always describe an event from a slightly different perspective, recasting the story to reveal new dimensions of the experience. Much experience is given little significance: much of what we do and experience is not worth telling a story about, and only with close questioning are we able to recall fleeting aspects of our experience. In addition, experience is sensual and affective to the core and exceeds objectification in symbolic forms.

Narratives not only report and recount experiences or events, describing them from the limited and positioned perspective of the present. They also project our activities and experiences into the future, organizing our desires and strategies teleologically, directing them toward imagined ends or forms of experience which our lives or particular activities are intended to fulfill. Lived experience and social activities thus have a complex relationship to the stories that recount them.

Stories have a complex relationship to experience not only for those who recall and tell the tales; that relationship is also problematic for anthropologists interested in the study of experience – or the study of social process or culture more generally. We understand the experience of others in some measure by the experiences provoked in us when we hear such stories, experiences which are affective, sensual, and embodied. Part of the task of anthropological writing is to retell stories in a fashion that will provoke a meaningful experiential response and understanding in the reader. But our own responses are themselves culturally grounded, embedded in quite a different structure of aesthetic or emotional response than that of the members of the society being described (see Becker 1979).

Unni Wikan tells the story of her discovery of the grief of a young Balinese girl at the sudden death of the young woman's fiancé. Her public demeanor was "stage-managed" in a form familiar to those who have read Geertz on Bali. Her self-presentation was "smooth"; "she shone and sparkled" (Wikan 1987: 349). In more intimate moments, however, the young woman shared her sense of loss and grief with the anthropologist, as well as her fears that any expression of her sadness would be met with ridicule, her friends mocking her as a "widow." But how are we to interpret this case of a young girl who appears on the surface to be more culturally different than intimate experience reveals? To what extent is our intuition of the meaning of the story based on an American or European view – culturally idiosyncratic, perhaps – that the private sharing of grief is one of the deepest forms of human intimacy, that it provides access to a deeper under- standing of the experience of others, of what "really happened," than the expression of other emotions – anger or fear, for example – or than the public enactments of emotions can provide? Are we thus misled by our culturally informed intuitions in reading Wikan's account of her story and intuiting what the young Balinese woman really felt or experienced? I tend to think Wikan has the better of this particular argument with Geertz about the nature of some aspects of Balinese "psychology," but there is the potential for serious confusion in such analyses of the quality of lived experience derived from stories we tell from field research.

Similarly, the telling of illness stories is often a highly personal and intimate matter in North American society, and such stories constitute a genre of popular and conventional literature in Western culture.[9] These stories and the meanings and values associated with illness and suffering in our own society shape our hearing and retelling of the experiences of illness in other societies. It is critical therefore that we submit to closer examination the telling of illness narratives, the interpretation of these by others in the societies we study, anthropological writing about such stories, the reactions of the audiences for whom we write, and thus ultimately the relation of culture, narrative, and experience. Otherwise, our own projections are likely to dominate our interpretations of others' experiences of suffering.

The past decade has seen the emergence of a small but growing literature on narrative dimensions of illness, care-seeking, and therapeutic process. One stream of this literature is from within medicine; several literary-minded clinicians have provided detailed clinical accounts or stories of the lives of those with serious illness, expanding on the traditional genre of the case history and developing a more elaborate form of illness stories which also reflect on what disease tells us about suffering and the human condition. For example, Oliver Sacks' accounts of persons with Parkinsonism (1973), migraine (1986), and other neurological disorders (1985) portray the human dimensions of quite dramatic medical conditions and the suffering they provoke from the perspective of a humanistic physician. These are not unlike, in some ways, those personal accounts of illness which have become an important genre in recent years, and which may serve as primary source material for our thinking about the narrative structuring of illness experience in our own society (see R. Murphy 1987 and DiGiacomo 1987 for reflective accounts by anthropologists on their own experiences). Howard Brody's recent book (1987) extends an analysis of such narratives in an added direction. He draws on literary accounts and refers briefly to the "narrativity" literature to argue explicitly for the importance of an awareness of the narrative dimensions of illness in medical ethics, suggesting that aspects of illness central to ethical reflection and decision making are better apprehended through stories of illness than through abstract and rule-governed philosophical discourse.

A second stream of writing on narrative and illness has recently emerged from qualitative sociology research, in particular among those who have worked in the ethnomethodology and conversation analysis traditions. Mishler, who has conducted detailed studies of doctor–patient dialogue (1986a), has gone on to make a strong case for the narrative structure of conversation and to elaborate a fundamental critique of survey interviewing based on his analysis (1986b).[10] Williams' (1984) analysis of "narrative reconstruction" in chronic illness experience has attracted attention and been widely referenced in sociological writing. A recent issue of *Social Science and Medicine* (Gerhardt 1990) on qualitative research on chronic illness draws on these and other forms of conversation analysis to study the experience of chronic illness in North America and Europe. For example, Riessman (1990) demonstrates the usefulness of close textual analysis of a biographical account of illness, and Robinson (1990) draws on the narrative literature for analyzing the life stories of persons with multiple sclerosis.

Anthropological and cross-cultural analyses of illness narratives are surprisingly few. Early's work on "therapeutic narratives" in Cairo was among the first by an anthropologist to focus explicit attention on the stories told about illness and care-seeking (Early 1982; cf. 1985, 1988). She sat with women in the traditional quarter of Cairo and listened as they told everyday stories of illness – of their children, family members, and themselves – and their efforts to find appropriate care. These stories, she argues, operate as a "middle level system between experience and theory." They allow the women she studied to develop an interpretation of the illness in relation to a local explanatory logic and the biographic context of the illness, to negotiate right action in the face of uncertainty, and to justify actions taken, thus embedding the illness and therapeutic efforts within local moral norms. More recently, Price (1987) and Garro (1992), both cognitive anthropologists, have demonstrated how cultural knowledge and scripts for care-seeking are encoded in illness narratives, whether naturally occurring or elicited through interviews (in Ecuador and North America respectively). Mattingly (1989) has made the most extensive and explicit use of narrative theory to explore the story/experience relationship and the use of narratives by clinicians (American occupational therapists, in her case) to organize their practice and the experiences of those they treat.[11] She makes a strong case for the narrative structuring of clinical work, the role of clinicians in emplotting the illness experience and therapeutic work in which patients are engaged, as well as the importance of stories in shaping and evaluating their own work and clinical relationships.[12]

Kleinman (1988b) has combined the anthropological and clinical traditions, reflecting on persons with chronic illness whom he has seen as a physician and researcher. He uses anthropological analyses to show how "meaning is created in illness," how cultural values and social relations shape the experience of the body and sickness, and situate suffering in local moral worlds. He explores how experience is organized in narrative form, moving comparatively between North American and Chinese cases to demonstrate the importance of the social and cultural frames within which such narratives emerge. He argues that "the study of the experience of illness has something fundamental to teach each of us about the human condition" (p. xiii), and demonstrates how current practices in medicine have alienated the chronically ill from their care providers and led practitioners to relinquish "that aspect of the healer's art that is most ancient, most powerful, and most existentially rewarding" (p. xiv).

Much of the literature on illness narratives has addressed the structural characteristics of illness stories, their relation to life histories, the kinds of illness knowledge and values they encode, and what they reveal about the impact of illness on people's lives. In general, this "narrative turn" in writing on illness experience has benefited from broader interests in literary analysis in the humanities and social sciences. With the exception of Mishler and his colleagues and Mattingly, however, these authors have made rather little explicit use of literary critical theories of narrative and its interpretation. Although the issues many of these studies raise are important to my analysis as well, I take a somewhat different path into the subject here, continuing my examination of how illness and its experience are constituted through interpretive practices, and drawing explicitly on some aspects of narrative theory. In particular, I am interested in the relevance of "reader response" theory for analysis of stories that those who are ill tell us about their experience.

Anthropological analyses of narrative have been largely of two kinds: structuralist studies of folklore and mythology, and sociolinguistic studies of narrative performance. The Russian formalists and the structural linguists of the Prague school contributed to the French search for the fundamental narrative form. Propp (1968) argued that there are a limited number of basic character types and plot structures underlying all Russian folk tales. Lévi-Strauss (for example 1969) drew on Jakobson's distinction of horizontal and vertical axes to develop his comparative study of the fundamental structures of narrative.

Over against efforts to develop a structural theory of narrative, performance theorists and many literary theorists have argued for the essential temporal quality of narrative, its unfolding in time, its working through of a plight to a resolution through interactions of characters among whom consciousness of the nature of the situation is unevenly distributed, all in the medium of what Ricoeur (1981b) calls "narrative time." Victor Turner (1957, 1981) argued that such a narrative – or proto-narrative – structure lies beneath not only stories but social process itself, which moves relentlessly from a breach of an existing state to a crisis and redress. Narrative accounts, along with ritual, efforts at legal redress, and other social dramas, are organized in relation to the contradictions structured into societies (for example through kin systems), as well as to the "absolute indeterminacy" that becomes evident at moments of breach and crisis, Turner argues (1981: 153)[13] – and all this can only occur in time.

Temporality is present not only in the structure of narrative but in its perform-ance. Narrations and rituals are intersubjective processes, requiring performers and audiences along with "textual" forms, and have their effect as event within temporally lived experience (for example Bauman 1986; for relevant analyses of healing rituals see Schieffelin 1985 and Kapferer 1983).

Reading response theorists have elaborated on the temporal and intersubjective qualities of all narrative by giving special attention to the "phenomenology of the act of following a story" (Ricoeur 1981a: 277). Narrative is not simply that which is present in a completed story, whether a written text, a folk tale, or a story as told or performed. In order to constitute narrative, the story must be appropriated by a reader or an audience. Appropriation of this sort is not a passive receiving of an author's message (as much of the speech act theory seems to suggest); instead, as Iser (1978: 21) shows, "the reader 'receives' [the message of the text] by composing it." A plot, for example, is not simply present as the structure of a narrative but is created by readers moment by moment as they proceed through a text, finding themselves limited to "the blind complexity of the present" (Ricoeur 1981a: 279) and seeking to uncover and anticipate the structure and meaning of unfolding events. Both the art of narrating and the art of following a story thus require that we be able *"to extract a configuration from a succession,"* as Ricoeur says (1981a: 278), to engage in a form of aesthetic synthesis through which the whole – the story, the plot, the "virtual" text of the narrative – gradually comes into being.

Given this quality of narrative, Iser (1978: 22–23) argues, "the interpreter's task should be to elucidate the potential meanings of a text." Rather than identifying a single referential or authorized meaning, analysis involves "elucidating the process of meaning-production." Meaning-production is inherent in neither the text and its structure alone, nor in the activity of the reader alone, but in the inter-action between reader and text. Iser persuasively develops the hypothesis that "a literary text contains subjectively verifiable instructions for meaning-production, but the meaning produced may then lead to a whole variety of different experiences and hence subjective judgments" (1978: 25). Investigation of the synthetic processes involved in following a story – entering imaginatively into the world of the text, shifting viewpoints to follow the perspectives presented by the narrative and the narrator, reconfiguring and revaluing past events and actions of the characters in the story as the narrative unfolds, the personal discovery by the reader of significance and new meanings through the experience of reading a text, and the personal change the reader experiences as a result of such understanding – has produced a rich set of theoretical ideas and substantive findings. For reader response theorists, analysis of narrative thus turns on both the phenomenology of reading and on the characteristics of stories that provoke and constrain the reader's response.

It is my contention that reader response theory has special relevance for our investigation of illness narratives. The narrators of most illness stories which we as researchers are told, whether they are persons who are sick or their primary care-providers, are typically in the middle of a story. The narratives they produce are more akin to the "virtual text" of the reader of a story than the "actual" narrative text of a completed novel.[14] They are stories that change as events unfold. They point to the future with both hope and anxiety, and they often maintain several provisional readings of the past and the present. They may be expected, however, to be deeply cultural stories, if all that we have learned about culture and illness is reflected in the narratives people tell to make sense of their experience.

The narratology and reader response literature provide a number of technical distinctions and analytic constructs that can be used for the analysis of illness stories, either as elicited through interviewing or as observed in natural discourse settings. I return to the Turkish epilepsy narratives and examine them in relation to three analytic concepts from this literature: the "emplotting" of illness, through which an ordered story is sought and authored; the "subjunctivizing" qualities of the stories, including their openness to multiple readings and potential outcomes; and the "positioning of suffering" in the local discourse setting.

Emplotment and illness experience

Narrative theory describes two aspects of plot: plot as the underlying structure of a story, and "emplotment" as the activity of a reader or hearer of a story who engages imaginatively in making sense of the story. Both are relevant to the analysis of illness narratives.

Plot is that which gives order to a story. It is the sequential ordering of events and the relations that connect them to one another. In Meliha Hanim's story, the attack of her father is followed by her fainting, and that by a lifetime of fainting episodes which are deeply disturbing and associated with dreams or visions of the threatening knife. More than the frame of sequential relations, plot is the meaningful order through which experiences and events are joined together to make a story. Meliha Hanim's story was not one simply of a trauma and subsequent fainting, but of an ambiguous elopement or kidnapping, undertaken against her father's wishes, her father's retaliation, and a lifetime of resulting illness, a predicament which her husband has sought to resolve through a wide variety of efforts to find a cure.

"Plot as I conceive it," Peter Brooks (1984: xi) writes, "is the design and intention of narrative, what shapes a story and gives it a certain direction or intent of meaning. We might think of plot as the logic or perhaps the syntax of a certain kind of discourse, one that develops its propositions only through temporal sequence and progression."[15] Narrative "syntax," at least in Western literature and recent historiography,[16] has a distinctive form, which Ricoeur (1981a: 277) describes as follows:

> Let us say, to begin with, that a story describes a sequence of actions and experiences of a certain number of characters, whether real or imaginary. These characters are represented in situations which change [and to which] they react. These changes, in turn, reveal hidden aspects of the situation and the characters, giving rise to a new predicament which calls for thought or action or both. The response to this predicament brings the story to its conclusion.

Predicament, human striving, and an unfolding in time toward a conclusion are thus central to the syntax of human stories, and all of these, as we will see, are important to stories about illness experience.

From the perspective of readers or hearers of stories that are in process, plot is less a finished form or structure than an engagement with what has been told or read so far in relation to imagined outcomes that the story may bring – outcomes that are feared, longed for, or seem ironically or tragically inevitable. The "plot" for Meliha Hanim and her family was incomplete; not only was the illness on-going, but the family continued to try to find what is really happening, what the real story is, what story has the potential to invoke a cure. The reader is engaged imaginatively in constructing a "virtual plot," in attempting to extract configuration from what has been heard, in determining the nature of relationships among events and characters, separating the related from the irrelevant, conceiving potential outcomes in the world of the text. The activity of "emplotting" thus has a special affinity to the experience of persons with debilitating chronic illness, and the literature on this concept is especially useful in understanding their stories.

When I read the transcripts of the Turkish epilepsy interviews we conducted with an eye to "plot" and "emplotment," several things become apparent. First, the interviews consist in part, though not in total, of a corpus of stories of fainting or seizures, of other life experiences shown to be a cause or consequence of these episodes, and of efforts to find effective treatment. For nearly all those we interviewed, these episodes cohere as a larger narrative of an illness that has become a central organizing theme in the lives of the sufferers and their families. The most typical form portrays a predicament, associated with initial fainting episodes, followed in most cases by prolonged and persistent striving to find a cure, an unfolding of the illness within the life of the individual and family, and an imagined end juxtaposed to persistent illness. In some cases the initial "predicament" followed by a quest for cure is key to the entire story structure, while in others a life history of suffering is thematized as central to the structure of the story of the illness.

Second, several prototypical plot types can be identified among the illness narratives, as well as among the specific stories of which they are constituted. These have a distinctive cultural form, rooted in Turkish popular medical culture. They are present as the plot structures of the narratives we heard. They are also available as cultural resources for those in the midst of illness attempting to make sense of their experience; that is, they are possible stories one might reasonably tell about such an illness, potential plots giving order to the events one is experiencing.

Third, with few exceptions, the narratives are not complete, the stories not finished. They are told from "the blind complexity of the present as it is experienced" (Ricoeur 1981a: 278). In many cases, the actors were still engaged in the striving, in a quest for cure – in imagining alternative outcomes, evaluating the potential meanings of the past, and seeking treatments. Such tellers of the stories were thus akin to readers who are in the midst of a story. They approached the understanding of their predicament, of the story they were trying to make sense of, with an available body of typical plots – what Barthes calls the *déjà-lu*, the "already read" – drawn from their cultural repertoire. And they were still actively engaged in "emplotting" the condition from which they suffer, in seeking a plot open to a desired outcome.

In this section I outline five typical plot types found among the narratives we were told. I will go on in the next section to describe the representation of "subjunctivizing" elements in the stories, imagistic elements that suggest indeterminacy, an openness to possibility and the potential for change and healing in the lives of the sufferers.

Our research included thirty-two case studies. Of these, six were drawn from Ankara, thirteen from a town some distance from Ankara, and thirteen from a small village in the Ankara environs. Twelve of the sufferers were men or boys, twenty were women or girls; seven of the thirty-two were under the age of twelve. Twenty suffered (or had suffered) primary generalized or partial epileptic seizures, according to the research team, two were considered probable cases of epilepsy, and ten suffered fainting or seizures judged to be non-epileptic.

The stories we were told of the illness histories had several identifiable plot forms. Although other typologies of plot could be formulated, I want to suggest five plot types organized in terms of onset of the illness, its temporal unfolding in the sufferer's life, and the primary idiom for its expression.

The most common story form told how an illness began with a major emotional trauma associated with a frightening experience or a deep personal loss, which produced fainting that had continued intermittently for years following the experience. These plots were similar to those of "fright illness" we found in an Azerbaijani town in previous research (B. Good and M. Good 1982). In these narratives, the trauma associated with the beginning of the illness has a powerful effect on shaping the central meaning and configuration of the story. The temporal structure of the illness, with its traumatic onset often followed by an intense quest for cure, is central to this plot form. Meliha Hanim's story – of the threatened attack by her father – which I described in the beginning of this chapter, followed this pattern. Eleven of the thirty-two cases told stories of this form, and three others included stories of an emotional trauma as at least a possible source of their illness.

The second most common story form was of seizures beginning with a childhood fever or with an injury. High fevers in infancy, meningitis, an infant who fell from a bed, a young man beaten by a teacher – these were stories with their own drama of desperate efforts to find medical care, bitter memories of poor treatment from urban physicians and hospitals, remorse on the part of mothers for their failure to protect their children, and in several cases tragic outcomes with seizures associated with serious impairment or mental retardation. Although etiology often mirrors that of a medical narrative of these cases, the real drama of the stories often lay elsewhere. Eight of the thirty-two case accounts followed this form, and three others told stories of fevers or injury as potential origins of the seizures. Such stories were particularly prominent for persons whose illness had begun in childhood; stories told of all but two persons whose illness began before age twelve either followed this general form or (in two cases) described an attack by "evil eye" as producing fever secondarily.

Third most common (six persons) were cases of seizures that seemed to begin with no apparent cause. All of these were cases of generalized seizures that simply began – in all cases but one during early or late adulthood – in association with no recognized causal event. These stories were generally "unplotted," in a sense. The narratives focused on the effect of the illness on the life of the sufferer, but neither beginning nor potential ending were featured in the stories. They were organized less as quest stories than those in which discussions of beginnings were matched by a concern for outcome. It remains ambiguous whether lack of origin stories results simply from a particular style of emplotment, from a particular pattern of onset of seizures, or from a medicalization of the condition and thus a focus on physiological site rather than temporal order in a life history.

Fourth, a number of women told stories of a lifetime of sadness, poverty, and suffering in which episodes of "fainting" were persistent and prominent. These narratives combined a typical rhetoric of complaint, voiced in the idiom of sıkıntı (worry, suffering) and uzuntu (worry, pain, sorrow),[17] complaints of fainting (bayılma), stories of onset associated with life tragedies, and a lack of extensive care-seeking. Nearly all such cases were of women who initially screened positive for a history of seizures but were ultimately diagnosed as having psychological rather than epileptic seizures. However, these cases join together a rhetoric of suffering and tragedy with seizures – explicitly described as "fainting" – in a manner that shapes the meaning context of epileptic seizures more generally.

Finally, classical Middle Eastern stories of illness onset being caused by evil eye or being struck by jinns were the primary organizing feature of several of the narratives. Three case narratives were explicitly organized in this form; a fourth included such a story; and stories of encounters with religious healers and visits to shrines indicated that the potential for reading the epilepsy experience in such terms was widely present. This story form was held as a potential means of explaining seizures and thus configuring episodes and experience of illness for nearly all of those we interviewed.

These general plot forms were prominent structural features of the narratives we heard. They give stories coherence, order selection and sequence of episodes told, and make the accounts recognizable to others in the society. More than that, they are story forms available to individuals and families engaged in emplotting their experience – that is, in evaluating the potential sources of seizures or fainting, drawing into coherent relationship a number of life experiences, and anticipating the probable course of their illness and potential sources of efficacy. In a number of the cases, the stories we were told suggested that sufferers or family members held open the possibility not only of various possible endings to the story they were telling, but actively maintained several plots as potential ways of interpreting their illness. In the following section, I will examine more carefully the maintenance of competing plots as a strategy for "subjunctivizing reality." However, before going on, a recounting of three of the epilepsy narratives will illustrate the plot structures of the narratives we heard and provide the data for looking in more detail at the stories in light of reader response theory.

Zeki Bey

Zeki Bey was a thirty-two year old man whom we interviewed with his wife, a sister, and his mother in his house in an older *gecekondu* ("squatter settlement") that is now part of Ankara. He has been suffering epileptic seizures since he was seventeen years old. He told us the story of how the illness began.

ZEKI BEY: The news came to me this way. Early in the morning I left the house. My mother was with [my father in the hospital]. He died at 2:00 at night. I was in the car that usually brings me from work; . . . a car coming from the opposite direction signaled Ismail [the driver]. When the signal was given, I understood, I understood, I said my father died. Of course he pulled off to the right, talked, came back, got into the car, and we went. I wanted to drop by the hospital before going to work. And there, the second man came, and when he said "condolences" ("*başin sağolsun*"), "I lost myself."
ZEKI'S SISTER: At that time he fell down the stairs.
ZEKI BEY: And meanwhile, I came to myself. I hit a man, Ali Haydar also hit him, and I also hit him. We went down to the morgue; what could I do in the morgue, since he had died at 2:00. Before we didn't have a telephone at home, later, at night, I said where can I go, that place (street, or hospital) was *karişik* (mixed up), I didn't know, and when I hit that man, I was attacking him, I was going, he wouldn't let me embrace [my father's

body] ... when I found the bowl [for washing the dead] I was so upset (*sinirli* – nervous, upset) that I hit him in the forehead with it. Blood was everywhere, nothing could stop me, I wasn't seeing anything, because of being upset; because of being upset I did ... we hit the man, of course they were outside, they didn't know what was going on, what happened to me happened during that time, and after that it continued.

ZEKI'S SISTER: He fought with the guys there, he fell down the stairs to the second floor, he tumbled, his nose bled, he fell tumbling, they called him from downstairs ...

INTERVIEWER: When you were falling down the stairs, did you hit your head?

ZEKI BEY: I'm telling you, when I was falling it happened suddenly ... Before I got the bowl, I couldn't tell the difference between things. I got up ... I found the bowl, I just remember that I hit him on the forehead, and of course they took me out of there.

ZEKI'S SISTER: They gave him a "courage needle" (tranquillizer injection), they did it there. Until the death of my father, he had nothing. He wasn't even working. After that, he began to work.

Zeki Bey had had generalized seizures for fifteen years. Yet he told the story with immediacy, drama and poignancy. The death of his father and his mad, violent grief in the hospital served not only as the causal explanation of his illness. More importantly, it gave texture and meaning to the larger life story. His sister and the interviewer suggested the possibility of recasting the story as an injury narrative rather than a story organized around the initial emotional trauma, but he eloquently resisted. His illness had a powerful and meaningful beginning, which gave shape and coherence to the larger narrative.

Zeki Bey's seizures were reasonably well controlled – though at a cost. He was once treated by his "insurance doctor" with electroshock treatment, he told us, and has since been medicated with an extremely high dosage of phenobarbital. As a result, he suffers slurred speech and is often sleepy. He has been treated a number of times by *hoca*s, who have written curative prayers for him, but with no noticeable effect. He says they tell him his problem is caused by stepping on jinns, but he doesn't believe it. Meanwhile, he continues to work in a job at the municipality, where he is treated well by co-workers. His major concern is that he and his wife have had no children, and he wonders if either the illness or the medications are to blame. This, rather than treatment of the primary disease, organizes his interest in shaping the outcome of his illness story.

Omer

Omer was a six year old boy at the time of our research, who was diagnosed by the research team as suffering generalized, tonic–clonic seizures since infancy and prescribed anti-epileptic medication. He lives in an average village home with his mother and his father, who is a factory worker in Ankara, his paternal grandmother, and several other children. The boy's mother and grandmother participated in the interview.

The interview began with the grandmother expressing concern about what their village neighbors say about the boy – that he has difficulty speaking and understanding – and the gossip resulting from the visits from the medical research team.

They then launched immediately into describing how desperately they had sought care for him. "How many doctors we took him to, how many *hoca*s we took him to, we took him to [a *hoca*] in K—, we took him to [a shrine in] B—, everywhere they said 'he'll get better, he'll get better, he'll get better, he'll get better . . . '" "What is there in K—?" we asked. They said that it is a shrine (*yatır*) with a "deep *hoca*," that when they took the child there at age five he still could not speak, and that he had begun to speak after being taken to the shrine.

They told a story of their experience at the shrine – first in brief form, a story with gaps and contradictions, then following our questions a more elaborate version of the story.

> INTERVIEWER: What happened when you took him to the *yatır*?
> OMER'S MOTHER: We took him to the *yatır*, he slept there.
> OMER'S GRANDMOTHER: *Dede* ("grandfather, dervish, sheikh") said "he should sleep until he wakes." He said "he himself should wake up." We held the baby, he was sleeping until we arrived at K—.
> OMER'S MOTHER: [he said] we should stop when he woke up.
> OMER'S GRANDMOTHER: The *hoca* was offended. "You took the baby here before anyone gathered around him, before the baby recovered," he said. "You just came here for the trip," the *hoca* said. The baby, we came to K—, he said he came to consciousness (?). When you bring adults, they come quickly; they do not come quickly to children, but they do gather around them.

They went on to tell the story in more detail. The *yatır* is a place with tombs of saints and a fountain "that appeared from God." People who are paralyzed come and sleep there, and while they sleep, "they gather around that person; when they shake him, he wakes up."

"Who gathers around?" we asked.

"Whomever you see," Omer's mother said.

"*Jinns*, *peris*, unseen creatures that disturb people by gathering around them," the grandmother interjected.

"The person who goes there gets well," the mother said.

"She and I and his father, the three of us took the baby there in our arms. He slept there," the grandmother said.

The mother went on, "he slept very comfortably. If he had slept longer, he would have 'gone' (died?) . . . " But before he awoke, they took him to the cab – since they were paying by the hour, it was getting expensive – and left.

The story included a brief explanation that the *hoca* said the illness had begun because the child had "stepped on dirt" after evening prayer. It led immediately to another story of treatment at a different shrine, which concluded with the healer pronouncing, "by the time he is ten years old, he will get well."

A simple question about how old the child was when the illness began produced another story of the beginnings of the illness when the child was eight months old.

> MOTHER: In essence, it happened to him because of an evil eye. There is a woman in this village, if she looks at you she destroys you. That woman looked at him when he was eight months old, the next morning he couldn't speak. His mouth foamed.

GRANDMOTHER: His mouth foamed, he started doing like this.
MOTHER: When his mouth foamed the baby was unable to recover for three days, he couldn't speak, nothing, he died.

They went on to describe how the woman had stopped by and stayed for dinner one evening, though she was dirty from painting her house.

MOTHER: Before she left, I dressed the baby, I put on his white dress. The baby was all right. I brought him near her. "Where did you find this 'Bulgarian seed'? Where did you find this 'foreign seed'?" she asked.[18]
GRANDMOTHER: Don't even say it!
MOTHER: To the baby, she said just this. The baby didn't recover. In the morning he was seized with the illness. The evil eye was cast upon the child. . . . He was very beautiful. He was bright and clean. You should have seen him!

They went on to tell stories of trips to the doctor, of leaving the infant in the hospital, but of his failure to recover and his seizures continuing monthly. They told of his unruliness, their terrible anxieties about disciplining him, and their fears about what he may be like when he grows up. This led to stories by the grandmother of children she had who died in infancy, of her leaving her first husband when he took a second wife, and of the pension she received when her second husband died, which she now dedicates to the family. The visit drew to a close.

In this case, the underlying plot was of an innocent infant being struck by an evil eye, leading to a sudden fever, fainting, and an illness and disability which has persisted despite desperate efforts to find a cure. Stories recounted inadequate treatment at hospitals and some limited benefit from religious healers. Hope for resolution of the condition was mixed with serious anxiety about the child's future.

Kerim Bey

Kerim Bey was a twenty-six year old man, identified as epileptic by the research team, who had suffered generalized seizures since he was seventeen or eighteen years old. He lives with his wife and child on the third floor of a three story house, whose other floors are home to his parents and his brother with his wife and child. Kerim works as a security guard at a nearby factory. He responded to our initial questions about how the illness had begun with a clear story of a frightening experience that produced his initial fainting. His reflections on this experience later in the interview, as well as his wife's discussion of his illness during a separate interview, will be described in the following sections of this chapter.

"Do you remember how it started?" we asked. He answered with a story.

"Down below here there is a street. It was two or three o'clock at night. My brother's wife was having her baby. They told me to take the news to her mother and father. 'We are taking their daughter to the hospital, so they should have the news.' They woke me

and I got up. While my eyes were closed, I went out onto the asphalt, the main street. I went down three blocks. ! don't know if you saw the Employment Office building there. There I went to the left, then again turned to the right. After going 100, 150 meters, three black dogs – I don't know whether you watched the late night movie yesterday, what do you call those dogs?"
INTERVIEWER: "Doberman."
   "Three of those dogs came out. When they began barking, I suddenly was startled. I turned and ran from there back home. Here I fell and fainted. One year later, when I was jumping into the truck . . . I was on the truck in the evening . . . In the evening I had come from work, I had gone to cut the wood, I came, I took a shower, I got out of the shower, I ate garlicky *manti*. I slept so heavily that I didn't keep account of how long I slept. [In the evening I was unloading the truck.] I fell from the top of the truck, from seven and a half or eight meters, I fell from left to right. I had a fall that took my breath away. I landed on my father's chest. My father was ill. I was hanging from my sweater on one of the hooks of the truck. They took me immediately to the hospital doctor. He said, 'it is the initial stage of epilepsy.' He asked whether I had eaten garlicky *manti*. 'This is the beginning of epilepsy,' he said, 'don't allow him to worry about things, don't let him be anxious, don't let him have less than eight hours of normal sleep, don't wake him before he has had eight hours of sleep.' This kind of advice he gave."

This young man went on to describe how he is able to work as a security guard with the support of his superiors and fellow workers. ("The company doctor told my supervisor that I had to go on disability because I had epilepsy and I couldn't work as a security guard. But my supervisor rejected this; he said that my condition was no worse than his other workers who had diabetes, heart disease, or wore strong glasses.") Nonetheless, he feels his life is seriously constrained by the illness. He cannot seek other jobs, though he believes he is capable of doing them. He cannot consider going abroad – to Germany, for example – as many others have done to advance their personal or family well-being. "The problem is I can't accomplish the things that I want. I always have this fear that I might faint." Indeed, he does continue to have seizures, though he is on medication, in part associated with having to switch periodically between day and night work shifts. When he faints, he feels embarrassed. "I feel depressed. I feel angry. For instance when I recover from fainting I see my friends looking at me. They don't look down on me but still I don't want to be in that position. I always ask myself, 'Why am I fainting? Can't this be cured?' So I feel angry."
   He has had regular medical treatment and drug therapy. Still, he reports that one of his physicians "told me that if I had an operation I could get well. But nobody does this operation in Turkey, so he told me that I would have to go to Germany or the United States." By this means he continues to imagine a cure, a life without seizures or fear of them, and thus a life open to new possibilities. But this openness of the story is represented not only by his describing a possible medical treatment that could change the ending of the story, but by his maintenance of several over-lapping plots that make sense of the mysterious appearance of the frightening dogs, as became evident as the story unfolded.

"Subjunctivizing" elements in illness narratives

Narrative discourse accomplishes its effects by "recruiting the reader's imagination,"[19] by enabling or provoking the reader to enter the world presupposed by the text. The reader of a well told story grasps the situation from the points of view of the diverse actors of the drama, experiencing their actions and the story as indeterminate and open, even though the text or the story has a fixed structure and ending. Narrative succeeds by "subjunctivizing reality," a phrase I take from Bruner (1986: 26), by exploring the indeterminacy of reality and stimulating such exploration in the reader.[20] "To be in the subjunctive mode is . . . to be trafficking in human possibilities rather than in settled certainties," Bruner writes (1986: 26). A central task for the critic set out by reader response theory is to examine how a text stimulates readers' entry into the subjunctive world of its actors, draws them into the diverse perspectives of the actors, invites concern about how the story might turn out.

Illness stories contain subjunctivizing elements not merely because they are narrative in structure and are performed to elicit an imaginative and empathetic response from an audience. They also have such subjunctivizing elements because the narrators – the person with an illness, family members participating in their care, medical professionals – are in the midst of the story they are telling. As I have argued, those who told us stories of their experiences with epilepsy were actively engaged in making sense of the illness and in attempting to influence its outcome. They were deeply committed to portraying a "subjunctive world," one in which healing was an open possibility, even if miracles were necessary. The analogy of the reader in the midst of a story, drawn almost against his or her will into the world of the text and moving forward, reinterpreting the past in light of the emergent present and future, makes sense of several elements of the narratives we recorded. I want to mention just two aspects of the Turkish narratives that maintain "subjunctivity" and illustrate from the cases I have described.

First, the narratives maintained multiple perspectives and the potential for multiple readings. They contained stories of episodes associated with the onset of seizures or with encounters with care-providers that allowed multiple interpretations of the source of the illness, alternative readings of prognosis and course, and thus maintained the potential for cure. Often these perspectives were represented through juxtaposed stories, independent episodes in the larger narrative, with the narrator making no effort to establish the relations among stories or to select a single coherent interpretation. The narratives thus maintained multiple perspectives and disparate points of view, all representing aspects of the narrator's experience and the possibility of diverse readings of what had happened and what the future might hold. The provisional quality of the story thus has a creative potency. Several examples will illustrate.

The young man we called Kerim first told us the stories of his being frightened by the barking dogs as he was running across town, leading to his fainting, and of having had his first major seizure while working on a truck a year after this event.

Later in the interview he told of an encounter with a healer that suggested a radical reinterpretation of the "fright" story as he had first presented it.

He described a conversation with an acquaintance who was a *hoca* from a family of Sheyhs who live primarily in the Diyarbakir region in eastern Turkey, in which he had lamented that his illness could not be cured.

> I told him I was going to be married in September, and I will pay the necessary money to have an operation in the United States. The doctor here said that "two veins are inflamed," and for that he gave me the pills. He said you have an 80 percent chance of being better if you use them. I told this to my friend (the Sheyh). He was surprised. It was during Ramazan (the month of fasting), and he was going to Diyarbakir (in eastern Anatolia) for a visit. So he went there, and he asked the senior members of his family, who are *dede*s, and they said, "Did you do such and such?" He said, "I didn't." He did [the things they said]. Roughly speaking, since Ramazan, I haven't been ill.

His friend returned to the senior Sheyhs the next year, and was told to "do the same thing again."

> In my case this happened. We were sitting here like this. He doesn't treat everyone, also he doesn't treat for money. He does it as charity. . . . He lighted two candles. He put water [in a bowl]. The dogs which I saw when I was sleepy at that first incident, I closed my eyes, the same scene appeared. The man said that this is speaking with the jinns, according to the Koran. So the jinns tell the sheyh that I had walked on them and had killed their children. The jinns said, "That is why we disturb him, we make him ill. He can't be cured." The *hoca* began to tremble, he closed the book (the Qur'an), and said that he could not go on. He looked again in the water one week later. Later he again looked, and the jinns said, "OK, we won't disturb him anymore, but he has to pray such and such *suras*, before he goes out. We are always behind him." I said if I am not well by September, I will go to the doctor and explain the situation and tell him that the pills he prescribed didn't help, that they cause harm, so an operation, he took an x-ray for an operation. Let me have an operation . . .

Kerim Bey told us this story following an account of a mysterious experience he had had of seeing *Sarı Kız*, a "Golden Girl" (or pale, blonde, or "yellow" woman) late one night. When we asked whether the story had any relation to the original "fright" that caused his illness, he told the story of the jinns, framing it by saying it was from the perspective of "old custom" (*eski adet*).

The jinn story is told from the point of view of a religious healer. It provides a clear alternative to a more straightforward reading of the original event as a "fright" or "shock" that caused fainting and the eventual onset of epilepsy. But the framing of the story by a different account of the cause of the illness ("inflamed veins in the head"), presented from the perspective of a physician, maintains these alternate readings of the experience and alternate plot structures without resolving them. Indeed, later in the interview Kerim gave a very brief version of another experience that might be related to his epilepsy. ("Before I fell down from the truck, I had a fight with one of our neighbors. A stone hit my head. This might also cause my illness.")

For those of us who were told the story, as for Kerim himself, no single account, no single point of view adequately renders the experience. As Iser (1978: 109) writes, "The reader's wandering viewpoint is, at one and the same time, caught up in and transcended by the object it is to apprehend." Each story casts doubt on the others, or provides a potential alternative interpretation of the illness and of other stories about it. New experiences call for reinterpretation of past experiences and suggest new possibilities for the future, in life as in reading. ("It is clear, then, that throughout the reading process there is a continual interplay between modified expectations and transformed memories" [Iser 1978: 111].) But the *telos* and the desire that drive the story forward are not simply those of the imagination, as of the reader of a story. They are the desire for a cure in everyday time, an urgent desire to imagine and achieve an alternative outcome. The imagination of a possible cure – the surgical procedure in the United States, or coming to terms with the jinns – lends hope to the author and subjunctivity to the narrative.

The juxtaposition of contrasting and complementary perspectives on the illness, represented through the stories of personal trauma, fainting episodes, and encounters with healers, could be illustrated from many of the interviews. Meliha Hanim told of her illness beginning when her father came and threatened her with the knife, and organized her narrative in relation to that event. However, at the end, she and her husband discussed her "diabetes" and her current low salt diet for "high blood pressure," which seemed to be helping. She discussed physicians' treatments and prescriptions, and at the same time talked of a particularly memorable meeting with a healer at a shrine that led to relief "for a period of time." The conflicting implications of these stories were left unresolved. The mother and grandmother of Omer told of the child's illness beginning with a fever, but then incorporated that story into a larger story of the neighbor's evil eye. The *hoca*'s diagnosis was only noted in passing. Unsatisfactory experiences with doctors and hospitals are contrasted with the visit to the shrine, which led to the boy beginning to speak.

The diverse accounts of the illness in these narratives represent alternative plots, a telling of the story in different ways, each implying a different source of efficacy and the possibility of an alternative ending to the story. My point is not that persons having access to a plural medical system do not simply choose among alternative forms of healing but instead draw on all of them, often at the same time – by now a truism in medical anthropology. It is rather that stories of illness and healing experience which represent quite distinct and often competing forms of composing the illness are present in narratives precisely because they maintain the quality of subjunctivity and an openness to change. Those narratives of the tragic and hopeless cases, in particular of persons who were severely mentally retarded, showed little openness of this kind. Those who had simply accepted their illness as a chronic disease to be treated with medication also maintained little of the multiplicity that was present in the narratives I have been describing. For these, the disorder was a part of the "horizon" of their experience, rather than "thematized" as central to their lives.[21] However, the multiplicity of perspectives was particularly evident in the narratives of persons in the early stages or the "middle" of the story, those still actively engaged in reevaluating the past and seeking to open their future to change. For these, subjunctivity was a central element in their construction of the object of their suffering.

Subjunctivity was also represented in the narratives through stories of encounters with the mysterious – with what C. S. Lewis, in his lovely essay "On Stories," calls "the marvelous or supernatural" (1982: 12). Lewis argued (pp. 10–15) that one of the functions of art is "to present what the narrow and desperately practical perspectives of real life exclude." He was especially fond of children's stories and science fiction because they awaken in us a sense of the "idea of otherness" and thus of the creative imagination: "To construct plausible and moving 'other worlds' you must draw on the only real 'other world' we know, that of the spirit."

Illness narratives often include stories of experiences of the mysterious, stories which suggest the possibility of sources of potency which we seldom seek in everyday life. In the Turkish narratives, these were represented in stories of uncanny experiences, as well as those of encounters with healers and their vision of the "supernatural." For Meliha Hanim, the threat of her father, what she described as his "wickedness" (*ser*), was not a distant memory but a live and mysterious force, which erupted in her fainting spells and dreams. She described how two nights earlier she felt that she was going to be ill as she went to bed.

> "At that moment, they told me that somebody's son had died. Go over there, they said. I went there. What are you doing here? I said I don't know, I locked the door and came. They said that my landlord had died. It happened exactly like that. I was coming, actually, my husband in my dream had died. Did your father die? they said. My father also died. My father was saying, this knife with its black handle is your enemy, daughter, my father said in the dream."
>
> The daughter-in-law interrupted: "You see, the same knife, she still sees it in her dreams."
>
> "The same knife," she went on, "the knife in my father's hand, that night appeared in front of me again. They say that knife will kill you. I was screaming, screaming, screaming, I was sweating in my dream. I woke up and found myself in bed. I have been suffering from this for a long time, for forty years."

For the psychiatrist reader, this passage will raise questions about the possibility of dissociation or post-traumatic stress disorder as a diagnosis, rather than epilepsy or some other diagnosis. From a narrative point of view, what seems especially powerful is the sense of mysteriousness, of the active presence of the father's evil in memory and its irruption through "fainting" into Meliha Hanim's life.

In Kerim's account of his illness, the mysterious was present not only in his story of the healer who saw the jinns, but in his encounter with the *Sarı Kız*, which he described in response to a question about the relation between being startled or frightened and his "fainting."

> . . . it was about four months ago. I was assigned to the outside depot. We had a guard house there. It is in the cold of the winter. In the winter you have snow and rain. A friend

of mine, whom I like, said come, let's boil some tea, the place where we are is nearby
. . . I am sleepy [he said]. I said go and rest, you can sleep. . . . So I went to this place to
punch the clocks. That place is very dark and desolate. There are always birds. Suddenly
a cat appears; they call it a cat, but I don't know what it is. A sound came from the cat,
like a new born baby was crying, like a mourning song (*ağıt*). Something was there . . .
I said to myself, "My God, what is this sound?" I loaded my gun. I was ready to shoot.
. . . "Perhaps one of these is coming," I thought. I went to some other places.

Before, one of our friends had gone to that place. As a joke they told him there is a
Sarı Kız there, like a jinn, there is a *Sarı Kız*, they said, there is a baby. I remembered
these things. "Is there a cat?" I said. I loaded my gun. I was going to shoot it. I finished
my rounds. I came back to the guard house. We had decided that my friend and I would
meet there from 6:10 till 7. I boiled the tea. We had bread, breakfast and so forth, and
we drank tea. "Friend, I am going to go," I said. Just after I went out [of the guard
house], I fell down [in a seizure]. If I had fallen inside I could have fallen on the stove
and burned myself.

This story was told with no conclusions drawn. Kerim would almost certainly
have denied any explicit belief that encounters with the spirit world trigger his
fainting episodes, just as many deny that they believe what the *hoca*s tell them.
Such denials are not only a result of recognition that physicians and university
faculty (such as those conducting the interviews) consider such beliefs superstitious, but deep ambivalence about such "traditional beliefs" is part of the
Turkish cultural discourse on secularism. At the same time, uncanny experiences
associated with seizures and with visits to shrines are represented in vivid
memories and recounted as narratives. While not entirely "rational," the stories
represent the presence of the mysterious and the potential for change. Narratives
are especially appropriate to such representation. As C. S. Lewis wrote, "The story
does what no theorem can quite do. It may not be 'like real life' in the superficial
sense; but it sets before us an image of what reality may well be like at some more
central region" (1982: 15).

These two "subjunctivizing" elements in the illness narratives – the maintenance of alternative perspectives and the representation of the mysterious – are
by no means the only examples I could point to. The stories have "gaps," the
unspoken or unexplained, that represent unknown or unknowable dimensions of
reality that offer hope that potent, untapped sources of efficacy will yet be found.
The quest structure of the narratives – the stories of a search for cure from doctors
and shrines all over the country – presupposes subjunctivity. The openness of time
horizons – the representation of the future as a potent source for change and
healing – is a central subjunctivizing theme in many of the stories. And others
could be identified as well.

Taken together, these subjunctivizing "tactics" of narrative representation
provide insight into the nature of illness experience. Disease as represented in
biomedicine is localized in the body, in discrete sites or physiological processes.
The narratives of those who are subjects of suffering represent illness, by contrast,
as present in a life. Illness is grounded in human historicity, in the temporality of
individuals and families and communities. It is present as potent memories and as

desire. It embodies contradictions and multiplicity. As with aesthetic objects or complex narrative texts, illness cannot be represented all at once or from a single vantage. It is constituted, rather, as a "network of perspectives," in Iser's words. ("As the reader's wandering viewpoint travels between all these segments, its constant switching during the time-flow of reading intertwines them, thus bringing forth a network of perspectives, within which each perspective opens up a view not only of others but also of the intended imaginary object" [1978: 197].) And illness, present in imagination and experience, is constituted with an openness to change and to healing.

The narrative positioning of suffering

Before concluding this chapter, it is important to discuss briefly some aspects of the pragmatics of illness narratives. It would be a grave error to conceive illness narratives as the product of an individual subject, a story told by an individual simply to make sense of his or her life. Anthropological interviews conducted in clinical settings, with only interviewer and subject present, can easily produce the illusion that such is the setting in which stories have their natural lives. Indeed, my account of Brian's narrative of chronic pain in the last chapter gives little sense of the dialogical and intersubjective quality of his story and his experience. The interviews we undertook in Turkish homes, though far more formal than most of our ethnographic work, gave lie to such illusions. Meliha Hanim's story was first told to us by her daughter-in-law. Later she herself told a variant of the story, and again later her husband entered the discussion and told yet another version of their "eloping" and of his efforts to help his wife find care. The stories of the lad Omer were told exclusively by his mother and grandmother. Kerim's wife and sister-in-law told us stories indicating quite a different view of his illness from his own, as they discussed his condition when he was not with us. In nearly all the narratives we heard, family politics was not only present as a subtext of many of the stories, but was also central to the pragmatics of their telling. The narratives were intersubjective in a direct and obvious way: they were stories that utilized popular cultural forms to describe experiences shared by members of a family; the stories were dialogically constructed, told often by interwoven conversations of several persons, stories whose referents were often the experiences of persons other than the narrators; and they were stories positioned amidst authors, narrators, and audience.

The stories told with several family members present often seemed to represent a strategic compromise. The tensions resolved by a particular narrative form often reemerged in later variants of the stories or in the pragmatic and rhetorical dimensions of performance of the narratives. Again, I can only briefly illustrate some of the pragmatic dimensions of these illness narratives, beginning with the account of a woman I will call Emine.

We found our way to the home of a twenty-three year old woman in the provincial town we were working in, entered a central living room, and found ourselves amidst part of a large extended family of Kurdish background. Emine had been identified by the neurological research team as suffering fainting spells of psychological origin, "conversion reactions" they were labeled on the form. Emine sat in the middle of the room, enormous, quiet, appearing depressed, holding a child. She was surrounded by her in-laws – a strong, rather majestic woman who was mother of the family, an older son and his wife, and the youngest *gelin*, the most recent bride to come to the family, who sat shyly. Though we addressed our questions to Emine, she spoke only a few sentences throughout the "interview." Her mother-in-law and older sister-in-law quickly joined in describing her problem. She becomes *sıkıntı* whenever you say something to her, she takes things negatively. She becomes upset, she becomes numb, she faints. When did it start? She came three years ago, we don't know if she had it before she came. She is too fat. She doesn't like crowded places. Does she fall down when she faints? Yes. She feels depressed (*bunalıyor*). "I cry and then I feel better," Emine inserted. "I have pain in my back, in my arms, and in my breast."

Emine, we were told, came from a nearby Kurdish village three years ago to marry one of the sons of this family. This son – her husband – has mental problems. He was hospitalized and still takes medications. A previous wife left him. He fought and injured someone, but was not jailed because the doctor said he had schizophrenia. But he is fine now and works at the municipality as a cleaner.

And then the sister-in-law, joined by the mother-in-law, told another story. One day, the sister-in-law said, Emine explained to her that while she was in the field with her previous husband, she got sick, she felt dizzy, she didn't drink water until the following day. She fell into a faint. Whether it was from sun or nerves we don't know, the sister-in-law said.

We asked Emine to tell us the story, but the sister-in-law went on. Her first husband died. I don't know, perhaps she became ill because of that. She says that she has been ill since that time. They had been married for six months when the accident happened. Her first husband shot himself accidentally and she was with him. They were alone. He hung his gun in a tree, and when he reached for it to stand up, he shot himself. She was frightened, crying. She ran away. The shepherds found her. Did she recover from that terrible fright? Yes, she returned to the village and recovered. She was two months pregnant when the accident happened. She said she wouldn't get married if she had a baby boy. But the baby died after she gave birth to her. Then, of course, she got *uzuntu* again.

Emine was silent. Her story was told exclusively by those around her. Her Turkish wasn't so good, we were told, she speaks primarily Kurdish. She had left her family in the village, married the schizophrenic son of this extended family, joined a household that included four sons, three of whom were married, entered a family which though Kurdish in background spoke mostly Turkish. So naturally others answered our questions.

Few of the cases we studied were as dramatic as this. Emine's voice was appropriated by the family. She was not allowed to tell her story, perhaps even to have a story. She was the daughter-in-law, an outsider in a powerful family, only a year past being the youngest bride. Her story evoked a previous husband. She was fat. She had pain. Only in her silence, her depression, did she seem powerful. The image of her sitting quietly while others told her story reminded us of the role of local power relations in the pragmatics of narrative. Relations of power and gender are expressed not only in the structure of the story, in the point of view it assumes, but in the elementary framing of who is allowed to articulate the story, who has the authority to speak, to construct the illness which belongs not to an individual but to a family.[22]

I return for my final example to the case of Meliha Hanim. As I mentioned briefly, the story of her eloping with her husband and of her father's appearance with the knife was told several times, each framing the event somewhat differently, each positioning her suffering and the care provided by members of her family somewhat differently.

In the middle of our conversation, before Meliha Hanim's husband joined us, the daughter-in-law retold the story, reshaping its plot.

> About this elopement, she herself [that is Meliha Hanim] usually explains . . . Now my father-in-law – he had been married twice – because she didn't want to marry him, they prayed, he and one of his neighbors, they prayed on two figs, two ordinary figs, and a *hoca* prayed on them, in the old way of course. . . . They gave her those figs, and after she ate those figs, she didn't resist going with my father. Later, after they had gone a little ways . . . she was regretful that she had gone, and she wanted to return. When she wanted to return, of course there were two people that had taken her, my father and his friend. They threatened her with a gun. You have to go on with this, you have come this far and you have to go on. So she had to continue going on.

This story of the marriage situates Meliha Hanim's husband in a different relation to the original events of the illness than the previous story. Along with whispered comments to our research assistant, the story highlights his previous marriages and his treachery, passionate though it was. It also casts question upon his self-representation, in his story of the onset of her illness and his efforts to find effective treatment for her. He told the story as follows:

> . . . there were no *hoca*s, hajjis, doctors that I didn't take her to. There was a *hoca* in K. village, he was building a two story house. I gave him the money for the second story! But I found no cure. We thought she had epilepsy. . . . Actually, it's not proper to say this, I wanted to marry her, but her father wouldn't give her to me. We eloped. I was at work . . . fifteen days later he came and beat on the door with a knife, someone told her, "Oh my god, your father has come, he will kill you with the knife." They came into the house, her mother, may she rest in peace, said to the husband, "Ali, come in through the window." Because they locked the door, she didn't remember that there were bars over the window, so suddenly she fell to the floor. From then to now . . .

This story not only casts the gender relations differently than the previous versions, but situates the narrator, Meliha Hanim's husband, differently. In his concluding comments to us, he expressed his continuing devotion to his wife and to finding a cure for her.

"Does anyone ever say that her illness comes from jinns or *peris*?" we asked.

"Yes, of course," he replied. "Even a doctor in S— told me to take her to a *hoca*. I said 'Doctor Bey, I came to you as a last resort. I took her to *hocas*, to doctors. They recommended you, so we came here.' By that day's money – it was nearly fifteen years ago – I gave him 20,000 lira by that day's money. But I found no remedy. But until I die, I will continue to carry her on my shoulders. Let me die, not her. If she were to die, I couldn't continue, to go on. I will carry her on my shoulders until I am broken."

Meliha Hanim's husband was a man who had grown up in the village, moved to town, and worked in a factory. He was a gentleman, refined, seemingly sweet and affectionate to his wife. In light of the whispers about his previous marriages and his eye for other women, his expressions of dedication to his wife's care remained subject to alternative interpretations to the end. And so it was with all the illness stories we heard. They represented the narrator even as they told of the illness. Suffering was positioned in the field of social relations, in particular in the dynamics of Turkish family politics. The stories were shaped by the pragmatics of the social relations as well as by the intractability of the illness and its dramatic episodes.

Thus, the illness narratives represented "fainting" as residing amidst conflicted social relations. The stories themselves were "compromise formations," configurations that concealed dynamic relations as well as representing a coherent ordering of experience. Many of the stories are best viewed, as Brooks (1984: xiv) says of the narrative text, as "a system of internal energies and tensions, compulsions, resistances, and desires." In particular, in the Turkish case, such "energies and tensions" are present in the embedding of "fainting" in family relations – in gender relations, conflicts across generations, and among affines, especially new brides and their in-laws. This was evident in the stories themselves, in particular when variants were told, as well as in the pragmatics of their narration.

Other examples of the positioning of suffering through the pragmatics of story-telling could be illustrated. For a number of the women with non-epileptic fainting, their stories of how they fainted when they became nervous or anxious suggested that such episodes enhanced their power within their families, at the same time that it articulated a life of suffering. Stories told by family members or others, when the sufferer was absent, reminded us that most of the narratives we heard were told from the perspective of those who were ill. They were designed not to represent experience dispassionately, but to elicit a particular understanding or interpretation of the condition, and in some cases to elicit a particular intervention on their behalf by the interviewers.

My goal in this section has not been to provide a full set of categories for analyzing these issues, a full sociolinguistics or pragmatics of illness narratives, but to attempt to show that narrative theory provides new ways for anthropologists interested in illness narratives to engage a close reading of our interview transcripts and ethnographic observations.

The narrative shaping of illness

In this chapter, I have examined what we can learn about the cultural shaping of illness through a careful analysis of the stories people tell about their experience. Two kinds of conclusions are appropriate: first, a few words about what we can learn about epilepsy in Turkish culture from such analysis; and second, a more general review of the role of narrative in the shaping of illness.

I began this chapter with questions about the relation of "fainting" to "epilepsy" in Turkish culture provoked by Meliha Hanim's stories about her illness. Through the course of our research it became clear that epilepsy belongs in popular discourse to the larger domain of "fainting." This should come as no surprise, not only because fainting is less stigmatizing than epilepsy in Turkish culture. Although epilepsy is generally represented in biomedicine and in popular American medical culture as a disease with origins in a discrete location in the brain, clearly distinguishable from hysterical or functional fainting of psychological origins, this was not true as recently as the nineteenth century in Europe and America. Hypnotism, hysteria, and epilepsy were closely entwined in the history of European psychiatry, and the leading neurologists of the last half of the nineteenth century – Charcot with his colleague Paul Richer at the Salpetrière in Paris, and William Gowers at the National Hospital in London – devoted much of their writing and research to describing "hysteroepilepsy" and identifying seizures resulting from lesions in the cerebral cortex.[23] Indeed, recent work on "temporolimbic epilepsy" has again sought to expand the category epilepsy to include a wide variety of behavioral disorders which appear to be accompanied by unusual EEG findings from the temporolimbic region (see Spiers et al. 1985 for a summary). Thus the phenomenology does not allow a neat distinction of types or origins of seizures or "fainting."

"Fainting" as a cultural object condenses a network of meanings. This semantic network includes traumatic experiences of fright, shock, and loss; generalized expressions of suffering, anxiety and grief (*sıkıntı* and *uzuntu*); attacks by jinns and being struck by "bad glance" or evil eye; and severe forms of seizures, including those labeled epilepsy, as well as mental retardation and madness. These are linked to fainting not only symbolically, through various "semiotic connections," explanatory models, and idioms of distress. They are also joined through the special logic of narratives. Stories organized around prototypical plot forms find the mysterious origins of seizures in these diverse domains of experience. The "network of perspectives" available in these stories allows the "wandering viewpoint" to constitute an "intended imaginary object" that both exceeds and is exceeded by the dramatic behaviors and loss of consciousness associated with seizures (Iser 1978: 197). And these stories do not neatly distinguish epileptic and non-epileptic fainting.

The stories we were told also recall vivid experiences with physicians and healers. Nearly all those we interviewed had sought treatment from physicians, though their experiences were quite mixed. Some remained on standard anti-convulsive medications, some continued in active search for a treatment that would produce cure, and some had despaired of effective care. Nearly all had sought religious healing, and stories representing the healers' perspective enlarged the imaginative domain of the illness, though they were often told with skepticism and irony. Stories also told of shattered ambitions, loss of status and opportunity, and threats to family honor, all of which are part of the experience of recurrent seizures. At the same time, many epileptics continued to work, to be married and have children, and to have friendships they described as little influenced by their illness. These stories, as much as those about cause or about dramatic seizures, are included in the corpus of stories that constitute fainting as a domain of Turkish popular culture.

It is tempting for a medical social scientist to enumerate the cultural beliefs concerning the cause and workings of epilepsy, then compare these with beliefs in other societies. People of course reason about illness, and culture provides the logic of that rationality. I have resisted, however, focusing on the structure of reasoning. The transformation of these narratives and the modes of aesthetic response associated with stories into "beliefs" or "explanation" would be extremely misleading. The language of belief and rationality sets forth a whole chain of analytic assumptions associated with progressive science, authorizing the language of medicine and heightening the sense of distance between ourselves and the other, as I described in chapter 1. More than that, it describes quite poorly the similarities and differences across cultures in the narrative shaping of reality, the complex relations between story and experience, and the aesthetic response associated with stories and the constitution of illness as a cultural domain. It has been my claim that detailed attention to narrative and narrative forms of representing reality provides insight into the synthetic processes through which illness is constituted, while telling us a great deal about our practical concerns about the cultural shaping of illness associated with such dramatic disorders as epileptic seizures. This leads me to some final observations about the analysis of illness narratives.

There is an obvious reason for rejecting the analogy of illness and its interpretation to the reading of fiction. Illness is all too real, and its attendant fears and misery "cannot be wished away."[24] Any analogy of such experience to "fiction" has the potential to devalue suffering and misrepresent the very essence of the experience. However, disease as embedded in life can only be represented through a creative conceptual response. Its "thereness" in the body must be rendered "there" in the life. And this process, even more than the referential or "locutionary" processes of biomedical representation, requires an aesthetic response, an active, synthetic process of constituting in an effort to grasp what is certainly there but is indeterminate in form.

Literary scholars and philosophers since Aristotle have sought to reduce the gap between aesthetic objects and reality, by finding powerful references to reality and significance in poetry and fiction. Ricoeur (1981a: 274–296) argues similarly for reducing the gap between "fiction" and "history." Although illness experiences are far from "fictional," there are reasons to reduce the gap between fiction and reality in the context of cultural studies of illness – real illness in contemporary, living sufferers, not simply its representation in literature or tribal myths – by investigating the narrative qualities of illness in all its reality. Several reasons may be enumerated.

First, much of what we know about illness we know through stories – stories told by the sick about their experiences, by family members, doctors, healers, and others in the society. This is a simple fact. "An illness" has a narrative structure, although it is not a closed text, and it is composed as a corpus of stories. Second, stories are not only the means by which illness experience is objectified, communicated, and reported to others; they are also a primary means for giving shape to experience and making past experience available to sufferers themselves. Significant experience is stored in the stockhouse of memory as stories, and remembering and recounting those stories provide access to the attendant experiences.

Third, illness narratives – both the corpus of story episodes and the larger life "story" or illness narrative to which they contribute – have elements in common with fiction. They have a plot; succession is ordered as history or event, given configuration. They have indeterminacy and openness; therapeutic actions, motives of participants, the efficacy of interventions and events are open to reinterpretation as life goes on, revealing hidden aspects unavailable to the blindness of the present. There is no final judgment about their meaning or significance. Narratives are organized as predicament and striving and as an unfolding of human desire.

Fourth, illness stories once told break free of their original discursive or performative setting. They are "entextualized," in Ricoeur's (1981a: 197–221) sense of the word.[25] They are told and retold, made available to multiple "readers." Their effects and interpretations are unpredictable; they cannot be controlled by the author, by the teller of the tale.

Fifth, the sufferer is not only a narrator of stories but is, in several important senses, similar to a "reader." Those with an illness find themselves in the midst of "reading" a story, often helpless to affect its outcome, constantly revising interpretations, judgments, hopes, and expectations as the narrative time progresses. The illness can only be comprehended, constituted by a synthetic act, by giving larger sense to what can only be experienced in discrete moments and from limited perspectives. Medical treatments lead the sufferer into new imaginative worlds, whether into the specialized worlds of biomedicine or of other forms of healing. Quite new aspects of experience are "thematized," while others recede to the horizon. Illness is confrontational; it captures our attention. It is filled with "gaps," with the unknown and the unknowable, which provoke an imaginative response. All of these are characteristics which Ingarden (1973), Iser (1978), Ricoeur (1981a, 1984), and others have shown to be present in the phenomenology of reading.

Finally, illness and illness narratives have the potential to recast reality in relation to the unexpected, the non-ordinary, a predicament, the mysterious. Bruner (1986: 24) writes that "stories of literary merit . . . render the world newly strange, rescue it from obviousness, fill it with gaps that call upon the reader, in Barthes's sense, to become a writer, a composer of a virtual text in response to the actual. In the end, it is the reader who must write for himself what *he* intends to do with the actual text." And so with illness. At the same time that it offers suffering, pain, and misery, when illness is transformed as narrative it has the potential to awaken us to conventionality and its finitude, provoking a creative response and revitalizing language and experience.

C. S. Lewis argued that narratives must be organized as a series of events if we are to consider them as stories, but that this series "is only really a net whereby to catch something else. The real theme may be, and perhaps usually is, something that has no sequence in it . . . " (1982: 17). The struggle between plot and theme, between the succession of events and the grand ideas we feel are represented by this particular set of events, is as characteristic of life as of stories. And as in life, the grand ideas often elude the stories as well. No surprise, Lewis concludes (1982: 19). "If Story fails in that way does not life commit the same blunder? . . . If the author's plot is only a net, and usually an imperfect one, a net of time and event for catching what is not really a process at all, is life much more? . . . In life and art both, as it seems to me, we are always trying to catch in our net of successive moments something that is not successive." Stories, perhaps better than other forms, provide a glimpse of the grand ideas that often seem to elude life and defy rational description. Illness stories often seem to provide an especially fine mesh for catching such ideas. It is for this reason that anthropologists often turn to stories of illness and suffering to be awakened to the ideas we sense are present in the lives of others, present but not readily described.

7

Aesthetics, rationality, and medical anthropology

Shortly after I had finished writing the last major chapter of this book – on the narrative representation of illness – a former professor of mine asked what I had discussed in the Morgan Lectures. I replied that I was developing a theory of culture and illness from the perspective of aesthetics, examining how illness is formulated as an "aesthetic object." I later thought back on what I had said with considerable anxiety, because with the exception of reviewing some of the literature on narrativity the book hardly addresses the issue of aesthetics at all. Furthermore, this surely represents a small part of what this book has been about and a very partial way of conceiving a program for medical anthropology. Nonetheless, my rather offhand comment suggested an interpretation of where I had emerged after nearly two years of work on this project, and may serve as the starting point for work to come. Studies of narrative and story-telling, of art and the aesthetic response may ultimately have more to offer for comparative, cross-cultural studies of illness and healing than is immediately obvious, stimulating insights quite different than those provided by framing the field as the comparative study of human ecology or political economy or social structure or illness behavior.

When I responded to my friend's question that I had undertaken an analysis of illness as an "aesthetic object," I was not implying that illness is a thing of beauty, although there is an elaborate cultural aesthetic to healing activities (Roseman 1988, 1992) as there is to everyday forms of social life and bodily awareness, including illness (Desjarlais 1992a, 1992b). I was referring more specifically, however, to how we analyze the disjunction between disease as an object or condition of a physical body, as it is popularly (and medically) conceived, and disease as a presence in a life or in a social world. I was suggesting that theories of aesthetics, which explore the relation of the canvas and oil of a painting to the highly complex "aesthetic object" or work of art, or the relation of the printed text to the literary object, might provide a means for challenging our own cultural proclivity for naturalism and biological reductionism.

The aesthetic object is not reducible to the oil on the canvas or to a musical score or even its performance. It is also not reducible to a representation or reflection of these in the mind of the viewer or the musical audience. The aesthetic object is a particularly complex and dynamic form of relationship among these, a relationship which depends upon and yet transcends both performance and audience, reader and text, the material object and a reflective, sensuous response.[1] By way of analogy, disease is not simply a physiological or biological state of an individual human body. Neither is it a reflection of such a state in the experience of the sufferer or in a particular representation of disease – in the literature of the biomedical sciences, in the conversations of clinicians and the information produced by their technologies, in the host of "opinions" on the condition articulated in the social world, or in the documents produced by administrative and political bodies which have authority to classify disease and disability and to respond. Disease is a particularly complex and dynamic form of relationship among these, a synthetic object *par excellence*. Any cross-cultural study thus faces the methodological and theoretical challenge of investigating illness and healing with full awareness of this multiplicity and with methods that account for the synthesizing activities by which disease is made an object of personal, social, political, and medical significance.

The question I want to return to in these final remarks is how we go about such investigations. How do we take account of the "heterology" of illness, the multiplicity of voices and perspectives that enter conversation about disease and its treatment? How do we investigate how such voices not merely comment on but constitute illness and human suffering, as well as therapies and the alleviation of suffering? How is illness inserted into life, and why does it so often serve as the source of a society's reflections about the ultimate nature of reality and about what matters most in life? And what are the implications of how we address these issues for our epistemological and ethical concerns as we go about our research and writing?

As I gave my spur of the moment interpretation of the lectures, I was thinking explicitly of Wolfgang Iser's writing about how the reader's confrontation with a text provokes the constitution of aesthetic objects and the reader's entry into the world of the text. Iser argues that the literary object – a character in a novel, an event, a situation or dilemma – can never be given or comprehended in a single moment or from a single point of view. As he writes, " . . . the whole text can never be perceived at any one time. . . . The 'object' of the text can only be imagined by way of different consecutive phases of reading. . . . there is a moving viewpoint which travels along *inside* that which it has to apprehend" (Iser 1978: 108–109). Thus we come to know characters through the eyes and conversations of other actors in the drama. We see them respond to novel and fateful predicaments. Characters reveal themselves and develop through time, surprising us by their strengths or disappointing or outraging us by their vanity or miscalculations or their cruelty. No single perspective ever reveals them fully. Their manifold quality requires acts of synthesis on the part of the reader, an active response in which we enter the world of the text and draw together the divergent perspectives to constitute the character or the event as a whole, as an aesthetic object.

Characters are not natural objects of texts, only later interpreted by readers; characters as aesthetic objects require the synthesizing activities of readers for their formulation. It is my intuition that these activities may serve as a powerful model for how illness is constituted as a personal and social object, embedded within the lives of individuals and families, interpreted and responded to in the context of medical pluralism and the complexities and discord of contemporary medical institutions.

For Iser, the synthesizing activities of the reader are at the center of his investigation of the phenomenology of reading. It is my claim that analogous activities lie at the heart of the "formative principles" inherent in the constitution of illness within particular cultures. Reflections on this analogy and its implications for a program for medical anthropology will serve as my final remarks, drawing together issues addressed in these lectures. First, I will briefly examine the implications of medicine's "heteroglossia" or the presence of diverse voices and competing interpretations for the study of illness and healing, with a look at previous work on semantic networks. Second, I will make explicit my claims that we should make "interpretive practices" the basis for comparative studies, and indicate some rather surprising epistemological implications of addressing medicine via theories of aesthetics. Finally, I will return to the critique of instrumental reason, which I have been developing here, and conclude with a few remarks about the implications of this critique for the challenges facing medical anthropologists.

Lest I be misunderstood from the outset, let me preface these concluding remarks by making explicit one methodological principle which I take as given and which has been implicit in the organization of this book. My interest in symbolic forms and cultural practices or in "heterology" and aesthetics is not meant to discount comparative studies of medical systems or absolve medical anthropologists from the demands for controlled comparisons of disease and illness, studies which advance our understanding of the place of culture in shaping illness and mediating healing. And it is not meant to diminish the relevance of biology to our research. Anthropologists interested in the comparative study of illness and its treatment do well to move dialectically between a critical analysis of biomedical categories and knowledge, on the one hand, and operationalizations of such categories for the purposes of comparative, cross-cultural analysis, on the other (see B. Good 1992b). For example, I attempted in the third chapter to develop a critical analysis of medical knowledge as assimilated into the experience of medical students, arguing that what is taken as "natural" by the clinician is a very distinctive formulation of medicine's objects that results from carefully learned and regulated medical practices. On the other hand, in chapters 5 and 6, I reported on research in which formal criteria for "chronic pain" and "epilepsy," categories drawn from medicine, were used to select samples of individuals in order to investigate how these conditions are experienced and given voice through culturally distinctive narratives. Medical anthropologists must take very seriously the problem of defining units of analysis, if they are to make cross-cultural comparisons – on this I fully agree with Browner and her colleagues. And medicine, along with social theory and local ethnomedical systems, may serve as the source for such units. For example, extremely important contributions to our understanding of psychopathology have been made by anthropologists who operationalize the diagnostic criteria for "schizophrenia," identify samples, then investigate how social practices and cultural interpretations work their profound effects on the experience, social response, treatment, and course and prognosis of this troubling condition, as well as by those who have provided a cultural critique of this category from professional psychiatry. Similar contributions have been made by those who operationalized criteria for "susto," an ethnomedical category in Mexico, as the basis for research (Rubel 1964; Rubel, O'Nell and Collado Ardon 1984). What I have argued throughout this book, however, is that in both moments of this dialectic, critical attention should be given to the "formative" activities through which illness is constituted, made the object of knowledge and control, embedded in experience and social life, and transformed through therapies and the "work of culture." And I have argued that reductionist theories of culture, in various forms, undermine our best efforts to produce a coherent account of medical knowledge and ethically sensitive reflections on human suffering.

The "synthesis" of aesthetic objects: illness and "semantic networks" revisited

Theories of aesthetic response provide a potential model for investigating the relation of "disease" to the "network of perspectives" and competing interpretations brought to bear on symptoms and illness in all medical systems. They also serve to rethink some aspects of the study of semantic networks.

For Iser, the characters of the literary or dramatic text and the imaginary worlds which they inhabit are not entirely fixed by the text. The text is partially indeterminate. It provokes a response in the reader, and the characters – those denizens of the literary world – inhabit the imagination of the reader. But the characters are not simply figures of the mental life of the reader, or of a community of readers, any more than they are simply given by the text. They are constituted through a complex relation among text, reader, and the social and historical moment of each, at once dependent on and transcending these. The "synthesis" is not a single, final act of the reader, but an on-going process, joining memory and anticipation, a process imaged by Iser as a "moving viewpoint." As he wrote (1978: 107):

> The reader's wandering viewpoint is, at one and the same time, caught up in and transcended by the object it is to apprehend. Apperception can only take place in phases, each of which contains aspects of the object to be constituted, but none of which can claim to be representative of it. Thus the aesthetic object cannot be identified with any of its manifestations during the time-flow of the reading. The incompleteness of each manifestation necessitates syntheses, which in turn bring about the transfer of the text

to the reader's consciousness. The synthetizing process, however, is not sporadic – it continues throughout every phase of the journey of the wandering viewpoint.

These synthesizing activities must hold in tension the diverse and often divergent viewpoints from which the character or situation have been conveyed. The reader hears from one actor after another, enters imaginatively into their perspectives on the narrative drama, and from this vantage comes to know central characters. This "knowing" requires a synthesis that transcends any particularity.

> As the reader's wandering viewpoint travels between all these segments, its constant switching during the time-flow of reading intertwines them, thus bringing forth a *network of perspectives*, within which each perspective opens up a view not only of others but also of the intended imaginary object. Hence no single textual perspective can be equated with this imaginary object, of which it only forms one aspect. The object itself is a *product of interconnections* . . . (Iser 1978: 197; my emphases)

For individual sufferers, becoming acquainted with a major disease or chronic illness involves a similar process. We learn of a condition bit by bit – from a confused encounter with a physician, chance discussions with others who have a similar illness and covert responses of those who do not, popular literature and claims of "alternative" healing, as well as the unique and primary claims of our own embodied experience. We indeed learn to view illness from the perspectives of others, holding them in narrative tension. These opinions are not given all at once, but emerge over time – time which is fraught with anxiety and despair as well as moments of anticipation and hope. And no synthesis is ever complete. Illness narratives – stories patients and their families tell about the illness, as well as implicit narratives through which physicians emplot the therapeutic course facing their patients – construct their object by maintaining this multiplicity and taking a stance in relation to it. Illness is thus objectified, made an object of understanding and striving, both through narrative rendering and through acts of synthesis comparable to those of a reader.

But this is true not only for the individual who is sick or possessed or in pain, but for other actors in the medical drama. Even within medicine, there is never a single medical object. A tumor is clearly a material form, but viewed from within the medical world is resembles a "multiply stratified creation," as Ingarden described the work of art (Ingarden 1973, quoted in Casey 1973: xx). It is a gross mass, a histological condition conceived in relation to processes of normal and abnormal cellular growth, and a moment in a process of vascularization. It is a physiological condition, and a product of a genetic regulatory scheme which has "switched on" certain forms of growth. But it is much more than this as well. It is a part of the sensuous, lived body, a dramatic rupture of a life history, an object of intense diagnostic and therapeutic activity, and a politicized object of social attention. Any act of objectification is a moment of synthesis, but the "multiple strata" resist closure. For each actor involved, alternative representations and the complexity of the object challenge any particular formulation.

Acknowledgement of the multiple points of view through which we come to know disease does not imply that we cannot conduct cross-cultural studies, that no unit of analysis can serve for comparative hypotheses and research. We can quite usefully study the experience and response to cancer or epilepsy or chronic pain or depression across cultures, although such categories may be called into question as research proceeds.[2] But the empiricist program of studying culturally relative beliefs about natural disease objects is challenged on two counts – for its essentialist conception of disease and for a superficial analysis of how illness is cognized and comes to be known as a dimension of human experience and understanding. An insistence on recognizing the "network of perspectives," the "moving viewpoint," and the emergent activities of objectification and synthesis offers far more interesting opportunities for comparative studies.

In 1977 I introduced the notion "semantic network" to indicate that illness has meaning not simply through univocal representations that depict a disease state of the body, but as a "product of interconnections," in Iser's terms – a "syndrome" of experiences, words, feelings, and actions that run together for members of a society. The concept was elaborated in a set of papers, written in collaboration with Mary-Jo Good (B. Good and M. Good 1980, 1981, 1992; B. Good, M. Good, and Moradi 1985), in which we attempted to incorporate into our analysis the diverse meanings, voices, and experiences that are condensed by core symbols in the medical lexicon. We began by simply trying to make sense of a common complaint by women and men in the small Azeri town in Iran in which we worked that their "hearts" (*qalb*) were upset or uncomfortable or in distress (*narahat*). As we inquired about these complaints, a wide variety of explanations were given for specific cases of the illness. And as we mapped out in graphic form the relations among these explanations, they suggested several culturally specific domains of experience to be the referents of the complaint, rather than some medical condition or an unarticulated emotional injury or conflict. What we called semantic network analysis thus suggested a way of conceiving how diverse and apparently conflicting claims about the nature of a specific illness complaint could be synthesized and culturally objectified, formulated as an "object" of personal and social awareness. Based on this work, we investigated other categories in the medical lexicon of popular Iranian and American health culture, as well as core symbols of professional medicine.[3]

The analysis of "semantic networks" was conceived as a particular approach to semiotic or symbolic analysis. We attempted to represent cultural meaning in configurationist terms, in contrast both with naturalist or empiricist accounts, on the one hand, and with structuralist accounts of semiotics in terms of binary oppositions, on the other. Mapping out "networks" provided one way of systematically investigating and graphically representing semantic domains or semantic fields.[4] We sought to follow Izutsu's advice to "bring together, compare, and put in relation all the terms that resemble, oppose, and correspond with each other" (1966: 36). We argued that this provided a method for identifying meaningfully related domains of social life and experience, as well as semantic domains, that are essential to the translation of a term such as "heart distress," as it was used in Iranian medical discourses.[5]

Furthermore, we argued that semantic networks are cultural models that not only reflect or refer to specific domains of social life, but that are generative models as well. For example, body size has been linked to "self control" in American popular and medical culture in a relatively enduring fashion. The meaning of being "fat" in American society is inextricably linked to a large semantic domain associated with "self control." Widely differing popular and professional theories of obesity and dieting provide countless rationalizations for this deep cultural association, which is taken as natural or given. Semantic networks such as these are "deep" in the sense that they are largely outside of explicit cultural awareness, that they are enduring, appear to be natural, and are generative of popular and professional discourse and behavior. New elements – new diseases, new forms of therapy – can thus be incorporated into a medical system only by being integrated into existing semantic networks or by condensing new sets of relationships.[6]

Semantic network analysis was thus developed as a means for analyzing illness as a "network of perspectives" and a "product of interconnections," as a form of synthesis that condenses multiple and often conflicting social and semantic domains to produce "the meaning" of a complaint or an illness. Rethinking this work from the perspective of reader response theory or studies of the work of art, however, suggests at least two limitations to a semiotic account of these issues.

First, a semiotic theory of "synthesis" – of a symbol "condensing"[7] multiple meanings – is not mistaken, but from the perspective developed in this book, such a theory is partial and distinctly limited. Iser's analysis of the synthesis of the aesthetic objects of a narrative (a character, a dilemma, an event) as a process in which the reader confronts a text in all its indeterminacy, a set of activities through which the reader enters the world of the narrative and responds imaginatively to the diverse points of view as they unfold through time, and a process which maintains rather than dissolves (or resolves) the dynamic tensions in the constitution of the aesthetic object, suggests a number of issues to be explored in comparative medical studies. In particular, it suggests a way of advancing our analysis in a way that incorporates a recognition of the heteroglossia or multiplicity of voices present in the constitution of all illness.

The term "heteroglossia" has come into academic prominence recently through the work of Mikhail Bakhtin, the Russian literary critic, and his analysis of the dialogical quality of texts and their interpretation (Bakhtin 1981, 1984; see also Todorov 1984, Morson 1981). Bakhtin began with a recognition of the diversity of national, religious and scholarly tongues that entered literature at the end of the Middle Ages, enabling the emergence of the novel. He insisted on careful attention to the individuality of such voices, as well as the dialogue in which they engaged, in words that offer a challenge to ethnographers.

For the consciousness that lives in it, language is not an abstract system of normative forms but a concrete heterological opinion on the world. Every word gives off the scent of a profession, a genre, a current, a party, a particular work, a particular man, a generation, an era, a day, and an hour. Every word smells of the context and contexts in which it has lived its intense social life; all words and all forms are inhabited by intentions. (Quoted in Todorov 1984: 56–57)

Given the complexity of medical settings in which we work, providing a readable ethnographic account of the "concrete heterological opinions" present and of the contexts in which these voices have lived their "intense social life" is no mean task. Analyzing the diverse ways in which "heterological opinions" are synthesized, in which they are joined in the objectification of and response to disease, and investigating the implications of these processes for course of illness or therapeutic outcome are equally challenging. And here Bakhtin's image of dialogue – of dialogue among the voices in a text, of dialogue between these voices and the reader, of the dialogical quality of consciousness and the imagination – may serve to complement Iser's image of the "reader" as a model for research. Illness is not only constituted in the "wandering viewpoint" of the individual – the sufferer, a family member, a care-provider. It is also multiply constituted in ways that are often conflicting. Illness is essentially dialogical. It is "synthesized" in the narratives of Turkish families, fraught with gender and kinship politics. It is objectified as a specific form of disordered physiology in case presentations and conversations among physicians. But such objectification may be resisted or subverted by patients, by legal advocates, or by agents of insurance companies who authorize or refuse payments for specific treatments, all negotiating with one another in constituting the medical "object" and in addressing the material body. Thus, while core symbols in a medical lexicon may indeed condense or hold in tension a powerful network of meanings, the process of synthesis is not only semiotic, but social, dialogical, imaginative, and political. And so too should be our analyses.

Reference to Bakhtin suggests a second limitation of the semantic paradigm. Bakhtin recognized that in consciousness and in social life, as well as in literature, the multiplicity of voices about which he wrote are engaged in positioned dialogue. The analysis of Freud's writing by Bakhtin and his "circle of Freud" in terms of an "unauthorized consciousness" as distinguished from a "habitual, 'official' consciousness," written as it was during Stalinist repression, had potent political tones and served as a foundation for much of his later writing (Todorov 1988: 31; Volosinov 1976). Words not only carry with them the contexts in which they have lived; they are "inhabited by intentions," and these intentions are linked to structures of authority. Semantic network analysis has little way to represent the diversity of forms of authority and resistance associated with core elements in a medical system. We have argued that semantic networks are produced and reproduced precisely in struggles over "heart distress" or "competence" or "risk," struggles which reflect and reveal structures of power and authority. Furthermore, the fact that semantic networks are culturally "deep" and generative as well as enduring may provide one means for understanding how hegemonic forms are organized and reproduced.[8] However, this relationship between semantic structures and hegemonic power relations has not been fully developed. A purely semantic analysis of these issues is limited; however, semantic analysis can provide a means to further critical research.

One major challenge we face in cross-cultural studies is thus to investigate how diverse actors, each with attendant "voices," interpretive practices, forms of knowledge, and moral stances, contribute to the constitution of illness in personal experience and as an object of medical and social attention. I remain convinced that semantic networks serve as deep, generative cultural forms, playing a significant role in processes of objectification and synthesis, and that analysis of such networks contributes to our understanding of illness as a "product of inter-connections" rather than as a more or less accurate representation of disordered biology. Studies of literary or aesthetic objects suggest ways we might extend such analysis, providing new approaches to understanding how multiple points of view are joined and synthesized in narratives and negotiated in diverse dialogical settings. And recent critical studies offer important opportunities for research that attends more directly to distinctive medical voices and the "heterological opinions" they offer on the world and for extending our understanding of semantic networks and their role in the reproduction of hegemonic meanings and social relations.

The comparative study of interpretive practices: culture, illness, and medical knowledge

A theme that has run throughout these lectures has been an argument that we should conceive culture and reality as embedded in activity, in interpretive practices of members of a society interacting with the social and empirical world to formulate and apprehend reality in distinctive ways. I have argued that interpretive practices generate distinctive modes of experience, and that these in turn are associated with culturally distinctive forms of illness. And I have suggested that a primary task for comparative analysis is the identification of such practices, the analysis of how they mediate the experience of illness, and systematic cross-cultural investigation of their effects on the phenomenology and course of illness.

Many of medical anthropology's most dramatic examples of such research are found in studies of the so-called "culture bound syndromes." In many of these, a set of distinct cultural practices can be shown to exploit neurological or psycho-logical propensities that are found in members of all societies. For example, *latah* is a form of deviance found in Malay cultures (with similar forms present in several other Asian societies). When *latah* sufferers are startled, they engage in a highly stereotyped set of behaviors. They may echo words or behaviors of those who provoke (or startle) them, burst out with profanity or engage in long sequences of "*latah* behaviors," amusing an audience and shaming the sufferer.

Ronald Simons (1980), a psychiatrist and medical anthropologist, has provided evidence that this condition is an elaboration of the startle reflex. In all societies, some persons are "hyper-startlers." However, in Malay cultures, this neuro-biological potential is exploited – culturally and socially – to constitute a distinctive form of deviant behavior. Not all Malay hyper-startlers are provoked into becoming *latah*; only those who are socially vulnerable, especially low status widows, are likely to be labelled and treated as *latah*. The startle reflex thus mediates the condition, and many of the accompanying behaviors seem neuro-logically patterned. However, neurobiology is relatively indeterminate, with interpretive activities and social relations producing a distinctive cultural form of deviance or illness.

Possession and trance experience offer more complex examples of culturally specific elaborations of a mode of shaping and apprehending reality that is a broadly available human potential. Possession exploits dissociative processes that are cognitive potentials for at least some members of all societies; it may also reflect developmental responses to trauma that lower the threshold of intrusive dissociative experience, explaining both the social (and gendered) distribution of the condition as well as individual vulnerability to being possessed.

My point here, of course, is that these examples may serve as a model for research that investigates how specific interpretive practices, grounded in symbolic forms and modes of experience they mediate, are associated with distinctive forms of illness and "ethnobehavioral" syndromes. Whether we are investigating "functional" conditions such as these or infectious diseases or other medical conditions, the position developed in this book suggests we focus our research on cross-cultural comparisons of the formative practices of health care systems, rather than on beliefs and behaviors associated with given diseases. In addition, I have argued that the moment we attend carefully to such interpretive practices, whether of those who are ill or those who provide care, we find them to include narratives.

But the program outlined in this book goes considerably beyond a set of methods for studying how culture influences the experience and course of illness – empirical research on the extent and sources of the social and cultural relativity of illness and disease, research which thus critiques the rendering of such conditions as natural and universal in most biomedical writing. And the claim I am making for the relevance of aesthetics is not limited to my concern that we should pay far closer attention to the relation of narrative to illness experience. I have argued throughout these lectures that methodological difficulties reflect very real epistemological problems. I have attempted to probe the tensions and paradoxes within which we work – paradoxes present in my own framing of "possession" in relation to "neurological potentials" rather than in relation to the spirit world. I want to return here to my final reflections on the relevance of a theory of interpretive practices – and of narrative and aesthetics – for the epistemological issues facing medical anthropology.

"Medical anthropology" is a kind of oxymoron. The term "medical" usually denotes a realm of rationality and natural science, a realm in which culture is seen as an intrusion into scientific understanding and rational therapeutics. "Anthropology," on the other hand, designates a fundamentally historicist vision, a conviction that all knowledge is culturally located, relative to historical era and perspective. The issues raised by the juxtaposition of the natural sciences and historicism are thus especially acute in medical anthropology. They are heightened by our post-colonial concerns about how we should write about "science" in relation to other societies and ways of life.

I argued in the beginning of this book that for medical anthropologists, these theoretical concerns – shared widely with other anthropologists and social scientists – are closely tied to methodological and ethical considerations, lending them a special urgency. The authorization inherent in other ways of life and in radically other interpretations of human suffering, present among persons we anthropologists go off to live among, runs headlong into the powerful authorization of the biological sciences. The conflicts between medical representations of illness and local cultural interpretations of sickness and suffering are made more difficult because of the moral imperative we feel to use medical knowledge to relieve suffering and promote the welfare of those with whom we work. And our uneasiness is heightened by the growing dominance of instrumental reality in medical practice today. Unless we explicitly confront the empiricist claims of the biosciences, a coherent response to these paradoxes will remain impossible. I therefore take it to be a critical task for medical anthropologists to join in rethinking the theoretical foundations of comparative studies in this field, to develop a new language and methods for research which can both advance our empirical research and open the field to a more humane practice.

I began these lectures with a critique of common-sense theories of medical anthropology, arguing that a view of rationality which is embedded in a correspondence theory of knowledge – that is, one that conceives the source of rationality to be the match between propositions and the empirical world – has serious difficulties, however attractive it may be. I drew on Cassirer's philosophy of culture, Charles Taylor's writing on language, and the Boasian tradition of cultural analysis to argue that interpretive practices are formative, that symbolic forms mediate reality and all knowledge. Reality in this view is not that which precedes interpretation. It is rather that which resides amidst the interactions or relationships among the physical body, the lived body, and the interpretive activities of the sufferer, healers, and others in the social world. Medical knowledge, whether that of bench researchers, clinicians, health workers in an urban community, specialists of Tibetan meditation and healing, or Brazilian Indian shamans, is knowledge of distinctive aspects of reality mediated by symbolic forms and interpretive practices. Each depends upon a form of correspondence between language and the empirical world, where the "empirical world" refers to that which is found within human experience. However, as Hilary Putnam argues in his discussions of varieties of realism (which I quoted in chapter 4), the problem we face is not whether there is a correspondence between language and the empirical world, but that there are too many correspondences. Medical anthropologists are thus not limited to repeating comparative studies of the correspondence between (largely mistaken) cultural views and a reality to which we (and the medical sciences) have unique access. Instead, we have vital opportunities to investigate how local medical worlds – including those of biomedicine – formulate and respond to illness, comprehend aspects of reality, produce distinctive forms of medical knowledge, and shape a crucial dimension of human experience.

My contention has thus been that meaning and knowledge are always in reference to a world constituted in human experience, formulated and apprehended through symbolic forms and distinctive interpretive practices. This view neither contradicts our intuition that medical knowledge is progressive, nor implies that knowledge is subjective. The empirical world always transcends our knowledge; and technology, symbolic formations, and social practices open up worlds to our experience – and to knowledge. John Barrow (1988), in his book *The World Within the World*, makes the extremely interesting observation that although Newtonian mechanics works well locally (one can fly to the moon using Newton alone, he claims), we know (thanks to Einstein) that Newton was wrong. There is in this, he says (p. 110), a "salutary lesson. We can use a law of Nature for hundreds of years without any adverse results, and build an entire metaphysical view of Nature's mechanical workings upon it, yet find that it is just a little piece of a vast and entirely dissimilar scheme." The point is that we do not make up worlds through the interpretive practices that lie at the ground of all our knowledge. Symbolic practices and our technologies mediate knowledge. They open worlds to exploration; they open to understanding aspects of the natural world and worlds of human experience. And meaning and knowledge are always constituted in relation to such worlds of experience.

The approach I have developed here is thus not a form of subjectivism or voluntarism. Such positions are simply untenable for medical anthropologists. When we suffer disease, we confront the resistance of the real world as brute fact. The practices and technologies of health care systems mediate real, empirical knowledge, and some are far more effective than others. The alternative, however, is not simply a return to empiricism. The natural sciences themselves depend not only on an implicit view of the relation of truth and beauty – a view that orderly, harmonious theories are required to represent the order of nature (Chandrasekhar 1987) – but also on an understanding of reality as multifaceted and infinite. Perspectivism is rooted in reality itself. As Ortega y Gasset observed, "Reality, just because it is reality and exists outside of our individual minds, can only reach us by multiplying itself into a thousand faces or surfaces." Or again, "Reality cannot be observed except from the point of view to which each of us has been inescapably assigned in the universe. That reality and this point of view are correlative, and just as reality cannot be invented, so the point of view cannot be feigned either."[9] Although individuals or groups may have mistaken notions about disease, local worlds of medical knowledge cannot simply be judged by the measure of biomedical rationality.

In the course of the last several chapters, I have drawn an analogy between these epistemological arguments and a debate among literary theorists about the place of the text and the reader in interpretation, in particular about the nature and degree of indeterminacy of the aesthetic object. Iser takes a middle position between those who argue for a fixed, semiotic analysis of the text (the text therefore being determinate of a correct interpretation), and those who argue for virtual unlimited indeterminacy in the interpretive experience of diverse readers. Iser argues that the text systematically evokes experience, but that the aesthetic object is a relation between the text and the imaginative activities of the reader.[10] I have suggested by way of analogy that disease provides "subjectively verifiable instructions for meaning-production," as Iser (1978: 25) writes of the text, that disease and the material body place limits on our interpretation, and that medical encounters themselves shape our meaning-production. But Iser goes on to argue that "the meaning produced may then lead to a whole variety of different experiences and hence subjective judgments" (p. 25), and this too is true of disease. The "aesthetic object" is thus constituted in relation to the constraints and resistances inherent in reality, as well as local processes of meaning-making, and our research should focus on "elucidating the process of meaning-production" (1978: 23) as well as the structure of reality in comparative, cross-cultural studies.

Iser's analysis is relevant here not only for his view of the "resistance of the text" and the interpretive activities of the reader, but because of his claims about the underlying structure of indeterminacy inherent in all texts and its role in provoking the response of the reader. Iser argues convincingly that certain forms of indeterminacy – what he calls "blanks" and "negations" – are as powerful as the positive structures of the narrative in propelling the reader to "formulate" the world of the text. A "blank" is a "vacancy in the overall system of the text, the filling of which brings about an interaction of textual patterns" (Iser 1978: 182). Blanks are gaps in potential associations within the text – a plot line suddenly broken off, an abrupt introduction of new characters. Iser argues that these serve to "provoke and guide" the reader into creating associations and "referential fields." He also argues that blanks exist in the relation between the text and the reader's store of experience, challenging our sense of the "conceivable" and forcing us to reimagine the world. The "negation," on the other hand, is an active rejection of the anticipated – a challenge to the presumed norms of the text or the reader, passages that unmake the meaningful order seemingly presumed by an earlier passage. It therefore "situates the reader halfway between a 'no longer' and a 'not yet'" (p. 213). Again, Iser argues that negations or "deformations" – "tragic suffering, misery and disaster" – provoke the reader into imaginative interpretations that transcend any simple copying of reality. Thus, "meaning coincides with the emergence of the reverse side of the represented world" (p. 229).

Iser's discussion of negativity is extremely complex, and I have hardly done it justice here. However, his analysis is highly suggestive as we think about illness and the cultural imagination. The stories we heard in Turkey were filled with blanks and negations. Explanations were negated in the next moment, and obvious blanks were left in the accounts of the relations among episodes or apparently causal events. Anticipated resolutions of the seizures, healing promised by physicians and by religious healers, eagerly sought and hoped for, were negated time and again. And yet the image of healing was evoked. Stories were broken off midstream, and another passage with a differing account or perspective on the illness was introduced. The anticipated order of life was challenged. Often, any transcending vision was implied by the negation of the expected, if at all, rather than voiced as an affirmation or positive philosophy. Surely this is as common in the everyday, lived experience of illness as it is in the stories we tell.

We might even argue that illness has such a potent role in the cultural imagination of a community or a society precisely because of its negativity. The gaps among domains of experience, the breaks in meaning, are made painfully obvious. The taken-for-granted is negated. Potency shows itself at the limits of the determinate world far more than in its everyday forms. Although phenomeno- logical "resistance" – our experience of material objects in the world, or social forces that thwart our desires – serves as the basis for knowledge, the very preconditions of knowledge are formulated at the limits of such resistance, in face of the blanks and negations that give texture to all reality. Perhaps this is why illness and healing are wellsprings of the cultural imagination, rich sources of ritual and symbolic forms.

Iser argues that negativity – "the nonformulation of the not-yet-comprehended" – provokes a questioning of the world. And "if the reader is made to formulate the cause underlying the questioning of the world, it implies that he must transcend that world, in order to be able to observe it from outside." Herein lies its special power. "Whatever may be the individual contents which come into the world through a work of art, there will always be something which is never given in the world and which only a work of art provides: it enables us to transcend that which we are otherwise so inextricably entangled in – our own lives in the midst of the real world" (Iser 1978: 230).

The "interpretive practices" of which I have been writing are thus not simply causal explanations, as a long line of rationalist medical anthropology seems to suggest. They are diverse acts of the creative imagination – meanings made apparent as "the reverse side of the represented world," potency revealed as much by the indeterminate as by the determinate. Knowledge is formulated in relation to the negations of reality as well as to its provocations, and aesthetics is thus present in science as in other modes of experience. However, in our encounters with illness, the limitations of science quickly become apparent. Little wonder we feel we have more to learn than to teach when we bear witness to responses to suffering by persons of other religious, medical, and cultural traditions.

Medicine, rationality, and medical anthropology

Finally, some concluding remarks about culture, medicine, and rationality. In a little book entitled *The Presence of Myth*, recently translated into English, the Polish philosopher Kolakowski (1989) argues for the critical role of "the mythic" in meaningful human existence, and of the threat that instrumental rationality will appropriate and subjugate the mythological in modern culture. This threat has special meaning in contemporary medicine. Clinical medicine all too often instantiates a narrowly conceived instrumental reality. It does so quite subtly, I have argued, through the force of everyday practices – like writing in charts – through which the objects of medicine are constituted. It does so also by narrowing the scope of the clinical gaze to such an extent that many of the most crucial aspects of medical care – addressing social and economic conditions that produce a patient's disease and trigger costly interventions, placing priority on helping patients achieve a good death – are simply ignored as irrelevant to the domain of clinical practice.[11] Instrumental rationality is also instantiated through the institutionalization of norms governing what is talked about among physicians or among physicians and other health care providers, norms learned by medical students when they feel forced to grieve alone in a locked bathroom rather than be seen crying by other doctors when a patient they have cared for dies, norms which translate the awful truths spoken by an AIDS patient into the technical language of psychiatry, norms which limit speaking practices during medical rounds to the most immediate issues of diagnosis and technical services. In part, these practices serve to protect physicians, who must routinely confront mortality and pain in the context of ultimate uncertainty. In large measure, however, they grow out of a deeply empiricist vision of illness and a highly stratified structure of power relations, and they serve more to reproduce these than to protect or benefit either patients or care-providers.

Some physicians who heard the second Morgan Lecture (chapter 3 of this book) objected that my analysis of the management of moral drama through routine technical procedures was relevant only to tertiary care teaching hospitals and the experiences of interns and medical students. They argued that as physicians mature, in particular in their primary care activities, attention to the lifeworld becomes more and more prominent as a dimension of medical practice. This may be true for some. However, it ignores the dominance of instrumental rationality at medicine's intellectual core and in the most basic routines of practice, even in primary care. For many general medicine departments in American academic settings, rational decision theorizing has been embraced as the basic science of primary care, and in nearly all clinical teaching attention to issues of values is largely reserved for legal and ethical conflicts.

But it is not only in clinical medicine that instrumental rationality continues to advance and to appropriate the mythological. Instrumental rationality is the organizing modality for the classification and recording of diseases and treatments in a burgeoning bureaucracy of insurance agencies, medical records, and disability services. It pervades public health, where the consideration of human suffering, of local moral worlds, of the meaning of illness and rituals of affliction, seems oddly anachronistic and out of place. And all too often instrumental rationality is instantiated in the medical social sciences, where the language of behavior joins with narrowly experimental and epidemiological paradigms of science, displacing values to the margins. All of these contribute to what Habermas (1987a: 318ff.) calls "the colonization of the lifeworld" – the "cultural impoverishment of everyday communicative practice," "an elitist splitting-off of expert cultures from contexts of communicative action in daily life," and "the penetration of forms of economic and administrative rationality into areas of action that resist being converted over to the media of money and power" (p. 330).

I am convinced of the threat of the dominance of instrumental rationality to human freedom and to our experience of the meaningful, mythological, and transcendent dimensions of illness, healing, and human existence. This conviction lies at the heart of my interest in developing a critique of narrowly referential and empiricist views of culture, language, and meaning. The formulation of the medical social sciences and medical anthropology in the language of belief and rational behavior contributes, I am convinced, to the advancement of "cognitive-rationality" in matters of health and healing, and thus helps reproduce a narrow vision of medicine as the domain of instrumental rationality. I see as a central task for medical anthropology the opening up of our discourse to issues of existential concerns and humane values, as well as to our social commitments. A truly critical medical anthropology is not one which attends solely to issues of power and political economy, important as these are. In illness we confront ultimate human limits, and cross-cultural studies have the potential to awaken us to the presence of the soteriological in human culture, as well as the potential for its exploitation.

These issues are important for how we conceive a program for medical anthropology, both as research and as practical activity. In our relations with biomedicine, simply adding a bit of humanities to medical education or changing doctors' attitudes or even increasing the presence of social concerns in medical practice is hardly what is at stake. We have a more significant opportunity to help open up within medicine a region for vital research and practical activity, to contribute to the development of medicine as a theoretical and conceptual domain as well as a domain of humane practice. It is my conviction that making explicit the narrative and moral dimensions of routine clinical practice, investigating illness in the context of local moral worlds, and rethinking medicine's common-sense epistemological claims are means by which medical anthropologists may attempt to resist the encroachment of instrumental rationality into this domain of the lifeworld.[12] This is the larger project to which these lectures are dedicated.

And finally, I return to Lewis Henry Morgan. You may recall that I argued in the opening of these lectures (chapter 1) that Morgan's distinction between "descriptive" and "classificatory" kin systems grew out of his conviction that culture either reflects nature or refigures it. Morgan and his contemporaries were convinced that history and society progress or advance through the development of knowledge and forms of social organization that more clearly reflect the Natural Order. This claim, of course, authorized the point of view of the Victorians, who claimed to know what empirical reality or the Natural Order is really like. In the colonialist era, this authorization was mandate, validating Victorian societies while providing motivation for wide-ranging efforts to reorder other societies. But today, such an authorization is widely experienced as a burden. Scientific representations, including those of disease and the human body, undermine our efforts to take seriously the truth claims of other religious and healing traditions, even as they offer opportunities for better health. The hold of our own scientific convictions, joined with our growing alarm at the destructive consequences of much of science and technology, has provoked the sense of irony that so pervades anthropology today.

Within biomedicine and the medical sciences, there is seldom such a sense of irony. As a consequence, whereas medical anthropologists sometimes feel like remnants of out-moded Enlightenment thinking among our anthropological colleagues, among physicians and public health specialists we often feel like tiresome skeptics. Theirs is a sure method, a natural and realist epistemology, conviction of advancing knowledge and a surety that no end is in sight, only deeper understanding, more powerful therapeutics, positive benefits, and a readiness to engage in educating patients and society. Here we still find what Geertz calls "a salvational belief in the powers of science" (1988: 146; cf. Midgley 1992). We anthropologists sometimes feel as though we have been through the social revolution of the 1960s and the post-colonial era, and many of the physicians and medical scientists with whom we work have not. Where once we hoped for dramatic results from our anthropological insights, today we face the moral and epistemological dilemmas of other social activists – observers, participants, definers of the problems and champions of solutions, but now with the post-sixties awareness of the intractability of bad housing and violence, of inequities and declining living conditions, and thus of our impotence to produce dramatic change. Little wonder that our "epistemological hypochondria" and our critical reflections seem oddly placed amidst the optimism of molecular biology and the conviction of sure knowledge of the mechanisms of disease that is linked for the clinician with an intimacy with human suffering.

This cultural moment provides a context for the theoretical reflections of the Morgan Lectures and this book. It is also the context in which medical anthropology has come of age. And this coming of age has been quite remarkable in its scope and dynamism. A diverse set of issues is now addressed with a technical competence and theoretical complexity hardly imaginable in the early years of the field. More full length monographs have appeared in the past several years than in the previous three decades. Not only has the number of persons working explicitly in medical anthropology grown rapidly, but more and more anthropologists – and others from the social sciences and humanities – are working on topics of direct concern to those of us who have been in this field for some years.

Issues central to anthropology at large – critical accounts of cultural representations of gender and the body, ethnographies of embodied experience and the
senses, historical studies of modern science and colonialism or ethnographic
writing on contemporary science and post-modern societies, studies of culture and
biology, and research on development, the environment, and human ecology – are
increasingly addressed through investigations of medical phenomena. Indeed, as
I suggested in my opening comments, our active engagement in problems of
medicine and technology, health and development, and cultural responses to
human suffering may play a role in revitalizing anthropology at large.

Nonetheless, I have argued that the difficulties that arise from the competing
epistemological claims of the biosciences and local cultures continue to challenge
our anthropological writing and our applied work. In kinship studies, Morgan's
distinction between descriptive and classificatory systems was abandoned with
relative ease. In studies of medical systems, relinquishing analogous distinctions
remains more difficult. The stakes are higher, and the claims of biomedicine to
represent the Natural Order remain strong.

It should be remembered, however, that as Morgan came to know and admire
the Iroquois, he came to see their matrilineal (and therefore "classificatory") kin
system less as mistaken or unnatural and more as a creative refiguring of nature,
a system with a cultural logic and aesthetic that gave order to Iroquois society.
Contemporary anthropologists, who like Morgan work intimately with persons in
another society or subculture, are often faced with a similar dilemma. Unlike
many philosophers, who contrive imaginary worlds upon which to build their
arguments, we face epistemological concerns which are grounded in the ethics of
our conversations with members of another very real world. Forms of interpretation which simply reassert our own scientific or naturalist rationality are
profoundly inadequate.

Breaking down the sharp distinction between descriptive and classificatory
systems, between "history and fiction," or between belief and knowledge, is thus
crucial for anthropologists. For those of us engaged in comparative studies of
medicine, it will require on-going theoretical reflections and the development of
new concepts and methods for the field. Recent writing in the philosophy, history,
and sociology of science have taken steps in this direction and deserve the
attention of anthropologists. And I have argued in this chapter that studies of the
literary or aesthetic object also offer a rich language and set of ideas for us to
explore. Morgan's intuition that aesthetics offers a potential means for dissolving
– or reformulating – his epistemological quandary seems a good one. However,
this is not a "problem" which we will "solve." The essential qualities of medicine
as a symbolic form, an institution, and a moment in our lives – its joining of the
natural sciences and the narrative, of the rational and the deeply irrational, and of
physiology and soteriology, and its mediation of our experiences of negation and
ultimacy – will continue to challenge our formulations.

Morgan was, of course, also an activist – in part because of the very ideas of
social evolution that seem so untenable today. For those in medical anthropology,

the impulse to activism remains a significant motivating force. There are many forms of our activism and thus many voices and audiences. Some engage in the enterprise for the sake of comparative science; some to contribute to understanding and solving major health problems; some to provide voice to the voiceless and to empower the disenfranchised; some to reflect on the human condition; some to encourage a more humane medical practice. No wonder I spoke of medical anthropology as our field's London – where we come together over issues that matter to us in various ways, where we attempt to insert our academic research into diverse social settings, debates, and action fields.

It has been my goal in these lectures to outline some dimensions of theory for our field that can contribute to such activities.

Notes

1 Medical anthropology and the problem of belief

1 Relevant literature will be reviewed in following chapters. Examples include Arney and Bergen (1984), Arney (1982), Lock and Gordon (1988), Roberts (1981), Showalter (1985), Buckley and Gottlieb (1988), Martin (1987), and Jacobus, Keller, and Shuttleworth (1990).

2 See, for example, B. Good (1977); B. Good and M. Good (1980, 1981, 1982); B. Good, Herrera, M. Good, and Cooper (1985); B. Good, M. Good, and Moradi (1985); M. Good and B. Good (1988).

3 I initially used the phrase (B. Good 1977) with reference to Harrison's critique of what he called the "empiricist theory of language" (Harrison 1972), and we have continued to use the phrase, "the empiricist theory of medical language," to characterize a set of philosophical presuppositions in medicine and the medical social sciences (e.g., B. Good and M. Good 1981; B. Good, M. Good, and Moradi 1985), in spite of the potential for confusion associated with using the term "empiricist."

4 Cassirer (1955b). See chapters 3 and 4 of this book for a fuller discussion of the relevance of Cassirer's work to the issues discussed here.

5 Edwin Ardener (1982: 2) makes an argument similar to that which I will develop here, when he compares "missionaries" and "historical materialists," whose "violent attacks on the merest hint of cultural relativism" are derived, he argues, from their shared assurance that "the observer's vision is the truth."

6 See Caplan, Engelhardt, and McCartney (1981) for a collection of essays on this topic; see also Kleinman, Eisenberg, and Good (1978) and essays in Lock and Gordon (1988) relevant to a philosophical or cultural analysis of "the medical model."

7 See Taylor (1985a, 1985b, 1989). His essays "Language and Human Nature" and "Theories of Meaning" in volume I of his Collected Papers (1985a) are especially relevant to the argument I develop here. See also Shweder (1984a) for a discussion of the role of "Enlightenment" theories of rationality in anthropology, which he contrasts with the "romanticist counterpoint." Although I engage in a critique of some aspects of the "Enlightenment" analysis of culture and representation in the following pages, I am not advocating many aspects of "Romanticist" theories of language nor attempting to situate my discussion fully in relation to the history of theories of language. For a historical discussion of these issues, see Aarsleff (1982).

8 This is a brief and schematic representation of an extremely complex history of theories of language, summarizing Charles Taylor's (1985a) discussion.

9 Again, this schematic representation barely alludes to a host of philosophical debates.

In addition to Taylor (1985a, 1985b, 1989), classic formulations of this argument are found in Rorty (1979) and Putnam (1978, 1981, 1987, 1990). For a recent discussion in anthropology, see Shore (1991). Shore, along with Taylor, argues for a focus on "meaning construction," for theories that take as their starting point "the activity underlying meaningful uses of language" (Taylor 1985a: 251), which is quite close to what will be argued here.

10 For a relevant discussion of chronic pain, see the essays in M. Good et al. (1992).

11 Key texts in this debate include Wilson (1970), Horton and Finnegan (1973), Hookway and Pettit (1978), Hollis and Lukes (1982), Leplin (1984), and Doyal and Harris (1986). See also, for example, A. Rorty (1988), Sperber (1985), Shweder (1984a), Taylor (1985b: 134–151) and Tambiah (1990).

12 Favret-Saada's analysis of her almost accidental entry into witchcraft discourse, entry as a person who asks explicit questions and is thus a person of power, has important implications only hinted at here. The ethnographer is the questioner *par excellence*, and therefore assumes a position of power, one often confused with powers to "heal" or act on behalf of those questioned. Medical students become physicians, I argue in chapter 3, in part by engaging in certain speech acts, especially questioning and examining, which presume and reproduce a position of power. In a relevant passage in *The Archaeology of Knowledge*, Foucault (1972: 50) argues that investigation of how discourses produce (rather than passively represent) their objects must begin with the question "who is speaking? Who, among the totality of speaking individuals, is accorded the right to use this sort of language (*langage*)?" Forms of speaking presuppose the "right" to speak and thus a position within a system of power relations.

13 Personal conversation, and as part of an unpublished talk to the Department of Social Medicine, Harvard Medical School, in 1988. See Steedly (1993: ch. 1).

14 I am particularly grateful to Theresa O'Nell for her help in analyzing this text.

15 Although Needham (1972) raises many of the relevant philosophical issues using anthropological examples, he does not address the history of the concept in anthropology directly. The same is true in brief form for Hahn (1973). See Tooker (1992) for a recent discussion of these issues. Comaroff and Comaroff's (1991: 27–32) discussion of the history of the concept "consciousness" raises some issues parallel to those discussed here.

16 "Belief" was used explicitly in the cognitivist tradition to refer to mental representations for many years. Recently, the term "cultural knowledge" has largely replaced "belief" as an analytic category among cognitive anthropologists (see essays in Holland and Quinn 1987, for example), although discussion of the epistemological implications of the shift from analysis of "belief" to "cultural knowledge" is generally absent from the cognitive science and cognitive anthropology literature.

17 Not to mention "moral hypochondria," in Geertz's terms (1988: 137).

18 In addition to Favret-Saada (1980), see Pouillon (1982).

19 For a more general discussion of the view of "science as salvation" in Western civilization, see Midgley (1992).

20 Such examples are often given with little discussion, as though the authority of biomedical knowledge needs no comment. For example, Shweder (1984a: 8–9) asks "How should we interpret and represent the apparently false knowledge of an alien culture?" He goes on immediately: "The Bongo-Bongo tell you that eating the ashes of the burnt skull of the red bush monkey will cure epilepsy. What do you do with that? Do you render it as a 'belief,' adding that the Bongo-Bongo believe this strange false thing, that they fail to see that these things are unconnected?" The problem of what the Azande – for they are the source of Shweder's rhetorical question – considered the cause and cure

of epilepsy poses the issue of apparently false belief in its sharpest form. Unquestioned authority is yielded (by Shweder) to medicine's representation of illness, posing the standard challenge to relativism, framed as a problem of belief. (See chapter 6 of this book for a discussion of the problems of a naive medicalized view of epilepsy.)

21 Latour's *Science in Action* (1987) might serve as icon for this broad movement.

22 Steven Stich (1983) provides the strongest and most detailed case against the use of "belief" as an analytic category in philosophy, psychology, and cognitive science. He develops an extremely rich account of "belief" in Western folk psychology, exploring the set of linguistic practices in which our concepts of "belief" and "mind" are embedded. For example, he shows how our notions of "holism," that is our view that beliefs have meaning only within a network of other beliefs, "reference," and "causal pathways leading to beliefs" are all embedded in a folk psychology about beliefs as sentences stored in the mind, a position he holds cannot be defended in philosophical or psychological terms.

Stich goes on to argue that the assumptions about belief in our folk psychology have meaning only in relation to a set of language practices or our "way of life," and there-fore are unlikely to be meaningful in other societies. Indeed he suggests that Needham's analysis is correct, that "in many societies the background practices [built into our folk notion of belief] are sufficiently different that there just isn't anything looking all that much like prototypical cases of belief" (p. 218). For an ethnographic illustration of this, see Tooker (1992).

23 These issues will be reviewed in more detail in chapter 2. For a critique of studies of stress, see A. Young (1980). A critical review of care-seeking studies is found in B. Good (1986).

24 If an utterance is to be understood as reflecting a "belief," it must be assumed to be made sincerely. Such assumptions must be subject to what Hahn (1973: 215) calls "the ethnography of sincerity." That is, we are constantly in doubt about what the natives really believe.

25 I of course take this phrase from Obeyesekere, first articulated in his discussion of "depression" in Sri Lanka (1985) and elaborated in his Morgan Lectures (1990).

2 Illness representations in medical anthropology: a reading of the field

1 Benjamin Paul's *Health, Culture, and Community: Case Studies of Public Reactions to Health Programs* (1955) was the pivotal work in defining medical anthropology in these terms.

2 I have benefited in this section from my reading of an unpublished paper by Julia Paley (1991).

3 Benedict herself was careful to deny metaphysical claims about "society." In the essay under discussion here, she wrote: "Every society, beginning with some slight inclination in one direction or another, carries its preference farther and farther, integrating itself more and more completely upon its chosen basis, and discarding those types of behavior that are uncongenial" (1934: 72). However, she added a footnote to the term "society" as follows: "This phrasing of the process is deliberately animistic. It is used with no reference to a group mind or a superorganic, but in the same sense in which it is customary to say, 'Every art has its own canons.'" Despite such caveats, her differences with Sapir on the locus of culture and its relation to the individual were significant.

4 A passage in his "Cultural Anthropology and Psychiatry" seems directed at Benedict's formulation: " ... personalities are not conditioned by a generalized process of adjust-ment to 'the normal' but by the necessity of adjusting to the greatest possible variety of

idea patterns and action patterns according to the accidents of birth and biography"
(Sapir 1949 [1932]: 515).

5 Key papers arguing for the validity of the schizophrenia or psychosis "metaphor" (Noll
1983) for shamanism include Kroeber (1940), Devereux (1956, 1961), Silverman
(1967), and La Barre (1970). Examples of critiques of this position include Boyer
(1969), Handelman (1967, 1968), Peters (1981, 1982), and Noll (1983).

6 The best recent review of changing understandings of dissociation in American
psychiatry and the relevance of current "neo-dissociationist" theorizing for anthropological studies of possession and ecstatic states is found in Castillo (1993).

7 This topic is too wide-ranging to be reviewed in a footnote. Key collections include a
book edited by Simons and Hughes (1985) and a set of papers in *Social Science and
Medicine* edited by Kenny (1985). The discussions represented by these recent
collections go far beyond the early speculations about "ethnic psychoses" (Devereux
1980 [1965]). Key questions now include the extent of actual cultural diversity in the
expression and course of major mental illnesses, how to include the role of physiological and psychological processes in comparative cultural analyses, the cross-cultural
validity of specific diagnostic manuals (in particular, the American Psychiatric
Association's Diagnostic and Statistical Manuals III and IIIR), and how to classify the
diverse phenomena to which the terms "culture-bound disorders" or "culture-bound
syndromes" have been applied (see Kleinman 1988a: chs. 2 and 3 for an appraisal of
the field). Several general positions have served as the basis for hypotheses in the field.
A standard psychiatric formulation holds that biology provides the "final common
pathway" (Akiskal and McKinney 1973) through which diverse social phenomena are
channeled, and that psychiatric disease entities are universal, though prevalence, illness
behavior, and some aspects of phenomenology and prognosis may vary with culture. A
second position has held that specific forms of social organization, cultural meanings
and socialization create quite distinctive "common behavioral pathways" (Carr 1978;
Carr and Vitaliano 1985), which give psychopathology – and associated psychophysiological processes – distinctive forms across cultures. Other forms of "interactionism"
(Kleinman and B. Good 1985: ch. 1; Kleinman 1988a) have elaborated the mediation
of culture and biology, while some continue to argue that all psychopathology is
culture-bound (Gaines 1992a, 1992b).

8 Again, this field is too large to review in a footnote. H. Murphy (1982) and Kleinman
(1988a) are the best monograph-length critical reviews of the topic. See also Kleinman
and B. Good (1985) for papers on depression; B. Good and Kleinman (1985) for a
review of the literature on culture and anxiety disorders, and Guarnaccia, Good, and
Kleinman (1990) and Guarnaccia and Farias (1988) on anxiety disorders in Puerto
Rican culture; and Estroff (1981, 1989), Jenkins (1988a, 1988b, 1991), and Warner
(1985) for examples of the culture and schizophrenia literature.

9 The most interesting anthropological research testing hypotheses generated by an
explicit "social response" position has been carried out by Nancy Waxler (1974, 1977a,
1977b). Useful debates of these issues, in particular about the status of the category
"schizophrenia" and the role of culture in determining chronicity, include J. Murphy
(1976) and Waxler (1977a); Warner (1985, 1988) and Barrett (1988b); and a paper by
Cohen (1992) with responses by Sartorius, Waxler, Warner, and Hopper. The best
recent overall review of this debate is to be found in Hopper (1992).

10 Although many scholars contributed to the development of scholarship on medical
systems, including notably Arthur Kleinman and John Janzen, it is impossible to
overstate the contribution of Charles Leslie. Through his key writings on India (e.g.
1973, 1976a), his organization of the Wenner-Gren conference and his editing of the

conference papers as *Asian Medical Systems* (1976b), his role as editor of the medical anthropology section of *Social Science and Medicine*, his development of the University of California Press book series on the "Comparative Study of Health Systems and Medical Care," his contribution to the International Association for the Study of Traditional Asian Medicine, his efforts within the Society for Medical Anthropology, and perhaps most importantly his fostering of an international scholarly conversation into which he has continuously drawn young researchers, he has played a singular role in developing the field. For a retrospective account and partial rethinking of some of this work, see Leslie (1989). For an earlier review of the development of work on "medical systems," see Press (1980). The papers from the 1985 conference on Asian Medical Systems organized by Leslie in association with the American Anthropology Association meetings and supported again by the Wenner-Gren Foundation have just come to publication (Pfleiderer 1988; Leslie and Young 1992).

11 Reviews of the field in the past decade have almost without exception been devoted to specialized topics in the field. (Landy's 1983 review, totalling nearly 130 pages, appears to have been written about 1980 and hardly touches upon the significant developments of the field. By the early 1980s, it is almost unthinkable that one could write, as he did, that "a kind of evolutionary perspective, as Alland [1966, 1970] proposed, has achieved, I believe, a broad tacit consensus . . . " [Landy 1983: 187].) Reviews in the *Annual Review of Anthropology* alone include Worsley's review of the literature on "non-Western medical systems" (1982), Hahn and Kleinman on "biomedical practice and anthropological theory" (1983), Messer on culture and diet (1984), Dougherty and Tripp-Reimer on nursing and anthropology (1985), Davis and Whitten on culture and sexuality (1987), Heath on anthropology and alcohol studies (1987), Etkin on "ethnopharmacology" (1988), Paul on psychoanalytic anthropology (1989), Inhorn and Brown on "the anthropology of infectious disease" (1990), and Shipton on famine and food security in Africa (1990). Johnson and Sargent's (1990) recent collection includes nineteen essays, each essentially a review of special areas of medical anthropology.

12 Examples include Nichter (1989), Scheper-Hughes (1987), Packard (1989), Gussow (1989), Turshen (1989), Janes, Stall, and Gifford (1986), and Van der Geest and Whyte (1988).

13 I quote here from Welsch not to indicate a criticism of his essay, but to note how even in fairly critical analyses of "traditional medicine" and care-seeking patterns Rivers' formulation seems to capture the essence of the enterprise.

14 The study goes on to reject the validity of men's objection to using condoms: "Despite the fact that relatively few men report having used condoms, the majority claim that they tear, stay inside the woman's vagina, and decrease sexual pleasure. These negative attitudes must be based on conjecture rather than experience" (Bertrand et al. 1991: 58). "Experience" here denotes that of individuals, not a sense of shared knowledge or experience, and even a claim to decreased sexual pleasure is regarded as due to "unsubstantiated rumors."

15 Lepowsky also refers to "biomedical beliefs and practices" (p. 1049), but the overall logic of the argument is the juxtaposition of biomedicine with traditional beliefs, with the conclusion that use of the orderly's medicine may be rationalized in supernatural terms and utilized without threatening the native belief system.

16 For his own critical assessment of that work, see Alland (1987).

17 It is remarkable to note the regularity with which culture is analyzed as "belief systems" or "information," as well as the language of "control strategies," within the biocultural literature. See, for example, Moore et al. (1980: ch. 6), McElroy and Townsend (1985:

ch. 3), and Brown and Inhorn (1990). The joining of the analytic languages of adaptation and belief is explicit but is treated as almost obvious, needing no explication. For example, in an excellent review of "disease, ecology, and human behavior," Brown and Inhorn (1990: 195–196) write: "Cultural adaptations to diseases include behaviors and beliefs that function to limit morbidity and mortality in two general ways. First, some behaviors and beliefs have preventive functions by reducing exposure to disease organisms for certain segments of society. Second, others involve appropriate therapy for diseases, generally termed ethnomedicine."

18 It is ironic that "neofunctionalism" and "neoevolutionism," as well as the concept "adaptation," have received more critical scrutiny within ecological anthropology than ecologically oriented medical anthropology. See, for example, Orlove (1980) and Bargatzky (1984). For a fine response to medical ecology from the perspective of "critical" medical anthropology, see Singer (1989b). Dunn's analysis of the "adaptive efficacy" of both cosmopolitan medicine and traditional Asian medical systems is probably the most interesting formulation of the concept adaptation in relation to medical systems (Dunn 1976).

19 The critique of the Health Belief Model and studies of illness behavior are drawn in part from my paper, "Explanatory Models and Care-Seeking: A Critical Account" (B. Good 1986: 162–163, 169–170).

20 See Morsy (1990) for a review of the political economy literature, much of which is relevant to this issue.

21 In this formulation, I am implicitly contrasting the empiricist view with Taylor's (1985a) development of an intersubjective theory of language, in which sense is not separate from the subject, reference not distinct from sense, and therefore language not separable from the constituting actions of the subject. Subjects engage in constant efforts to authorize language and performance, to make "invocations" efficacious, and to account for actions in narrative terms. Taking such a perspective on care-seeking suggests a very different set of issues than those usually addressed in this literature. See Crandon-Malamud (1991) and Brodwin (1991) for examples of new approaches to care-seeking. A number of these issues will be developed in chapters 6 and 7.

I should state explicitly that the anthropological literature is diverse, and by no means do all studies of care-seeking fall prey to the difficulties I elaborate here.

22 See, for example, Gilman (1988), who argues in a psychological idiom that "how we see the diseased, the mad, the polluting is a reflex of our own sense of control and the limits inherent in that sense of control. Thus the relationship between images of disease and the representation of internalized feelings of disorder is very close" (p. 3). See also Herzlich and Pierret (1987) for a study of the representations of social reality invoked in theories and images of disease. This, of course, is a theme that runs throughout anthropological studies of sickness.

23 Charles Taylor writes that naturalistic accounts of meaning that arose during the Enlightenment were motivated by "the desire to overcome projection, and what we later call 'anthropomorphism', that promiscuous mixing of our own intuitions of meaning, relevance, importance with objective reality" (1985a: 249). This clearly is the aim of Sontag and others who would demystify disease. However, Taylor argues that purely designative theories of meaning and positive theories of knowing, which grew out of these Enlightenment motives, ignore "the activity underlying meaningful uses of language" (Taylor 1985: 251), hiding the constructive role of the language of science by treating it as pure depiction. These, he argues, are no longer philosophically tenable. And so it is with such anthropological theories.

24 As Sahlins goes on, "Either cultural practice is a behavioral mode of appearance of the

laws of natural selection, just like any 'species-specific behavior,' or else it is subsumed within a more general ecosystem which alone and as a totality enjoys the powers of self-regulation or 'mind' and those constraints are realized in cultural forms" (1976a: 101).

25 Anthropologists have always been interested in the obverse question – how the apparent order in the natural and social world structures perception, language, and culture – as well. However, since writings on scientific epistemology attended almost exclusively to this question, anthropologists in the Boasian tradition posed the hypothesis of the primacy of language and culture to counter such positivist views of representation. Cognitivists are now returning to balance the traditional Boasian question by asking again how the material and social worlds structure perception, language, and culture.

26 In 1972, Keesing stated this critique for cognitive anthropologists in general in more pointed language: "Cognitive anthropology has so far been an Alice in Wonderland combination of sweepingly broad aspirations and ludicrously inadequate means. We have been cheerfully and optimistically using high school algebra to explore the most profound mysteries of the natural world" (quoted in Keesing 1987: 369).

27 Or as Quinn and Holland (1987: 14) write: "Notwithstanding the primacy attributed to referential meaning in the western positivist/empiricist tradition, what one needs to know to label things in the world correctly did not prove to be the most salient part of cultural meaning."

28 Stich's (1983) analysis of "belief" in folk and professional psychology can be read as an example of such an analysis.

29 Garro goes some distance beyond Sperber's slogans about "the epidemiology of beliefs" (Sperber 1985, 1990), providing a method for investigating both consensus and variability in the conceptualization of illness among members of a society, rather than focusing on ontological assertions about culture as ultimately mental – read "neural" – and therefore material.

30 Again, there are exceptions. For example, Garro (1990) has combined cognitive studies with more general ethnographic writing on changes in Ojibway culture, and Strauss and Quinn are currently attempting to use Bakhtin as a theoretical bridge between cognitive representations of society and the political management of discourse (for example, Strauss 1992). It remains to be seen how this effort will influence the field.

31 Although many studies subsequent to Kleinman's early writing on explanatory models used the concept as the equivalent of the more traditional health belief model, this was not true in general of the best work in the meaning-centered tradition. It is my view that Allan Young's critique (1981) of "EM theories" as a version of "rational man theory" is appropriate for the health belief research but misrepresents the interpretive tradition.

Linda Garro (personal correspondence) distinguishes explicitly between "cultural models," which are shared cultural understandings, and "explanatory models," specific to a given situation or a particular explanation of an illness episode. I prefer to use the term "explanatory models" in a more generic sense, following Engelhardt's (1974) seminal discussion of the role of explanatory models in scientific theorizing. Explanatory models, however widely shared, are drawn on by individuals to frame or explain or make sense of specific illness occurrences. However, as I argue in chapter 6, explanation should not be privileged over narrative representations, which may indeed precede and be ontologically prior to explanation.

32 I will return to the issues of the presence of multiple discourses and perspectives as essential constituting features of illness, in particular in chapter 7. Part of the passage

from which this brief phrase is drawn is as follows: "In language, there is no word or form left that would be neutral or would belong to no one: all of language turns out to be scattered, permeated with intentions, accented. For the consciousness that lives in it, language is not an abstract system of normative forms but a concrete heterological opinion on the world" (Bakhtin, "Slovo v romane," quoted in Todorov 1984: 56).

33 See, for example, B. Good and M. Good (1980). Mary-Jo Good's current work on "competence" (M. Good 1985; M. Good and B. Good 1989), "risk" (in obstetrical discourse), and "hope" (M. Good, B. Good, Schaffer, and Lind 1990) represents a joining of our original semantic analysis to studies of political economy and micro-analyses of power relations.

34 Studies which refer explicitly to the semantic network concept include Kleinman's writings on Chinese illness categories and care-seeking patterns (Kleinman 1980), Bibeau's (1981) analysis of Ngbandi disease categories, Blumhagen's (1980) rather formal studies of the category "hypertension" among American primary care patients, Amarasingham's (1980) analysis of a case of madness and care-seeking in Sri Lanka, Farmer's (1988) study of "bad blood" in Haiti, Pugh's (1991) study of the semantics of pain in Indian culture, Murray and Payne's (1989) analysis of the meanings of AIDS in contemporary American epidemiology, and Strauss's (1992) analysis of political beliefs of individual Americans. For an analysis of causal reasoning about diarrheal disease in Kenya that uses the concept semantic network without explicit reference to this tradition, see Patel, Eisemon, and Arocha (1988).

35 For collections of essays important to the emergence of the "critical" approach, see the symposium on "Critical Approaches to Health and Healing in Sociology and Anthropology," *Medical Anthropology Quarterly* (old series) 17 (5), Nov. 1986; special issues of *Social Science and Medicine* on "Marxist Perspectives" (vol. 28, no. 11, 1989) and "Critical Medical Anthropology: Theory and Research" (vol. 30, no. 2, 1990); and special collections in *Medical Anthropology Quarterly* (new series) on "Gramsci, Marxism, and Phenomenology: Essays for the Development of Critical Medical Anthropology" (vol. 2, no. 4, Dec. 1988 [Frankenberg 1988a]) and on "The Political Economy of Primary Health Care in Costa Rica, Guatemala, Nicaragua, and El Salvador" (vol. 3, no. 3, Sept. 1989 [Morgan 1989]).

36 The clearest discussion of the concept "hegemony" which I have read is to be found in Raymond Williams, *Marxism and Literature* (1977) in a chapter entitled "Hegemony." Here he distinguishes among the concepts hegemony, ideology, and culture in a concise and explicit manner. He argues that hegemony is "in the strongest sense a 'culture', but a culture which has also been seen as the lived dominance and subordination of particular classes" (p. 110). At stake in the debates between interpretive and critical medical anthropologists is not simply the role of power manifest in and constituted through various forms of discourse, but rather the question of whether interpretations of culture must refer ultimately to "the massive historical and immediate experience of class domination and subordination, in all their different forms" (Williams 1977: 112), that is whether class relations or domination are the decisive issues in a given cultural analysis or indeed are decisive in all cultural analyses.

37 Personally I find Jean Comaroff's analyses of a South African people (e.g. Comaroff 1985) and Allan Young's current work on a Post-Traumatic Stress Disorder Unit (e.g. Young 1990) to be especially convincing. From the interpretive tradition, Kleinman (1986) provides a particularly forceful analysis of neurasthenia that joins macro-societal analysis to the micro-analytics of power relations, and these to an interpretation of human suffering as voiced in a particular historical moment. The essays in the

special issue of the *American Ethnologist* on Medical Anthropology in 1988 (Greenwood et al. 1988) reflect the importance of both the critical and interpretive paradigms during the past decade.

38 Sindzingre, commenting on the papers in the special issue on Gramsci, Marxism, and phenomenology in *Medical Anthropology Quarterly*, provides a French perspective on this literature. She writes (1988: 447): "American Marxist texts give voice to a tradition, reflect a style, define a special, indeed critical frame of discourse; nevertheless, though purportedly critical, they take for granted basic concepts (mode of production, domination, imperialism, etc.) that have become exotic for European (notably French) readers." Although sympathizing with their critique of culturalism and methodological individualism, she rejects "going back (regressing) to a concept of mystification (undertaken by a Machiavellian subject)" that understands "culture as nothing but a means of manipulation" (p. 452). For a brief critique of the concepts "mystification" and "reification" from within the critical tradition, see Allan Young's commentary on Taussig's use of these terms (Young 1982: 275–277).

39 Pappas, himself a physician, seems to have experienced his own training in this way. He writes (1990: 202):

What I as a student . . . found most difficult about clinical work was the assumption of control over the patient's body during the exam. . . . Descriptions of the simple techniques of percussion, auscultation, and palpation do not convey the intimacy of the physical exam, which unlike even sex, requires near total surrender of the body. The patient becomes the docile body to be manipulated and explored; robbed of autonomy so completely as almost to obliterate the meaning of being an actor.

The clash between doctors and patients is not only over different ideas about illness and health. The awareness of the elemental power over the human body is an important source of anxiety, grievance, and discontent in the doctor–patient interaction. It is the source of much of the criticism of the medical profession . . .

This conclusion is surely mistaken. Anxiety there is about the physical exam, anxiety by all parties involved. But it is exploitation of that intimacy, whether through callous indifference or incompetence or through the enforcing of sexist images of women during birthing or through taking advantage of patients' vulnerability that is at stake in most criticism of the medical profession, not the percussion and palpation of the physical exam.

40 I am paraphrasing Lakoff and Johnson (1980: 4–5), here, where they note that an argument is quite a different thing when the metaphors underlying its conceptualization are drawn from the imagery of warfare, as in the United States, rather than for example from the image of a dance. It is not uncommon, incidentally, for physicians to refer to a developing relationship with their patients as a kind of dance.

3 How medicine constructs its objects

1 The "New Pathway" (or New Pathway to General Medical Education) was an experimental curriculum that was offered to twenty-four Harvard Medical School students beginning in the fall of 1985 and to forty students in the following year, and with some modifications has now become the common curriculum for Harvard medical students. The project was stimulated by Dean Daniel C. Tosteson, who in 1982 brought together several groups of faculty, students, and administrators to work toward the design and implementation of a new curriculum. Dean Tosteson outlined his call for new approaches to medical education in the Alan Gregg Memorial Lecture to the American Association of Medical Colleges in 1980 (Tosteson 1981), a position supported and elaborated in Harvard President Derek Bok's 1984 Annual Report to the

Board of Overseers (Bok 1984). The new curriculum shifted basic science teaching to a problem-based approach, organized largely through small group tutorials. A "Patient–Doctor" curriculum was also organized to support the teaching of the social sciences relevant to medical care, preventive medicine, and medical ethics. Changes were also introduced into the clinical clerkships. Beginning with the class entering in 1987, the New Pathway curriculum (or the "Common Pathway") was made available to all students.

The educational reform and the research reported in this chapter were supported by a major grant from the Kaiser Family Foundation. Descriptions of aspects of the educational project are available in Office of Educational Development, Harvard Medical School (1989) and Colvin and Wetzel (1989). Reports of our research are available in M. Good and B. Good (1989) and B. Good and M. Good (forthcoming).

Special thanks are owed to Leon Eisenberg, James Adelstein, and Dan Goodenough for support for this project, as well as to the students and faculty who participated in the interviews and allowed me to join in their tutorials and laboratories.

2 Sherry Ortner's 1984 essay "Theory in Anthropology Since the Sixties" labeled most clearly the emergence of "practice" as an analytic category within anthropology. She showed that attention to practice in American anthropology grew out of dissatisfaction with the semiotic analyses of symbolic anthropology and the institutional determinism of structural Marxism and political economy analyses. Drawing on the social theory of Bourdieu (1977), Giddens (1979), Sahlins (1981), Raymond Williams (1977), and others, Ortner placed the new attention to practice in the context of enduring questions about the relation of structure and agency. She argued that rather than juxtaposing individual and society, recent critical studies of "practices" allow new understanding of "how society and culture themselves are produced and reproduced through human intention and action" while still attending to society as "objective reality" and humans as "social product" (1984: 158).

The attention within anthropology to practices as mediating agency and structure has counterparts in the philosophy and sociology of science (e.g. Rouse 1987 and Latour 1987). Much of this literature continues to refer to both the "archaeological" and "genealogical" writings of Foucault on "discursive practice" (cf. Dreyfus and Rabinow 1982) and Bourdieu's writings on practice and reproduction (Bourdieu 1978; Bourdieu and Passeron 1977).

3 For related critical readings of Foucault, see Taylor (1985b: 152–184) and Habermas (1987b: 238–293). Both analyze the absence of subjectivity and experience in his theory; in addition, they point out the dangers of Foucault's "cryptonormativism," that is his rejection of the need to spell out his critical conception of power and domination in relation to an explicit theory of human freedom.

4 Chapter 2 reviews some of the literature relevant to this project, particularly under the heading of meaning-centered analyses in medical anthropology. Kleinman's 1973 essay, "Medicine's Symbolic Reality: A Central Problem in the Philosophy of Medicine," was one of the earliest statements of issues involved in the analysis of medicine as symbolic formation; it remains a seminal statement of issues to be addressed. Other works which contribute to understanding how medicine is constituted as a "symbolic formation" in Cassirer's terms include V. Turner (1967) (especially ch. 9, "Lunda Medicine and the Treatment of Disease," pp. 299–358), G. Lewis (1975, 1976), A. Young (1976), Tambiah (1977), Bosk (1979), Kleinman (1980), B. Good and M. Good (1980), Lock (1980), Comaroff (1982), Csordas (1983), Ohnuki-Tierney (1984), Hahn (1985), Scheper-Hughes and Lock (1987), Farmer (1988), Gordon (1988), Kirmayer (1988), and Nichter (1989).

5 The joke later gets turned around to defend the limits of one's competence. A student whose father is a hand surgeon says that he used to tell his kids when they got sick, "you'll have to go to the pediatrician. I didn't attend class the day they talked about that!"

6 The "medicalization" of the body has been the subject of a burst of attention in sociology, anthropology, and feminist studies. See, for example, B. Turner (1984), Scheper-Hughes and Lock (1987), Suleiman (1986), and Jacobus, Keller, and Shuttleworth (1990).

7 Classic accounts in the sociology of the anatomy lab are found in Becker et al. (1961) and Fox (1988: 51–77). Recent essays include Lella and Pawluch (1988) and Hafferty (1988, 1991).

8 In the 1989 Dunham Lectures at Harvard Medical School, Sir David Childton Phillips, Professor of Molecular Biophysics at Oxford University, explored the "famous protein-folding problem," which he called "the last unsolved problem of molecular biology" (Harvard Medical Area Focus, April 13, 1989). The first lecture, which reportedly "provided the first three-dimensional structure of an enzyme," was described by a reporter as follows: "The difficulty lies in deducing a three-dimensional protein configuration from a linear sequence of amino acids. It is like guessing the architecture of a building from a list of the lumber and glass that will go into it." Dr. Phillips reportedly went on to describe imaging techniques that have facilitated structural analyses and the classification of proteins into structural families.

9 Lewontin, Rose, and Kamin (1984) provide a powerful explication of the ideological basis of biological determinism and the research agendas it yields – studies of genetic bases of IQ, gender differences, and schizophrenia, for example. They argue that those pursuing this research program "are committed to the view that individuals are ontologically prior to society and that the characteristics of individuals are a consequence of their biology" (p. 35). When linked to molecular biology and genetics, this yields the "claim that the gene is ontologically prior to the individual and the individual to society" (p. 59). These authors attempt, through a critical review of the research in these areas, to show that this ideological commitment produces "findings" and claims not supported by the data. For a polemical critique of sociobiology in anthropology, see Sahlins (1976b).

10 Lest this quotation be misinterpreted, I should note that this was from one of the most caring, sensitive, philosophically inclined students in the class.

11 Barrett (1988a), analyzing the construction of schizophrenia in psychiatric practices, provides a rich and detailed analysis of the relation between medical interviewing and writing in the medical chart. He shows the extent to which writing precedes rather than records conversation, and he draws on Smith (1974) to argue that medical charts construct the patient as a "documentary reality." This analysis derives in large measure from Foucault's brilliant discussion of "the examination" (1977: 170–194). The following line from Foucault (p. 191) could serve as summary of much of the recent research on the discursive practices of clinical medicine: "The examination, surrounded by all its documentary techniques, makes each individual a 'case': a case which at one and the same time constitutes an object for a branch of knowledge and a hold for a branch of power." However, in Foucault's analysis, not only is "the will to power" held to be ontologically prior to "the will to knowledge," but knowledge and therapy are largely reduced to an exercise of power and the relations in which they are embedded. For a critique of this view, see Habermas (1987b: 266–293). In my view, attention to power relations need not presume such a reduction.

Ricoeur provides a perspective on the dialectic between speaking and writing, in his discussion of the "text" and "entextualization," which serves as an interesting complement to Foucault's analysis (Ricoeur 1981a: chs. 5 and 8). See Kuipers (1989: 109–112) for a review of recent anthropological analyses of entextualization in medical settings. I return to a discussion of these issues in relation to narrative and illness in chapter 6.

12 See Anspach (1988) for a discussion of case presentations in two intensive care nurseries and an obstetrics and gynecology service. See also Arluke (1978), Bosk (1979: ch. 3), and Mizrahi (1984).

13 These issues will be discussed in detail in chapter 6, where I draw on the narrativity literature to analyze illness narratives.

14 A fourth year student who had just received a letter promising him the internship and residency position he had hoped for told me he felt freed of much of the scrutiny he had endured for the past two years. Other students, he said, now called him a "FYBIGMI," acronym for "Fuck You Buddy I've Got My Internship"!

15 For an alternative reading of how deeply involved clinical work often is in "emplotting" therapeutic courses and illness experience, of how central "narrative time" may be to clinical work with those with serious chronic or life-threatening conditions, see Mattingly (1989, 1991, forthcoming) and M. Good et al. (forthcoming).

16 Indeed, precisely such a critique, as outlined in President Bok's "report on medical education," served as one of the primary justifications for the development of Harvard's new curriculum (see Bok 1984).

17 Habermas's analysis of the "colonization of the lifeworld" or "internal colonization" is developed as a critical elaboration of Weber's theses on rationalization (Habermas 1987a: 303–373). Habermas argues that "capitalist modernization follows a pattern such that cognitive-rationality surges beyond the bounds of the economy and state into other, communicatively structured areas of life and achieves dominance there at the expense of moral–political and aesthetic–practical rationality" (p. 304). He criticizes Weber for an ambiguous use of the expression "rationalization," for not clearly distinguishing between "action rationality" and "system rationality" (p. 307). And he holds that "disenchantment" and "alienation" are not structurally necessary accompaniments of secularization and increasing societal complexity. Instead he credits "the cultural impoverishment of everyday communicative practice" to "an elitist splitting-off of expert cultures from contexts of communicative action in daily life" and "the penetration of forms of economic and administrative rationality into areas of action that resist being converted over to the media of money and power" (p. 330).

My claim here is that the routine management of such a threatening event as the madness of the AIDS patient described represents precisely such a "splitting-off of expert culture" from the common concerns of the lifeworld – of both patient and physicians. I suggest further that medicine's appeal comes in large measure from its offer of a technical "salvation," and that this rationalized soteriology increasingly penetrates or "colonizes" the lifeworld of persons who are sick and their families.

4 Semiotics and the study of medical reality

1 Cassirer never tired of attributing to Kant a revolution in the conception of philosophy, in terms of which "philosophers were freed from having to attain a reality more profound (or more immediate) than the only one given in experience, either as encountered or as reflected upon by the only valid methods of scientific synthesizing" (Hamburg 1949: 90), which thus relieved philosophy of the burden of ontological metaphysics.

2 Cassirer gave specific content to his thesis that "symbolic forms are organs of reality."

Hamburg (1949: 84) outlines three aspects of the theory. First, Cassirer held that "no meaning can be assigned to any object outside the cultural (mythical, artistic, common sense, scientific) contexts in which it is apprehended, understood, or known." Objects only come to meaning from a perspective rooted in a given symbolic form, through which we experience the world and come to knowledge. Second, Cassirer held that "no meaning can be assigned to any object except in reference to the pervasive symbolic-relation types of space, time, cause and number which 'constitute' objectivity in all domains . . . " (Hamburg 1949: 84). Cassirer argued throughout his work for a relational rather than substantialist understanding of symbols and knowledge (cf. Bourdieu's [1989: 15] discussion). In part, this relational view was an elaboration of the Kantian categories. But for Cassirer, the relational characteristic of the symbolic was more general, as I will discuss below. Third, Cassirer developed and elaborated a theory of the relationship between the "sensuous" (*Sinnliches*) and the "sense" (*Bedeutung*, meaning) it embodies. According to Hamburg (p. 84), "no meaning can be assigned to any object without . . . assuming a representative relationship – expressed in the symbol-concept – which . . . would be said to hold between given 'sensuous' moments, on the one hand, and a (in principle) non-sensuous 'sense' moment, on the other." This embodiment of meaning in the senses, which served to further Cassirer's understanding of the types of knowledge distinctive to the symbolic forms, will be especially fruitful in our thinking about the role of the cultural in shaping illness and in anthropological interpretations of the formation of the objects of medical knowledge within medicine as a symbolic form.

3 Mary-Jo and I have often used the videotape of this case for teaching medical students and residents. The analysis that follows was worked out in collaboration with Mary-Jo and in conversation with students.

4 The physician's words are transcribed in italics. When his conversation overlapped hers, his comments will be inserted into her discourse in square brackets.

5 See Tambiah (1990: ch. 6) for a critical review of philosophical discussion of commensurability and translation of cultures in the context of the rationality and relativism debate.

6 The literature on this topic is voluminous, especially that relating to humoral medicine in Hispanic cultures. See Temkin (1973) for a history of Galenism. Tedlock (1987) provides the best recent review of the issues under discussion on humoral medicine in Latin America. See Laderman (1981) for an especially useful discussion of Islamic humoral medicine in the Malay context. A special issue of *Social Science and Medicine* (vol. 25, no. 4, 1987) was recently devoted to "Hot–Cold Food and Medical Theories: Cross-Cultural Perspectives." And George Foster has recently reviewed and partially reinterpreted his own seminal writing on the legacy of Hippocratic medicine in Spanish-American communities (Foster 1988).

7 Unless otherwise noted, transliterations are in Azeri Turkish. Because writing in Turkish was forbidden under the Pahlevi dynasty, Iranian Azeri shows significant regional variation and no single written form. Transliteration here is from popular spoken Azeri in Maragheh during the 1970s.

8 Among previous publications especially relevant to this discussion are M. Good (1977, 1978, 1980), B. Good (1976a, 1976b, 1977, 1981), M. Good and B. Good (1988), and B. Good and M. Good (1981, 1982, 1992).

9 See M. Good (1980) for a detailed discussion of these issues.

10 The discussion that follows combines a reading of classical Greek sources, particularly Galen's *On the Usefulness of the Parts of the Body* (May 1968, vols. I and II; hereafter referenced as Galen, *Usefulness*, I or II); classical Islamic medical texts, particularly

Ibn Sina's *Canon of Medicine* (Gruner 1930; hereafter referenced as Ibn Sina, *Canon*); popular Islamic commentaries on the classic tradition, including Elgood's translation (1962) of al-Suyutti's *Tibb-ul-Nabbi* or Medicine of the Prophet (referenced as al-Suyutti, *Tibb-ul-Nabbi*) and Levey's translation (1967) of al-Ruhawi's *Practical Ethics of the Physician* (referenced as al-Ruhawi, *Ethics*); and various commentaries on Greek and Galenic–Islamic medicine.

The scholarly translation of the Galenic tradition and its elaboration in Islamic science is reasonably well understood (see, for example, Nasr 1968, Browne 1921, Siddiqi 1959). In the fifth century A.D. a group of Nestorian Christians were expelled from their school in Edessa by the Byzantines and took copies of Greek scholarship – notably of Hippocrates and Galen – to Jundi Shapur (near contemporary Ahwaz in Iran) where they continued their translations into Syriac and founded a hospital (see Whipple 1967). The Arab invasions left the school and hospital intact, and with the flowering of Muslim learning in Baghdad under the Abbasids, the learning of Jundi Shapur was carried to the Muslim capital. Greek works and learning were also brought to Baghdad from Alexandria and other centers of Hellenistic learning (Meyerhoff 1937). In Baghdad, in particular from about 850 through 1100 A.D., the great Islamic philosopher/physicians developed the classical system of Islamic medicine, adhering closely to the Galenic humoral schema. During this period, medical scholarship, hospitals, and medical schools were developed in the Middle East, North Africa, and Spain.

In Iran, the Islamic–Galenic tradition reached its peak during the period of the Safavids (sixteenth through the early eighteenth centuries). Classical Arabic texts were translated in Persian and new texts composed. Hospitals were built in major cities, and pharmacology and surgery (with anesthesia) reached their apex in Iran (Elgood 1951, 1966). Islamic–Galenic medicine, which always retained the designation "Greek" (*Tibb Unani* or Greek medicine), was practiced as both professional and popular medicine in Iran through the 1930s (see B. Good 1976b, 1981). Physicians (*hakims*), who mixed and dispensed medications, were found in towns and cities throughout Iran. By the 1970s, *hakims* no longer practiced in Iran. Galenic–Islamic medicine was practiced by folk specialists – herbal medicine sellers, neighborhood specialists in cupping, midwives, bonesetters – and was part of popular health culture.

11 "The nutritive faculty is that whereby the aliments are transformed into the likeness of the thing nourished, thereby replacing the loss incidental to the process of life," according to Ibn Sina (*Canon*: 113).

12 In Persian and Arabic the term *ruh* is the translation of the Greek *Pneuma*. *Ruh* is also used generally for man's immortal soul, although Ibn Sina and some others use the term *nafs*.

13 The May translation of Galen regularly uses the terms "coction" and "concoction," from the Latin *concoctus*, past participle of *concoquere* or "to cook together."

14 There is some discrepancy in the sources as to whether the transformations that occur in the veins and the heart represent separate stages of digestion. Formally, Ibn Sina conceives the third stage as occurring in the blood vessels (*Canon*: 91). Both the Greek and Islamic sources indicate that a further cooking of some blood occurs in the heart, where it is combined with the vital *pneuma* or *ruh*.

15 These residues of the digestive processes are linked to Islamic purity laws in the *Tibb-ul-Nabbi* ("Medicine of the Prophet") treatises (see below). Thus, the transformation of raw aliment produces both living tissue and polluted or impure waste products.

16 The theory that putrid air causes epidemics continued to be popular, even in nineteenth-century America. The cholera epidemics of 1832 and 1849 were ascribed to the putrid

air in the slums of large cities such as New York. Any who could afford to do so left the cities for higher ground where the air is pure and healthy (Rosenberg 1962: 73–78, 172).

17 The general rule to be followed is to evacuate the abnormal humor through the normal channel of exit from the affected organ when possible (e.g., for morbid humors in the ducts of the liver, evacuation through the intestines) (Ibn Sina, *Canon*: 474). The second procedure, based on the structural principles of the attraction of the near or of the opposites, is as follows: "(i) by attraction from a distant place, (ii) by attraction to a neighboring place." Thus, bleeding hemorrhoids in a woman may be treated by increasing menstrual flow (near) or by blood-letting from veins in the upper part of the body (distant) (*Canon*: 475–476). Blood-letting is used to reduce a superabundance of all humors, or it may be used for an excess of atrabilious humor in the blood. Thus, venesection may continue as long as the blood is black and thick (*Canon*: 479, 503, 607). Emesis (vomiting) is particularly useful to remove bile or phlegm from the upper part of the stomach, purgation to remove humors from the lower stomach and intestines. Enemas are useful for acting on the intestines or the organs which impair the liver and cause fever. Cupping is particularly useful for drawing humors from one part of the body to another, for drawing an "inflammatory process" from deep parts to the surface where they will be accessible to treatment, to divert such an inflammation from a major organ to a lesser one, or to draw blood into an organ to warm it and disperse the humors (*Canon*: 511).

18 The decisive evidence was the finding that "male and female twins are often found in the same part of the uterus: this we have observed sufficiently by dissection in all the Vivipara, both land-animals and fish" (Lloyd 1973: 173).

19 See, in particular, Nasr (1964, 1968). See also B. Good (1977) and B. Good and M. Good (1992).

20 Quoted from the *Rasa'il* of the Ikhwan al-Safa (the "Brethren of Purity"), in Nasr (1968: 97).

21 In a later passage, al-Ruhawi (*Ethics*: 48) provides an even more detailed depiction of the qualities corresponding to the four ages of mankind.

Some people have divided age into four divisions and have said that the complexion of each one is similar to the complexion of the mixtures of the body and its parts, and related to the seasons of the year. They have declared that in childhood there is heat and moisture similar to the complexion of blood, air, and the season of spring; in the young there is heat and dryness like the complexion of yellow bile, fire, and the season of summer; in the mature man's age, there is coldness and moisture like the nature of phlegm, water, and the season of winter; in the aged, there is coldness and dryness like the nature of black bile, soil, and autumn.

22 For a critical analysis of just such issues of translatability and commensurability, see Tambiah (1990: ch. 6).

23 In an important introduction to the ideas of Russian psychologists, especially Vygotsky, Rogoff (1984) outlined the challenge of a social view of cognition and cognitive practices. Soviet psychology argues, she showed, that rather than beginning with individual psychology, then adding social influences, cognitive studies should instead focus on "the social unit of activity, from which individual functioning springs" (Rogoff 1984: 5). For further elaboration of these ideas, see Rogoff and Lave (1984), Wertsch (1985, 1991) and Lave (1988).

24 It is relevant here to remark on Cassirer's view of the relational quality of symbols and knowledge, in particular in his analysis of the symbolic "function." This term he derived from mathematical formulations, rather than the functionalism of the social sciences, and it involved him in a controversy with his teacher, Hermann Cohen

(Gawronsky 1949: 21–22). Cohen attempted to establish the infinitesimal numbers as an absolute element; Cassirer demonstrated that in number theory, any number has value only as a relation. For example, "five is only five in relation to one, yet it is an infinite number in relation to an infinitesimal one, and an infinitesimal number in relation to an infinite one" (Gawronsky 1949: 21). Cassirer (1923) went on to demonstrate the fruitfulness of such a "functionalist" rather than "substantivist" view not only of numbers, but of all theoretical knowledge. This perspective, in Gawronsky's (1949: 21) gracious language, "freed the principles and methods of human reason from the shadow of absoluteness and disclosed their functional nature as flexible instruments of human knowledge." The "function" contains a point of view and direction, which serves as the basis for measurement of similarity among elements and their arrangement according to affinity. "The ideal connections spoken of by logic and mathematics are the permanent lines of direction, by which experience is oriented in its scientific shaping. The function of these connections is their permanent and indestructible value, and is verified as identical through all changes in the accidental material of experience" (Cassirer 1923: 323). Thus, Cassirer demonstrated the validity for scientific knowledge of what structuralists have elaborated for the analysis of elements in mythology, totemism, or ritual, that such elements have their meaning not as absolutes, as representations of concrete substance, but as elements in a field of relations.

25 See Barth (1987) for a critique of these forms of structuralist analysis and a reformulation in terms of the production, reproduction, and creative reworking of a tradition of cultural knowledge.

26 Ortner (1974) provided an early critical analysis of structuralist accounts of the nature/culture opposition in relation to gender. The edited collection by MacCormack and Strathern (1980) includes a series of discussions of the issue in various ethnographic domains. For more recent discussions, see Butler (1990), Epstein (1988), Harding (1986), and Suleiman (1986).

27 He goes on, "Aristotle considers the female to be like a deformed male, and it is this conviction, rather than any empirical considerations, that underlies his doctrine that males are hotter than females" (Lloyd 1966: 59). See Bottéro (1991) for a discussion of Ayurvedic theories of semen and semen loss, which are quite similar to the Hippocratic theories in form and implication.

28 This paragraph and the following are drawn from B. Good and M. Good (1992: 267–268).

5 The body, illness experience, and the lifeworld: a phenomenological account of chronic pain

1 I am referring here to the distinction in Scheper-Hughes and Lock (1987), repeated in Lock and Scheper-Hughes (1990), between the "individual body," the "social body," and the "body politic." When objective pathology cannot account for the pain, complaints lack legitimacy even among close friends and family members; it is therefore a disorder of the "social body." The enormous difficulty of determining who should receive disability payments, given the lack of correlation between objective signs and the experience of pain, leads constantly to struggles between pain sufferers and physicians and administrators. Such payments are also subject to budgetary politics of the meanest kind (see Osterweis et al. 1987). Pain and its experience is thus present in the "body politic."

2 Fortunately there are exceptions. See, for example, Schieffelin (1976), Rosaldo (1984), Keyes (1985), and Abu-Lughod (1986). For a review of the literature on funeral rituals, on the other hand, see Huntington and Metcalf (1979) and Bloch and Parry (1982).

3 This research is described in our book *Pain as Human Experience: An Anthropological Perspective* (M. Good et al. 1992). The introduction to the book (Kleinman et al. 1992) provides a review of the literature on culture and pain, and a description of the various studies that were part of the larger research program.

   The specific case – that is, the transcript of the interview – which I analyze in this chapter has served as the basis for several formal presentations and for my chapter in the pain book (B. Good 1992a). The study from which it was drawn was conducted with Linda Garro, principal investigator, and Karen Stephenson, with the support of National Institute of Mental Health training grant MH 18006 and a small research grant from the Department of Social Medicine, Harvard Medical School. Although the data and analysis here overlap with that chapter, here I attempt to spell out in greater detail the theoretical and methodological issues involved in studying illness experience.

4 This young man described his problem as arising from "TMJ" or "temporomandibular joint disorder." Although he was recruited to the study as one of a group of persons who saw their pain and dysfunction as deriving from disorders of the jaw joint, he is not selected for this case study because he is representative of the larger TMJ sample. Indeed, in many ways he is different from most sufferers of jaw joint disorders. For example, he is much more explicit about having a history of psychological problems and of seeking treatment from counselors than is true of most members of that sample and of most persons who identify their problems as caused by TMJ. He was selected for this case study rather because of his remarkable ability to convey the felt quality of a lifeworld threatened with dissolution.

5 A much more complete discussion of the narrative literature and what it has to offer for the analysis of illness stories is provided in chapter 6. For a collection that introduces these issues, see Mitchell (1981).

6 This position derives from Schutz's discussion of "multiple realities" (Schutz 1971). It was elaborated by Geertz in analyses of religion (1973: 87–125) and common sense (1983: 73–93). Tambiah (1990: 84–110) returns to the nature of "multiple orderings of reality" in his discussion of Lévy-Bruhl and the problem of translations across cultures.

7 Csordas (1990) provides a rich analysis of Merleau-Ponty's conception of the "body," and calls for the development of "embodiment" as an analytic category in anthropology. He draws on the theoretical formulations of Merleau-Ponty and Bourdieu, in an effort to move beyond Hallowell and Mauss, whose writings reflect an earlier interest in phenomenology and the body. Csordas provides a review of recent writings on embodiment in anthropology, and undertakes an analysis of Catholic charismatic healing from this perspective. His forthcoming monograph will extend these analyses into a full conceptual account of embodiment as a category for medical anthropology.

8 In addition to Csordas (1990), see Spicker and Pellegrino (1984), Frank (1986), Scheper-Hughes and Lock (1987), Kirmayer (1988), Jackson (1989: 119–155), Ots (1990), Devisch (1990), Pandolfi (1990), and Gordon (1990).

9 Attention to the senses as an ethnographic domain, for example in Stoller (1989), Howes (1989), and Roseman (1990), represents a renewed interest in embodied experience and its cultural shaping, an interest absent in both social structural analyses and cognitive theories of culture.

10 Husserl described his methodological approach to investigating the lifeworld as follows:

   I begin . . . by questioning that which has in me, under the heading "world," the character of the conscious, the experienced, and the intended, and which is accepted by me as being; I ask what it looks like in it being accepted thus; I ask how I became conscious of it, how I may describe it,

...; how what is subjective in this way manifests itself in different modes, what it looks like in itself, ... how it is to be described, what kind of achievement it is that brings about in me a world of this typical existential character. (Husserl, quoted in Brand 1967: 209)

11 See Holzner (1972) for a discussion of the shock of dramatic disruptions of everyday experience. First person narratives of major illness often describe the author's memory of the subtle shift not simply in experience of self but in the appearance of the world. Recall William Styron's comments quoted in the opening page of this chapter. Paul Tsongas (1984: 31) described a more sudden shift in his experience of the world, on the day he was told he had lymphoma: "I was in Washington and in the United States Senate, but I wasn't. My world was no longer expansive and reaching, but closed and shrinking."

12 I refer here to the focus on language and culture in the American tradition, represented by Whorf (1956) and Hallowell (1955), and to Mauss's writings on *les techniques du corps* or "body techniques" (1979: 95–123) and Bourdieu's writing on *habitus* and the "socially informed body" (1977). For a discussion, see Csordas (1990).

13 Robert Murphy (1987: 12) provides a vivid description of this experience, as he tells of the onset of the disease that led inexorably to his paralysis.

As Simone de Beauvoir wrote, anatomy may not be destiny, but it is indeed an unstated first assumption in all our enterprises. ... illness negates this lack of awareness of the body in guiding our thoughts and actions. The body no longer can be taken for granted, implicit and axiomatic, for it has become a problem. It no longer is the subject of unconscious assumption, but the object of conscious thought.

14 Again, Robert Murphy (1987: 58) described eloquently that feeling for the chronically ill who adapt to the special world of the hospital.

Visitors to those long hospitalized often find that the patients are rather indifferent to news of the outside world, preferring instead to talk about other patients in the room, their doctors, and the events of the floor. Visitors find themselves speaking to disinterested listeners, and the conversations have two subject matters, two universes of discourse. ... Visits tend to become minor rituals, the settings of an interplay between alienation and agonized attempts to maintain solidarity.

15 For a discussion and review of the literature, see Kleinman et al. (1992).

16 In the biography of his illness, *Heading Home*, Senator Paul Tsongas described his great impatience with the lack of urgency others felt about dealing with pressing social problems, once he discovered he had cancer. At a school committee meeting, prior to his making public his disease, he exploded in anger at a committee member who was refusing to move ahead with a reform project. His vehemence surprised himself as much as others.

That night I reflected upon what had happened. I realized that the lymphoma had given me a sense of urgency. I had come to realize that a person's stay on earth was truly temporary. Before, while I knew it was temporary, I felt it was infinite. There would always be time to do something. But now I had spent three weeks thinking about and negotiating with the reality that we are all going to die. ... The earth was timeless, not those who inhabited it. What had to be done had to be done now. (1984: 113–114)

His time perspective had shifted, and he felt alienated from ordinary reality and its inhabitants. "I felt like an intruder – as if this world had gone somewhere, leaving me behind" (p. 79).

17 This phrase is drawn from the subtitle to Scarry's book, *The Body in Pain: The Making and Unmaking of the World.*

18 Nigerian novelist Chinua Achebe has explored this theme in his essay on Tutuola's *The Palm-Wine Drinkard* (Achebe 1988: 100–112).

The reader may, of course, be so taken with Tutuola's vigorous and unusual prose style or beguiled by that felicitous coinage, "drinkard," that he misses the social and ethical question being proposed: What happens when a man immerses himself in pleasure to the exclusion of all work; when he raises pleasure to the status of work and occupation and says in effect: "Pleasure be thou my work!"? *The Palm-Wine Drinkard* is a rich and spectacular exploration of this gross perversion, its expiation through appropriate punishment and the offender's final restoration. That's what the story is about. (p. 112)

19 These issues are explored in the essays in M. Good et al. (1992).

20 See, for example, Fox (1959; 1988: 381–412, 645–671), G. Lewis (1975), Leslie (1976b), A. Young (1976), Kleinman (1988b), Farmer (1988), Harris (1989).

6 The narrative representation of illness

1 The overall research was supported by the Pharma International Division of Ciba Geigy, and conducted by an international group of neurologists, epidemiologists, and social scientists, under the rubric of the International Community Based Epilepsy Research Group (ICBERG). Research was conducted in Ecuador, Turkey, Pakistan, and Kenya. Ciba Geigy provided scientific, organizational, and logistical support for local researchers in the conduct of the epidemiological study. For the ethnographic study in Turkey, they provided access to the case lists and findings of the clinical evaluations and sociological questionnaires, covered basic expenses, and provided transportation for the research team.

Our Turkish colleagues in the project included Professor İsen Toğan Arıcanlı, Professor Zafer İlbars, Professor A. Güvener, and Dr. İlker Gelişen. Two students, Nevzat Durak and Ajlan Ozkaraduman, participated in and transcribed the interviews.

A description of the methods of the overall project is provided in Shorvon et al. (1991). Findings of the Turkish project are to be found in Güvener et al. (1990).

2 See Shorvon and Farmer (1988) for a review. A recent World Health Organization report estimates 0.5 to 4 percent of any population will experience epilepsy, and that out of 50 million cases world-wide, "at least half are either not properly treated or not treated at all" (World Health Organization 1990).

The Turkish epidemiological study screened 11,497 persons, conducted clinical interviews with 947 persons identified as potential cases, and made confirmed diagnoses of epilepsy in 81 persons. This translated into prevalence rates of 4.6, 8.7, and 9 per 1,000 in urban, semiurban, and rural communities respectively. Twenty-four of the cases (30%) were under anti-epileptic therapy at the time of the survey; twenty-two (27%) had used anti-seizure medications in the past, and thirty-five (43%) had never received drug treatment for their condition (Güvener et al. 1990).

3 Social science literature on cultural interpretations of epilepsy and its stigmatization outside of North America and Europe is surprisingly scant. The only full ethnography on seizure disorders is the Levy, Neutra, and Parker (1987) study of the Navajo. Recent studies of stigmatization caused by perceived contagion of epilepsy in Africa include Awaritefe (1989) and Nkwi and Ndonko (1989). Studies from North America and Europe include Schneider and Conrad (1980, 1981, 1983) and Kirchgassler (1990).

4 The World Health Organization recommends beginning treatment programs with the use of phenobarbitone, then using alternative or adjunctive drugs for those persons who fail to respond to phenobarbitone. Their report suggests that the great majority of cases can be managed for an average of $5 US per patient per year (World Health Organization 1990). Some have argued that phenobarbitone causes reduced levels of cognitive functioning, mediated through cerebral glucose metabolism (Theodore et al.

1986), and that alternative drugs, while more expensive, are also more effective and cause fewer cognitive side effects.

In the Kenya portion of the ICBERG study, a selection of 302 patients were randomized and treated with either carbamazepine or phenobarbitone for one year (Feksi et al. 1991). Of the patients who completed the trial 53 percent were seizure-free in the 6–12 month study period, and a quarter were free of seizures during the whole 12 months. No differences were found in efficacy of the two medications.

5 All names used here are pseudonyms. In Turkish, a name like "Meliha Hanim" combines a given name (Meliha) and a form of address (Hanim = Ms.). For men, the form of address, combined with a given name, is "Bey."

6 It was often difficult to determine precisely whether descriptions of seizures being "like sleep" truly indicated the lack of tonic and clonic features, whether they referred to the post-ictal phase of the seizure, or whether the description was meant to minimize the severity of the condition.

7 The "c" in Turkish is pronounced as "j." Thus *hoca* is pronounced as "hoja."

8 The classic text on the mimetic question from literary criticism is of course Erich Auerbach's *Mimesis: The Representation of Reality in Western Literature* (1953). More recent discussions include those by historian Hayden White (1981), philosopher Paul Ricoeur (1984), and psychologist Jerome Bruner (1986, 1990). All derive ultimately from reflections on Aristotle's *Poetics*. See also Mattingly (1989: ch. 3).

9 See Anatole Broyard's review essay on Western literary accounts of illness and its experience, a reading given special veracity by his own illness and special poignancy by his recent death (Broyard 1992).

10 See the appendix to Mishler's *Research Interviewing* (1986), "Suggested Readings in Narrative Analysis," for a useful review of literature relevant for medical anthropology.

11 Much of my thinking about narrative studies was stimulated by Cheryl Mattingly's thesis (1989) and by conversations with her. See also Mattingly (1991, forthcoming) and Mattingly and Fleming (forthcoming).

12 See also M. Good et al. (forthcoming) for an analysis of the narrative structuring of time horizons in clinical work with cancer patients. Anthropological studies of narratives from the Middle East, relevant to this chapter but not specifically on illness experience, include Bilu (1988) and Meeker (1979).

13 Turner (1981: 153) refers explicitly to Sally Falk Moore's argument that "the underlying quality of social life should be considered to be one of theoretical absolute indeterminacy" (Moore 1978: 48). He goes on (p. 159) to link his general argument about the dialectic between structure and unstructure to Moore and Meyerhoff's argument (in *Secular Ritual*) about social process moving "between the formed and the indeterminate."

14 See Bruner (1986: ch. 2) for an elaboration of Iser's distinction between "virtual" and "actual" text, as I use it here.

15 Ricoeur (1981a, 1984) makes a strong argument for narrative having both temporal and atemporal or non-chronological orders of significance. On the one hand, plot orders events and actions. "It 'grasps together' and integrates into one whole and complete story multiple and scattered events . . . " (1984: x), ordering events in time and showing their relation to one another. On the other hand, " . . . the activity of narrating does not consist simply in adding episodes to one another; it also constructs meaningful totalities out of scattered events" (Ricoeur 1981a: 278), pointing to an underlying meaning or significance that inheres in the totalities, the "moral of the story."

16 Becker, in an analysis of the "textual coherence" of the Javanese shadow theatre or

wayang, defines plot as "a set of constraints on the selection and sequencing of dramatic episodes or motifs" (1979: 216–217). He goes on to demonstrate that the constraints that structure the *wayang* differ quite dramatically from those identified by Aristotle as characteristic of tragic drama. His analysis suggests the importance of cultural differences in narrative structure. At the same time, it broadens the definition of plot beyond that which I find useful for the analysis of illness narratives.

17 The Tarhan Kitabevi large Turkish–English dictionary (1959) gives as primary meanings for *sıkıntı* "worry, trouble, embarrassment, suffering, weariness, distress, penury, difficulty, annoyance," and for *üzüntü* "worry, care, anxiety, trouble, nuisance, grief, pain, sorrow."

18 "Bulgarian Turks," those living in Turkey who migrated from Bulgaria, are known to be blonde and blue-eyed and especially beautiful. They may also be referred to as "foreign."

19 The phrase is taken from Bruner (1986: 25) and his discussion of Iser's view of the indeterminate relation of reader and text.

20 The phrase might also be derived from Victor Turner's distinction between the "subjunctive" mode of antistructure and the "indicative" mode of structure (1981: 159). He writes:

In preliminary rites of separation the initiand is moved from the indicative quotidian social structure into the subjunctive antistructure of the liminal process and is then returned, transformed by liminal experiences, by the rites of reaggregation to social structural participation in the indicative mood. The subjunctive, according to *Webster's Dictionary*, is always concerned with "wish, desire, possibility, or hypothesis"; it is a world of "as if," ranging from scientific hypothesis to festive fantasy. It is "if it *were* so," not "it *is* so." The indicative prevails in the world of what in the West we call "actual fact," though this definition can range from a close scientific inquiry into how a situation, event, or agent produces an effect or result to a layperson's description of the characteristics of ordinary good sense or sound practical judgment.

21 See Iser (1978: 96–103) for a discussion of the interaction of theme and horizon in the experience of the reader.

22 Basil Sansom, in a fine essay entitled "The Sick Who Do Not Speak" (1982), describes quite a different "appropriation" of the voice of the sick by the community among the Aborigines of Darwin fringe camps. Here, because truly sick persons are possessed by a sickness, their voices cannot be trusted. Consequently their story belongs to the "community of suffering" that cared for them during the illness. The retelling of this story is done only among members of that community. If the story is to be told anew, it is done quite formally and carefully, for the act of retelling draws the hearer into the community who cared for and care for the person who suffered.

23 See Thornton (1976) for a quirky history of the historical relationships among hypnotism, hysteria, and epilepsy. For a brief account of Charcot and Gowers on "hysteroepilepsy," see Massey and McHenry (1986). For an interesting account of Charcot and his work by an American physician who made a pilgrimage to the Salpetrière to observe Charcot and his work, see Morton (1880).

24 This phrase refers to Berger and Luckmann's classic definition of "reality" as a "quality appertaining to phenomena that we recognize as having being independent of our own volition (we cannot 'wish them away')" and of knowledge as the certainty that such phenomena are real and "possess specific characteristics" (1966: 1).

25 Quite appropriate criticism of the formalism implied by the "culture as text" analogy often pays little attention to Ricoeur's formulation in what is the primary source for much of the cultural analysis that draws on this analogy. In "The Model of a Text: Meaningful Action Considered as a Text" (1981a: 197–221), Ricoeur begins with an

analysis of the difference between spoken discourse and text. "Entextualization" frees discourse from its conversational context, makes the speaker's words available to an audience diverse in space and time. The speaker loses control of the words and their interpretations, as well as of the presentation of self. And the referential world of the text surpasses the situation of the spoken discourse. The same is true, Ricoeur argues, of social action that becomes "entextualized." An act has consequences beyond the initial situation of the action, as it is recorded, remembered, and described by those who participated or only heard secondary accounts of the action. And narrativization, I would argue, is one of the primary means by which illness is "entextualized." Stories of illness are told from person to person, recorded in medical charts as well as in community memory. No wonder such care is taken by a sufferer and his or her family in crafting a story that will represent the illness and its bearer in the most advantageous light. And no wonder such stories are so open to contest.

7 Aesthetics, rationality, and medical anthropology

1 In addition to Iser's analysis of the aesthetic object in narrative, which I have discussed in some detail in the last chapter, I am also referring here to the work of Ingarden (1973) and Dufrenne (1973), both of whom preceded Iser in developing detailed phenomenological accounts of aesthetic experience and aesthetic objects in music, painting, architecture and film. Ingarden in particular attempts to place his analysis of aesthetic objects in these fields in relation to his studies of the literary work of art.

2 See Cohen (1992a, 1992b) for an account of how an effort to study Alzheimer's Disease and senile dementia in India broke down, and his interpretation of the implications of such difficulties. See also how O'Nell's (1991, 1992) investigation of "depression" among the Flathead led to a partial deconstruction of this category.

3 These have included analyses of "back pain" (B. Good and M. Good 1980), of "depression" in Iranian culture (B. Good, M. Good, and Moradi 1985), and of "competence," "hope," and "risk" in American medicine (M. Good 1985, M. Good et al. 1990, M. Good et al. forthcoming). For a further review, see chapter 2, pp. 54–55.

4 The term "semantic networks" is used in contemporary psycholinguistics, but with a quite different meaning. There it is used to designate theories of how lexical items are stored in memory and how they are processed to produce sentences (see Johnson-Laird, Herrmann, and Chaffin 1984 for a review; see also Evens 1988 for a recent collection of studies). Theories of semantic fields or domains are explicitly rejected in this literature as inadequate for "building lexicons for parsing and text generation" (Evens 1988: 2).

5 Although drawing on survey research and clinical data, our semantic network research has been broadly interpretive and has drawn on diverse sources to produce a macro-cultural account of medical knowledge rather than an account of individual cognition. No single methodology has been developed in medical anthropology for eliciting and analyzing semantic networks, and partly as a result of this, cognitive anthropologists have not, until very recently, investigated the relation between individual semantic networks and those shared cultural forms analyzed by symbolic anthropologists. Given recent interest in "connectionist" analyses (Strauss 1988; D'Andrade 1992), and Strauss's analysis of networks of individuals' political beliefs (1992), new work at the interface of cognitive and interpretive approaches might emerge.

6 For example, compare Murray and Payne (1989) and Farmer (1990a, 1990b) for discussions of the entry of "AIDS" (or "sida") into American and Haitian semantic networks.

7 Our analysis drew on Victor Turner's seminal work on the "polysemic" quality of

Ndembu ritual symbols, which in turn drew on Freud's analysis of the "condensation" of meanings by dream symbols (Turner 1967).

8 I cannot elaborate this point here. The meanings associated with "hot" and "cold" in Islamic physiology are linked to a hegemonic representation of gender, indeed provide a grounding to the apparent naturalness of gender inequality, as I attempted to show in chapter 4. The semantic network associating back pain with malingering and unwillingness to work (B. Good and M. Good 1981) is grounded in and helps reproduce an ideology of individual responsibility and the legitimacy of claims of the work place. The semantic network which AIDS has come to occupy, and which is constantly reproduced in public discourse, powerfully supports hegemonic representations of Haiti (Farmer 1992) and of homosexuality, poverty, and ethnicity in North America.

9 These passages, from Ortega's essay "Verdad y perspectiva," are quoted in Julian Marias's notes on a paragraph in Ortega's *Meditations on Quixote* (Ortega y Gasset 1961: 171).

10 See Eco (1992) for a related argument from the perspective of semiotics.

11 Waitzkin (1991) has demonstrated this convincingly, showing how the process is subtly woven through clinical interactions.

12 Far too many medical anthropologists are contributing to this enterprise to attempt to reference their work. Not surprisingly, as I write this I am thinking in particular of my colleagues Arthur and Joan Kleinman (1991), especially their work on human suffering and "local moral worlds," Leon Eisenberg (1986), Mary-Jo Good (M. Good et al. 1990), and Cheryl Mattingly (1989).

References

Aarsleff, Hans. 1982. *From Locke to Saussure. Essays on the Study of Language and Intellectual History.* Minneapolis: University of Minnesota Press.

Abad, B., and E. Boyce. 1979. Issues in Psychiatric Evaluations of Puerto Ricans: A Sociocultural Perspective, *Journal of Operational Psychiatry*, 10: 28–39.

Abu-Lughod, Lila. 1986. *Veiled Sentiments: Honor and Poetry in a Bedouin Society.* Berkeley: University of California Press.

1990. The Romance of Resistance: Tracing Transformations of Power through Bedouin Women, *American Ethnologist*, 17: 41–55.

Achebe, Chinua. 1988. Work and Play in Tutuola's *The Palm-Wine Drinkard.* In *Hopes and Impediments: Selected Essays*, pp. 100–112, New York: Doubleday.

Ackerknecht, Erwin H. 1946. Natural Diseases and Rational Treatment in Primitive Medicine, *Bulletin of the History of Medicine*, 19: 467–497.

Akiskal, H. S., and W. T. McKinney. 1973. Depressive Disorders: Toward a Unified Hypothesis, *Science*, 182: 20–29.

Alland, Alexander. 1966. Medical Anthropology and the Study of Biological and Cultural Adaptation, *American Anthropologist*, 68: 40–51.

1970. *Adaptation in Cultural Evolution: An Approach to Medical Anthropology.* New York: Columbia University Press.

1987. Looking Backward: An Autocritique, *Medical Anthropology Quarterly*, 1: 424–431.

Amarasingham, Lorna Rhodes. 1980. Movement among Healers in Sri Lanka: A Case Study of a Sinhalese Patient, *Culture, Medicine and Psychiatry*, 4: 71–92.

Anspach, Renee R. 1988. Notes on the Sociology of Medical Discourse: The Language of Case Presentation, *Journal of Health and Social Behavior*, 29: 357–375.

Ardener, Edwin. 1982. Social Anthropology, Language and Reality. In David Parkin (ed.), *Semantic Anthropology*, pp. 1–14, London: Academic Press.

Arluke, Arnold. 1978. Roundsmanship: Inherent Control on a Medical Teaching Ward, *Social Science and Medicine*, 14A: 297–302.

Arney, William Ray. 1982. *Power and the Profession of Obstetrics.* Chicago: University of Chicago Press.

Arney, William Ray, and Bernard J. Bergen. 1984. *Medicine and the Management of Living. Taking the Last Great Beast.* Chicago: University of Chicago Press.

Auerbach, Erich. 1953. *Mimesis: The Representation of Reality in Western Literature.* Princeton: Princeton University Press.

Austin, J. L. 1962. *How to Do Things with Words.* Oxford: Oxford University Press.

Awaritefe, A. 1989. Epilepsy: The Myth of a Contagious Disease, *Culture, Medicine and Psychiatry*, 13: 449–456.

Baer, Hans. 1986. The Replication of the Medical Division of Labor in Medical Anthropology: Implications for the Field, *Medical Anthropology Quarterly*, 17: 63–65.

Bakhtin, Mikhail. 1981. *The Dialogic Imagination. Four Essays by M. M. Bakhtin*. Edited by Michael Holquist. Translated by Caryl Emerson and Michael Holquist. Austin: University of Texas Press.

1984. *Rabelais and His World*. Translated by Helene Iswolsky. Bloomington: Indiana University Press.

Bargatzky, Thomas. 1984. Culture, Environment, and the Ills of Adaptationism, *Current Anthropology*, 25: 399–415.

Barrett, Robert J. 1988a. Clinical Writing and the Documentary Construction of Schizophrenia, *Culture, Medicine and Psychiatry*, 12: 265–299.

1988b. Interpretations of Schizophrenia, *Culture, Medicine and Psychiatry*, 12: 357–388.

Barrow, John D. 1988. *The World Within the World*. Oxford: Clarendon Press.

Barth, Fredrik. 1987. *Cosmologies in the Making: A Generative Approach to Cultural Variation in Inner New Guinea*. Cambridge: Cambridge University Press.

Bauman, Richard. 1986. *Story, Performance and Event: Contextual Studies of Oral Narrative*. Cambridge: Cambridge University Press.

Becker, A. L. 1979. Text-Building, Epistemology, and Aesthetics in Javanese Shadow Theatre. In A. L. Becker and Aram A. Yengoyan (eds.), *The Imagination of Reality: Essays in Southeast Asian Coherence Systems*, pp. 211–241. Norwood, NJ: ABLEX.

Becker, Howard S., Blanche Geer, Everett C. Hughes, and Anselm L. Strauss. 1961. *Boys in White: Student Culture in Medical School*. Chicago: University of Chicago Press.

Benedict, Ruth. 1923. The Concept of the Guardian Spirit in North America, *Memoirs of the American Anthropological Association*, 29: 1–97.

1934. Anthropology and the Abnormal, *Journal of General Psychology*, 10: 59–82.

Berger, Peter L., and Thomas Luckmann. 1966. *The Social Construction of Reality*. New York: Doubleday.

Bernstein, Richard J. 1976. *The Restructuring of Social and Political Theory*. Philadelphia: University of Pennsylvania Press.

Bertrand, Jane T., Bakutuvwidi Makani, Susan E. Hassig, Kinavwidi Lewu Niwembo, Balowa Djunghu, Mbadu Muanda, and Chirwisa Chirhamolekwa. 1991. AIDS-Related Knowledge, Sexual Behavior, and Condom Use among Men and Women in Kinshasa, Zaire, *American Journal of Public Health*, 81: 53–58.

Bibeau, Gilles. 1981. The Circular Semantic Network in Ngbandi Disease Nosology, *Social Science and Medicine*, 15B: 295–307.

Bilu, Yoram. 1988. Rabbi Yaacov Wazana: A Jewish Healer in the Atlas Mountains, *Culture Medicine and Psychiatry*, 12: 113–135.

Bloch, Maurice, and Jonathan Parry. 1982. *Death and the Regeneration of Life*. Cambridge: Cambridge University Press.

Blumhagen, Dan. 1980. Hyper-tension. A Folk Illness with a Medical Name, *Culture, Medicine and Psychiatry*, 4: 197–227.

Bok, Derek. 1984. President's Report on Medical Education, *Harvard University Gazette*, 79 (33): 1–12.

Bosk, Charles. 1979. *Forgive and Remember: Managing Medical Failure*. Chicago: University of Chicago Press.

Bottéro, Alain. 1991. Consumption by Semen Loss in India and Elsewhere, *Culture, Medicine and Psychiatry*, 15: 303–320.

Bourdieu, Pierre. 1977. *Outline of a Theory of Practice*. Cambridge: Cambridge University Press.

   1989. Social Space and Symbolic Power, *Sociological Theory*, 7: 14–25.

Bourdieu, Pierre, and Jean-Claude Passeron. 1977. *Reproduction In Education, Society and Culture*. Sage Studies in Social and Educational Change, vol. 5. London: Sage Publications.

Boyer, L. Bryce. 1969. Shamans: To Set the Record Straight, *American Anthropologist*, 71: 307–309.

Brand, Gerd. 1967. Intentionality, Reduction, and Intentional Analysis in Husserl's Later Manuscripts. In Joseph J. Cockelmans (ed.), *The Philosophy of Edmund Husserl and Its Interpretation*, pp. 197–217.

Brodwin, Paul Eric. 1991. Political Contests and Moral Claims: Religious Pluralism and Healing in a Haitian Village. Ph.D. Dissertation, Department of Anthropology, Harvard University.

Brody, Howard. 1987. *Stories of Sickness*. New Haven: Yale University Press.

Brooks, Peter. 1984. *Reading for the Plot. Design and Intention in Narrative*. New York: Vintage Books.

Brown, Peter J., and Marcia C. Inhorn. 1990. Disease, Ecology, and Human Behavior. In Thomas M. Johnson and Carolyn F. Sargent (eds.), *Medical Anthropology: A Handbook of Theory and Method*, pp. 187–214.

Browne, Edward G. 1921. *Arabian Medicine*. Cambridge: Cambridge University Press.

Browner, C. H., Bernard R. Ortiz de Montellano, and Arthur J. Rubel. 1988. A Methodology for Cross-Cultural Ethnomedical Research, *Current Anthropology*, 29: 681–702.

Broyard, Anatole. 1992. *Intoxicated By My Illness, and Other Writings on Life and Death*. New York: Clarkson Patter.

Bruner, Jerome. 1986. *Actual Minds, Possible Worlds*. Cambridge, MA: Harvard University Press.

   1990. *Acts of Meaning*. Cambridge, MA: Harvard University Press.

Buckley, Thomas, and Alma Gottlieb. 1988. *Blood Magic. The Anthropology of Menstruation*. Berkeley: University of California Press.

Butler, Judith. 1990. *Gender Trouble: Feminism and the Subversion of Identity*. New York: Routledge.

Caplan, Arthur L., H. Tristram Engelhardt, Jr., and James J. McCartney. 1981. *Concepts of Health and Disease. Interdisciplinary Perspectives*. Reading, MA: Addison-Wesley.

Carr, David. 1986. *Time, Narrative, and History*. Bloomington, IN: Indiana University Press.

Carr, John E. 1978. Ethno-Behaviorism and the Culture-Bound Syndromes: The Case of Amok, *Culture, Medicine and Psychiatry*, 2: 269–293.

Carr, John E., and Peter P. Vitaliano. 1985. The Theoretical Implications of Converging Research on Depression and the Culture-Bound Syndromes. In Arthur Kleinman and Byron Good (eds.), *Culture and Depression*, pp. 244–266.

Casey, Edward S. 1973. Translator's Foreword to Mikel Dufrenne, *The Phenomenology of Aesthetic Experience*, pp. xv–xlii. Evanston, IL: Northwestern University Press.

Cassirer, Ernst. 1923. *Substance and Function, and Einstein's Theory of Relativity*. Translated by William Curtis Swabey and Maria Collins Swabey. Chicago: The Open Court Publishing Co.

   1933. Le Langage et la Construction du Monde des Objets, *Journal de Psychologie Normale et Pathologique*, 30: 18–44.

   1946. *Language and Myth*. New York: Dover Publications (1953 edition).

1955a. *The Philosophy of Symbolic Forms. Vol. 1: Language.* New Haven: Yale University Press.

1955b. *The Philosophy of Symbolic Forms. Vol. 2: Mythical Thought.* New Haven: Yale University Press.

Casson, R. 1983. Schemata in Cognitive Anthropology, *Annual Review of Anthropology*, 12: 429–462.

Castillo, Richard Joseph. 1991. Culture, Trance and Mental Illness: Divided Consciousness in South Asia. Ph.D. Dissertation, Department of Anthropology, Harvard University.

1993. Spirit Possession in Southeast Asia: Dissociation or Hysteria? *Culture, Medicine and Psychiatry* (in press).

Chandrasekhar, Subrahmanyan. 1987. *Truth and Beauty: Aesthetics and Motivations in Science.* Chicago: University of Chicago Press.

Chen, Lincoln C. 1986. Primary Health Care in Developing Countries: Overcoming Operational, Technical, and Social Barriers, *The Lancet*, Nov. 29, 1986: 1260–1265.

Chrisman, Noel J. 1977. The Health Seeking Process: An Approach to the Natural History of Illness, *Culture, Medicine and Psychiatry*, 1: 351–377.

Clark, Margaret. 1959. *Health in the Mexican-American Culture.* Berkeley: University of California Press.

Clatts, Michael C., and Kevin M. Mutchler. 1989. AIDS and the Dangerous Other: Metaphors of Sex and Deviance in the Representation of Disease, *Medical Anthropology*, 10: 105–114.

Clement, Dorothy C. 1982. Samoan Folk Knowledge of Mental Disorders. In A. J. Marsella and G. M. White (eds.), *Cultural Conceptions of Mental Health and Therapy*, pp. 193–213. Dordrecht, Holland: D. Reidel Publishing Co.

Clements, Forrest E. 1932. Primitive Concepts of Disease, *University of California Publications in American Archeology and Ethnology*, 32: 185–252.

Cockelmans, Joseph J. 1967. *The Philosophy of Edmund Husserl and Its Interpretation.* Garden City, NY: Doubleday.

Cohen, Lawrence. 1992a. No Aging in India. Ph.D. Dissertation, Department of Anthropology, Harvard University.

1992b. No Aging in India. The Uses of Gerontology, *Culture, Medicine and Psychiatry*, 16: 123–161.

Colson, Anthony C., and Karen E. Selby. 1974. Medical Anthropology, *Annual Review of Anthropology*, 3: 245–262.

Colvin, Robert B., and Miriam S. Wetzel. 1989. Pathology in the New Pathway of Medical Education at Harvard Medical School. *A.J.C.P.*, October (Supplement 1): 523–520.

Comaroff, Jean. 1982. Medicine: Symbol and Ideology. In P. Wright and A. Treacher (eds.), *The Problem of Medical Knowledge*, pp. 49–68. Edinburgh: Edinburgh University Press.

1985. *Body of Power, Spirit of Resistance. The Culture and History of a South African People.* Chicago: University of Chicago Press.

Comaroff, Jean, and John Comaroff. 1991. *Of Revelation and Revolution. Vol. 1: Christianity, Colonialism, and Consciousness in South Africa.* Chicago: University of Chicago Press.

Corin, Ellen E. 1990. Facts and Meaning in Psychiatry. An Anthropological Approach to the Lifeworld of Schizophrenics. *Culture, Medicine and Psychiatry*, 14: 153–188.

Crandon-Malamud, Libbet. 1991. *From the Fat of Our Souls: Social Change, Political Process, and Medical Pluralism in Bolivia.* Berkeley: University of California Press.

Crapanzano, Vincent. 1992. *Hermes' Dilemma and Hamlet's Desire: On the Epistemology of Interpretation.* Cambridge, MA: Harvard University Press.

Csordas, Thomas J. 1983. The Rhetoric of Transformation in Ritual Healing, *Culture, Medicine and Psychiatry*, 7: 333–376.

   1988. Elements of Charismatic Persuasion and Healing, *Medical Anthropology Quarterly*, 2: 102–120.

   1990. Embodiment as a Paradigm for Anthropology, *Ethos*, 18: 5–47.

Csordas, Thomas J., and Arthur Kleinman. 1990. The Therapeutic Process. In T. Johnson and C. Sargent (eds.), *Medical Anthropology: A Handbook of Theory and Method*, pp. 11–25.

D'Amico, Robert. 1989. *Historicism and Knowledge*. New York: Routledge.

D'Andrade, Roy G. 1976. A Propositional Analysis of U.S. American Beliefs about Illness. In K. A. Basso and H. A. Selby (eds.), *Meaning in Anthropology*, pp. 155–180. Albuquerque: University of New Mexico Press.

   1992. Cognitive Anthropology. In T. Schwartz, G. White, and C. Lutz (eds.), *The Social Life of Self: Directions in Psychological Anthropology*. Cambridge: Cambridge University Press.

Das, Veena. 1993. Moral Orientations to Suffering: Legitimation, Power, and Healing. In L. C. Chen, A. Kleinman, and N. C. Ware (eds.), *Health and Social Change in International Perspective*. Oxford: Oxford University Press.

Davidson, Donald. 1974. Belief and the Basis of Meaning, *Synthese*, 27: 309–323.

   1980. *Essays on Actions and Events*. Oxford: Clarendon Press.

Davis, D. L., and R. G. Whitten. 1987. The Cross-Cultural Study of Human Sexuality, *Annual Review of Anthropology*, 16: 69–98.

Delaney, Carol. 1987. Seeds of Honor, Fields of Shame. In David Gilmore (ed.), *Honor and Shame and the Unity of the Mediterranean*, pp. 35–48. American Anthropological Association, Special Publication 22. Washington, DC: American Anthropological Association.

Desjarlais, Robert R. 1992a. Yolmo Aesthetics of Person, Health and "Soul Loss," *Social Science and Medicine*, 34: 1105–1117.

   1992b. *Body and Emotion: The Aesthetics of Illness and Healing in the Nepal Himalayas*. Philadelphia: University of Pennsylvania Press.

Devereux, George. 1956. Normal and Abnormal: The Key Problem of Psychiatric Anthropology. In J. B. Casagrande and T. Gladwin (eds.), *Some Uses of Anthropology: Theoretical and Applied*, pp. 23–48. Washington, DC: Anthropological Society of Washington.

   1961. Shamans as Neurotics, *American Anthropologist*, 63: 1088–1090.

   1980 [1965]. Schizophrenia: An Ethnic Psychosis or Schizophrenia without Tears. In G. Devereux (ed.), *Basic Problems of Ethnopsychiatry*, pp. 214–236. Chicago: University of Chicago Press.

Devisch, Rene. 1990. The Therapist and the Source of Healing among the Yaka of Zaire, *Culture, Medicine and Psychiatry*, 14: 213–236.

DiGiacomo, Susan. 1987. Biomedicine as a Cultural System: An Anthropologist in the Kingdom of the Sick. In Hans Baer (ed.), *Encounters with Biomedicine*, pp. 315–346. New York: Gordon and Breach Science Publishers.

Dougherty, Molly C. and Toni Tripp-Reimer. 1985. The Interface of Nursing and Anthropology, *Annual Review of Anthropology*, 14: 219–241.

Douglas, Mary. 1975. *Implicit Meanings: Essays in Anthropology*. London: Routledge and Kegan Paul.

Doyal, Len, and Roger Harris. 1986. *Empiricism, Explanation and Rationality. An Introduction to the Philosophy of the Social Sciences*. London: Routledge and Kegan Paul.

Dreyfus, Hubert L., and Paul Rabinow. 1982. *Michel Foucault: Beyond Structuralism and Hermeneutics*. Chicago: University of Chicago Press.

Dufrenne, Mikel. 1973. *The Phenomenology of Aesthetic Experience*. Translated by Edward S. Casey. Evanston, IL: Northwestern University Press.

Dunk, Pamela. 1989. Greek Women and Broken Nerves in Montreal, *Medical Anthropology*, 11: 29–46.

Dunn, Fred L. 1976. Traditional Asian Medicine and Cosmopolitan Medicine as Adaptive Systems. In Charles Leslie (ed.), *Asian Medical Systems: A Comparative Study*, pp. 133–158.

Early, Evelyn Aleene. 1982. The Logic of Well-Being: Therapeutic Narratives in Cairo, Egypt, *Social Science and Medicine*, 16: 1491–1497.

1985. Catharsis and Creation: The Everyday Narratives of Baladi Women of Cairo, *Anthropological Quarterly*, 58: 172–181.

1988. The Baladi Curative System of Cairo, Egypt, *Culture, Medicine and Psychiatry*, 12: 65–83.

Ebigbo, P. O. 1982. Development of a Culture Specific (Nigeria) Screening Scale of Somatic Complaints Indicating Psychiatric Disturbance, *Culture, Medicine and Psychiatry*, 6: 29–43.

Eco, Umberto. 1992. *Interpretation and Overinterpretation*. Cambridge: Cambridge University Press.

Eisenberg, Leon. 1986. Mindlessness and Brainlessness in Psychiatry, *British Journal of Psychiatry*, 148: 497–508.

Elgood, Cyril. 1951. *A Medical History of Persia*. Cambridge: Cambridge University Press.

1962. Tibb-ul-Nabbi or Medicine of the Prophet: Being a Translation of Two Works of the Same Name, *Osiris*, 13: 33–192.

1966. *Safavid Surgery*. Oxford: Pergamon Press.

Engel, George L. 1977. The Need for a New Medical Model: A Challenge for Biomedicine, *Science*, 196: 129–136.

Engelhardt, H. Tristram. 1974. Explanatory Models in Medicine: Facts, Theories, and Values, *Texas Reports on Biology and Medicine*, 32: 225–239.

Epstein, Cynthia Fuchs. 1988. *Deceptive Distinctions: Sex, Gender, and the Social Order*. New Haven: Yale University Press.

Estroff, Sue. 1981. *Making It Crazy*. Berkeley: University of California Press.

1989. Self, Identity, and Subjective Experience of Schizophrenia: In Search of the Subject, *Schizophrenia Bulletin*, 15: 189–196.

Etkin, Nina L. 1988. Ethnopharmacology: Biobehavioral Approaches in the Anthropological Study of Indigenous Medicines, *Annual Review of Anthropology*, 17: 23–42.

Evans-Pritchard, E. E. 1937. *Witchcraft, Oracles and Magic among the Azande*. Oxford: Oxford University Press.

Evens, Martha Walton. 1988. *Relational Models of the Lexicon: Representing Knowledge in Semantic Networks*. Cambridge: Cambridge University Press.

Fabrega, Horacio. 1970. On the Specificity of Folk Illnesses, *Southwestern Journal of Anthropology*, 26: 304–314.

1972. Medical Anthropology. In B. J. Siegel (ed.), *Biennial Review of Anthropology*. Stanford: Stanford University Press.

Fabrega, Horacio, and Daniel B. Silver. 1973. *Illness and Shamanistic Curing in Zinacantan: An Ethnomedical Analysis*. Stanford: Stanford University Press.

Farmer, Paul. 1988. Bad Blood, Spoiled Milk: Bodily Fluids as Moral Barometers in Rural Haiti, *American Ethnologist*, 15: 62–83.

1990a. AIDS and Accusation: Haiti, Haitians, and the Geography of Blame. In Douglas A. Feldman (ed.), *Culture and AIDS*, pp. 67–91. New York: Praeger.

1990b. Sending Sickness: Sorcery, Politics, and Changing Concepts of AIDS in Rural Haiti, *Medical Anthropology Quarterly*, 4: 6–27.

1992. *AIDS and Accusation: Haiti and the Geography of Blame*. Berkeley: University of California Press.

Farmer, Paul, and Byron Good. 1991. Illness Representations in Medical Anthropology: A Critical Review and a Case Study of the Representation of AIDS in Haiti. In J. A. Skeltons, R. T. Croyle, and R. Eiser (eds.), *The Mental Representation of Health and Illness*.

Farmer, Paul, and Arthur Kleinman. 1989. AIDS as Human Suffering, *Daedalus*, 118 (2): 135–160.

Favret-Saada, Jeanne. 1980. *Deadly Words. Witchcraft in the Bocage*. Cambridge: Cambridge University Press.

Feksi, A. T., J. Kaamugisha, J. W. A. S. Sander, S. Gatiti, and S. D. Shorvon. 1991. Comprehensive Primary Health Care Antiepileptic Drug Treatment Programme in Rural and Semi-Urban Kenya, *The Lancet*, 337: 406–409.

Finkler, Kaja. 1983. *Spiritist Healers in Mexico*. South Hadley, MA: Bergin and Garvey.

Fisher, Sue, and Alexandra Dundas Todd (eds.). 1983. *The Social Organization of Doctor–Patient Communication*. Washington, DC: Center for Applied Linguistics.

Foster, George M. 1987a. World Health Organization Behavioral Science Research: Problems and Prospects, *Social Science and Medicine*, 24: 709–715.

1987b. Bureaucratic Aspects of International Health Agencies, *Social Science and Medicine*, 25: 1039–1048.

1988. The Validating Role of Humoral Theory in Traditional Spanish-American Therapeutics, *American Ethnologist*, 15: 120–135.

Foster, George M., and Barbara Gallatin Anderson. 1978. *Medical Anthropology*. New York: Wiley.

Foucault, Michel. 1970. *The Order of Things. An Archaeology of the Human Sciences*. New York: Random House.

1972. *The Archaeology of Knowledge*. New York: Harper and Row.

1973. *The Birth of the Clinic. An Archaeology of Medical Perception*. New York: Random House.

1977. *Discipline and Punish: The Birth of the Prison*. New York: Vintage Books.

1978. *The History of Sexuality. Vol. 1: An Introduction*. New York: Random House.

1980. *Power/Knowledge*. Edited by Colin Gordon. New York: Pantheon.

Fox, Renée C. 1959. *Experiment Perilous: Physicians and Patients Facing the Unknown*. Glencoe, IL: Free Press.

1988. *Essays in Medical Sociology: Journeys into the Field* (2nd edn.). New York: Wiley.

Frake, Charles O. 1961. The Diagnosis of Disease Among the Subanun of Mindanao, *American Anthropologist*, 63: 113–132.

1962. *The Ethnographic Study of Cognitive Systems*. Washington, DC: The Anthropological Society of Washington.

Frank, Gelya. 1986. On Embodiment: A Case Study of Congenital Limb Deficiency in American Culture, *Culture, Medicine and Psychiatry*, 10: 189–219.

Frankenberg, Ronald. 1988a. Gramsci, Marxism, and Phenomenology: Essays for the Development of Critical Medical Anthropology. Edited by R. Frankenberg. Special Issue of *Medical Anthropology Quarterly*, 2 (4): 324–459.

1988b. Gramsci, Culture, and Medical Anthropology: Kundry and Parsifal? or Rat's Tail to Sea Serpent? *Medical Anthropology Quarterly*, 2: 324–337.

1988c. "Your Time or Mine?" An Anthropological View of the Tragic Temporal Contradictions of Biomedical Practice, *International Journal of Health Services*, 18: 11–34.

Freidson, Eliot. 1961. *Patients' Views of Medical Practice*. New York: Russell Sage Foundation.

1970. *Profession of Medicine: A Study of the Sociology of Applied Knowledge*. New York: Dodd, Mead and Co.

Gaines, Atwood D. 1979. Definitions and Diagnoses, *Culture, Medicine and Psychiatry*, 3: 381–418.

1982. Cultural Definitions, Behavior and the Person in American Psychiatry. In A. Marsella and G. White (eds.), *Cultural Conceptions of Mental Health and Illness*, pp. 167–192. Dordrecht, Holland: D. Reidel Publishing Co.

1992a. Ethnopsychiatry: The Cultural Construction of Psychiatries. In A. D. Gaines (ed.), *Ethnopsychiatry: The Cultural Construction of Folk and Professional Psychiatries*. Albany, NY: SUNY Press.

1992b. From DSM-I to III-R; Voices of Self, Mastery and the Other: A Cultural Constructivist Reading of U.S. Psychiatric Classification, *Social Science and Medicine*, 35: 3–24.

Garro, Linda. 1986a. Intracultural Variation in Folk Medical Knowledge: A Comparison between Curers and Non-Curers, *American Anthropologist*, 88: 351–370.

1986b. Decision-Making Models of Treatment Choice. In Sean McHugh and T. Michael Vallis (eds.), *Illness Behavior: A Multidisciplinary Model*, pp. 173–188. New York: Plenum Press.

1988. Explaining High Blood Pressure: Variation in Knowledge about Illness, *American Ethnologist*, 15: 98–119.

1990. Continuity and Change: The Interpretation of Illness in an *Anishinaabe* (Ojibway) Community, *Culture, Medicine and Psychiatry*, 14: 417–454.

1992. Chronic Illness and the Construction of Narrative. In Mary-Jo DelVecchio Good, Paul E. Brodwin, Byron J. Good, and Arthur Kleinman (eds.), *Pain as Human Experience: An Anthropological Perspective*, pp. 100-137.

1993. Perspectives in the Health and Health Care of Canada's First Peoples, *Culture, Medicine and Psychiatry*, 17.

Gawronsky, Dimitry. 1949. Ernst Cassirer: His Life and His Work. In Paul Arthur Schilpp (ed.), *The Philosophy of Ernst Cassirer*, pp. 1–37. Evanston, IL: Library of Living Philosophers, Inc.

Geertz, Clifford. 1973. *The Interpretation of Cultures*. New York: Basic Books.

1983. *Local Knowledge. Further Essays in Interpretive Anthropology*. New York: Basic Books.

1988. *Works and Lives. The Anthropologist as Author*. Stanford, CA: Stanford University Press.

Gerhardt, Uta (ed.). 1990. Qualitative Research on Chronic Illness. Special Issue of *Social Science and Medicine*, 30: 1149–1263.

Giddens, Anthony. 1979. *Central Problems in Social Theory: Action, Structure and Contradiction in Social Analysis*. Cambridge: Cambridge University Press.

Gilman, Sander L. 1988. *Disease and Representation: Images of Illness from Madness to AIDS*. Ithaca, NY: Cornell University Press.

Glick, L. B. 1967. Medicine as an Ethnographic Category: The Gimi of the New Guinea Highlands, *Ethnology*, 6: 31–56.

Good, Byron J. 1976a. Medical Change and the Doctor–Patient Relationship in an Iranian
    Provincial Town. In Khodadad Farmanfarmaian (ed.), *The Social Sciences and
    Problems of Development*, pp. 244–260. Princeton, NJ: Princeton University Program
    in Near Eastern Studies.
    1976b. The Professionalization of Medicine in an Iranian Provincial Town. In Madeleine
    Leininger (ed.), *Transcultural Health Care Issues and Conditions*, pp. 51–65.
    Philadelphia, PA: F. A. Davis Co.
    1977. The Heart of What's the Matter. The Semantics of Illness in Iran, *Culture,
    Medicine and Psychiatry*, 1: 25–58.
    1981. The Transformation of Health Care in Modern Iranian History. In Michael E.
    Bonine and Nikki R. Keddie (eds.), *Modern Iran: The Dialectics of Continuity and
    Change*, pp. 59–82. Albany, GA: SUNY Albany Press.
    1986. Explanatory Models and Care-Seeking: A Critical Account. In Sean McHugh and
    T. Michael Vallis (eds.), *Illness Behavior: A Multidisciplinary Model*, pp. 161–172.
    New York: Plenum Press.
    1992a. A Body in Pain – The Making of a World of Chronic Pain. In Mary-Jo
    DelVecchio Good, Paul E. Brodwin, Byron J. Good, and Arthur Kleinman (eds.), *Pain
    as Human Experience: An Anthropological Perspective*, pp. 29–48.
    1992b. Culture and Psychopathology: Directions for Psychiatric Anthropology. In
    Theodore Schwartz, Geoffrey M. White, and Catherine A. Lutz (eds.), *The Social Life
    of Self: New Directions in Psychological Anthropology*. Cambridge: Cambridge
    University Press.
Good, Byron J., and Mary-Jo DelVecchio Good. 1980. The Meaning of Symptoms: A
    Cultural Hermeneutic Model for Clinical Practice. In Leon Eisenberg and Arthur
    Kleinman (eds.), *The Relevance of Social Science for Medicine*, pp. 165–196.
    Dordrecht, Holland: D. Reidel Publishing Co.
    1981. The Semantics of Medical Discourse. In Everett Mendelsohn and Yehuda Elkana
    (eds.), *Sciences and Cultures. Sociology of the Sciences*, vol. 5, pp. 177–212.
    Dordrecht, Holland: D. Reidel Publishing Co.
    1982. Toward a Meaning-Centered Analysis of Popular Illness Categories: "Fright
    Illness" and "Heart Distress" in Iran. In Anthony J. Marsella and Geoffrey M. White
    (eds.), *Cultural Conceptions of Mental Health and Therapy*, pp. 141–166. Dordrecht,
    Holland: D. Reidel Publishing Co.
    1992. The Comparative Study of Greco-Islamic Medicine: The Integration of Medical
    Knowledge into Local Symbolic Contexts. In Charles Leslie and Allan Young (eds.),
    Paths to Asian Medical Knowledge, pp. 257-271.
    Forthcoming. "Learning Medicine": The Constructing of Medical Knowledge at
    Harvard Medical School. In Shirley Lindenbaum and Margaret Lock (eds.), *Analysis
    in Medical Anthropology*, Berkeley: University of California Press.
Good, Byron, Mary-Jo DelVecchio Good, and Robert Moradi. 1985. The Intepretation of
    Dysphoric Affect and Depressive Illness in Iranian Culture. In Arthur Kleinman and
    Byron Good (eds.), *Culture and Depression*, pp. 369–428.
Good, Byron J., Henry Herrera, Mary-Jo DelVecchio Good, and James Cooper. 1985.
    Reflexivity, Countertransference and Clinical Ethnography: A Case from a
    Psychiatric Cultural Consultation Clinic. In Robert Hahn and Atwood Gaines (eds.),
    Physicians of Western Medicine, pp. 177–192.
Good, Byron, and Arthur Kleinman. 1985. Epilogue: Culture and Depression. In
    A. Kleinman and B. Good (eds.), *Culture and Depression*, pp. 491-505.
Good, Mary-Jo DelVecchio. 1977. Social Hierarchy in Provincial Iran: The Case of Qajar
    Maragheh, *Journal of Iranian Studies*, 10: 129–163.

1978. Women in Provincial Iran and Turkey. In Lois Beck and Nikki Keddie (eds.), *Women in the Muslim World*, pp. 482–500. Cambridge, MA: Harvard University Press.

1980. Of Blood and Babies: The Relationship of Popular Islamic Physiology to Fertility, *Social Science and Medicine*, 14B: 147–156.

1985. Discourses on Physician Competence. In Robert Hahn and Atwood Gaines (eds.), *Physicians of Western Medicine*, pp. 247–268.

1990. The Practice of Biomedicine and the Discourse on Hope: A Preliminary Investigation into the Culture of American Oncology. In Beatrix Pfleiderer and Gilles Bibeau (eds.), *Anthropologies of Medicine: A Colloquium on West European and North American Perspectives*. Heidelberg, Germany: Vieweg.

Good, Mary-Jo DelVecchio, Paul E. Brodwin, Byron J. Good, and Arthur Kleinman (eds.). 1992. *Pain as Human Experience: An Anthropological Perspective*. Berkeley: University of California Press.

Good, Mary-Jo DelVecchio, and Byron J. Good. 1988. Ritual, the State, and the Transformation of Emotional Discourse in Iranian Society, *Culture, Medicine and Psychiatry*, 12: 43–63.

1989. "Disabling Practitioners": Hazards of Learning to be a Doctor in American Medical Education, *Journal of Orthopsychiatry*, 59: 303–309.

Good, Mary-Jo DelVecchio, Byron J. Good, Tseunetsugu Munakata, Yasuki Kobayashi, and Cheryl Mattingly. Forthcoming. Oncology and Narrative Time, *Social Science and Medicine*.

Good, Mary-Jo DelVecchio, Byron J. Good, Cynthia Schaffer, and Stuart E. Lind. 1990. American Oncology and the Discourse on Hope, *Culture, Medicine and Psychiatry*, 14: 59–79.

Good, Mary-Jo DelVecchio, Linda Hunt, Tseunetsugu Munakata, and Yasuki Kobayashi. 1993. A Comparative Analysis of the Culture of Biomedicine: Disclosure and Consequences for Treatment in the Practice of Oncology. In Peter Conrad and Eugene Gallagher (eds.), *Medicine Across Societies*. Philadelphia: Temple University Press.

Goodenough, Ward. 1956. Componential Analysis and the Study of Meaning, *Language*, 32: 195–216.

1981. *Culture, Language, and Society*. Menlo Park, CA: Benjamin/Cummings.

Goodman, Nelson. 1978. *Ways of Worldmaking*. Indianapolis: Hackett Publishing Co.

Gordon, Deborah R. 1988. Tenacious Assumptions in Western Medicine. In Margaret Lock and Deborah Gordon (eds.), *Biomedicine Examined*, pp. 11–56.

1990. Embodying Illness, Embodying Cancer, *Culture, Medicine and Psychiatry*, 14: 275–297.

Greenwood, Davydd, Shirley Lindenbaum, Margaret Lock, and Allan Young (eds.). 1988. Theme Issue: Medical Anthropology, *American Ethnologist*, 15 (1): 1–167.

Gruner, O. Cameron. 1930. *A Treatise on The Canon of Medicine of Avicenna, Incorporating a Translation of the First Book*. London: Luzac and Co.

Guarnaccia, Peter, and Pablo Farias. 1988. The Social Meanings of Nervios: A Case Study of a Central American Woman, *Social Science and Medicine*, 26: 1223–1231.

Guarnaccia, Peter J., Byron J. Good and Arthur Kleinman. 1990. A Critical Review of Epidemiological Studies of Puerto Rican Mental Health, *American Journal of Psychiatry*, 147: 1449–1456.

Gussow, Zachary. 1989. *Leprosy, Racism, and Public Health: Social Policy in Chronic Disease Control*. Boulder, CO: Westview Press.

Güvener, Adnan, Aysel Işık, Zafer İlbars, and İlker Gelişen. 1990. Orta Anadolu Bölgesinde Epidemiyolojik, Klinik ve Sosyokültürel Yönleriyle Epilepsi Araştırması,

Turkiye Klinikleri Tip Bilimleri Araştırma Dergisi, 8: 151–159. [Epidemiological, Clinical and Sociocultural Aspects of Epilepsy in a Community Based Survey in Central Anatolia, *Turkish Journal of Research in Medical Sciences*, 8: 151–159].

Habermas, Jurgen. 1984. *The Theory of Communicative Action. Vol. 1: Reason and the Rationalization of Society*. Translated by Thomas McCarthy. Boston: Beacon Press.

1987a. *The Theory of Communicative Action. Vol. 2: Lifeworld and System: A Critique of Functionalist Reason*. Translated by Thomas McCarthy. Boston: Beacon Press.

1987b. *The Philosophical Discourse on Modernity*. Translated by Frederick G. Lawrence. Cambridge, MA: MIT Press.

Hafferty, Frederic W. 1988. Cadaver Stories and the Emotional Socialization of Medical Students, *Health and Social Behavior*, 29: 344–356.

1991. *Into the Valley: Death and the Socialization of Medical Students*. New Haven: Yale University Press.

Hahn, Robert A. 1973. Understanding Beliefs: An Essay on the Methodology of the Statement and Analysis of Belief Systems, *Current Anthropology*, 14: 207–229.

1985. A World of Internal Medicine: Portrait of an Internist. In R. A. Hahn and A. D. Gaines (eds.), *Physicians of Western Medicine*, pp. 51–111.

Hahn, Robert A., and Atwood Gaines (eds.). 1985. *Physicians of Western Medicine*. Dordrecht, Holland: D. Reidel Publishing Co.

Hahn, Robert A. and Arthur Kleinman. 1983. Biomedical Practice and Anthropological Theory: Frameworks and Directions, *Annual Review of Anthropology*, 12: 305–333.

Hallowell, A. Irving. 1955. The Self and its Behavioral Environment, and The Ojibwa Self and its Behavioral Environment. In *Culture and Experience*, pp. 75–110, 172–182. New York: Schocken Books.

Hamburg, Carl H. 1949. Cassirer's Conception of Philosophy. In Paul Arthur Schilpp (ed.), *The Philosophy of Ernst Cassirer*, pp. 73–119. Evanston, IL: Library of Living Philosophers, Inc.

Handelman, Don. 1967. The Development of a Washo Shaman, *Ethnology*, 6: 444–464.

1968. Shamanizing on an Empty Stomach, *American Anthropologist*, 70: 353–356.

Harding, Sandra. 1986. *The Science Question in Feminism*. Ithaca: Cornell University Press.

Harris, Grace Gredys. 1989. Mechanism and Morality in Patients' Views of Illness and Injury, *Medical Anthropology Quarterly*, 3: 3–21.

Harrison, Bernard. 1972. *Meaning and Structure: An Essay in the Philosophy of Language*. New York: Harper and Row.

Heath, Dwight B. 1987. Anthropology and Alcohol Studies: Current Issues, *Annual Review of Anthropology*, 16: 99–120.

Herzlich, Claudine, and Janine Pierret. 1987. *Illness and Self in Society*. Baltimore: Johns Hopkins University Press.

Himmelstein, David, and Stephanie Woolhandler. 1986. Cost without Benefit: Administrative Waste in U.S. Health Care, *New England Journal of Medicine*, 314: 441–445.

Holland, Dorothy, and Naomi Quinn (eds.). 1987. *Cultural Models in Language and Thought*. Cambridge: Cambridge University Press.

Hollis, Martin, and Steven Lukes. 1982. *Rationality and Relativism*. Oxford: Basil Blackwell.

Holzner, Burkart. 1972. *Reality Construction in Society*. Cambridge, MA: Schenkman Publishing Co.

Hookway, Christopher, and Phillip Pettit. 1978. *Action and Interpretation. Studies in the Philosophy of the Social Sciences*. Cambridge: Cambridge University Press.

Hopper, Kim. 1992. Some Old Questions for the New Cross-Cultural Psychiatry, *Medical Anthropology Quarterly*, 5: 299–330.

Horn, Joshua S. 1972. *Away With All Pests: An English Surgeon in People's China, 1954–1969*. New York: Bantam Books.

Horton, Robin. 1967. African Traditional Thought and Western Science, 1, *Africa*, 37: 50–71.

Horton, Robin, and Ruth Finnegan. 1973. *Modes of Thought: Essays upon Thinking in Western and Non-Western Societies*. London: Faber.

Howes, David. 1989. Review of Alain Corbin, The Foul and the Fragrant: Odor and the French Social Imagination, *Culture, Medicine and Psychiatry*, 13: 89–97.

Hughes, Charles. 1968. Ethnomedicine. In *International Encyclopedia of the Social Sciences*. New York: Free Press.

Huntington, R., and Peter Metcalf. 1979. *Celebrations of Death: The Anthropology of Mortuary Ritual*. Cambridge: Cambridge University Press.

Hutchins, Edward. 1980. *Culture and Inference: A Trobriand Case Study*. Cambridge, MA: Harvard University Press.

Ingarden, Roman. 1973. *The Literary Work of Art: An Investigation on the Borderlines of Ontology, Logic, and Theory of Literature*. Translated by George G. Grabowicz. Evanston, IL: Northwestern University Press.

Inhorn, Marcia C., and Peter J. Brown. 1990. The Anthropology of Infectious Disease, *Annual Review of Anthropology*, 19: 89–117.

Iser, Wolfgang. 1978. *The Act of Reading. A Theory of Aesthetic Response*. Baltimore: Johns Hopkins University Press.

Izutsu, Toshihiko. 1966. *Ethico-Religious Concepts in the Qur'an*. Montreal: McGill University Press.

Jackson, Michael. 1989. *Paths toward a Clearing: Radical Empiricism and Ethnographic Inquiry*. Bloomington, IN: Indiana University Press.

Jacobus, Mary, Evelyn Fox Keller, and Sally Shuttleworth. 1990. *Body/Politics. Women and the Discourses of Science*. New York: Routledge.

Janes, Craig R., Ron Stall and Sandra M. Gifford (eds.). 1986. *Anthropology and Epidemiology*. Dordrecht, Holland: D. Reidel Publishing Co.

Janz, N. K., and M. H. Becker. 1984. The Health Belief Model: A Decade Later, *Health Education Quarterly*, 11: 1-47.

Janzen, John. 1978a. The Comparative Study of Medical Systems as Changing Social Systems, *Social Science and Medicine*, 12: 121–129.

1978b. *The Quest for Therapy in Lower Zaire*. Berkeley: University of California Press.

1987. Therapy Management: Concept, Reality, Process, *Medical Anthropology Quarterly*, 1: 68–84.

Jenkins, Janis H. 1988a. Ethnopsychiatric Interpretations of Schizophrenic Illness: The Problem of *Nervios* within Mexican-American Families, *Culture, Medicine and Psychiatry*, 12: 301–329.

1988b. Conceptions of Schizophrenia as a Problem of Nerves: A Cross-Cultural Comparison of Mexican-Americans and Anglo-Americans, *Social Science and Medicine*, 12: 1233–1243.

1991. The 1990 Stirling Award Essay: Anthropology, Expressed Emotion, and Schizophrenia, *Ethos*, 19: 387–431.

Jenkins, Janis H., and Marvin Karno. 1992. The Meaning of Expressed Emotion: Theoretical Issues Raised by Cross-Cultural Research, *American Journal of Psychiatry*, 149: 9–21.

Johnson, Thomas M., and Carolyn F. Sargent (eds.). 1990. *Medical Anthropology: A Handbook of Theory and Method*. New York: Greenwood Press.

Johnson-Laird, P. N., D. J. Herrmann, and R. Chaffin. 1984. Only Connections: A Critique of Semantic Networks, *Psychological Bulletin*, 96: 292–315.

Kapferer, Bruce. 1983. *A Celebration of Demons: Exorcism and the Aesthetics of Healing in Sri Lanka*. Bloomington: Indiana University Press.

Kaufman, Sharon R. 1988. Toward a Phenomenology of Boundaries in Medicine: Chronic Illness Experience in the Case of Stroke, *Medical Anthropology Quarterly*, 2: 338–354.

Keesing, Roger M. 1987. Models, "Folk" and "Cultural": Paradigms Regained? In D. Holland and N. Quinn (eds.), *Cultural Models in Language and Thought*, pp. 369–393.

Kenny, Michael G. (ed.). 1985. Culture Bound Syndromes. Special Issue of *Social Science and Medicine*, 21 (2): 163–228.

Kermode, Frank. 1966. *The Sense of an Ending. Studies in the Theory of Fiction*. Oxford: Oxford University Press.

Keyes, Charles F. 1985. The Interpretive Basis of Depression. In Arthur Kleinman and Byron Good (eds.), *Culture and Depression: Studies in the Anthropology and Cross-Cultural Psychiatry of Affect and Disorder*, pp. 153–174.

Kirchgassler, K. U. 1990. Change and Continuity in Patient Theories of Illness: The Case of Epilepsy, *Social Science and Medicine*, 30: 1313–1318.

Kirmayer, Laurence J. 1988. Mind and Body as Metaphors: Hidden Values in Biomedicine. In M. Lock and D. Gordon (eds.), *Biomedicine Examined*, pp. 57–93.

Kleinman, Arthur. 1973a. Toward a Comparative Study of Medical Systems, *Science, Medicine and Man*, 1: 55–65.

    1973b. Medicine's Symbolic Reality: On the Central Problem in the Philosophy of Medicine, *Inquiry*, 16: 206–213.

    1974. Cognitive Structures of Traditional Medical Systems, *Ethnomedicine*, 3: 27–49.

    1977. Depression, Somatization and the New Cross-Cultural Psychiatry, *Social Science and Medicine*, 11: 3–10.

    1980. *Patients and Healers in the Context of Culture. An Exploration of the Borderland between Anthropology, Medicine, and Psychiatry*. Berkeley: University of California Press.

    1986. *Social Origins of Distress and Disease: Depression, Neurasthenia, and Pain in Modern China*. New Haven: Yale University Press.

    1988a. *Rethinking Psychiatry: From Cultural Category to Personal Experience*. New York: The Free Press.

    1988b. *The Illness Narratives: Suffering, Healing and the Human Condition*. New York: Basic Books.

Kleinman, Arthur, Paul Brodwin, Byron Good, and Mary-Jo DelVecchio Good. 1992. Pain and Human Experience: An Introduction. In M. Good, P. Brodwin, B. Good, and A. Kleinman (eds.), *Pain as Human Experience: An Anthropological Perspective*, pp. 1–28.

Kleinman, Arthur, Leon Eisenberg, and Byron Good. 1978. Culture, Illness, and Care: Clinical Lessons from Anthropologic and Cross-Cultural Research, *Annals of Internal Medicine*, 88: 251–258.

Kleinman, Arthur, and Byron J. Good (eds.). 1985. *Culture and Depression: Studies in the Anthropology and Cross-Cultural Psychiatry of Affect and Disorder*. Berkeley: University of California Press.

Kleinman, Arthur, and Joan Kleinman. 1991. Suffering and its Professional Transformation: Toward an Ethnography of Experience, *Culture, Medicine and Psychiatry*, 15: 275–301.

Kleinman, Arthur, Peter Kunstadter, E. Alexander, and James Gale (eds.). 1976. *Medicine in Chinese Cultures: Comparative Studies of Health Care in Chinese and Other Societies.* Washington, DC: U.S. Government Printing Office for Fogarty International Center, N.I.H.

Kleinman, Arthur, and L. H. Sung. 1979. Why Do Indigenous Practitioners Successfully Heal? A Follow-Up Study of Indigenous Practice in Taiwan, *Social Science and Medicine*, 13: 7–26.

Kolakowski, Leszek. 1989. *The Presence of Myth.* Translated by Adam Czerniawski. Chicago: University of Chicago Press.

Kortmann, Frank. 1990. Psychiatric Case Finding in Ethiopia: Shortcomings of the Self Reporting Questionnaire, *Culture, Medicine and Psychiatry*, 14: 381–391.

Kroeber, A. L. 1940. Psychotic Factors in Shamanism, *Character and Personality*, 8: 204–215.

Kuipers, Joel C. 1989. "Medical Discourse" in Anthropological Context: Views of Language and Power, *Medical Anthropology Quarterly*, 3: 99–123.

Kunstadter, Peter. 1976. Do Cultural Differences Make Any Difference? Choice Points in Medical Systems Available in Northwestern Thailand. In A. Kleinman et al. (eds.), *Medicine in Chinese Cultures: Comparative Studies in Health Care in Chinese and Other Societies*, pp. 351–384.

La Barre, Weston. 1970. *The Ghost Dance: Origins of Religion.* New York: Delta.

Laderman, Carol. 1981. Symbolic and Empirical Reality: A New Approach to the Analysis of Food Avoidances, *American Ethnologist*, 8: 468–493.

1987. The Ambiguity of Symbols in the Structure of Healing, *Social Science and Medicine*, 24: 293–301.

1991. *Taming the Wind of Desire: Psychology, Medicine, and Aesthetics in Malay Shamanistic Performance.* Berkeley: University of California Press.

Lakoff, George, and Mark Johnson. 1980. *Metaphors We Live By.* Chicago: University of Chicago Press.

Landy, David. 1983. Medical Anthropology: A Critical Appraisal. In Julio Ruffini (ed.), *Advances in Medical Social Science, vol. 1*, pp. 185–314. New York: Gordon and Breach.

Latour, Bruno. 1987. *Science in Action. How to Follow Scientists and Engineers through Society.* Cambridge, MA: Harvard University Press.

Lave, Jean. 1988. *Cognition in Practice: Mind, Mathematics and Culture in Everyday Life.* Cambridge: Cambridge University Press.

Lella, Joseph W., and Dorothy Pawluch. 1988. Medical Students and the Cadaver in Social and Cultural Context. In M. Lock and D. Gordon (eds.), *Biomedicine Examined*, pp. 125–153.

Leplin, Jarrett. 1984. *Scientific Realism.* Berkeley: University of California Press.

Lepowsky, Maria. 1990. Sorcery and Penicillin: Treating Illness on a Papua New Guinea Island, *Social Science and Medicine*, 30: 1049–1063.

Leslie, Charles. 1973. The Professionalizing Ideology of Medical Revivalism. In Milton Singer (ed.), *Entrepreneurship and Modernization of Occupational Cultures in South Asia.* Durham, NC: Duke University Press.

1976a. *Asian Medical Systems: A Comparative Study.* Berkeley: University of California Press.

1976b. The Ambiguities of Medical Revivalism in Modern India. In Charles Leslie (ed.), *Asian Medical Systems*, pp. 356–367. Berkeley: University of California Press.

1989. Indigenous Pharmaceuticals, the Capitalist World System, and Civilization, *Kroeber Anthropological Society Papers*, 69–70: 23–31.

Leslie, Charles, and Allan Young (eds.). 1992. *Paths to Asian Medical Knowledge.* Berkeley: University of California Press.

Levey, Martin. 1967. Medical Ethics of Medieval Islam with Special Reference to Al-Ruhawi's "Practical Ethics of the Physician," *Transactions of the American Philosophical Society*, NS, 57 (3): 1–100. Philadelphia: American Philosophical Society.

Lévi-Strauss, Claude. 1963. *Structural Anthropology.* New York: Basic Books.

    1969. *The Raw and the Cooked. Introduction to a Science of Mythology, vol. 1.* Chicago: University of Chicago Press.

    1985. *The View from Afar.* New York: Basic Books.

Levy, Jerrold E., Raymond Neutra, and Dennis Parker. 1987. *Hand Trembling, Frenzy Witchcraft, and Moth Madness. A Study of Navajo Seizure Disorders.* Tucson: University of Arizona Press.

Lewis, C. S. 1982 [1966]. *On Stories and Other Essays on Literature.* Edited by Walter Hooper. San Diego: Harcourt Brace Jovanovich.

Lewis, Gilbert. 1975. *Knowledge of Illness in a Sepik Society.* London: Athlone Press.

    1976. A View of Sickness in New Guinea. In J. B. Loudon (ed.), *Social Anthropology and Medicine*, A.S.A. Monograph 13. London: Academic Press.

Lewontin, R. C., Steven Rose, and Leon J. Kamin. 1984. *Not In Our Genes: Biology, Ideology, and Human Nature.* New York: Pantheon Books.

Lienhardt, Godfrey. 1961. *Divinity and Experience. The Religion of the Dinka.* New York: Oxford University Press.

Lin, Tsung-Yi, Kenneth Tardiff, George Donetz, and Walter Goresky. 1978. Ethnicity and Patterns of Help-Seeking, *Culture, Medicine and Psychiatry*, 2: 3–14.

Littlewood, Roland. 1992. Humanism and Engagement in a Metapsychiatry. Review of Arthur Kleinman, *Rethinking Psychiatry: From Cultural Category to Personal Experience*, *Culture, Medicine and Psychiatry*, 16: 395–405.

Lloyd, G. E. R. 1966. *Polarity and Analogy.* Cambridge: Cambridge University Press.

    1973. Right and Left in Greek Philosophy. In Rodney Needham (ed.), *Right and Left: Essays on Dual Symbolic Classification*, pp. 167–186. Chicago: University of Chicago Press.

Lock, Margaret. 1980. *East Asian Medicine in Urban Japan: Varieties of Medical Experience.* Berkeley: University of California Press.

    1990. On Being Ethnic: The Politics of Identity Breaking and Making in Canada, or, *Nevra* on Sunday, *Culture, Medicine and Psychiatry*, 14: 237–254.

Lock, Margaret, and Deborah Gordon. 1988. *Biomedicine Examined.* Dordrecht, Holland: Kluwer Academic Publishers.

Lock, Margaret, and Nancy Scheper-Hughes. 1990. A Critical-Interpretive Approach in Medical Anthropology: Rituals and Routines of Discipline and Dissent. In T. Johnson and C. Sargent (eds.), *Medical Anthropology: A Handbook of Theory and Method*, pp. 47–72.

Loudon, J. B. 1976. Introduction. In J. B. Loudon (ed.), *Social Anthropology and Medicine*, pp. 1–48. A.S.A. Monograph 13. London: Academic Press.

Lovejoy, Arthur. 1936. *The Great Chain of Being.* Cambridge, MA: Harvard University Press.

Lukes, Steven. 1970. Some Problems about Rationality. In Bryan R. Wilson (ed.), *Rationality*, pp. 194-213.

Lutz, Catherine. 1985. Depression and the Translation of Emotional Worlds. In A. Kleinman and B. Good (eds.), *Culture and Depression*, pp. 63–100.

1988. *Unnatural Emotions: Everyday Sentiments on a Micronesian Atoll and Their Challenge to Western Theory.* Chicago: University of Chicago Press.

MacCormack, Carol, and Marilyn Strathern (eds.). 1980. *Nature, Culture and Gender.* Cambridge: Cambridge University Press.

Maiman, L. A., and M. H. Becker. 1974. The Health Belief Model: Origins and Correlates in Psychological Theory. In M. H. Becker (ed.), *The Health Belief Model and Personal Behavior*, pp. 9–26. Thorofare, NJ: Slack.

Marcus, George, and Michael Fischer. 1986. *Anthropology as Cultural Critique. An Experimental Moment in the Human Sciences.* Chicago: University of Chicago Press.

Maretzki, Thomas W. 1985. Biomedicine and Naturopathic Healing in West Germany: A Historical Ethnomedical View of a Stormy Relationship, *Culture, Medicine and Psychiatry*, 9: 383–422.

1989. Cultural Variation in Biomedicine: The *Kur* in West Germany, *Medical Anthropology Quarterly*, 3: 22–35.

Martin, Emily. 1987. *The Woman in the Body. A Cultural Analysis of Reproduction.* Boston: Beacon Press.

Massey, E. Wayne, and Lawrence C. McHenry. 1986. Hysteroepilepsy in the Nineteenth Century: Charcot and Gowers, *Neurology*, 36: 65–67.

Mattingly, Cheryl. 1989. Thinking with Stories: Story and Experience in a Clinical Practice. Ph.D. Thesis, Massachusetts Institute of Technology.

1991. The Narrative Nature of Clinical Reasoning, *Journal of American Occupational Therapy*, 45: 998–1005.

Forthcoming. Therapeutic Emplotment, *Social Science and Medicine.*

Mattingly, Cheryl, and M. Fleming. Forthcoming. *Forms of Inquiry in a Therapeutic Practice.* Philadelphia: F. A. Davis.

Mauss, Marcel. 1979. *Sociology and Psychology: Essays.* Translated by Ben Brewster. London: Routledge and Kegan Paul.

May, Margaret Tallmadge. 1968. *Galen: On the Usefulness of the Parts of the Body.* Translated from the Greek with an Introduction and Commentary by M. T. May, vols. 1 and 2. Ithaca: Cornell University Press.

McElroy, Ann, and Patricia K. Townsend. 1985. *Medical Anthropology in Ecological Perspective.* Boulder, CO: Westview Press.

McKinlay, John B. 1986. A Case for Refocusing Upstream: The Political Economy of Illness. In P. Conrad and R. Kern (eds.), *The Sociology of Health and Illness: Critical Perspectives*, pp. 484–498. New York: St. Martin's Press.

Mechanic, David. 1982. *Symptoms, Illness Behavior, and Help-Seeking.* New York: Prodist.

1986. Illness Behavior: An Overview. In Sean McHugh and T. Michael Vallis (eds.), *Illness Behavior: A Multidisciplinary Model*, pp. 101–109. New York: Plenum Press.

Meeker, Michael. 1979. *Literature and Violence in North Arabia.* Cambridge: Cambridge University Press.

Merleau-Ponty, Maurice. 1962. *Phenomenology of Perception.* London: Routledge and Kegan Paul.

1964. Cézanne's Doubt. In Maurice Merleau-Ponty, *Sense and Non-Sense*, pp. 9–25. Evanston, IL: Northwestern University Press.

Messer, Ellen. 1984. Anthropological Perspectives on Diet, *Annual Review of Anthropology*, 13: 205–249.

Meyerhoff, Max. 1937. On the Transmission of Greek and Indian Science to the Arabs, *Islamic Culture*, 2: 17–29.

Midgley, Mary. 1992. *Science as Salvation: A Modern Myth and its Meaning*. London: Routledge.

Minuchin, Salvador, Bernice Rosman, and Lester Baker. 1978. *Psychosomatic Families: Anorexia Nervosa in Context*. Cambridge, MA: Harvard University Press.

Mishler, Elliot. 1986a. *The Discourse of Medicine: Dialectics of Medical Interviews*. Norwood, NJ: ABLEX.

    1986b. *Research Interviewing: Context and Narrative*. Cambridge, MA: Harvard University Press.

Mitchell, W. J. T. (ed.). 1981. *On Narrative*. Chicago: University of Chicago Press.

Mizrahi, Terry. 1984. Coping with Patients: Subcultural Adjustments to the Conditions of Work among Internists-in-Training, *Social Problems*, 32: 156–165.

Moerman, Daniel E. 1983. Physiology and Symbols: The Anthropological Implications of the Placebo Effect. In Lola Romanucci-Ross, Daniel E. Moerman, and Laurence R. Tancredi (eds.), *The Anthropology of Medicine: From Culture to Method*. New York: Praeger.

Moore, Lorna G., Peter W. Van Arsdale, JoAnn E. Glittenberg, and Robert A. Aldrich. 1980. *The Biocultural Basis of Health: Expanding Views of Medical Anthropology*. Prospect Heights, IL: Waveland Press.

Moore, Sally Falk. 1978. *Law as Process*. London: Routledge and Kegan Paul.

Moore, Sally Falk, and Barbara G. Myerhoff (eds.). 1977. *Secular Ritual*. Assen: Van Gorcum.

Morgan, Lynn M. 1987. Dependency Theory in the Political Economy of Health: An Anthropological Critique, *Medical Anthropology Quarterly*, 1: 131–155.

    1989. The Political Economy of Primary Health Care in Costa Rica, Guatemala, Nicaragua, and El Salvador. Edited by L. Morgan. Special Issue of *Medical Anthropology Quarterly*, 3 (3): 227–282.

    1990. The Medicalization of Anthropology: A Critical Perspective on the Critical-Clinical Debate, *Social Science and Medicine*, 30: 945–950.

Morson, Gary Saul. 1981. *Bakhtin: Essays and Dialogues on His Work*. Chicago: University of Chicago Press.

Morsy, Soheir. 1978. Sex Roles, Power, and Illness in an Egyptian Village, *American Ethnologist*, 4: 137–150.

    1980. Body Concepts and Health Care: Illustrations from an Egyptian Village, *Human Organization*, 39: 92–96.

    1990. Political Economy in Medical Anthropology. In Thomas M. Johnson and Carolyn F. Sargent (eds.), *Medical Anthropology: A Handbook of Theory and Method*, pp. 26–46.

Morton, William J. 1880. Hystero-Epilepsy – Its History, Etc. A Letter to the Editor of *The Medical Record* (A Weekly Journal of Medicine and Surgery, George F. Shrady, editor, New York: William Wood and Company), 18: 246–248.

Murphy, H. B. M. 1982. *Comparative Psychiatry: The International and Intercultural Distribution of Mental Illness*. New York: Springer-Verlag.

Murphy, Jane M. 1976. Psychiatric Labeling in Cross-Cultural Perspective, *Science*, 191: 1019–1028.

Murphy, Robert F. 1987. *The Body Silent*. New York: Henry Holt.

Murray, Stephen O., and Kenneth W. Payne. 1989. The Social Classification of AIDS in American Epidemiology, *Medical Anthropology*, 10: 115–128.

Nasr, Seyyed Hossein. 1964. *An Introduction to Islamic Cosmological Doctrines*. Cambridge, MA: Harvard University Press.

    1968. *Science and Civilization in Islam*. New York: New American Library.

Navarro, Vicente. 1989. Why Some Countries Have National Health Insurance, Others
    Have National Health Services, and the U.S. Has Neither, *Social Science and
    Medicine*, 28: 887–898.
Needham, Rodney. 1972. *Belief, Language and Experience*. Chicago: University of
    Chicago Press.
Nichter, Mark. 1980. The Layperson's Perception of Medicine as Perspective into the
    Utilization of Multiple Therapy Systems in the Indian Context, *Social Science and
    Medicine*, 14B: 225–233.
    1981. Idioms of Distress: Alternatives in the Expression of Psychosocial Distress. A
    Case Study from South India, *Culture, Medicine and Psychiatry*, 5: 5–24.
    1989. *Anthropology and International Health: South Asian Case Studies*. Dordrecht,
    Holland: Kluwer Academic Publishers.
Nichter, Mark, and Carolyn Nordstrom. 1989. A Question of Medicine Answering: Health
    Commodification and the Social Relations of Healing in Sri Lanka, *Culture, Medicine
    and Psychiatry*, 13: 367–390.
Nkwi, Paul Nchoji, and Flavius Tioko Ndonko. 1989. The Epileptic Among the Bamileke
    of Maham in the NDe Division, West Province of Cameroon, *Culture, Medicine and
    Psychiatry*, 13: 437–448.
Noll, Richard. 1983. Shamanism and Schizophrenia: A State-Specific Approach to the
    "Schizophrenia Metaphor" of Shamanic States, *American Ethnologist*, 10: 443–459.
Obeyesekere, Gananath. 1985. Depression, Buddhism, and the Work of Culture in Sri
    Lanka. In Arthur Kleinman and Byron Good (eds.), *Culture and Depression*,
    pp. 134–152.
    1990. *The Work of Culture: Symbolic Transformation in Psychoanalysis and Anthro-
    pology*. Chicago: University of Chicago Press.
Office of Educational Development, Harvard Medical School. 1989. The New Pathway
    to General Medical Education at Harvard University, *Teaching and Learning in
    Medicine*, 1: 42–46.
Ohnuki-Tierney, Emiko. 1981. *Illness and Healing among the Sakhalin Ainu – A Symbolic
    Interpretation*. London and New York: Cambridge University Press.
    1984. *Illness and Culture in Contemporary Japan: An Anthropological View*.
    Cambridge: Cambridge University Press.
O'Nell, Theresa DeLeane. 1991. Undisciplined Hearts: Depression and Moral Imagination
    on the Flathead Reservation. Ph.D. Dissertation, Harvard University.
    1992. "Feeling Worthless": An Ethnographic Investigation of Depression and Problem
    Drinking at the Flathead Reservation, *Culture, Medicine and Psychiatry*, 16 (4):
    447–470.
Ong, Aihwa. 1987. *Spirits of Resistance and Capitalist Discipline: Factory Women in
    Malaysia*. Albany: State University of New York Press.
    1988. The Production of Possession: Spirits and the Multinational Corporation in
    Malaysia, *American Ethnologist*, 15: 28–42.
Onoge, Omafume. 1975. Capitalism and Public Health: A Neglected Theme in the Medical
    Anthropology of Africa. In S. Ingman and A. Thomas (eds.), *Topias and Utopias of
    Health*, pp. 219–232. The Hague: Mouton.
Orlove, Benjamin S. 1980. Ecological Anthropology, *Annual Review of Anthropology*, 9:
    235–273.
Ortega y Gasset, José. 1961. *Meditations on Quixote*. New York: W. W. Norton.
Ortner, Sherry B. 1974. Is Female to Male as Nature is to Culture? In Michelle Zimbalist
    Rosaldo and Louise Lamphere (eds.), *Woman, Culture, and Society*, pp. 67–87.
    Stanford: Stanford University Press.

1984. Theory in Anthropology Since the Sixties, *Comparative Studies in Society and History*, 26: 126–166.

Osterweis, M. et al. 1987. *Pain and Disability*. Washington, DC: National Academy Press.

Ots, Thomas. 1990. The Angry Liver, the Anxious Heart and the Melancholy Spleen: The Phenomenology of Perceptions in Chinese Culture, *Culture, Medicine and Psychiatry*, 14: 21–58.

Packard, Randall M. 1989. *White Plague, Black Labor: Tuberculosis and the Political Economy of Health and Disease in South Africa*. Berkeley: University of California Press.

Paley, Julia. 1991. From the "Spirit of the People" to the "Genius of a People": The Links between German Philosophy and American Cultural Anthropology in the Late 19th and Early 20th Centuries. Special Paper, Department of Anthropology, Harvard University.

Pandolfi, Mariella. 1990. Boundaries Inside the Body: Women's Sufferings in Southern Peasant Italy, *Culture, Medicine and Psychiatry*, 14: 255–273.

Pappas, Gregory. 1990. Some Implications for the Study of the Doctor–Patient Interaction: Power, Structure, and Agency in the Works of Howard Waitzkin and Arthur Kleinman, *Social Science and Medicine*, 30: 199–204.

Patel, Vimla L., Thomas O. Eisemon, and Jose F. Arocha. 1988. Causal Reasoning and the Treatment of Diarrhoeal Disease by Mothers in Kenya, *Social Science and Medicine*, 27: 1277–1286.

Paul, Benjamin D. 1955. *Health, Culture, and Community: Case Studies of Public Reactions to Health Programs*. New York: Russell Sage Foundation.

Paul, Robert A. 1989. Psychoanalytic Anthropology, *Annual Review of Anthropology*, 18: 177–202.

Peters, Larry. 1981. *Ecstasy and Healing in Nepal*. Malibu, CA: Undena Publications.
    1982. Trance, Initiation and Psychotherapy in Tamang Shamanism, *American Ethnologist*, 9: 21–46.

Pfleiderer, Beatrix (ed.). 1988. Permanence and Change in Asian Health Care Traditions. Special Issue of *Social Science and Medicine*, 27: 413–567.

Podelefsky, Aaron, and Peter J. Brown. 1991. *Applying Cultural Anthropology: An Introductory Reader*. Mountain View, CA: Mayfield Publishing Co.

Polgar, Steven. 1963. Health Action in Cross-Cultural Perspective. In H. E. Freeman, Sol Levine, and L. G. Reeder (eds.), *Handbook of Medical Sociology*. Englewood Cliffs, NJ: Prentice-Hall.

Popper, Karl. 1972. *Objective Knowledge: An Evolutionary Approach*. Oxford: Clarendon Press.

Pouillon, Jean. 1982. Remarks on the Verb "To Believe". In Michel Izard and Pierre Smith (eds.), *Between Belief and Transgression. Structuralist Essays in Religion, History and Myth*. Translated by John Leavitt, pp. 1–8. Chicago: University of Chicago Press.

Press, Irwin. 1980. Problems in the Definition and Classification of Medical Systems, *Social Science and Medicine*, 14B: 45–57.

Price, Laurie. 1987. Ecuadorian Illness Stories: Cultural Knowledge in Natural Discourse. In Dorothy Holland and Naomi Quinn (eds.), *Cultural Models in Language and Thought*, pp. 313–342.

Propp, V. 1968. *Morphology of the Folktale*. Austin: University of Texas Press.

Pugh, Judy F. 1991. The Semantics of Pain in Indian Culture and Medicine, *Culture, Medicine and Psychiatry*, 15: 19–43.

Putnam, Hilary. 1978. *Meaning and the Moral Sciences*. Boston: Routledge and Kegan Paul.

1981. *Reason, Truth and History*. Cambridge: Cambridge University Press.

1987. *The Many Faces of Realism. The Paul Carus Lectures*. LaSalle, IL: Open Court.

1990. *Realism with a Human Face*. Cambridge, MA: Harvard University Press.

Quinn, Naomi. 1987. Convergent Evidence for a Cultural Model of American Marriage. In D. Holland and N. Quinn (eds.), *Cultural Models in Language and Thought*, pp. 173–192.

Quinn, Naomi, and Dorothy Holland. 1987. Culture and Cognition. In D. Holland and N. Quinn (eds.), *Cultural Models in Language and Thought*, pp. 3–40.

Rhodes, Lorna Amarasingham. 1990. Studying Biomedicine as a Cultural System. In T. Johnson and C. Sargent (eds.), *Medical Anthropology: A Handbook of Theory and Method*, pp. 159–173.

Ricoeur, Paul. 1981a. *Hermeneutics and the Human Sciences*. Edited and translated by John B. Thompson. Cambridge: Cambridge University Press.

1981b. Narrative Time. In W. J. T. Mitchell (ed.), *On Narrative*, pp. 165–186.

1984. *Time and Narrative*, vol. 1. Translated by Kathleen McLaughlin and David Pellauer. Chicago: University of Chicago Press.

Riessman, Catherine Kohler. 1990. Strategic Uses of Narrative in the Presentation of Self and Illness: A Research Note, *Social Science and Medicine*, 30: 1195–1200.

Rivers, W. H. R. 1913. Massage in Melanesia. *Proceedings of the Seventeenth International Congress of Medicine*, London, August 1913.

1924. *Medicine, Magic, and Religion*. London: Kegan Paul, Trench, Trubner.

Roberts, Helen. 1981. *Women, Health and Reproduction*. London: Routledge and Kegan Paul.

Robinson, Ian. 1990. Personal Narratives, Social Careers and Medical Courses: Analysing Life Trajectories in Autobiographies of People with Multiple Sclerosis, *Social Science and Medicine*, 30: 1173–1186.

Rodmell, S. 1987. The Health Education Response to AIDS, *Radical Community Medicine*, 31: 15–20.

Rogoff, Barbara. 1984. Introduction: Thinking and Learning in Social Context. In Barbara Rogoff and Jean Lave (eds.), *Everyday Cognition: Its Development in Social Context*, pp. 1–8.

Rogoff, Barbara, and Jean Lave. 1984. *Everyday Cognition: Its Development in Social Context*. Cambridge, MA: Harvard University Press.

Romanucci-Ross, Lola. 1969. The Hierarchy of Resort in Curative Processes: The Admiralty Islands, Melanesia, *Journal of Health and Social Behavior*, 10: 201–209.

Rorty, Amélie Oksenberg. 1988. *Mind in Action: Essays in the Philosophy of Mind*. Boston, MA: Beacon.

Rorty, Richard. 1979. *Philosophy and the Mirror of Nature*. Princeton: Princeton University Press.

Rosaldo, Renato. 1984. Grief and the Headhunter's Rage: On the Cultural Force of Emotions. In E. Bruner (ed.), *Text, Play, and Story: The Construction and Reconstruction of Self and Society*, pp. 178–195. Washington, DC: American Ethnological Society.

Roseman, Marina. 1988. The Pragmatics of Aesthetics: The Performance of Healing among Senoi Temiar, *Social Science and Medicine*, 27: 811–818.

1990. Head, Heart, Odor, and Shadow: The Structure of the Self, the Emotional World, and Ritual Performance among Senoi Temiar, *Ethos*, 18: 227–250.

1992. *Healing Sounds from the Malaysian Rain Forest: Temiar Music and Medicine*. Berkeley: University of California Press.

Rosenberg, Charles E. 1962. *The Cholera Years*. Chicago: University of Chicago Press.

Rosenstock, I. M. 1974. Historical Origins of the Health Belief Model. In M. H. Becker (ed.), *Health Belief Model and Personal Health Behavior*, pp. 1–8. Thorofare, NJ: Slack.

Rouse, Joseph. 1987. *Knowledge and Power: Toward a Political Philosophy of Science*. Ithaca, NY: Cornell University Press.

Rubel, Arthur J. 1960. Concepts of Disease in Mexican-American Culture, *American Anthropologist*, 62: 795–814.

1964. The Epidemiology of a Folk Illness: Susto in Hispanic America, *Ethnology*, 3: 268–283.

Rubel, Arthur J., and Michael R. Hass. 1990. Ethnomedicine. In Thomas M. Johnson and Carolyn F. Sargent (eds.), *Medical Anthropology: A Handbook of Theory and Method*, pp. 115–131.

Rubel, Arthur J., Carl W. O'Nell, and R. Collado Ardon. 1984. *Susto: A Folk Illness*. Berkeley: University of California Press.

Rubenstein, Robert A., and Sandra D. Lane. 1990. International Health and Development. In Thomas M. Johnson and Carolyn F. Sargent (eds.), *Medical Anthropology: A Handbook of Theory and Method*, pp. 367–390.

Sacks, Oliver. 1973. *Awakenings*. New York: E. P. Dutton.

1985. *The Man Who Mistook His Wife for a Hat and Other Clinical Tales*. New York: Summit Books.

1986. *Migraine: Understanding a Common Disorder*. Berkeley: University of California Press.

Safa, Kaveh. 1988. Reading Saedi's *Ahl-e Hava*: Pattern and Significance in Spirit Possession Beliefs on the Southern Coasts of Iran, *Culture, Medicine and Psychiatry*, 12: 85–111.

Sahlins, Marshall. 1976a. *Culture and Practical Reason*. Chicago: University of Chicago Press.

1976b. *The Use and Abuse of Biology: An Anthropological Critique of Sociobiology*. Ann Arbor: University of Michigan Press.

1981. *Historical Metaphors and Mythical Realities: Structure in the Early History of the Sandwich Islands Kingdom*. Ann Arbor: University of Michigan Press.

Sansom, Basil. 1982. The Sick Who do not Speak. In David Parkin (ed.), *Semantic Anthropology*. A.S.A. Monograph 22. London: Academic Press.

Sapir, Edward. 1949 [1929]. The Status of Linguistics as a Science. In David G. Mandelbaum (ed.), *Selected Writings of Edward Sapir in Language, Culture and Personality*, pp. 160–166. Berkeley: University of California Press. (Originally published in *Language*, 5 (1929), 207–214.)

1949 [1932]. Cultural Anthropology and Psychiatry. In David G. Mandelbaum (ed.), *Selected Writings of Edward Sapir in Language, Culture and Personality*, pp. 509–521. Berkeley: University of California Press.

Sarbin, Theodore R. (ed.). 1986. *Narrative Psychology: The Storied Nature of Human Conduct*. New York: Praeger.

Sargent, Carolyn Fishel. 1989. *Maternity, Medicine, and Power: Reproductive Decisions in Urban Benin*. Berkeley: University of California Press.

Scarry, Elaine. 1985. *The Body in Pain. The Making and Unmaking of the World*. New York: Oxford University Press.

Scheper-Hughes, Nancy. 1987. *Child Survival*. Dordrecht, Holland: D. Reidel Publishing Co.

1988. The Madness of Hunger: Sickness, Delirium and Human Needs, *Culture, Medicine and Psychiatry,* 12: 429–458.

1990. Three Propositions for a Critically Applied Medical Anthropology, *Social Science and Medicine,* 30: 189–197.

Scheper-Hughes, Nancy, and Margaret M. Lock. 1987. The Mindful Body: A Prolegomenon to Future Work in Medical Anthropology, *Medical Anthropology Quarterly,* 1: 6–41.

Schieffelin, Edward L. 1976. *The Sorrow of the Lonely and the Burning of the Dancers.* New York: St. Martin's Press.

1985. Performance and the Cultural Construction of Reality, *American Ethnologist,* 12: 707–724.

Schneider, Joseph W., and Peter Conrad. 1980. Medical and Sociological Typologies: The Case of Epilepsy, *Social Science and Medicine,* 15A: 211–219.

1981. In the Closet with Illness: Epilepsy, Stigma Potential and Information Control, *Social Problems,* 28: 34–44.

1983. *Having Epilepsy: The Experience and Control of Illness.* Philadelphia: Temple University Press.

Schutz, Alfred. 1971. On Multiple Realities. In *Collected Papers. Vol. 1: The Problem of Social Reality,* pp. 207–259. The Hague: Martinus Nijhoff.

Scotch, Norman. 1963. Medical Anthropology. In B. J. Siegel (ed.), *Biennial Review of Anthropology.* Stanford: Stanford University Press.

Scott, James. 1985. *Weapons of the Weak: Everyday Forms of Peasant Resistance.* New Haven: Yale University Press.

1990. *Domination and the Arts of Resistance: Hidden Transcripts.* New Haven: Yale University Press.

Shipton, Parker. 1990. African Famines and Food Security: Anthropological Perspectives, *Annual Review of Anthropology,* 19: 353–394.

Shore, Bradd. 1991. Twice-Born, Once Conceived: Meaning Construction and Cultural Cognition, *American Anthropologist,* 93: 9–27.

Shorvon, S.D., and P. J. Farmer. 1988. Epilepsy in Developing Countries: A Review of Epidemiological, Sociocultural, and Treatment Aspects, *Epilepsia,* 29 (Suppl. 1): S36–S54.

Shorvon, S. D., Y. M. Hart, J. W. A. S. Sander, and F. van Andel. 1991. *The Management of Epilepsy in Developing Countries: An "ICBERG" Manual.* London: Royal Society of Medicine Services.

Showalter, Elaine. 1985. *The Female Malady. Women, Madness, and English Culture, 1830–1980.* New York: Pantheon Books.

Shweder, Richard A. 1984a. Anthropology's Romantic Rebellion against the Enlightenment, or There's More to Thinking than Reason and Evidence. In R. Shweder and R. LeVine (eds.), *Culture Theory,* pp. 27–66.

1984b. Preview: A Colloquy of Culture Theorists. In R. Shweder and R. LeVine (eds.), *Culture Theory,* pp. 1–24.

Shweder, Richard A., and Robert A. LeVine. 1984. *Culture Theory. Essays on Mind, Self, and Emotion.* Cambridge: Cambridge University Press.

Siddiqi, M. Z. 1959. *Studies in Arabic and Persian Medical Literature.* Calcutta: Calcutta University Press.

Silverman, Julian. 1967. Shamanism and Acute Schizophrenia, *American Anthropologist,* 69: 21–31.

Simons, Ronald C. 1980. The Resolution of the *Latah* Paradox, *Journal of Nervous and Mental Disease,* 168: 195–206.

Simons, Ronald C., and Charles C. Hughes (eds.). 1985. *The Culture-Bound Syndromes: Folk Illnesses of Psychiatric and Anthropological Interest.* Dordrecht, Holland: D. Reidel Publishing Co.

Sindzingre, Nicole. 1988. Comments on Five Manuscripts, *Medical Anthropology Quarterly*, 2: 447–453.

Singer, Merrill. 1989a. The Coming of Age of Critical Medical Anthropology, *Social Science and Medicine*, 28: 1193–1203.

1989b. The Limitations of Medical Ecology: The Concept of Adaptation in the Context of Social Stratification and Social Transformation, *Medical Anthropology*, 10: 223–234.

1990. Reinventing Medical Anthropology: Toward a Critical Realignment, *Social Science and Medicine*, 30: 179–187.

Skeltons, J. A., R. T. Croyle, and R. Eiser (eds.). 1991. *The Mental Representation of Health and Illness.* Springer-Verlag Series, Contributions to Psychology and Medicine. New York: Springer-Verlag.

Smith, Dorothy E. 1974. The Social Construction of Documentary Reality, *Sociological Inquiry*, 44: 257–268.

Smith, Wilfred Cantwell. 1977. *Belief and History.* Charlottesville: University of Virginia Press.

1979. *Faith and Belief.* Princeton: Princeton University Press.

Snow, Loudell. 1974. Folk Medical Beliefs and their Implications for Care of Patients, *Annals of Internal Medicine*, 81: 82–96.

Sontag, Susan. 1977. *Illness as Metaphor.* New York: Farrar, Straus and Giroux.

1989. AIDS and Its Metaphors. New York: Farrar, Straus and Giroux.

Sperber, Dan. 1985. *On Anthropological Knowledge.* Cambridge: Cambridge University Press.

1990. The Epidemiology of Beliefs. In Colin Fraser and Georg Gaskell (eds.), *The Social Psychological Study of Widespread Beliefs*, pp. 25–44. Oxford: Clarendon Press.

Spicker, Stuart F., and Edmund D. Pellegrino (eds.). 1984. Embodiment and Rehabilitation. Special Issue of *The Journal of Medicine and Philosophy*, 9 (1).

Spiers, Paul A., Donald L. Schomer, Howard W. Blume, and M-Marsel Mesulam. 1985. Temporolimbic Epilepsy and Behavior. In M-Marsel Mesulam (ed.), *Principles of Behavioral Neurology*, pp. 289–326. Philadelphia: F. A. Davis.

Staiano, Kathryn Vance. 1986. *Interpreting Signs of Illness: A Case Study in Medical Semiotics.* Berlin: Mouton de Gruyter.

Steedly, Mary Margaret. 1993. *Hanging Without a Rope: Narrative Experience in Colonial and Neocolonial Karoland.* Princeton: Princeton University Press.

Stich, Stephen P. 1983. *From Folk Psychology to Cognitive Science. The Case Against Belief.* Cambridge, MA: MIT Press.

Stocking, George S., Jr. 1968. *Race, Culture, and Evolution: Essays in the History of Anthropology.* New York: Free Press.

Stoller, Paul. 1989. *The Taste of Ethnographic Things: The Senses in Anthropology.* Philadelphia: University of Pennsylvania Press.

Strauss, Claudia. 1988. Culture, Discourse, and Cognition: Forms of Belief in Some Rhode Island Working Men's Talk About Success. Ph.D. Thesis, Department of Anthropology, Harvard University.

1992. What Makes Tony Run? Schemas as Motives Reconsidered. In Roy D'Andrade and Claudia Strauss (eds.), *Human Motives and Cultural Models*, pp. 197–224. Cambridge: Cambridge University Press.

Sturtevant, William C. 1964. Studies in Ethnoscience, *American Anthropologist*, 66: 99–131.

Styron, William. 1990. *Darkness Visible: A Memoir of Madness*. New York: Random House.

Suleiman, Susan Ruban (ed.). 1986. *The Female Body in Western Culture: Contemporary Perspectives*. Cambridge, MA: Harvard University Press.

Tambiah, Stanley Jeyaraja. 1977. The Cosmological and Performative Significance of a Thai Cult of Healing Through Meditation, *Culture, Medicine and Psychiatry*, 1: 97–132.

1985. *Culture, Thought, and Social Action. An Anthropological Perspective*. Cambridge, MA: Harvard University Press.

1990. *Magic, Science, Religion, and the Scope of Rationality*. Cambridge: Cambridge University Press.

Tarhan Kitabevi. 1959. *Turkce–Ingilizce Buyuk Lugat (A Comprehensive Turkish–English Dictionary)*. Ankara: Tarhan Kitabevi.

Taussig, Michael T. 1980. Reification and the Consciousness of the Patient, *Social Science and Medicine*, 14B: 3–13.

Taylor, Charles. 1985a. *Human Agency and Language. Philosophical Papers 1*. Cambridge: Cambridge University Press.

1985b. *Philosophy and the Human Sciences. Philosophical Papers 2*. Cambridge: Cambridge University Press.

1989. *Sources of the Self. The Making of the Modern Identity*. Cambridge, MA: Harvard University Press.

Tedlock, Barbara. 1987. An Interpretive Solution to the Problem of Humoral Medicine in Latin America, *Social Science and Medicine*, 24: 1069–1083.

Temkin, Owsei. 1973. *Galenism: Rise and Decline of a Medical Philosophy*. Ithaca, NY: Cornell University Press.

Theodore, William H., Giovanni DiChiro, Richard Margolin, Don Fishbein, Roger J. Porter, and Rodney A. Brooks. 1986. Barbiturates Reduce Human Cerebral Glucose Metabolism, *Neurology*, 36: 60–64.

Thornton, E. M. 1976. *Hypnotism, Hysteria and Epilepsy: An Historical Synthesis*. London: William Heinemann Medical Books Ltd.

Todorov, Tzvetan. 1984. *Mikhail Bakhtin: The Dialogical Principle*. Translated by Wlad Godzich. Theory and History of Literature, vol. 13. Minneapolis: University of Minnesota Press.

Tooker, Deborah E. 1992. Identity Systems of Highland Burma: "Belief," Akha *Zan*, and a Critique of Interiorized Notions of Ethno-Religious Identity, *Man*, 27: 799–819.

Tosteson, Daniel C. 1981. Science, Medicine, and Education. The Alan Gregg Memorial Lecture, *Journal of Medical Education*, 56: 8–15.

Trautmann, Thomas R. 1987. *Lewis Henry Morgan and the Invention of Kinship*. Berkeley: University of California Press.

Tsongas, Paul. 1984. *Heading Home*. New York: Vintage Books.

Turner, Bryan S. 1984. *The Body and Society: Explorations in Social Theory*. Oxford: Basic Blackwell.

Turner, Victor. 1957. *Schism and Continuity in an African Society: A Study of Ndembu Village Life*. Manchester: Manchester University Press.

1967. *The Forest of Symbols: Aspects of Ndembu Ritual*. Ithaca, NY: Cornell University Press.

1981. Social Dramas and Stories about Them. In W. J. T. Mitchell (ed.), *On Narrative*, pp. 137–164.

Turner, Victor W., and Edward M. Bruner (eds.). 1986. *The Anthropology of Experience.* Urbana, IL: University of Illinois Press.

Turshen, Meredeth. 1977. The Impact of Colonialism on Health and Health Services in Tanzania, *International Journal of Health Services*, 7: 7–35.

1984. *The Political Ecology of Disease in Tanzania.* New Brunswick, NJ: Rutgers University Press.

1989. *The Politics of Public Health.* New Brunswick, NJ: Rutgers University Press.

Van der Geest, Sjaak, and Susan Reynolds Whyte (eds.). 1988. *The Context of Medicines in Developing Countries: Studies in Pharmaceutical Anthropology.* Dordrecht, Holland: Kluwer Academic Publishers.

Van Schaik, Eileen. 1988. Paradigms Underlying the Study of Nerves as a Popular Illness Term in Eastern Kentucky, *Medical Anthropology*, 11: 15–28.

Volosinov, V. N. 1976. *Freudianism: A Critical Sketch.* Translated by I. R. Titunik and edited in collaboration with Neal H. Bruss. Bloomington: Indiana University Press.

Waitzkin, Howard. 1981. The Social Origins of Illness: A Neglected History, *International Journal of Health Services*, 11: 77–103.

1991. *The Politics of Medical Encounters: How Patients and Doctors Deal with Social Problems.* New Haven: Yale University Press.

Waitzkin, Howard, and B. Waterman. 1974. *The Exploitation of Illness in Capitalist Society.* Indianapolis: Bobbs-Merrill.

Warner, Richard. 1985. *Recovery From Schizophrenia: Psychiatry and Political Economy.* Boston, MA: Routledge and Kegan Paul.

1988. Response to Dr. Barrett, *Culture, Medicine and Psychiatry*, 12: 390–395.

Warwick, Ian, Peter Aggleton and Hilary Homans. 1988. Constructing Commonsense – Young People's Beliefs about AIDS, *Sociology of Health and Illness*, 10: 213–223.

Waxler, Nancy E. 1974. Culture and Mental Illness: A Social Labeling Perspective, *Journal of Nervous and Mental Disease*, 159: 379–395.

1977a. Is Mental Illness Cured in Traditional Societies? A Theoretical Analyis, *Culture, Medicine and Psychiatry*, 1: 233–253.

1977b. Is Outcome Better for Schizophrenia in Non-Industrialized Societies? *Journal of Nervous and Mental Disease*, 167: 144–158.

Weber, Max. 1946. *From Max Weber: Essays in Sociology.* Translated and edited by H. H. Gerth and C. Wright Mills. New York: Oxford University Press.

Wellin, Edward. 1977. Theoretical Orientations in Medical Anthropology: Continuity and Change Over the Past Half-Century. In David Landy (ed.), *Culture, Disease, and Healing: Studies in Medical Anthropology*, pp. 47–58. New York: Macmillan.

Welsch, Robert L. 1983. Traditional Medicine and Western Medical Options among the Ningerum of Papua New Guinea. In Lola Romanucci-Ross, Daniel E. Moerman, and Laurence R. Tancredi (eds.), *The Anthropology of Medicine: From Culture to Method*, pp. 32–53. New York: Praeger.

Wertsch, James V. 1984. *Vygotsky and the Social Formation of Mind.* Cambridge, MA: Harvard University Press.

1991. *Voices of the Mind: A Sociocultural Approach to Mediated Action.* Cambridge, MA: Harvard University Press.

Whipple, Allen O. 1967. *The Role of the Nestorians and Muslims in the History of Medicine.* Princeton: Princeton University Press.

White, Geoffrey. 1982a. The Ethnographic Study of Cultural Knowledge of "Mental Disorder." In Anthony J. Marsella and Geoffrey M. White (eds.), *Cultural Conceptions of Mental Health and Therapy*, pp. 69–95. Dordrecht, Holland: D. Reidel Publishing Co.

1982b. The Role of Cultural Explanations in "Somatization" and "Psychologization," *Social Science and Medicine*, 16: 1519–1530.

White, Hayden. 1981. The Value of Narrativity in the Representation of Reality. In W. J. T. Mitchell (ed.), *On Narrative*, pp. 1–24.

White, Leslie. 1959. *Introduction to Lewis Henry Morgan: The Indian Journals 1859–62.* Ann Arbor: University of Michigan Press.

Whorf, Benjamin Lee. 1956. Science and Linguistics. In *Language, Thought and Reality*, pp. 207–219. Cambridge, MA: MIT Press.

Wikan, Unni. 1987. Public Grace and Private Fears: Gaiety, Offense, and Sorcery in Northern Bali, *Ethos*, 15: 337–365.

1991. Toward an Experience-Near Anthropology, *Cultural Anthropology*, 6: 285–305.

Williams, Gareth. 1984. The Genesis of Chronic Illness: Narrative Reconstruction, *Sociology of Health and Illness*, 6: 175–200.

Williams, Raymond. 1977. *Marxism and Literature*. Oxford: Oxford University Press.

Wilson, Bryan R. (ed.). 1970. *Rationality*. New York: Harper and Row.

Woolhandler, Steffie, and David U. Himmelstein. 1989. Ideology in Medical Science: Class in the Clinic, *Social Science and Medicine*, 28: 1205–1209.

World Health Organization. 1990. Initiative of Support to People with Epilepsy. Division of Mental Health, Document WHO/MNH/MND/90.3. Geneva: World Health Organization.

Worsley, Peter. 1982. Non-Western Medical Systems, *Annual Review of Anthropology*, 11: 315–348.

Yalman, Nur. 1964. The Structure of Sinhalese Healing Rituals, *Journal of Asian Studies*, 23: 115–150.

Young, Allan. 1976. Some Implications of Medical Beliefs and Practices for Social Anthropology, *American Anthropologist*, 78: 5–24.

1980. The Discourse on Stress and the Reproduction of Conventional Knowledge, *Social Science and Medicine*, 14B: 133–146.

1981. When Rational Men Fall Sick: An Inquiry into some Assumptions Made by Medical Anthropologists, *Culture, Medicine and Psychiatry*, 5: 317–335.

1982. The Anthropologies of Illness and Sickness, *Annual Review of Anthropology*, 11: 257–285.

1990. Moral Conflicts in a Psychiatric Hospital Treating Combat-Related Posttraumatic Stress Disorder (PTSD). In George Weisz (ed.), *Social Science Perspectives on Medical Ethics*, pp. 65–82. Dordrecht, Holland: Kluwer Academic Publisher.

Young, James. 1978. Illness Categories and Action Strategies in a Tarascan Town, *American Ethnologist*, 5: 81–97.

1980. A Model of Illness Treatment Decisions in a Tarascan Town, *American Ethnologist*, 7: 106–131.

1981. *Medical Choice in a Mexican Village*. New Brunswick, NJ: Rutgers University Press.

Young, James, and Linda Garro. 1982. Variation in the Choice of Treatment in Two Mexican Communities, *Social Science and Medicine*, 16: 1453–1466.

Zimmerman, Francis. 1987. *The Jungle and the Aroma of Meats: An Ecological Theme in Hindu Medicine*. Berkeley: University of California Press.

Author Index

Subject Index